Plague and Pleasure

Modern statue of Pius II in Pienza Cathedral.
Photo credit: Luke Ashworth-Sides.

Plague and Pleasure

THE RENAISSANCE WORLD OF PIUS II

Arthur White

Foreword by Michael Lewis

The Catholic University of America Press
Washington, D.C.

The paper used in this publication meets the minimum requirements of American National Standards for Information Science—Permanence of Paper for Printed Library Materials, ANSI Z39.48-1984.
∞

Library of Congress Cataloging-in-Publication Data
White, Arthur, 1942–
Plague and pleasure : the renaissance world of Pius II / Arthur White ; with a foreword by Michael Lewis.
pages cm
Includes bibliographical references and index.
ISBN 978-0-8132-2681-1 (pbk. : alk. paper) 1. Pius II, Pope, 1405–1464. 2. Renaissance. 3. Europe—History—476–1492.
I. Title.
BX1308.W45 2014
282.092—dc23 2014023647

publication sees a grant from
Figure Foundation

I dedicate this book to my wife, Gail Brockett White, who is the *sine qua non* of my life and of everything I do; and to the Episcopal School of Acadiana, where I taught for nineteen years. High school cannot be paradise; but it comes closest at ESA.

Contents

Illustrations

Foreword

Michael Lewis

The time was the mid-1970s, a period now viewed by many amateur historians as the Dark Ages. I was a high school sophomore at the Isidore Newman School in New Orleans. Arthur White—thirty-five years later I can't think of him as anything but "Dr. White"—new to the school, was already a legendary history teacher. He was then teaching a class on the history of the Middle Ages unlike any history any of us had ever been taught: not chiefly names and dates to be memorized but ideas and passions to be grasped and felt. His history had body odor and excrement, carnal love and gruesome death. Someone once said that it's a wonder that history as told by professional historians is so boring, given that so much of it must be invented. Dr. White's history gave rise to something like the opposite reaction: this stuff is so earthy and real, there was no way he could be making it up.

His lectures were also strangely kinetic events: he skipped back and forth in front of the class as he spoke, his sleeves rolled up to expose the forearms of a welterweight. He brought so much life and energy to the Middle Ages that, even when my adolescent brain flickered and my eyelids drooped, I wished I weren't going to miss what I was about to miss. I seldom missed it, however. The moment Dr. White spotted a student's head descending upon his tiny desk he'd position himself in front of that desk, like a field goal kicker lining up the ball with the goalposts. With a great flourish he would then boot the bottom of the desk—sending both desk and student flying through the air. The crowd always went wild. The student, newly awakened, would laugh and return to the past. I think a lot of us left Dr. White's class with a sense that the Middle Ages was the period in human history most difficult to sleep through.

Dr White's book hit me a bit like a kick under my desk. He's said something fresh and new on a subject I didn't imagine there was anything fresh and new left to say. And he's done it by telling the story of a single fifteenth-century man, Aeneas Silvius Piccolomini. As a young man Aeneas distinguished himself with his love of sex and rock 'n' roll (or, at least, erotic poetry) and with his special gift for office politics and insults (he calls Venetians "companions of fish"). As an old man he distinguished himself by being elected pope and naming himself Pius II. Dr. White's idea is to use Aeneas's life as a lens on the period. This turns out to be a lovely idea, and he executes it with startling effect.

"The Myth of the Renaissance is one of the most significant invasions of myth into the realm of history that has ever existed," White writes. What he means by this, first, is that much of what we celebrate about the Renaissance arises not from some general improvement in human nature but from the trauma of the plague—or, as Dr. White puts it, "the morbid obsession with death and decay and, more importantly, the search for mental escape from stressful thoughts." The secularism we associate with the Renaissance, for instance, is less a denial of the importance of God than the opposite, "because God was part of the fearful reality that people were trying to escape."

What Dr. White means by his thesis statement, also, is that much of what we celebrate about the Renaissance was not peculiar to the Renaissance but to the Middle Ages.

I suppose it is not surprising that, when Dr. White set out to write a book about the Renaissance, he wound up with a defense of the Middle Ages. There's now a clear pattern of the most impassioned feeling for the medieval period expressing itself in southern Louisiana. In a strange way Dr. White's history belongs on the same shelf with John Kennedy Toole's *Confederacy of Dunces* and Walker Percy's *Lancelot.* What is surprising is that thirty-five years after I first heard Dr. White bring the human past back to life, his voice is as fresh and clear and interesting to me as ever.

Preface

For over two hundred years a myth has overshadowed our culture's understanding of the Italian Renaissance, distorting not only our conceptions of the Renaissance and the Middle Ages but also our ideas about the origins and character of modernity. Everyone knows the story: it proclaims that an ignorant, primitive, oppressive, and stagnant Middle Ages was overthrown in fifteenth-century Italy by daring, curious, freewheeling, freethinking humanists who ushered in the modern age of secularism, individualism, discovery, and freedom of thought, paving the way for science, technology, democracy, and all other blessings of modernity. This myth is still a powerful force in our society, validating whatever we currently define as "modern" and branding whatever seems to obstruct the modern with the derogatory epithet "medieval." Among serious scholars of history this "Myth of the Renaissance" has long lost its credibility. Nevertheless, it remains the *only* widely known narrative of medieval and Renaissance history. It is long overdue for replacement with a more accurate narrative that reflects the rehabilitation of the Middle Ages and the de-romanticizing of humanism achieved by twentieth-century scholarship. Attempting to replace the myth with a more accurate narrative is the purpose of this book.

Ironically, the myth owes part of its longevity to the fact that "master narratives" or "metanarratives"—broad interpretations covering long sweeps of history—have become unfashionable among most professional historians. Historians today seek to do justice to the distinctness of each event and the uniqueness of each individual in the past. Any generalization tends to blur these distinctions—the broader the scope of the generalization, the more these individual components are obliterated. Historians are also sensitive to the uncertainty of their material. It is commonly a laborious, scholarly process to establish even quite simple facts. A date or a name can require digging through archives to find documents that have to be compared to other documents from other archives. If the simple facts are that uncertain, how uncertain is a generalization about a century? For that matter, how many generalizations can we make with certainty and unanimity even about the present decade? How then can we be certain of generalizations made on the basis of the surviving evidence from five centuries ago? Moreover, the exponential growth of historical knowledge over the last century has made the volume of material that ought to be considered when making judgments about a lengthy time period prohibitively overwhelming.

Nevertheless, we cannot do without master narratives. Consider: What can we teach high school students or undergraduates *except* a metanarrative? Since very few of those students will major in history or pursue it in graduate school, what will they ever know of history other than a metanarrative? What, then, will form the historical perspective that influences their own sense of identity, their judgments of others, their sense of causation, their cultural values and their votes? What I mean to imply is that we inevitably *have* metanarratives, and it behooves us to get them as right as we can. What the average educated citizen needs from historians is the generalized narrative that tells them who they are, where they came from, why things are the way they are, and why people who differ from them think the way they do. Our minds, like nature, abhor a vacuum. If prudent historians will not give us a broad outline of what happened in history, we will snatch at one from somewhere else, such as Erich von Daniken's story of ancient men from outer space or Dan Brown's fictitious intrigues. More likely we will just make do with whatever narrative is left over from the last time historians were producing them. Thus, the avoiding of metanarratives has only allowed outdated ones, such as the Myth of the Renaissance, to continue occupying the field.

In attempting to replace the Myth of the Renaissance with a more accurate interpretation, I am well aware that I cannot do justice to the virtually infinite number of concrete events and specific individuals upon which all generalizations must rest. There is no escape from having to make a subjective selection among the factors that might be, and ought to be, considered and included in such a generalized view. The very nature of the task insures that this book will omit more than it includes and will rely upon many unproven assumptions. Even though I tremble before the pitfalls, the attempt remains necessary; otherwise, a myth that has been contradicted by firm research on many fronts will carry the day by default.

Historians no longer accept the Middle Ages as a millennium of "darkness." Beginning with Charles Homer Haskins's 1927 book, *The Renaissance of the Twelfth Century,* we have gradually come to understand that the High Middle Ages (roughly the twelfth and thirteenth centuries) were not part of a thousand-year "Dark Ages" but rather a dynamic, prosperous, productive period of unusually *rapid* economic, demographic, technological, intellectual, institutional, and cultural growth. In a long lifetime of study and writing, the late Paul Oskar Kristeller (1905–1999) succeeded in convincing students of Renaissance humanism that there never was a humanist ideology during the Renaissance. Humanists of that period did not teach secularism, or individualism, or respect for Man and his capacities, or the liberation of the human spirit—they did not even teach "humanism," since that word was not invented until the nineteenth century.[1] They taught Latin and sometimes Greek. A humanist was a man who revered and tried to imitate the Latin language as the ancient Romans wrote it and who taught others to do the same. The rehabilitation of the High Middle Ages and Kristeller's scholarly, non-ideological concept of the humanists will get more attention in the first chapter, but they make it obvious that we cannot avoid formulating a new and very different narrative of the Renaissance.

To condense such a sweeping project to the scope of a readable book addressed to the general public requires some drastic principle of selection, as if we were to seek one thread out of a tapestry to serve as a representative of the whole. The thread I have chosen as a sample of my thesis is the life of one fairly representative humanist, Aeneas Silvius Piccolomini (1405–1464), who in 1458 became Pope Pius II. Aeneas/Pius (as we may call him for now) was, among other things, a prolific writer of treatises, letters, and fiction. But what makes him knowable enough to serve as a guide to his period is a remarkable autobiographical record written during his papacy. The *Commentaries on the Memorable Things that Happened in His Times* is part memoir, part diary.[2] It is, like other autobiographical writings, riddled with self-deceptions and efforts to

1. The term "humanism" was coined by the German educator F. J. Neithammer; Paul Oskar Kristeller, *Renaissance Thought and Its Sources,* ed. Michael Mooney (New York: Columbia University Press, 1979), 22.

2. *Pius II, Commentarii rerum memorabilium quae temporibus suis contigerunt* (Rome: 1584); *The Commentaries of Pius II,* trans. Florence Alden Gragg, introduction and notes by Leona C. Gabel, in *Smith College Studies in History,* Books I–XIII, vols. 22, 25, 30, 35, 43 (Northampton, Mass.: Smith College, 1936–1957); henceforth abbreviated as *Comm.,* Smith.

manipulate its author's image; but even so, the author's flaws (such as his amazing vanity) stand out unmistakably, as do his amiability, his kindness to the poor, and his fundamental good intentions. We will need to pry at times into the emotions of individuals and their subjective reactions to events around them; Pius's *Commentaries* are at least somewhat more open and frank about such matters than most other fifteenth-century writings. The life of Aeneas/Pius illustrates many, though not all, of the key aspects of the Renaissance. Aeneas was a practicing humanist, was involved in all the tumult of Italian politics, waged war as pope, fled from (and once actually caught) the plague, participated in extravagant festivals, enjoyed Roman ruins, loved natural beauty, patronized architects, and transformed his native village into a showpiece of the new architecture. Each of these things was in some way representative of the period and serves to illustrate the interpretation I want to present. He also left gaps: aspects of the period (such as painting) in which he took no interest that I will have to fill in other ways.

Following the life of an individual will help somewhat to overcome one of the perils of generalization by keeping us in touch with the untidiness of history, the personal quirks, the happenstances, the contradictoriness of real people and real events. Nevertheless, a single life, even one that exemplifies many Renaissance behaviors, cannot give a picture of how varied those behaviors could be or how widely prevalent they were. For that reason I have found it necessary to pause several times in the narrative of Pius's life to look at other examples of significant themes. Alternating with narrative biographical segments there will be chapters on private rooms (*studioli*), festivals, ideal cities, villas and gardens, and painting. This book is not a biography. Pius is a means here, not the end. There are certain aspects of his life I will largely omit. Aeneas/Pius was entangled in the affairs of every European region except Scandinavia and usually Britain. The affairs of France, Burgundy, Germany, Bohemia, Hungary, and the Balkan countries will get only minimal attention in this book, even when they engrossed the energies of its protagonist.

Although I have no personal taste for controversy, this will probably be a controversial book. I know that many people will feel disoriented without the Myth of the Renaissance and that for some it has almost a religious significance. Voltaire, who originated the Renaissance myth, intended it as a bludgeon with which to attack Christianity. Crusading secularists still use it that way, as in a bumper sticker I have seen that said, "Religion ruled in the Dark Ages." I do not think the interpretation I will offer supports any current ideology, religious, political, or economic. It is not the business of history to do so. History should, if anything, challenge our contemporary assumptions by showing us that there are other ways to be human besides the ones we can observe today, and it should remind us that we are as much tossed about by events and dependent upon our unproven and unexamined assumptions as any previous generation. Insofar as our ideals are valid, they do not need spurious support from a mythologized past; insofar as they are invalid, we should welcome critique from our predecessors.

Some academics may object to the unashamedly popular tone of this book. Unfortunately, in the field of history, new ideas generated behind ivy-covered walls are very likely to stay there. It is not like that in the sciences: if a paleontologist has evidence that dinosaurs were warm-blooded, it gets picked up by the news media and brought before the public. That does not happen very often in history, at least not for interpretive issues. The rehabilitation of the Middle Ages, or Kristeller's revelation that humanists were students of classical Latin with no discernible ideology, has been long established among scholars while remaining almost invisible to most people. Expert knowledge does not always have to be broadly shared, but the experts must not allow outdated conceptions, left unchallenged, to mislead the public. Whether my interpretations are correct or not, I hope they may at least move the discussion of the Renaissance from the place where it seems to be stuck and extend it beyond academe into public awareness.

SOME DEFINITIONS

Before launching into the book proper I want to specify the way that I will use the key words "humanist," "humanism," and "Renaissance," whose meanings have become so elastic in general use that using them in a precise way may often be ambiguous.

Humanist: Following Paul Oskar Kristeller, I will use "humanist" to mean a person in the fourteenth through sixteenth centuries who studied and taught grammar, rhetoric, poetry, history, or ethics as written by Greek and Roman authors and who wrote with a deliberate effort to imitate the Latin of these classical writers.

Humanism: Although this word did not exist during the Renaissance, it is too convenient to dispense with. I will use it to mean nothing more than the common practices of the humanists without implying secularism, individualism, or any other ideological connotations.

Renaissance: I will use "Renaissance" in two ways: (1) referring to a cultural change; and (2) referring to the period of time when that change occurred. I think it legitimate to extend "Renaissance" to sixteenth-century cultural developments anyplace in Europe that were inspired and influenced by those in Italy, but in this book I will never use "Renaissance" to refer to anything outside of Italy. *Renaissance as a cultural change* will refer to (1) the transformation of language and literature wrought by Italian humanists in the fourteenth through sixteenth centuries and (2) the changes in visual arts and architecture during the fifteenth and sixteenth centuries. *Renaissance as a period of time* will be limited to the fifteenth century (quattrocento) and the sixteenth century (cinquecento).[3] The literary aspects of the Renaissance certainly began in the fourteenth century with Petrarch and Boccaccio, but the visual arts and architecture did not begin to respond significantly to humanist influence until after 1400. These arts are so integral to our concept of the Renaissance that I think it is misleading to apply the period label before arts and letters converged on parallel paths.

3. Italians and authors writing about Italy use *trecento,* "the three hundreds," to refer to the fourteenth century (1300s), *quattrocento,* "the four hundreds," to refer to the fifteenth century (1400s), and *cinquecento,* "the five hundreds," to refer to the sixteenth century (1500s). All of these will be used throughout this book.

Acknowledgments

Priority in gratitude goes to the late Charles Till Davis of Tulane University, who first got me interested in the interpretation of the Renaissance. I am profoundly grateful to Trevor Lipscombe, director of the Catholic University of America Press, who decided to take a chance on me and my book and who has guided it to fruition. I am also grateful to Theresa Walker, managing editor at the Catholic University of America Press, who guided me through the publication process. I am grateful to the two anonymous readers to whom the press sent the last manuscript. Both made plentiful suggestions that have improved the book in every direction and rescued me from numerous pitfalls. Special thanks also go to Aldene Fredenburg, who did the copyediting, for her care and diligence, and especially for her patience. I am also grateful to Sarah Ritchey of the University of Louisiana at Lafayette and to Mark Richard, Fr. Philip Rogers, Brian McIntyre, and the late Jan Nelson of the University of Alabama, who read all or part of the manuscript in its early stages and gave much-needed direction and encouragement. I could not have done any significant part of this project without the backing of Robert Carriker, my department chairman at the University of Louisiana at Lafayette. Many thanks go to the interlibrary loan department at the Edith Dupré Library at the same university, to its head, Deborah L. Johnson, and especially to Yolanda Landry and Dan Phillips, who obtained 113 books and articles for me, including some I never expected to find in North America. I am much indebted to Paolo Ragusa of the Istituto Italiano in Florence, who taught me the Italian language, and to Danny Osborne, who accompanied me on that venture. A very special contributor to this book is Luke Ashworth-Sides, who not only took many fine photographs, some of which appear in these pages, but who also did all the driving on remote roads in Italy as we sought to track down monasteries, ruins, campsites, springs, and abandoned villages, retracing the travels of Pius II. For all the errors, omissions, lapses of judgment, and other defects of this book I have only myself to thank. For forty-six years of daily support, patience, and longsuffering, as well as great joy, I thank my beloved wife, Gail. Above all I thank the grace and mercy of God.

Plague and Pleasure

Central Italy in the Time of Pius II. Courtesy of Arthur White.

I

The Myth of the Renaissance

NOT LONG AGO I went into an office at my university and told the lady behind the desk that I would be teaching a course on the Italian Renaissance in the fall semester. She brightened with recognition and enthusiastically proclaimed, "We all know what history teaches!" I returned her smile and waited to learn what history was all about. Raising her hand as high as she could, she announced, "First, everything went *way up* with the Greeks and Romans." Then, plunging her hand to mid-thigh, she continued, "but they came *crashing* down with the Middle Ages." Again her hand soared skywards: "and then they went *zooming* up again with the Renaissance." Holding her hand in the air a moment, she waved it indecisively and added, "and it sort of piddled out from there." Some might not agree that we have "piddled out" since the Renaissance, but her "up/crash/zoom" summary of Western history remains the story that "everyone knows." It is a pity, then, that it is not true.

Most of us learned in school that, around the year 1400, something called "humanism" dawned in Italy, banishing medieval darkness and bathing the world in the fresh new light of the Renaissance. For most modern people the word "humanism" carries a strong positive charge. Many people proudly label themselves as "humanists," meaning that they respect their fellow humans, treat them benevolently and tolerantly, and have faith in their essential goodness, their intelligence, and their capacity to accomplish great things. Whether or not they add the word "secular" in front of "humanism," most self-described "humanists" today would say that they doubt, deny, or ignore the existence of God. Most people learn that this secular humanism first appeared in the Italian Renaissance, and that, when it did, it liberated mankind's natural powers, stimulated the economy, freed people to be individuals, led to the birth of all branches of intellectual inquiry, and left proof of its confident new spirit in countless masterpieces of art.

It is jarring, therefore, to discover that people who lived during the Italian Renaissance never heard of "humanism," a word that was not coined until the nineteenth century. All they had was the word "human*ist*," which meant no more than a person well-versed in Roman and sometimes Greek literature who studied, taught, or wrote grammar, rhetoric, poetry, history, or ethics, subjects we still call "the humanities." These *studia humanitatis,* as they were known, had been part of the medieval academic curriculum since the late eleventh century. Academic subjects, like all the discourse of the church, the law, and most of the higher business of government, were taught, studied, and written about in the still living, still evolving Latin language. Today, when we think of the language used in law, academic disciplines, and theology, we think of dull, over-complicated lingo laden with technical jargon. These same qualities characterized the Latin used in those fields in the Middle Ages. Students of literature, whose first love is the beauty and clarity of language, usually despise such specialized jargons. This was also true of humanists who taught and studied Latin literature in the Middle Ages and the Renaissance. A fourteenth-century Italian, Francesco Petrarca (1304–1374; "Petrarch" in English), later called "the father of humanism," insisted that this medieval specialist's Latin was "barbarous" and that, to recover its lost beauty and eloquence, the Latin language must revert faithfully to the grammar and vocabulary of the ancient Romans. This was the most prominent facet of Petrarch's general belief that—except in religion—the ancient world had been superior to the present in every way. The cure for present ills, according to Petrarch, was to carry every aspect of life except religion back to the time of Cicero. He wrote in a letter:

> I have dwelt single-mindedly on learning about antiquity, among other things because this age has always displeased me, so that, unless love for dear ones pulled the other way, I always wished to have been born in any other age whatever, and to forget this one and I always tried to transport myself mentally to other times.[1]

1. Francesco Petrarca, "To Posterity," Rerum senilium libri (hereafter Sen.) XVIII.1, in *Letters of Old Age: Rerum senilium libri, I–XVIII,* trans. Aldo S. Bernardo, Saul Levin,

Coluccio Salutati, one of Petrarch's disciples, was chancellor of Florence from 1375 until his death in 1406. The propaganda that Salutati wrote for Florence in the revived Roman Latin was so effective that Florence's great enemy, Giangaleazzo Visconti, Duke of Milan, is reported to have said that he feared Salutati's pen more than a troop of horsemen.[2] Salutati's success set a precedent, not only that the Florentine chancellor must always be a prominent classical humanist, but also that every state in Italy, including the papacy, must employ humanists as chancellors and secretaries.[3] Salutati fostered a circle of younger humanists, including Poggio Bracciolini, Niccolò Niccoli, and Leonardo Bruni, who were evangelists for the cause of returning the Latin language to its "classic" stage of development. By the beginning of the fifteenth century (the quattrocento, as Italians call it),[4] public business was carried on exclusively in the polished, highly artificial, humanist Latin. As a result, aristocrats, the class who directed public affairs, hired humanist tutors to educate their sons in this neo-Latin and the classical culture that went with it. By the second quarter of the quattrocento mastery of the revived Roman Latin became a conspicuous class marker that clearly separated the ruling classes, with their humanist education, from lesser sorts who lacked it. Classical education continued to distinguish "gentlemen" from their inferiors until the European aristocracies immolated each other in the trenches during the First World War.

Humanists used their artificially revived language to write on many subjects, but, aside from their shared reverence for antiquity, they had no more agreement among themselves than users of polished English or French would have today. Because humanists were primarily concerned with the *form* of language, not its content, they were unlikely to develop a common philosophy or doctrine of "humanism"—which is why the "ism" form of the word never developed during the Renaissance. The linguistic purism of the humanists implied nothing at all about man and

---

and Reta A. Bernardo (Baltimore and London: Johns Hopkins University Press, 1992), 2:673–74.

2. Hans Baron, *The Crisis of the Early Italian Renaissance* (1955; repr. Princeton: Princeton University Press, 1966), 37–38; Lauro Martines, *The Social World of the Florentine Humanists 1390–1460* (Princeton: Princeton University Press, 1963), 252.

3. Charles Edward Trinkhaus, *The Scope of Renaissance Humanism* (Ann Arbor: University of Michigan Press, 1983), 16.

4. The terms "trecento" for the 1300s, "quattrocento" for the 1400s, and "cinquecento" for the 1500s are widely used in writing about the Renaissance and will often appear in these pages.

his place in the world or about religion or the lack of it. The only beliefs that humanists held in common were their allegiance to the Roman past and their conformity to classical grammar, vocabulary, and orthography. Paul Oskar Kristeller, the twentieth-century historian who reestablished our understanding of this original conception of a humanist, concluded "that the Italian humanists on the whole were neither good nor bad philosophers, but no philosophers at all."[5] "If we try to sum up their arguments and conclusions," Kristeller wrote, "leaving aside citations, examples, and commonplaces, literary ornaments, and digressions, we are frequently left with nearly empty hands."[6]

Judging history according to the purity of Latin letters, the humanists divided it into three epochs: classical antiquity, the golden age that could be emulated but not surpassed; the present, which was imitating that ancient excellence and was called "modern" (from *moderna,* meaning "current and up-to-date"); and, lying between these bright periods, the "ages in the middle" when men wrote "barbarous Latin." When sculptors, architects, and painters under humanist influence began to adopt Roman forms in their works, they adopted this same periodization. In a parallel with the literary men, artists rejected Gothic art and architecture from the recent past as "barbaric." In the quattrocento and cinquecento painters developed linear perspective and other skills unknown to antiquity and far excelled the Romans in convincingly depicting three-dimensional objects on a two-dimensional surface; but they still saw themselves as reviving a glorious antiquity. In the mid-sixteenth century, during the last phase of the Renaissance, the pioneer art historian, Giorgio Vasari, in his *Lives of the Most Eminent Painters, Sculptors, and Architects* (1550 and 1568), described the new art as a "rebirth" following the age of barbarism. His Italian word for rebirth, *rinascita,* translated into French and then borrowed into English, became our word "Renaissance." Throughout the quattrocento and cinquecento, love of the ancient, pride in the modern, and disdain for the intervening "barbarism" applied *only* to arts and letters. No one claimed that there had been any comparable "rebirth" in the economy, science, government, "worldliness," the church, or the character of their fellow citizens. They proclaimed themselves to be better artists and writers than their medieval predecessors, but not better *humans.*

5. Kristeller, *Renaissance Thought: The Classic, Scholastic and Humanist Strains* (New York: Harper Torchbooks, 1955), 99–100.

6. Kristeller, *Renaissance Thought: Sources,* 28.

The idea that the Italian Renaissance had been a *general* rebirth affecting every facet of human life was unheard of until two centuries after the Renaissance ended, and in France, not Italy.[7] It first took shape in the mind of François-Marie Arouet (1694–1778), better known as Voltaire, who used the concept as a weapon against religion. In the century before Voltaire, Galileo had proven that the geocentric model of the universe—devised in antiquity and generally accepted in the Middle Ages and Renaissance alike—was wrong and that the planets actually orbited around the sun, not the earth.[8] Not much later, Newton's discovery of invariable, mathematically quantifiable laws of physics seemed to lay nature's secrets open to human Reason (which thereupon began to be capitalized). A by-product of this scientific revolution was a confident faith that, if obstacles to the operation of Reason were only removed, Reason would reveal all knowledge and produce solutions to all problems. Voltaire was an effective and passionate propagandist for the Enlightenment, as this new faith was called. Although Voltaire was a deist who believed in a divine Creator, he thought that the greatest obstacles to the free operation of Reason were religion and tradition, which he saw as lingering aftereffects of the "barbarous" Middle Ages. Therefore, he believed that the Renaissance, which had ended the Middle Ages, must also have begun the destruction of religion and the liberation of Reason.

It was an article of faith for Voltaire that the Renaissance had rejected Christianity and thereby unleashed the power of man. He asserted (without evidence) that in fifteenth- and sixteenth-century Italy only the common people still adored the Christian mysteries, while the better classes mocked them.[9] Voltaire also believed, without evidence, that this partial removal of the Christian albatross led to sudden economic prosperity and increasing freedom; indeed, as Voltaire said, "everything tended toward perfection."[10] As for the Middle Ages, "*ces siècles grossiers*" (those gross centuries), when Christianity had dominated, "It is only necessary to know the history of that age in order to scorn it."[11] In the light of this

7. The much abbreviated account of the evolution of the traditional view of the Renaissance given here is indebted throughout to Wallace Ferguson, *The Renaissance in Historical Thought: Five Centuries of Interpretation* (New York: Houghton Mifflin, 1948).

8. Copernicus (1473–1543) advocated the heliocentric theory before Galileo, but Galileo was the first to demonstrate its clear superiority to older theories.

9. Voltaire (François-Marie Arouet), *Essai sur les moeurs et l'esprit des nations* (Paris: Editions Garnier Frères, 1963), 71.

10. Voltaire, *Siècle de Louis XIV* (Paris: Flammarion, n.d.), 6.

11. Voltaire, *Essai,* 11.

liberation Voltaire called upon his contemporaries to "erase the infamy" (*ecrasez l'infame*) of Christianity and replace it with the "natural religion" of deism, in which God's only role was to create the rational Laws of Nature and endow men with Reason in order to discover them.

From this admittedly simplified and inadequate summary of a complex intellectual revolution, it is clear enough that the Enlightenment itself originated "secular humanism," but its leaders, like a newly prominent family, had a natural (though irrational) yearning for a distinguished pedigree. Voltaire believed he had found this noble ancestry in Renaissance Italy. Voltaire created the underlying structure for the "Myth of the Renaissance," which has had many variations, but whose essential idea is that the Renaissance began modernity by liberating man's natural powers from the shackles that had enchained them during the medieval darkness. Faith in this myth virtually requires those who accept it to believe that all facets of human life withered during the Middle Ages and that all sprang into glorious new life with the Renaissance.

Properly used, the word "myth" does not necessarily imply falsehood. Whether a myth is literally true or not is simply irrelevant to its function as myth. Myths explain and justify deeply cherished faiths and transmit them to the next generation in simplified, memorable form. They are powerful and necessary if we are to define and transmit ideals—in fact, they are probably inseparable from having ideals at all. The function of history, however, is quite different: it serves the study of human nature by providing a record of actual human behavior in an almost infinite variety of situations. The two functions always have the potential for conflict: myth exists to reinforce and transmit our presuppositions and lacks any capacity for self-criticism; the study of history ought to be a constant "reality check," using historical information to continually criticize and correct our presuppositions. We cannot function without presuppositions, which is why we need myths; but we must continually criticize, reevaluate, and adjust them, which is why we need history. The Myth of the Renaissance is one of the most significant invasions of myth into the realm of history that has ever existed.

Since Voltaire first created it, the myth of a Renaissance liberation from the shackles of the Middle Ages has been expanded and readjusted again and again to illustrate the advantages of whatever aspect of modernity is currently fashionable—secularism, individualism, science, democracy, materialism, and capitalism, to name a few. The concept of modernity—now six centuries old—is continually changing. As succeeding "modern" ideals have come to the fore, each has deposited a fresh sedimentary layer on top of Voltaire's bedrock. The acknowledged "classic" among post-Voltairian interpretations of the Renaissance is *The Civilization of the Renaissance in Italy,* published in 1860 by the Swiss historian Jacob Burckhardt, in which he eloquently summed up the strata that had accumulated by his time. For Burckhardt's generation the romantic image of the heroic, creative individual was far more important than the rationalism cherished by the Enlightenment. Burckhardt's vision rests upon three concepts. The first, "The Development of the Individual" (one of Burckhardt's chapter titles), asserts that Renaissance Italians were the first people since antiquity to value their own individuality and to believe that their individual actions could change and control the world around them. The second concept, "The Discovery of the World and of Man" (another chapter title) claims that Renaissance people were the first since antiquity to enjoy the beauty of nature, explore its secrets, and understand and improve their political and social conditions. Burckhardt's third point is that, taken together, "The Development of the Individual" and "The Discovery of the World and of Man" constitute modernity. Burckhardt contrasts this with the Middle Ages.

> In the Middle Ages both sides of human consciousness—that which was turned within as that which was turned without—lay dreaming or half awake beneath a common veil.... In Italy this veil first melted into air; an *objective* treatment and consideration of the state and of all the things of this world became possible. The *subjective* side at the same time asserted itself with corresponding emphasis; man became a spiritual *individual* and recognized himself as such (italics are Burckhardt's).[12]

Since Burckhardt's time the Myth of the Renaissance has become ingrained in the self-image of Western civilization. Nevertheless, since the 1920s, historians of the Middle Ages have successfully demonstrated that, during the twelfth and thirteenth centuries, often called the High Middle Ages, Western Europe not only recovered from the setbacks it suffered during and after the fall of the Roman Empire, but in countless ways advanced beyond antiquity.[13] Considering the discoveries of histo-

12. Jacob Burckhardt, *The Civilization of the Renaissance in Italy,* trans. S. G. C. Middlemore, introduction by Peter Burke (London: Penguin, 1990), 98.

13. Charles Homer Haskins's book appeared in 1927. In the opening line Haskins acknowledged the revolutionary nature of his thesis: "The title of this book will appear to many to contain a flagrant contradiction. A renaissance in the Twelfth Century!"; Haskins, *The Renaissance of the Twelfth Century* (Cleveland, Ohio: Meridian, 1968), v.

rians over the last hundred years or so, it is hard to escape the conclusion that the High Middle Ages are the *foundational* period in the development of European civilization and that most of what has developed since then has been built upon those medieval foundations, not Renaissance ones. By the mid-twentieth century, historians of science had shown that the High Middle Ages, not the Renaissance, had established the Western tradition of experimental science in place of Greek methods that (with some well-publicized exceptions) were usually speculative and deductive. After this medieval period of scientific interests the Italian Renaissance, interested more in literature than in sciences, came (again, with some exceptions) as an "anticlimax."[14] Western successes in commerce, manufacture, and technology—activities that play a central role in most people's concept of modernity—have their historical roots in the Middle Ages, not in the Renaissance. The water, wind, and tidal mills of the medieval West harnessed sources of power other than human and animal muscle on a scale never reached by any previous civilization and applied these to industrial processes such as fulling cloth, operating bellows, tanning leather, sawing wood, making paper, and making mash for beer. Antiquity had known only the water mill, which was rarely utilized; in the thirteenth century there were 120 mills in and around the Flemish industrial town of Ypres.[15] The medieval invention of the pivoted axle made it possible to build four-wheeled vehicles larger and more stable than two-wheeled carts. (Roman roads were straight because, without axles, carts were difficult to turn.) On the sea, stern-post rudders and lateen sails and the compass improved shipping and opened the way for exploring the oceans and what lay beyond them.

In the High Middle Ages international trade routes flourished. Flanders and Florence wove fleeces from English and Spanish sheep into textiles and then shipped the cloth to the Baltic and the Middle East, as well as throughout Western Europe. Silk could either be imported from China or grown and woven into cloth at Lucca. Cities such as Frankfurt, Augsburg, Prague, Lübeck, and Hamburg flourished in regions that had been outside the reach of Rome but were now part of the heartland of the new civilization. Britain and Gaul, among the most underdeveloped

14. George Sarton, "Science in the Renaissance," in *The Civilization of the Renaissance*, edited by James Westfall Thompson, George Rowley, Ferdinand Schevill, and George Sarton (Chicago: University of Chicago Press, 1929), 75–76.

15. Lynn White, *Medieval Technology and Social Change* (1962; repr. New York: Oxford, 1978), 88–89; Jean Gimpel, *The Medieval Machine: The Industrial Revolution of the Middle Ages* (Aldershot, UK: Wildwood House, 1988), 1–2.

Roman provinces, became seats of powerful kingdoms. Italy's geographical position, between the older urban economies of the Levant and the rapidly developing ones across the Alps, enabled it to dominate long-distance trade, exporting Western cloth and importing Eastern luxury goods.[16] The value of goods passing through the port of Genoa doubled between 1214 and 1274 and then quadrupled on top of that between 1274 and 1293.[17] Using Eastern bases acquired during the crusades as well as permanent branches in European hubs, Italians merchants and bankers could move money and credit from London to Antioch, making Italy the unquestioned center of international banking.

Roman engineering had never attempted anything as daring as the Gothic cathedrals that suspended stone vaults upon a spider's web of slender piers and buttresses. The first universities came into being, teaching thousands a sophisticated, rigorous curriculum. At Toledo in Spain and at the universities, scholastics (as the humanists labeled the professors who dominated the universities) translated hundreds of works by ancient Greek writers and sought to use them as a foundation for new advances in science and philosophy. People read with eyeglasses for the first time, and weight-driven clocks began to standardize the length of the hours. It is impossible and fruitless to try to determine what culture was "most advanced" at what date, but Europe in the High Middle Ages was approximately as innovative and productive as Athens, Rome, China, India, Islam, or any other civilization of its time or earlier. The society that achieved all this was definitely not "asleep under a veil."

But if the Middle Ages were not "dark" or "asleep"; if the twelfth and thirteenth centuries were as productive and creative as any of the centuries that came after them; if "humanism" was about Latin grammar rather than about modern secularism, why did writers in the fifteenth and sixteenth centuries speak of their own time as a "rebirth"? Here, for example, is Matteo Palmieri (1406–1475), a Florentine humanist who ecstatically celebrates this "rebirth."

> Where was the painter's art till Giotto tardily restored it? A caricature of the art of human delineation! Sculpture and architecture, for long years sunk to the merest travesty of art, are only to-day in process of rescue from obscurity.... Of letters and liberal studies at large it were best to be silent

16. Richard A. Goldthwaite, *Wealth and the Demand for Art in Italy 1300–1600* (Baltimore: Johns Hopkins University Press, 1993), 13–14.

17. Daniel Waley, *The Italian City-Republics* (New York: McGraw-Hill, 1969), 37.

> altogether. For these, the real guides to distinction in all the arts, the solid foundation of all civilization, have been lost to mankind for eight hundred years and more. It is but in our own day that men dare boast that they see the dawn of better things.... Now, indeed, may every thoughtful spirit thank God that it has been permitted to him to be born in this new age so full of hope and promise, which already rejoices in a greater array of nobly-gifted souls than the world has seen in the thousand years that have preceded it.[18]

For all his enthusiasm, Palmieri speaks in this passage *only* about painting, sculpture, architecture, letters, and the *studia humanitatis:* these fields undoubtedly *did* undergo an important change: letters beginning in the fourteenth century and visual arts at the opening of the fifteenth century. Arts and letters constituted the entirety of the *rinascita* or Renaissance before Voltaire; Italians of the quattrocento and cinquecento (unless they were flattering a prince or a city) never spoke of "rebirth" in any other arena. In politics, economics, the church, and human nature their view was more often than not pessimistic. Those who want to understand the Renaissance historically are left then with a question that no one has seriously tried to answer. If human nature and society did *not* undergo a fundamental, revolutionary change in fourteenth- and fifteenth-century Italy, why did art and literature change so profoundly?

One of the prejudices arising from the Myth of the Renaissance is the assumption that the Renaissance could only be caused by something good. By definition, a golden age has no important imperfections, so that a search for its cause quickly becomes an effort to identify which of its many glories made everything else "tend to perfection." Instead of asking the open-ended question, "What caused the Renaissance?" we have asked only the loaded question, "What *good* thing caused the Renaissance?" The answer usually corresponds to what the author believes is the most desirable thing in his own period, such as secularism (Voltaire), individualism (Burckhardt), or political liberty and participation (Baron). Yet the most conspicuous change in the *objective* conditions of life in Italy between 1300 and 1400—that is, between the approximate end of the High Middle Ages and the approximate beginning of the artistic Renaissance—is not a good thing: it is, in fact, the return of plague to Europe after a six-century absence.

18. Matteo Palmieri, "On Civil Life," quoted in William H. Woodward, in *Studies in Education during the Age of the Renaissance, 1400–1600* (Cambridge: Cambridge University Press, 1906), 67.

The ingrained custom of ascribing all evils to the Middle Ages has made the words "medieval plague" inseparable in our minds. The disease usually thought to be bubonic plague first appeared in the Mediterranean region in 541–542 in the reign of the Byzantine emperor Justinian. This "First Pandemic" or "Plague of Justinian" lasted for generations, but was last mentioned in Western European sources in 767.[19] For nearly six centuries after that, including the High Middle Ages, Europe remained remarkably free of epidemic diseases.[20] The plague returned with a vengeance in the infamous "Black Death" of 1347–1352. The plague and its effects will get fuller treatment in the next chapter, but we must notice here something that textbooks and surveys seldom mention and never emphasize. After 1347–1352, the plague returned again and again at very frequent intervals everywhere in Europe throughout the period of Italy's Renaissance. These Renaissance plagues often blanketed all or much of Italy and often claimed the lives of large percentages of the population. A French scholar, Jean-Noel Biraben, in his study *Les hommes et la peste,* has attempted to list, by year and locality, every outbreak of plague in Europe (Biraben's listings for Italy are given in the appendix). We may be certain that Biraben's listings are incomplete, since he omits the outbreaks that figure most prominently during the papacy of Pius II (Rome, Viterbo, Bolsena, Abbadia in 1462 and Ancona in 1464). Yet, even by Biraben's incomplete listing, plague was raging someplace in Italy in *68 percent* of the years from 1348 to 1600—a span including all of the Italian Renaissance.[21]

These facts have profound significance for anyone trying to assess the differences between the Italian or European mentality in the High Middle Ages and in the Renaissance. *No one* in twelfth- and thirteenth-century Italy feared the plague or had any experience of its ravages. *Everyone* in late-fourteenth-, fifteenth-, and sixteenth-century Italy lived in constant fear of the plague; virtually everyone would have lost friends and loved ones to the disease; and almost everyone would have personally witnessed the horrors of a community held in its grip. Unless everything we now know about post-traumatic stress disorder (PTSD) was somehow suspended during this period, the outlook and attitudes of

19. William H. McNeill, *Plagues and Peoples* (New York: Anchor, 1977), 141.

20. John Kelly, *The Great Mortality: An Intimate History of the Most Devastating Plague of All Time* (New York: Harper Collins, 2005), 43–44; Robert S. Gottfried, *The Black Death: Natural and Human Disaster in Medieval Europe* (New York: Free Press, 1983), 12.

21. Jean-Noel Biraben, *Les hommes et la peste en France et dans les pays européens et mediterranéens,* appendix 4 (Paris: Mouton, 1975), 1:394–99.

everyone during this time must have been affected to some degree. Yet it is rare to find any writer interpreting the mentality of Italy during the Renaissance who acknowledges the plague and its effects.[22]

An oddity of periodization comes to our assistance here. The division of history into ancient, medieval, and modern epochs, with "the Renaissance" as the first phase of the latter, originated, as we have seen, with Italian humanists who were talking only about arts and letters. Many historians now recognize that this is a clumsy, arbitrary division, but, like the arrangement of letters on the keyboard (designed originally to slow typists down), it is easier to deal with its deficiencies than to replace it. One of the resulting quirks is that the line between "medieval" and "Renaissance" is drawn at different dates in Italy from elsewhere. Some authors begin the Italian Renaissance in the fourteenth century; others (as in this book) begin it in the fifteenth century; but everyone agrees that the Renaissance in Northern Europe did not fully arrive until the *sixteenth* century. Thus, north of the Alps, the fourteenth and fifteenth centuries are the "Late Middle Ages." While cultural historians have been squeamish about besmirching the Renaissance with plagues and wars, they have felt free to address the cultural effects of similar plagues, wars, and other disasters occurring at the same time in northern, "late medieval" Europe.

One of the great classics of early-twentieth-century historical writing, Johan Huizinga's *Autumn of the Middle Ages* (1919), focuses on the late-medieval mentality of northern France and the Netherlands, the part of northern Europe that was economically and socially most similar to Italy, and explains how that mentality shaped the rich literature and art this region produced at that time. Our concern in this book is with Italy; but it seems quite likely that Huizinga's observations in a region socially similar to Italy and subject to the same pattern of frequent plague and continual war would have parallels to developments in Italy during the same period of time. The thesis of this book is that the par-

22. Some historians have done very enlightening research on the emotional impact of the Black Death. Among them are Samuel K. Cohn, especially in *Cultures of Plague: Medical Thinking at the End of the Renaissance* (Oxford: Oxford University Press, 2010); David Herlihy, in several books and articles, including *The Black Death and the Transformation of the West* (Cambridge, Mass., and London: Harvard University Press, 1997); Sharon T. Strocchia, in *Death and Ritual in Renaissance Florence* (Baltimore: Johns Hopkins University Press, 1992); and art historian Millard Meiss, in his *Painting in Florence and Siena after the Black Death* (Princeton University Press, 1951). But even these generally do not extend their purview to the plague recurrences after the Black Death and do not apply their findings to the Renaissance per se.

allels are real, striking, and extremely significant. We will spend most of this book observing those parallels in the life of a single person, Aeneas Silvius Piccolomini (1405–1464), who became Pope Pius II in 1458. But before we can trace such parallels in his life we must briefly consult Huizinga to identify the factors and characteristics he recognized in Flanders that we expect to find also in Italy.

In the fourteenth and fifteenth centuries most of the Netherlands and much of northern France came under the rule of the Valois dukes of Burgundy, a cadet branch of the French royal family whose possession of the French Duchy of Burgundy gave them their title. The heart of the Burgundian state and its culture was Flanders, a region now split between Belgium and France. In the Middle Ages the county of Flanders and adjoining areas were more highly urbanized and economically advanced than any other part of Europe outside Italy. Flemish cities specialized in the production of woolen cloth and luxury textiles such as tapestries (called "arras" in many European languages after one of those cities). From the prosperity of Flanders and its neighbors, the Burgundian dukes derived a wealth that raised them to the forefront of European affairs. The ducal dynasty, its court, and its culture reached their apogee at the same time that Pius II reigned as pope. His contemporary, Duke Philip the Good (1419–1467), enjoyed a revenue estimated at 900,000 ducats, twice the revenue of the pope, four times the revenue of Florence, equaled among Italian states only by Venice.[23] Philip, his father, grandfather, and son all spent extravagantly on their court: clothes, jewels, buildings, festivals, tournaments, banquets, and art.[24] Philip the Good patronized the artist Jan van Eyck, one of the founders of a school of painters who united a Gothic aesthetic to an extremely detailed realism that was much admired and often imitated in Italy.[25]

Huizinga devotes little time to describing the plagues, wars, and

23. Otto Cartellieri, *The Court of the Dukes of Burgundy* (New York: Haskell House, 1925), 16. The income of Venice about half a century later is estimated at 1,150,000 ducats; Lauro Martines, *Furies: War in Europe, 1450–1700* (London and New York: Bloomsbury Press, 2013), 186. The ducat and the florin, the most common coins in the period, were approximately equal in worth. Radical economic change over the last half a millennium makes it impossible to estimate a modern value.

24. The dynasty consists of Philip the Bold (1363–1404), John the Fearless (1404–1419), Philip the Good (1419–1467), and Charles the Rash (1467–1477).

25. The term "Northern Renaissance," sometimes applied to this school of art, perpetuates the denial of medieval achievements in order to attach all good things to the Renaissance. It also invites confusion with the northern art influenced by Italy in the sixteenth century. Something like "Late Gothic Realism" would be much preferable.

instability that preyed upon the minds of the people he studied; he assumes that his readers know enough about the ever-recurrent plagues, the Hundred Years' War, and the struggles between the Burgundian dukes and the French monarchy. Instead, he concentrates on the dreary, pessimistic outlook that these tragedies instilled. In the period he studies, he tells us, "There is not only weariness with the world, but also an actual dread of life, a fearful shrinking away because of life's inevitable suffering."[26] Among his illustrations of this is the poetry of Eustache Deschamps (1346–1406), who describes the age in which he lives.

> Time of mourning and of temptations,
> Age of tears, of envy and of torment.
> Time of languor and of damnation,
> Age that brings us to the end.
> Time full of horror which does all things foolishly,
> Lying age, full of pride and envy,
> Time without honor and without true judgment.
> Age of sadness which shortens life.[27]

Huizinga rightly tells his readers that torrents of verses in this mournful key flowed from the pens of writers in these centuries—dreary verse whose sustained popularity would be inconceivable unless it echoed the mentality of the literate classes.[28] Adding to the terrors of the time, Huizinga sees a collapse of political morality in which arrogant, egocentric men and women observed the most exquisite courtesy while practicing murder, abduction, and cruelty for unabashedly selfish ends. "The unlimited arrogance of Burgundy!" Huizinga exclaims. Its history, he says, is "a poem of heroic pride." There "the splendor of painting, sculpture, and music flower, [while] the most violent code of revenge ruled and the most brutal barbarism spread among the aristocracy and burghers."[29] As we shall see, the life of Pius II in Italy shows innumerable examples of similarly despicable behavior. Burckhardt and his disciples make a point of emphasizing such dastardly political behavior in Italy as a sign of individualism![30]

In such an age, when plague stalked the city streets, when war was

26. Johan H. Huizinga, *The Autumn of the Middle Ages,* trans. Rodney J. Payton and Ulrich Mammitzsch (Chicago: University of Chicago Press, 1996), 35.

27. Quoted in ibid., 32.

28. Ibid., 32–33.

29. Ibid., 24–25.

30. For example, Burckhardt, *Civilization,* 35–39.

never more than a province away, when today's ally could be tomorrow's assassin, the fear of death entered into men's bones and lingered there. Like a latent disease, it could rush into their minds and chill their thoughts at the most unexpected moments. It was the period when the word "macabre" first appeared, a word describing the prevailing obsession with skeletons, rotting flesh, and the doom of youth and beauty. "It seems," Huizinga says, "as if the late medieval mind could see no other aspect of death than that of decay."[31] Huizinga's most vivid example of this morbid obsession with death is the Cemetery of the Innocents in Paris, dedicated to the children of Bethlehem, butchered at Herod's command. King Louis XI donated what was supposed to be the entire body of one of these murdered infants as a relic for the church.[32] In the center of this complex was a cemetery presided over by a large figure of Death, which is now at the Louvre. Burial, however, was only a preliminary here; after a few years the corpses were dug up so that the sacred ground could be reused. The skeletons then joined the growing heaps of bones and skulls in great bins above the Hall of Columns that surrounded the cemetery on three sides.[33] Sheltered beneath these ghoulish receptacles, people promenaded among the columns and contemplated the frescoes on the walls, which displayed a particularly fulsome *danse macabre.* The *danse macabre,* or "dance of death," was a common subject for art. In it skeletons and partially rotting corpses called *transis* dance with living men and women of every age and rank, leading them away to their graves. In the paintings at the Cemetery of the Innocents forty such figures were waltzed away by skeletal or decomposing versions of themselves. Under each couple, warning verses drove home the message of life's vanity and the equality of all in death.[34] This doleful place was one of the popular resorts of Paris. Shopkeepers set up their stalls in the Hall of Columns; friars preached there; women of easy virtue plied their trade; and an elderly female hermit had her cell on the side of the church.[35]

In this age of plague and war, dwelling on death and decay seemed to be no more than facing up to the realities of the human condition. Nevertheless, very few people could take a steady diet of that kind of real-

31. Huizinga, *Autumn,* 156.

32. Ibid., 169–70.

33. Ibid., 170. During a siege in 1590, the starving people of Paris ground these bones into a meal and ate the bread they made from it; Lauro Martines, *Furies,* 127.

34. Huizinga, *Autumn,* 165–66 and 170.

35. Ibid., 170.

ity. More often than not, instead of wallowing in gloom and fear, people sought some kind of mental defense, refuge, or escape from the depression that constantly threatened them. The Franco-Burgundian elite chose, in Huizinga's words, "to color life with lustrous tones, to live in a dreamland of shining fantasies, and to soften reality in the ecstasy of the ideal."[36] If facing reality meant dwelling on the threat of plague, the brevity and insecurity of life, the repellence of decaying corpses, people would, as often as possible, seek an alternative. The alternative to reality can only be *un*reality—an imaginary ideal, a dream, a fantasy. A dream or fantasy requires a theme—we can only dream or fantasize *about* something. Huizinga acknowledges the existence of a "bucolic" theme, by which he means the enjoyment of nature. Huizinga does not have much to say about this theme, but we will see that it was very important to Pius II. The preferred fantasy theme among Huizinga's Burgundians was the ideal of chivalry and courtly love. Chivalry and courtly love, two distinct but intertwined concepts, had evolved during the High Middle Ages as the feudal classes of Europe sought ideals to guide and justify their own behavior and their dominant place in society. Chivalry, put simply, was the behavior of ideal knights: skilled in warfare, strong, fearless, honorable, loyal, devout, defenders of the defenseless, champions of Christendom against the infidel. It was the medieval variant of the ethic found in warrior castes from the *Iliad* to Japanese samurai. Courtly love was the ideal behavior of knights and ladies toward one another. It had originated in the late eleventh century, when troubadours entertained predominately female audiences (husbands and fathers were away fighting) with tales of knights falling under the thrall of the ladies they adored. In courtly love the lady was expected to be cool and aloof, at least in the first stage of the relationship; and it was up to her to decide when and how the relationship advanced. The knight, on the other hand, inspired by his love for the lady and his desire to win her esteem, must perform feats of courage and skill, typically exhibited at tournaments. As long as the lady remained disdainful, the knight must be brokenhearted—a state of mind he should express in an ever-flowing stream of poetry. In twelfth-century courts led by two powerful women, Eleanor of Aquitaine (1122–1204) and her daughter, Marie of Champagne (1145–1198), the behaviors of courtly love were "enforced" on the knights in "courts of love" according to a somewhat tongue-in-cheek rulebook written by the court chap-

36. Ibid., 37–38.

lain.[37] Chivalry and courtly love first became the dominant themes of upper-class literature during the High Middle Ages, but this dominance suffered hardly any decline before the satire of Cervantes's *Don Quixote* in the seventeenth century, and they were still available when Tennyson wrote *Idylls of the King* in the nineteenth century. By the middle of the fourteenth century this theme had generated a whole imaginary world, furnished with enchanted castles, caves and forests, dragons, ogres, witches and wizards, quests, giants and dwarves, emblems, colors—all the paraphernalia that still bestows a medieval atmosphere on fantasies such as *Harry Potter* and *Lord of the Rings.* It was a pervasive motif everywhere in Italy during the Renaissance, but it has been largely ignored in general interpretations of the period.

An artificial, unreal parallel world can only function as a mental refuge if it can be made to *seem* real. To achieve that "seeming" is a very expensive undertaking that requires a great deal of leisure time and wealth to expend on art, architecture, and other "props" necessary to the performance. Art, literature, architecture were the most common means available for making the unreal seem real before film and the digital age—and, of course, only the most realistic art could perform this function. Chivalry and courtly love were forms of playacting from their beginnings: thus, they were ready-to-hand for the elaboration produced under the stresses of the fourteenth- and fifteenth-century plagues and wars. Huizinga consistently portrays the resulting expressions as unnaturally excessive and overblown. This is because "the greater the contrast with the misery of daily life, the more indispensible the festival and the stronger the means required to bestow splendor on life by virtue of the ecstasy of beauty and enjoyment that lights up the darkness of reality."[38] "The tension between the forms of life and reality is extremely high; the light is false and overdone."[39]

The culminating examples of these charades are the festivals of the court: tournaments, banquets, and entrances to cities by the most important personages. Among these, one of the most famous was the "Feast of the Pheasant" that Philip the Good gave in Lille on February 17, 1454, as an occasion for himself and his courtiers to pledge themselves to go on crusade. Constantinople had fallen to the Turks nine

37. Andreas Capellanus, *The Art of Courtly Love: With Introduction, Translation, and Notes by John Jay Perry* (New York: Columbia University Press, 1990).

38. Huizinga, *Autumn,* 303.

39. Ibid., 39.

months before, and Pope Nicholas had declared a crusade. Crusading had a special place in the mythology of chivalry; fighting the infidel was the highest calling and the moral duty of every knight. Philip's father, John the Fearless, had earned his flattering nickname from his courage in battle in 1396 at the disastrous Crusade of Nicopolis in Hungary. Constantinople was too distant from the Burgundian lands for Philip to have any practical interest in its fate, but the reputation he nurtured for his court as a kind of second Camelot required that he respond magnificently to its fall. That crusade and Philip the Good's role in it would become central issues in Pius II's papacy. Pope Pius II also engaged in tournaments, banquets, and state entries that differ little in spirit from these Franco-Burgundian extravaganzas.

Huizinga emphasizes the interconnection, even the fusion, of art and life in fifteenth-century France and Burgundy.[40] Art was not isolated from life as an object of contemplation, but was an integral part of the environment in which people lived; it served purposes that were seen as practical. An altarpiece existed to inspire devotion, to proclaim some aspect of Christian faith, and, not incidentally, to proclaim the glory and piety of the donor who commissioned it. Courtly art—palaces, the paintings, sculptures, tapestries, and furniture they contained, along with the associated ceremonies, banquets, tournaments, and processions—all existed to proclaim the glory of the prince and his justice, his clemency, his knightly prowess, his piety, his lineage, his wealth.[41] Art had always had essentially practical functions, even in the days of cave painting, and this was still true in the Middle Ages and Renaissance. But now art had the expanded task of transforming the real world into a fictional ideal. "Art," Huizinga says, "had the task of embellishing the forms in which life was lived with beauty." But—and the distinction is important—"What was sought was not art itself, but the beautiful life."[42] The beautiful life in late medieval France and Flanders must of course be Christian, but on its secular side the beautiful life meant the imagined world of chivalry and courtly love.

Huizinga frequently refers to similarities between Burgundian and Italian culture in the fifteenth century, but, writing when Burckhardt's version of the Myth of the Renaissance reigned unchallenged, he always yields superiority to the Italians.[43] Nevertheless, he says, "the line be-

40. Ibid., 311–13.
41. Ibid., 296–97.
42. Ibid., 296.
43. Ibid., 39, 42, 76, 136, 388, among others.

tween the Middle Ages and the Renaissance is too sharply drawn. The passionate desire to dress life in beauty, the refinement of the art of living, the colorful products of a life lived in imitation of an ideal are much older than the Italian *quattrocento.*"[44] "The whole aristocratic life of the later Middle Ages, whether one thinks of France and Burgundy or of Florence, is an attempt to play out a dream."[45] Huizinga says it was the same dream, chivalry and courtly love, both in Italy and the North. "France and Burgundy always play the piece in the old style. Florence composes on the set theme a new and more beautiful variation."[46] Here, I must differ from Huizinga; the chivalry/courtly love theme was very important in Renaissance Italy, but Italy's innovations are not associated with that theme as often as with another idealized dreamworld, that of ancient Rome.

Italy in the fourteenth and fifteenth centuries had as much or more plague and war as any part of transalpine Europe and would continue to suffer from both during the sixteenth century, when France and Spain launched invasions that extinguished Italy's political independence. As in the rest of Europe, war and plague engendered melancholy, morbidity, and a taste for the macabre. Italians, like the French and Burgundians, offset their melancholy by escaping into an idealized dreamworld that they sought to replicate in their own lives. Although many factors made Italy's cultural expressions distinct from those of the North, the distinction that lay at the core of those differences was that the two regions chose divergent themes to follow and imitate. While transalpine Europe dreamed of Camelot, Italians dreamed of Rome in its heyday and imitated it assiduously in literature and art. The difference in theme was certainly not absolute; we will see many examples of the popularity of chivalry in Italy. The classics were also welcomed in the North, as illustrated in Philip the Good's order of chivalry based upon the classical story of Jason and the Golden Fleece. Because they all served the same emotional need to escape from a worrisome reality, the escapist themes, including the less prominent bucolic theme, were emotionally interchangeable. Petrarch, for example, was the supreme courtly love poet of his century and a powerful influence on all courtly love poetry after him, but he is also the one who sounded the clearest clarion call to revert to Latin as the Romans had spoken it. In one of his letters Petrarch

44. Ibid., 39. "Much older" here apparently means only a century, since Huizinga never ventures earlier than 1300.

45. Ibid., 42.

46. Ibid., 42.

clearly marks the path that led from revulsion toward present-day reality to the embrace of antiquity.

> While I write I become eagerly engaged with our greatest writers ... and willingly forget those among whom my unlucky star destined me to live; and to flee from these I concentrate all my strength (on) following the ancients instead. For just as the very sight of my fellows offends me greatly, so the recollection of magnificent deeds and outstanding names gives me such incredible and unmeasurable delight that ... many would be stupefied to learn that I find greater pleasure in being with the dead than with the living.[47]

The same mechanism that operated for Petrarch during the fourteenth century when the Renaissance was still in embryo continued to work for Machiavelli in the sixteenth century. Machiavelli, writing to a friend, describes his readings in ancient authors in a way that reveals the same imitative, role-playing quality that Huizinga discerned in the North.

> On the coming of evening I return to my house and enter my study; at the door I take off the day's clothing, covered with mud and dust, and put on garments regal and courtly; and reclothed appropriately, I enter the ancient courts of ancient men, where, received by them with affection, I feed on that food which is only mine and which I was born for, where I am not ashamed to speak with them and to ask them the reason for their actions; and they in their kindness answer me; and for four hours of time I do not feel boredom, I forget every trouble, I do not dread poverty, I am not frightened by death; entirely I give myself over to them.[48]

In this book we will watch similar mechanisms working in the life of a representative figure of the Italian quattrocento, Aeneas Silvius Piccolomini, later Pope Pius II. His life, like most Italian lives during the Renaissance, was marked by periodic outbreaks of plague and almost continuous involvement in war. Before we launch into following these escapist mechanisms in his life, we need to look more closely at plague and war and the reactions to them in Renaissance Italy—an aspect of Italian life that has been consistently excluded from many interpretations.

47. Francesco Petrarca, *Rerum familiarum libri I–VIII* (hereafter *Fam.*), Book VI, *Petrarch to Giovanni Colonna, Avignon, 25 Sept., 1342*(?), trans. Aldo S. Bernardo (Albany: State University of New York Press, 1975), 4:314–15.

48. Machiavelli to Francesco Vettori, December 10, 1513, in *The Letters of Machiavelli: A Selection of His Letters,* by Niccolò Machiavelli, ed., trans. Allan Gilbert (New York: Capricorn, 1961), 142.

2

The Four Horsemen

THE ROMAN PEACE in the first and second centuries A.D. and the flourishing of Roman culture that accompanied it had coincided with a period of comparative respite from the scourges of famine, plague, war, and death. The High Middle Ages had benefitted from a similar hiatus. But in the fourteenth century these "Four Horsemen of the Apocalypse" came galloping back for several centuries of unusually intense affliction. Famine was the first to reappear. Climate change contributed to this as Europe moved from an unusually mild climactic cycle into what is now called the "Little Ice Age." In 1303 and again in 1306 and 1307, the Baltic Sea froze.[1] Crops failed across northern Europe from Ireland to Hungary in 1315–1317.[2] The rapid population growth during the High Middle Ages depended partly upon the clearing and developing of new agricultural land. But, even after all the available land had been put to use, the population continued growing. Peasants could only feed the swelling numbers by planting wheat on land formerly used for other crops or for pasture. Like the rice monocultures of Asia, this "wheat monoculture" made survival overly dependent on one crop. Thus, climate change fell upon an overpopulated Europe that had no margin between sufficiency and starvation.

Wheat crops failed in England in 1291–1293, while yields dropped by half in France and Germany. Regional famines became common,

1. Gottfried, *Black Death,* 24.

2. Lynn White, "Death and the Devil," in *The Darker Vision of the Renaissance: Beyond the Fields of Reason,* edited by Robert S. Kinsman, 26–27 (Berkeley: University of California Press, 1974).

but in 1309 there was continent-wide famine for the first time in 250 years. Between 1316 and 1322, famine may have reduced Europe's population by 10 to 15 percent.[3] The distress reached its peak in the 1340s; the crops failed in Tuscany in 1346, and hailstorms damaged the wheat in the following year. Penitential processions, some of them lasting for three days, wound through the streets of Florence and Siena, begging the Almighty for relief.[4] With some hyperbole, the Florentine Giovanni Morelli recalled in his memoirs for 1347 that there had been people who "lived on herbs and on the roots of herbs and on vile plants ... and the entire countryside was filled with persons who went about grazing like cattle on the grass."[5] Worse was coming; those weakened by malnutrition were quickly finished off by a more efficient killer that made its debut later that year—the Black Death.

In the years 1347–1353 the disease usually thought to be bubonic plague swept through Europe, claiming the lives of at least half the population. "Black Death" is a modern term; contemporaries called it "the Great Death" or "the Great Pestilence."[6] Our sources do not permit certainty about the numbers killed; for most of the twentieth century scholars accepted an estimate that about a third of the European population died.[7] Recent studies have pointed out that the statistics we have been using probably undercount the death rate.[8] Local demographic studies since about 1960 have tended to confirm a much higher estimate of mortality in the Black Death.[9] Recent estimates for Florence, one of the best-documented localities, are now in the range of 55 to 65 percent.[10] Italy as a whole fell into a range of between 50 and 60 percent.[11] It now seems likely that the *majority* of Europeans, perhaps 60 percent of the total, died in the Black Death between 1347 and 1353.[12] No other

3. Gottfried, *Black Death,* 26–28.

4. Meiss, *Painting in Florence,* 64.

5. David Herlihy and Christiane Klapisch-Zuber, *Tuscans and Their Families: A Study of the Florentine Catasto of 1427* (New Haven: Yale University Press, 1985), 89.

6. William Naphy and Andrew Spicer, *The Black Death and the History of Plagues 1345–1730* (Stroud, Gloucestershire, UK: Tempus, 2000), 53.

7. Ole J. Benedictow, *The Black Death, 1346–1353: The Complete History* (Woodbridge, Suffolk, UK: Boydell Press, 2004), 380.

8. Benedictow, *Black Death,* 257–73. Tax and other official records consistently underreport deaths among women, children, and the very poor—groups that probably had the highest mortality. It is also likely that death rates were much higher in the countryside, where the vast majority of the population lived, than in the comparatively well-documented cities.

9. Ibid., 246.

10. Ibid., 291–92.

11. Ibid., 307.

12. Ibid., 383.

event or series of related events—not even the two world wars and the systematic butcheries of Hitler and Stalin—have ever slaughtered such a high proportion of the European population.[13] And, although the epidemic took eight years to spread to every corner of the continent, its duration in any given place was usually only five to six months, during which time the survivors watched half or more of their family, friends, and fellow citizens perish.

There have always been "plagues" of various sorts; but we can identify none before the sixth century A.D. that showed the distinctive symptom of buboes: dark, hard swellings of the lymph glands in the groin and armpit as they clog up and become bloated with microbes. The first plague with bubonic symptoms in the West was the "Plague of Justinian" or "First Pandemic." In its initial outbreak in 541 at Constantinople, the Byzantine capital lost an estimated 40 percent of its people. In the outbreak of 599–600, Italy and southern Gaul lost an estimated 15 percent of their population.[14] In Rome the greatest outbreak was in 590, when penitential processions led through the city by Pope Gregory the Great produced a miraculous vision of the Archangel Michael standing atop Hadrian's tomb and sheathing his sword. A statue of the angel was erected on the site of the vision, so that Hadrian's tomb became, as it is today, the "Castel Sant'Angelo."[15] In 680 relics of St. Sebastian brought an end to the outbreak that was ravaging Pavia, laying the foundations for Sebastian's later emergence as a "plague-saint."[16] The cumulative demographic collapse both from repeated plagues and the collapse of the Roman social order in Western Europe may have reduced the population by as much as 50 to 75 percent.[17] Although the First Pandemic continued up to the twelfth century in the Middle East, it disappeared in the West after 767, probably because the small, scattered populations reduced the spread of all kinds of infectious diseases.[18] Even when the population expanded again in the High Middle Ages, contagious

13. Ibid., 69.

14. Naphy and Spicer, *Black Death,* 21–22.

15. Ibid., 23.

16. Sheila Barker, "The Making of a Plague Saint: Saint Sebastian's Imagery and Cult before the Counter-Reformation," in *Piety and Plague from Byzantium to the Baroque,* edited by Franco Mormando and Thomas Worcester (Kirksville, Mo.: Truman State University Press, 2007), 92.

17. Naphy and Spicer, *Black Death,* 21–22.

18. Kelly, *Great Mortality,* 44; Naphy and Spicer, *Black Death,* 22; McNeill, *Plagues and Peoples,* 113–14.

disease remained unusually rare. The gap of six centuries before the plague returned to Western Europe was long enough for vivid memory of the plague (except for St. Gregory's and St. Sebastian's miracles) to have died out.[19] Almost all observers in Europe in 1347–1353 believed that they were witnessing something unprecedented in human history.[20]

In early October 1347, at Messina in Sicily, the Franciscan chronicler Michele da Piazza recorded what may have been the first European landfall of the Second Pandemic, where it arrived aboard twelve Genoese galleys. Michele tells us that "The Genoese carried such a disease in their bodies that if anyone so much as spoke with one of them he was infected with the deadly illness and could not avoid death." The Messinians expelled the Genoese, but the disease was already on the loose. The extreme contagion, attested by every witness, amazed everyone. Michele wrote that "breath spread the infection among those speaking together, with one infecting the other, and it seemed as if the victim was struck all at once by the affliction and was, so to speak, shattered by it." He continues:

> This shattering impact, together with the inhaled infection, caused the eruption of a sort of boil, the size of a lentil, on the thigh or arm, which so infected and invaded the body that the victims violently coughed up blood, and after three days' incessant vomiting, for which there was no remedy, they died—and with them died not only anyone who had talked with them, but anyone who had acquired or touched or laid hands on their belongings.[21]

In Italy local chroniclers tell us that in Genoa six out of seven died, at Bologna and Padua two out of three; Piacenza lost half its people, while seven out of ten perished in Pisa.[22] In Orvieto people died at a rate of five hundred a day until half the population was gone. The surviving Orvietans added fifty new dates of religious observance to their calendar and, in fear of God, turned their remaining energies toward rushing the completion of their cathedral.[23] Few places suffered more than Siena, a

19. McNeill, *Plagues and Peoples,* 111.

20. Samuel K. Cohn, *The Black Death Transformed: Disease and Culture in Early Renaissance Europe* (London: Arnold, 2002), 224–26.

21. Michele da Piazza, *Cronaca* (selections), in *The Black Death,* edited and translated by Rosemary Horrox (Manchester, UK, and New York: Manchester University Press, 1994), 36.

22. Johannes Nohl, *The Black Death: A Chronicle of the Plague,* trans. C. H. Clark (1926; repr. New York: Ballantine, 1960), 33.

23. Carpentier, *Une ville devant,* 109.

great city of about sixty thousand people, where about 60 percent died.[24] In the Sienese government four of the nine priors died, along with the *podestà* (chief judicial officer), the captain of war, and two of the four financial directors.[25] A Sienese survivor, Agnolo di Tura, has left us a very personal description of the city's desolation.

> In this time began the Great Mortality, the greatest, and most obscure, and most horrible imaginable; and it lasted till October, 1348. It was of such a secret character that men and women died almost without warning. A swelling appeared in the groin or the armpit, and while they were talking they fell dead. The father would not attend to his son; one brother fled from the other; the wife abandoned her husband; for it was said that to catch the disease it sufficed to look upon a victim or to feel his breath. And it must have been so indeed, since so many perished in the months of May, June, July, and August, that it was impossible to find anyone to bury the dead. Neither relatives nor friends nor priests nor friars accompanied them to the grave, nor was the office of the dead recited. He who lost a relative or a house-mate, as soon as the breath had left the body, took him by night or day, and with two or three to lend a hand, carried him to the church, and with his helpers buried the corpse as best he could, covering it with just enough earth to save it from the dogs. And in many places of the city trenches were dug, very broad and deep, and into them the bodies were thrown and covered with a little earth; and thus layer after layer until the trench was full; and then another trench was commenced. And I, Agnolo di Tura, called Grasso, with my own hands buried five of my children in a single trench; and many others did the like. And many dead there were so ill-covered that the dogs dug them up and ate them, dispersing their limbs through the city. And no bells rang and nobody wept no matter what his loss, because almost everyone expected death.... And people believed and said: This is the end of the world.[26]

Agnolo was not being metaphorical in speaking of "the end of the world." Gabriele de' Mussis of Piacenza describes God's decree: "I shall wipe man, whom I created, off the face of the earth."[27] When the Florentine chronicler Giovanni Villani died, his brother Matteo took up where

24. Benedictow, *Black Death,* 307.

25. Meiss, *Painting in Florence,* 65–66.

26. Quoted in Ferdinand Schevill, *Siena: The Story of a Medieval Commune* (New York: Charles Scribner's Sons, 1909), 210–11.

27. De' Mussis, *Historia de Morbo* (selections), in Horrox, *Black Death,* 18.

Giovanni had left off, intending, as he said, to record "the extermination of mankind."[28]

There were anomalies that are still unexplained. Milan, with a population of as much as 100,000, lost "only" 15,000 people. There the despot Bernabò Visconti walled up whole families in their homes at the first sign of infection, but the mystery of why Milan escaped relatively lightly remains unsolved.[29] In Venice, the largest city in Europe, the population of 120,000 to 150,000 suffered a loss estimated at 60 percent.[30] The leaders of the republic fled, and no quorum for business could be assembled in the Great Council. The state awarded honors to any physicians who remained on duty.[31] After the epidemic ended, the doge invited foreigners to come repopulate the city, offering citizenship after two years of residence.[32]

In the introduction to the *Decameron,* Giovanni Boccaccio wrote the best-known account of the Black Death. Between his account and that of Gabriele de' Mussis in Piacenza we can reconstruct the range of symptoms that victims endured. De' Mussis says that "out of the blue, a kind of chilly stiffness troubled their bodies. They felt a tingling sensation, as if they were being pricked by the points of arrows."[33] After this, the buboes began to form, typically in the armpit or groin, growing ever more firm and solid. Boccaccio describes them as "egg-shaped, whilst others were roughly the size of the common apple."[34] As this happened, de' Mussis continues, "its burning heat caused the patients to fall into an acute and putrid fever, with severe headaches." Some victims developed an "intolerable stench.[35] In others there was vomiting of blood. Boccaccio and de' Mussis both describe other smaller swellings scattered over the body, which Boccaccio called *gavòccioli.*[36] A particularly deadly symptom mentioned by Boccaccio but not by de' Mussis was "dark blotches and bruises" all over the body, "sometimes large and few in number, at other times tiny and closely spaced."[37] Although some vic-

28. Meiss, *Painting in Florence,* 65–66.

29. Naphy and Spicer, *Black Death,* 35–36.

30. Gottfried, *Black Death,* 47–48.

31. Francis Aidan Gasquet, *The Black Death of 1348 and 1349* (London: George Bell, 1908), 35–36.

32. Nohl, *Black Death,* 33.

33. De' Mussis, *Historia de Morbo,* 24.

34. Giovanni Boccaccio, *The Decameron,* trans. G. H. McWilliam (London: Penguin, 1972), 50.

35. De' Mussis, *Historia de Morbo,* 24.

36. Ibid., 24; Boccaccio, *Decameron,* 50.

37. Boccaccio, *Decameron,* 50.

tims died quickly or within a day, Boccaccio and de Mussis both confirm that it took three to five days for most to die. Those who fell into a coma or those who had swellings or stench had no hope; but de' Mussis reports that some who had only the fever were able to recover.[38] Even today only about 20 percent of those with the common, bubonic form of the plague survive. The other forms, pneumonic and septicaemic, have almost no survivors.

The church was powerless to help. In the middle of March 1348 Pope Clement VI granted plenary absolution for all who died before Easter, provided they confessed and were contrite. But many would have found no priests alive or willing to hear their confessions.[39] The monastic orders, living together in close quarters, suffered particularly high casualties. Thirty thousand Franciscans died in Italy.[40] Petrarch's brother, Gerardo, was the sole survivor among the monks at the Certosa of Montrieux.[41] In the end, Pope Clement followed the advice of his doctors and fled to a country estate, where he kept fires blazing in all the rooms throughout the heat of summer.[42]

Witnesses unanimously emphasized the extreme contagion that affected animals as well as humans. Michele da Piazza in Messina said that "not just one person in a house died, but the whole household, down to the cats and the livestock."[43] Boccaccio says that when the healthy had contact with the sick, the disease would "rush upon" them "with the speed of a fire racing through dry or oily substances." Clothing and other possessions seemed as toxic as the dying victims themselves. In a memorable anecdote Boccaccio describes what happened when two pigs fell upon the rags of a deceased pauper.

> In their wonted fashion, the pigs first of all gave the rags a thoroughgoing mauling with their snouts after which they took them between their teeth and shook them against their cheeks. And within a short time they began to writhe as though they had been poisoned, then they both dropped dead to the ground, spread-eagled upon the rags that had brought about their undoing.[44]

38. De' Mussis, *Historia de Morbo,* 25.
39. Gasquet, *Black Death of 1348 and 1349,* 47.
40. Ibid., 36 and 52.
41. Nohl, *Black Death,* 39.
42. Gasquet, *Black Death of 1348 and 1349,* 51.
43. Da Piazza, *Cronaca,* 36.
44. Boccaccio, *Decameron,* 51.

In Piacenza Gabriele de' Mussis tells how people fleeing from Genoa rapidly infected his city. Fulco della Croce, a citizen of Piacenza, gave shelter to a Genoese friend who arrived already ill. The Genoese guest died that night "and then straightaway Fulco with his whole household and many of his neighbors died, too." De' Mussis reports that in Bubbio people died simply from buying merchandise from those who were fleeing Genoa. In the same town a victim made his confession and had a notary draw up his will before witnesses; the next day, the dying man, the priest, the notary, and the witnesses "were all buried together."[45]

This extreme contagion so unanimously reported throughout the four centuries of the Second Pandemic directly contradicts the way plague is known to spread today: through the clumsy mechanism of fleas that bite infected rats and subsequently bite humans. This, along with the lack of any reports of dying rats as a warning sign for plague, has led Samuel K. Cohn, among others, to challenge the established view that the Plague of Justinian and the Black Death were the same disease as the modern bubonic plaque caused by the microbe *Yersinia pestis*.[46] The twentieth-century view that *Yersinia pestis* is to blame for all occurrences of plague with bubonic symptoms has stout defenders, but the question is again open to debate.[47]

Agnolo di Tura in Siena, Michele da Piazza in Messina, de' Mussis in Piacenza, and Boccaccio in Florence all report indignantly that families often abandoned their infected members to die alone. Marchionne di Coppo Stefani, also in Florence, reports that relatives would place food and water by the sick person's bedside "so that you don't have to wake me during the night" and then decamp as soon as the victim was asleep.[48] Consequently, "many who died did not confess or receive the last rites; and many died by themselves and many died of hunger."[49] De' Mussis imagines the appeal of a child neglected by its mother: "Mother, where have you gone? Why are you so cruel to me when only yesterday

45. De' Mussis, *Historia de Morbo,* 21.

46. See Cohn, *Black Death Transformed* and *Cultures of Plague;* but also Graham Twigg, *The Black Death: A Biological Reappraisal* (New York: Schocken, 1985); Gunnar Karlsson, *Iceland's 1100 Years: The History of a Marginal Society* (Reykjavik, Iceland: Mál og menning, 2000); Norman Cantor, *In the Wake of the Plague: The Black Death and the World It Made (New York: Perennial/Harper Collins, 2002)*; and Susan Scott and Christopher Duncan, *Return of the Black Death: The World's Greatest Serial Killer* (Chichester, UK, and Hoboken, N.J.: Wiley, 2004).

47. The stoutest defender is probably Ole J. Benedictow.

48. Kelly, *Great Mortality,* 110.

49. Quoted in Benedictow, *Black Death,* 285.

you were so kind?" and "Come here, I'm thirsty, bring me a drink of water. I'm still alive. Don't be frightened. Perhaps I won't die. Please hold me tight, hug my wasted body. You ought to be holding me in your arms."[50]

When the dying finally ended, it left behind an empty, echoing world. Petrarch asked, "Where are our dear friends now? . . . There was a crowd of us, now we are almost alone."[51] Everywhere were ghost towns, abandoned and deteriorating buildings, overgrown fields, broken fences, roofless barns, and the return of forest. About one in ten villages in Tuscany were abandoned.[52] Although scattered cases still occurred, the survivors assumed that they had witnessed a unique outpouring of divine rage like the biblical flood. Petrarch said that "happy posterity, who will not experience such abysmal woe . . . will look upon our testimony as a fable."[53] But the Black Death was only the spectacular introduction to a four-hundred-year plague era. Only the Black Death of 1347–1353 reached every corner of Europe in a single, rapidly moving outbreak, but many later visitations covered large regions or even vast swathes of the continent. Every year saw outbreaks somewhere in Europe, and every locality experienced plague again and again for at least the first two centuries of the Second Pandemic. From 1400 to 1600 the plague raged somewhere in Europe during every year but one.[54] In Italy Venice had an outbreak in 1357, but most of the peninsula was not ravaged again until 1361–1363, when the *pesta secunda* in Pisa, Pistoia, and Florence, among other places, killed, on average, about 20 percent of the population.[55] In 1369–1371 the *pesta tertia* took an additional 10 to 15 percent. These returning outbreaks disabused the population of any illusion that the Black Death was a single, unique phenomenon. People had to habituate themselves to a life that was far more frightening and precarious than before.[56] Petrarch wrote to Boccaccio in September of 1363: "The year 1348 . . . was one of mourning for us. Now we realize

50. De' Mussis, *Historia de Morbo,* 22.

51. Kelly, *Great Mortality,* 12.

52. Peter Burke, *The Italian Renaissance: Culture and Society in Italy* (Cambridge: Polity Press, 1986), 225.

53. Philip Ziegler, *The Black Death* (New York: John Day, 1969), 45.

54. Ellen Schiferl, "Iconography of Plague Saints," *Fifteenth-Century Studies* 6 (1983): 205. The fortunate year was 1445.

55. Naphy and Spicer, *Black Death,* 40–41; Gottfried, *Black Death,* 130.

56. Carpentier, *Une ville devant,* 34.

that it is only the beginning of our mourning, for since then this evil force, unequaled and unheard of in human annals through the centuries, has never ceased, striking everywhere on all sides, on the left and right, like a skilled warrior."[57] As we have seen, plague is documented in Italy during at least 68 percent of the years from 1348 to 1600.[58] No matter where it appeared, plague cut off trade with the afflicted places and generated fear about where it might spread next. Petrarch spoke for a dozen generations of Europeans in saying, "even though danger may not be present, fear does not vanish."[59]

Although the later visitations of plague varied greatly in intensity and in geographical reach, there is no doubt that some were as deadly in the affected areas as the initial Black Death. The plague of 1400, spread far and wide by pilgrims coming to Rome for the Jubilee Year, was among the worst. In Rome six hundred to eight hundred were dying daily, most of them pilgrims.[60] Florentine undertakers officially reported 10,406 deaths, but the recordkeeping system seems to have broken down, and the usually reliable Giovanni Morelli estimated the dead at twenty thousand.[61] In Pistoia, where the documentation is better, half the population died both in the city and in the surrounding districts.[62] The food shortages that came in the wake of the plague indicate general disruption in the countryside.[63] In Padua in 1405, 18,000 died out of a population of 34,200.[64] When the plague finally relented in Padua, a Venetian army appeared before the walls to conquer the city when its resistance would be feeblest. This intersection of plague and war was very common.

During the widespread plague of 1449–1452, Milan bore the brunt of war, famine, and plague together. Filippo Maria Visconti, Duke of Milan, died suddenly in 1447, leaving a disputed succession claimed by

57. Petrarch, *Sen.* III.1.79–80.

58. Biraben, *Hommes et la peste,* 394–99; see appendix below.

59. Petrarch, *Fam.* IV.12.208.

60. Alfonso Corradi, *Annali delle epidemie occorse in Italia dale prime memorie fino al 1850: Complilati con varie note e dichiarazioni,* ed. U. Stefanutti (1863; repr. Bologna: Ristampa fotomeccanica, 1972), 1:245.

61. Herlihy and Klapisch-Zuber, *Tuscans,* 269.

62. Herlihy, *Medieval and Renaissance Pistoia,* excerpt (1967), in Bowsky, *Black Death,* 62–63.

63. Gene Brucker, *The Civic World of Early Renaissance Florence* (Princeton: Princeton University Press, 1977), 170.

64. Estimate by Karl Julius Beloch, *Bevölkerungsgeschichte Italiens* (Berlin and Leipzig, 1961), 67–74, cited in Biraben, *Hommes et la peste,* 1:186.

Francesco Sforza, a mercenary general married to Filippo Maria's illegitimate daughter. The Milanese, nevertheless, established the self-governing Ambrosian Republic. The result was a long, bitter war involving most of the cities of northern Italy. Sforza besieged Milan in 1450, leading to severe famine inside the city. Starvation broke the republic's resistance, and Sforza entered Milan as duke. Sforza restored the food supply, but, the very next year, plague devastated Milan, killing 30,000 citizens.[65]

Another particularly virulent outbreak of plague visited Italy in 1478, lasting in different places until 1482.[66] The Venetian territories were reported to suffer 300,000 dead over eight years of plague.[67] In Florence, destabilized by the Pazzi conspiracy against Lorenzo de' Medici and at war with the pope, Luca Landucci wrote on Christmas Eve 1478, "What with terror of the war, the plague, and papal excommunication, the citizens were in sorry plight. They lived in dread, and no one had any heart to work. The poor creatures could not procure silk or wool, or only a little, so that all classes suffered."[68] The next year, when the plague struck Rome, the pope fled and stayed away thirteen months, but the famous humanist Platina, in charge of the Vatican library, was left behind and died.[69] An important figure in the life of Pius II, Federico da Montefeltro, Duke of Urbino, who had made his city a center of Renaissance culture, was another victim.[70]

When the French invaded and temporarily conquered Naples in 1494, Italy became and remained for forty years "the cockpit of Europe," a battleground on which France and Spain fought for possession of the Duchy of Milan and the Kingdom of Naples, to which they each had a claim. The sack of Rome in 1527 and the siege of Florence in 1529 and 1530 ignited terrible plagues. In the Florentine plague of 1527, 30,000 people died—at least a quarter of the population.[71] Churches and convents were converted into hospitals, and six hundred huts were built

65. Diana Robin, *Filelfo in Milan: Writings 1451–1477* (Princeton: Princeton University Press, 1991), 104.

66. *Cultures of Plague,* 13.

67. Nohl, *Black Death,* 32.

68. Luca Landucci, *A Florentine Diary from 1450 to 1516 by Luca Landucci Continued by an Anonymous Writer til 1542, with Notes by Iodoco del Badia,* trans. Alice de Rosen Jervis (1927; repr. Hallandale, Fla.: New World, 1971), 26.

69. Corradi, *Annali delle epidemie,* 1:327.

70. Ibid., 1:328.

71. Ibid., 1;399; Cecil Roth, *The Last Florentine Republic* (London: Methuen, 1925), 76.

to isolate the sick outside the walls.[72] A document entitled "Description of the Plague at Florence in the Year 1527" comes to us in Machiavelli's handwriting. It is probably not his composition, but a copy he made of an account by his friend Lorenzo di Filippo Strozzi, whose additions and corrections appear on Machiavelli's copy.[73] Strozzi's description shows that the ambience of a city stricken with plague had shown no improvement since 1348.

> Our pitiful Florence now looks like nothing but a town which has been stormed by the infidels and then forsaken. One part of the inhabitants, ... have retired to distant country houses; one part is dead, and yet another part is dying. Thus the present is torment, the future menace, so we contend with death and only live in fear and trembling. The clean, fine streets which formerly teemed with rich and noble citizens are now stinking and dirty; crowds of beggars drag themselves through them with anxious groans and only with difficulty and dread can one pass them. Shops and inns are closed, at the factories work has ceased, the law courts are empty, the laws are trampled on. Now one hears of some theft, now of some murder. The squares, the market places on which the citizens used frequently to assemble, have now been converted into graves and into the resort of the wicked rabble.... If by chance relations meet, a brother, a sister, a husband, a wife, they carefully avoid each other. What further words are needed? Fathers and mothers avoid their own children and forsake them.... A few provision stores are still open, where bread is distributed, but where in the crush plague boils are also spread. Instead of conversation ... one hears now only pitiful, mournful tidings—such a one is dead, such a one is sick, such a one has fled, such a one is interned in his house, such a one is in hospital, such a one has nurses, another is without aid, such like news which by imagination alone would suffice to make Aesculapius sick.[74]

After 1530, when the wars became less frequent, the plague entered a new era in which occurrences became rarer, only one or very few cities being affected, with outbreaks occurring in eighteen out of forty-three years between 1533 and 1575. Nevertheless, when the next major attack came in the years 1575 through 1578, it invaded from both the southern and northern ends of the peninsula and claimed enormous numbers.[75]

72. Roth, *Last Florentine Republic,* 75.

73. Pasquale Villari, *The Life and Times of Machiavelli,* trans. Linda Villari (1891; repr. St. Claire, Mich.: Scholarly Press, 1969), 373.

74. Nohl, *Black Death,* 216–17.

75. Cohn, *Cultures of Plague,* 19–20.

In 1576 Milan lost 17,329, according to official records; Venice lost between a quarter and a third of its population; and the much smaller city of Brescia lost 17,396 out of between 45,000 and 46,000 people. Henceforth this pattern would hold: fewer, but particularly severe, plagues. In the plague of 1629 to 1633, among the worst in this later phase, Venice lost almost as many as in 1555–1556, but out of a reduced population, while Milan lost about half its estimated 100,000 people.[76] The last of Italy's widespread catastrophic plagues was in 1656–1657, in which Naples was devastated. Messina, among the first to be infected in 1347, had the dubious honor four hundred years later of experiencing Italy's last cataclysmic plague in 1742–1744. The last recorded outbreak was at the small town of Noja, in the province of Bari, in 1815–1816.[77]

While plague was a horrifying new type of disaster, war also grew in scale, frequency, and ferocity during the fourteenth through sixteenth centuries and probably played an equal role with plague in keeping the Italian population in continual stress. Although short, small wars had been endemic throughout Europe in the High Middle Ages, Italy, scene of the long struggle between popes and Holy Roman emperors and the endless quarrels between cities and civil upheavals within them, had already been one of the most violent regions of the continent. With the beginning of the Hundred Years' War between England and France in 1337, European warfare grew larger and more destructive. The Hundred Years' War impacted Italy because whenever there was a lull in the fighting in France the mercenary captains led their armies to Italy, where they became "free companies" supporting themselves on the loot of a rich country or holding entire cities for ransom. Military adventurers such as the Conte Lando (a German, Landau), Fra Moriale, the Company of the Hat, and the Company of St. George kept the countryside in terror and put cities under threat. Siena paid ransoms of 275,000 florins to save itself from attack.[78] Another German, Werner of Urslingen, wore a medal around his neck inscribed "Enemy of God, and of all Charity and Mercy."[79] The Englishman John Hawkwood (d. 1394) was a transitional figure; originally the leader of a marauding company, he settled into regular employment, first with the papacy, which was trying to control the ever-turbulent and rebellious Papal States, and later with

76. Biraben, *Hommes et la peste,* 1:86.
77. Ibid.
78. Meiss, *Painting in Florence,* 68.
79. Nohl, *Black Death,* 162.

Florence, where the painter Uccello immortalized him after his death by a fresco in the cathedral.[80] Hawkwood thus became a prototype of the *condottieri* (literally "contractors"), men whose army was a business enterprise and whose services were hired out to the Italian states under the terms of a business contract (*condotta*). The demand for the *condottieri's* services stemmed from the fact that the workers, artisans, and merchants of the Italian cities had little taste for abandoning commercial pursuits for military adventures. The use of *condottieri* increased rapidly in the fourteenth century. Florence, lacking spare manpower after the Black Death, ended military service for its citizens in 1351.[81] The urban aversion to combat provided an opportunity for rural nobles, who delighted in war, to equip and train landless peasants or hire unemployed veterans to form professional armies that the cities could hire. Italian noble families such as the Orsini and Colonna of Rome gradually wrested control of this highly profitable business from the foreign "free companies." In the fifteenth century the army business became the near-monopoly of the rulers of small city-states such as Urbino, Mantua, Ferrara, and Rimini.[82] The most successful *condottiere* was certainly Francesco Sforza, who, as we have seen, made himself Duke of Milan and one of the greatest powers of Italy in 1450.

Humanists, in imitation of their ancient forbears, were loud in their praise of military virtues and wove laurel wreaths in verse for any victorious commander, but they generally had only condemnation for the *condottieri* system itself. Petrarch raged against the *condottieri;* Salutati branded them as "outcasts who had entered into a perpetual conspiracy against peace and order"; Pietro Bembo condemned their bad Latin as well as their disorderly conduct; Alamanno Salviati wrote that men of that "occupation disgust me, because they are our natural enemies, and despoil all of us, and their only thought is to keep the upper hand and drain us of our wealth."[83] In the cinquecento, when the much larger hosts of France and Spain were accustomed to brushing aside Italian armies like crumbs from a picnic, Machiavelli blamed the *condottieri* and advocated replacing them with citizen-soldiers modeled on early

80. William Caferro, *Mercenary Companies and the Decline of Siena* (Baltimore and London: Johns Hopkins University Press, 1998), 13–14; Mallett, *Mercenaries and Their Masters: Warfare in Renaissance Italy* (Totowa, N.J.: Rowman and Littlefield, 1974), 40; Meiss, *Painting in Florence,* 68.

81. Baron, *Crisis of the Early Italian Renaissance,* 433.

82. Mallett, *Mercenaries,* 209.

83. Ibid., 208–10.

Rome. To discredit the *condottieri* he originated the misleading legend that they conducted "bloodless war" out of a desire not to risk or damage their armies through fighting. As Michael Mallett, a modern scholar of war in Renaissance Italy, tells us, this legend is a "compound of exaggeration and misunderstanding." Machiavelli illustrated his point with utterly fictional battle casualties: he says, for example, that at the Battle of Anghiari in 1440 only "one man was killed and he fell off his horse and was trampled to death," yet modern research establishes that there were about nine hundred deaths between the two sides. At the Battle of Molinello in 1467, Machiavelli said there were no deaths at all, whereas the local chroniclers report "that for days afterwards the whole countryside smelt of death as the bodies rotted in the ditches."[84]

It is true, however, that warfare in Renaissance Italy did not center on battles; it was waged primarily by looting and devastation, whose economic effects could bring the small states of Italy to their knees more quickly than battlefield defeats.[85] Armies lived off the land; even the peaceful passage of an army, with horses, pack animals, and camp followers as well as soldiers to feed, would eat up all the food and fodder in a district within a few days.[86] Italian agriculture, whose olives, vineyards, and herds required more long-term investment than cereal crops, was especially vulnerable to the attentions of the *guastatori* ("devastators") attached to the mercenary armies.[87]

Productive peasants, such as those whom Landucci saw fleeing from Lombardy in 1483, quickly became refugees. "It was a most pitiful sight to see these poor people pass, with a wretched little donkey, and their miserable household possessions: saucepans, frying pans, etc. One wept to see them barefoot and ragged; it is the cursed wars which have caused all this."[88] The effects of the *guastatori* could be long-lasting. In the quattrocento the area around Pisa had a reputation for desolation that it owed to wars that had destroyed the drainage system and left it subject to flooding.[89] Worse still were the effects of foreign invasion after 1494. Two of Henry VIII's envoys traveling through Lombardy in 1529 wrote home:

84. Ibid., 196–97. Battle statistics from this period are never very reliable. "Figures for the dead at the Battle of Agnadello (1509) varied from 6,000 to 20,000; at Ravenna (1512) from 10,000 to 30,000; and at Marignano (1518) from 18,000 to 30,000"; Lauro Martines, *Furies,* 176.

85. Mallett, *Mercenaries,* 191.

86. Lauro Martines, *Furies,* xi.

87. Mallett, *Mercenaries,* 191 and 228.

88. Landucci, *Florentine Diary,* 38–39.

89. Mallett, *Mercenaries,* 229.

> The most goodly country for corn and vines that may be seen, is so desolate, in all way that we saw [not] one man or woman laborers in the field, nor yet creature stirring, but in great villages five or six miserable persons ... in this mid way is a town ... all destroyed and in manner desolate ... [in Pavia] the children crying about the streets for bread, and the dying for hunger ... there is no hope many years that Italy shall be anything well restored, for want of people.[90]

In a land of city-states and fortresses, sieges were at least as crucial to warfare as field battles. Siege-craft changed as quattrocento Italy found itself in the middle of the gunpowder revolution. The earliest official reference to cannon comes from Florence in 1326. Twenty-four years later Petrarch commented that "now they are become as common as any kind of arms."[91] Before gunpowder medieval advances in fortification gave castles and walled cities enormous advantages over those who besieged them. Cannon at first only increased those advantages. Defenders could keep their artillery in place, ready for use; besiegers could require weeks to drag their ponderous guns into position. Once in place their rate of fire and accuracy left much to be desired. Technical improvements and the use of field fortifications gradually shifted the balance in favor of the attack, because accurate cannon fire could batter down the best medieval fortifications in a few weeks.[92]

But throughout the Renaissance the surest way to capture a city was to starve it out. This was the method the Florentines used against Pisa in 1406. The Pisans ate dogs, cats, rats, mice, and roots and made "bread" out of dried grass ground into a powder. In the meantime, siege engines pelted Pisa with stones. They also hurled into the city a captured soldier, tied into a compact ball. The curious who went up to the bloody heap in the street could read the attached message: "This is the kind of death that awaits anyone else who comes out of Pisa."[93] The victim's crime had been leaving the city—besiegers wanted to keep as many mouths inside as possible to eat up the available supplies. Beseiged cities, on the other hand, tried to expel such "useless mouths." Whose mouths were useless? Certainly, the indigent poor; but what about children, the sick, the elderly, and women—were the wives and children of the rich as "useless" as those

90. State Papers Foreign for the Reign of Henry VIII, National Archive, VII, 1849, 226, quoted in Robert Lopez, *The Three Ages of the Italian Renaissance* (Charlottesville: University Press of Virginia, 1970), 39.

91. Quoted in Gimpel, *Medieval Machine,* 228.

92. Mallett, *Mercenaries,* 162–63.

93. Lauro Martines, *Furies,* 4–5.

of the poor?[94] One of the most powerful institutions in Siena was the Hospital of Santa Maria della Scala, but it could not protect its inmates during the siege of 1554. Seven hundred of its charges were convoyed out of the city, but an attack on one of these convoys massacred more than 250 children ages six through ten. Later the last forty-five children in the hospital were also expelled, but the besiegers drove them back.[95]

God help the city that fell by storm! The customs of war dictated mercy for towns that surrendered when called upon to do so, but those captured by military action were put to the sack. Soldiers, eagerly led by their officers, stole everything of value, including the virtue of the women. The most horrible atrocities awaited anyone who tried to hide or protect their possessions. In the sack of Brescia in 1512 several priests were burned alive; the tormentors of the nobleman Cristoforo Guaineri hacked off his arms before roasting him over coals; Antonio del Sacre Fonte, a wealthy merchant, was flayed alive.[96]

Handheld firearms were slower to come into use than artillery. A type called the *sciopetto,* three to four feet long and too cumbersome for use in the field, may have existed before the end of the thirteenth century. It was a matter of note when Emperor Sigismund brought five hundred men specialized in the use of guns to his coronation at Rome in 1433.[97] In 1460 Pius II himself describes a *sciopetto* as a curiosity that he expects his readers never to have seen. "It is of iron or copper as long as a man, as thick as the fist, almost entirely hollow." After giving the ingredients for gunpowder, he continues: "Then a small ball of lead the size of a filbert is inserted in the front end. The fire is applied through a small hole in the back part and this explodes the powder with such force that it shoots out the ball like lightning with a report like a clap of thunder."[98] In the 1480s a more advanced gun, the trigger-operated arquebus, became widespread and helped to tip the balance in most armies away from the crossbow in favor of guns. In the next decade even cavalry began to use guns. No one has done a scientific comparison of the range, speed, or accuracy of fifteenth-century crossbows and firearms, but the firearm was cheaper to make and required less skill to use than the crossbow, and this seems to have been its chief advantage.[99]

94. Ibid., 106.

95. Ibid., 108.

96. Ibid., 61.

97. Mallett, *Mercenaries,* 156.

98. Pius II, *Commentarii rerum memorabilium quae temporibus suis contigerunt* IV, in *Comm.,* Smith), IV.323–24.

99. Mallett, *Mercenaries,* 157–58.

In naval war technological change was much less evident; galleys, usually triremes (propelled by three banks of oars), ruled the seas just as they had done when Athens fought the Persians at Salamis (480 B.C.). Quattrocento galleys did not ram each other as in ancient warfare, but served as fighting platforms for men armed with projectile weapons, crossbows, or firearms. These warriors included soldiers and officers, but sailors and often oarsmen were also armed. Oarsmen, therefore, were not slaves but earned decent wages.[100] For some, rowing was a career, but large expeditions often resorted to forced impressments.[101]

War during the Renaissance was crushingly expensive, and even the wealthiest states staggered under the burden. The papacy in the fourteenth century spent about 60 percent of its revenue on war, a proportion that was probably typical of other Italian states, as well.[102] In her wars against Filippo Maria Visconti, Duke of Milan, Florence may have spent three and a half million florins in 1427–1428, an amount ten times greater than the state revenue. This forced the imposition in 1427 of the *catasto,* a tax on wealth hailed by modern historians as a breakthrough in the rational exploitation of national resources, but probably not so cherished by Florentine taxpayers. Yet costs continued to escalate. Pope Martin V staged campaigns in 1421/22 and 1428/29 for 160,000 to 170,000 ducats a year; Paul II, successor of Pius II, spent half a million on the siege of Rimini in 1469—about double the papal revenue for the year.[103] Naval war was even more expensive. In Catalonia in the early quattrocento a large galley cost six to seven thousand florins to build and another six thousand to arm and sail. Including food and pay for soldiers and crew, a fleet of twenty vessels in a state of readiness cost over a quarter million florins a year.[104] Warships and merchant vessels differed only in equipment, not basic design. Thus, any large naval venture would purchase merchant ships, commandeer them, or receive them as donations or on loan and reequip them for war.[105] But if pay fell too far behind (and it was always in arrears), loaned or donated ships might return to civilian trade.[106]

We cannot understand Renaissance society without understand-

100. Mallett, *The Florentine Galleys in the Fifteenth Century* (Oxford: Clarendon, 1967), 29–30.

101. Alan Ryder, *The Kingdom of Naples under Alfonso the Magnanimous: The Making of a Modern State* (Oxford: Clarendon, 1976), 312–14.

102. Mallett, *Mercenaries,* 50.

103. Ibid., 227–28.

104. Ryder, *Kingdom of Naples,* 302–3.

105. Ibid., 296–97.

106. Ibid., 302–3.

ing that war was inextricably woven into the culture. Medieval chivalric culture had glorified war as the proper and natural pursuit of all males of the ruling classes. As real wars became more brutal, waged by paid professionals and by masses of peasantry whose crossbows or guns mowed down their victims without regard to personal valor, this make-believe world of noble knights and fair maidens was uncoupled from reality, becoming a mythology analogous to the tales of Olympian gods. Not only did the military ideal of chivalry continue unabated through the Renaissance, the revival of Roman culture and literature promoted an even sterner view of the warrior-male that could only reinforce the culture's bellicose orientation. In the later quattrocento, all the courts of Italy except the Roman curia were centered upon princes who were, or had been, active warriors. Tournaments and other military displays were popular with all classes in every city. Architects busied themselves designing fortifications; artists covered wedding chests (*cassone*) and the walls of upper-class palazzi with scenes of sieges, tournaments, and battles. Military treatises laden with antique Latin terminology flowed from the pens of humanists.[107] It used to be a commonplace to say that the Peace of Lodi in 1454 provided an age of peace that allowed the Renaissance to flourish. It is true that the "balance of power" enshrined in that treaty assured that no Italian power again sought, as Giangaleazzo and Filippo Maria of Milan and Ladislas of Naples had sought, to impose conquest or hegemony on the rest of the peninsula, but it hardly ushered in an age of serenity. In his six-year reign (1458–1464) during the post-Lodi period, Pius II faced rebellion in the Papal States, a succession war in Naples, a war with Sigismondo of Rimini, and preparations for a crusade against the Turks.

Plague and war elicited the same reactions in Italy that Huizinga identified in France and Flanders: the morbid obsession with death and decay and, more importantly, the search for mental escape from stressful thoughts. Most of our attention will be fixed on the escapist elements that were more common and more culturally productive and provided the emotional impulse behind the Renaissance, but this chapter devoted to tragedy and disaster may be the best place to briefly survey morbid and macabre reactions in Italy.

Something along the same lines as the Cemetery of the Innocents in Paris (described in the previous chapter) once existed at St. Paul's in

107. Robin, *Filelfo in Milan,* 57–58.

London and in Florence in the "Cloister of Bones" at S. Maria Nuova, where Fra Bartolommeo painted a *Last Judgment* in the 1490s that is now at the Museo di San Marco.[108] None of these charnel houses survive, but, to experience a similar atmosphere, let the visitor to Pisa leave the crowds at the leaning tower and pass behind the glaring white walls of the Campo Santo, the enclosed burial ground of the city. There he will find three fourteenth-century frescoes, removed for preservation to an adjoining room, that were among the earliest to bring together many of the themes of macabre art. The most striking is the central fresco, the *Triumph of Death,* in which, for the first time in a work of art, a figure visually personifies the abstract concept of Death. This personification is not yet the familiar Halloween skeleton, but a ferocious female with talons and enormous bat wings whose white hair and black drapery lash and swirl behind her. Armed with a scythe, she swoops down upon an unsuspecting group of elegantly dressed courtiers amusing themselves with musical instruments.[109] Below the doomed courtiers sit pitiful cripples dressed in rags who beg in vain for Death to free them from their misery.[110]

To the left of the courtiers we see the mounted figures of three lords and their entourage returning from the hunt. They pull up short in front of three coffins, one containing a fresh corpse, one a bloated, decomposing cadaver, and the third a skeleton. The horses, along with their riders, stare in horror; one of the lords holds his nose and mouth, overcome by the stench. Behind the coffins stands a grim old hermit, St. Macarius, holding a banderole that warns the huntsmen, "Your vainglory will be crushed! Behold the death of pride!"[111] This is one of many artistic representations of a poem, *The Legend of the Three Living and the Three Dead,* which exists in many versions going back into the thirteenth century.[112] Next to the *Triumph of Death* fresco in Pisa is a *Last Judgment* in which the Divine Judge ignores the token representation of heaven and turns all his angry attention toward the elaborately

108. Martin Wackernagel, *The World of the Florentine Renaissance Artists: Projects and Patrons, Workshop and Art Market* (Princeton: Princeton University Press, 1981), 128.

109. James M. Clark, *The Dance of Death in the Middle Ages and Renaissance* (Glasgow: Jackson, Son, 1950), 56.

110. John T. Paoletti and Gary M. Radke, *Art in Renaissance Italy* (New York: Harry N. Abrams, 1997), 142.

111. Pietro Vigo, *Le Danze Macabre in Italia* (Bergamo: Istituto Italiano D'Arti Grafiche, 1901), 52–53.

112. Elina Gertsman, "Visualizing Death: Medieval Plagues and the Macabre," in *Piety and Plague: From Byzantium to the Baroque,* edited by Franco Mormando and Thomas Worcester, 71 (Kirksville, Mo.: Truman State University Press, 2007).

depicted tortures of hell.[113] The third fresco consists of vignettes of hermits and ascetics intended to show that extreme asceticism is the only way to avoid the terrors portrayed in the other pictures. Scholars have disagreed about the date and authorship of these frescoes, but they were probably executed during the years immediately after the Black Death. Another personified *Triumph of Death* and a separate fresco of *The Three Living and the Three Dead* were painted at Subiaco shortly after the Black Death, but, since Pius II encountered them, we will defer describing them until he takes us there. The Subiaco artist was probably Sienese, and Pius may also have seen a similar scene that once existed near Siena itself in the Church of S. Francesco at Lucignano.[114]

Petrarch wrote a poem called "The Triumph of Death" as part of a series of "Triumphs." Artists frequently illustrated the poem, in which a female personification of Death rides in a car pulled by black oxen over a field carpeted with corpses.[115] This poem, widely known in Italy, is probably why "The Triumph of Death" was the most common subject for macabre art in Italy. Its popularity rose in the quattrocento with a fresco (now in the Galleria Regionale) executed about 1445 for Alfonso I of Sicily at the Palazzo Sclafani at Palermo. The figure of Death at Palermo is a skeleton armed with bow and arrows, riding a horse that is dead and rotting, yet bursting with energy. Decomposing corpses like this horse are called *transis,* from the Italian verb *transire,* "to pass away." This horrifying beast gallops furiously across the wall as Death's arrows strike down monarchs, princes, and prelates while the elderly and crippled beg fruitlessly for an end to their suffering.[116]

The *danse macabre* theme, in which persons of all sorts and conditions are waltzed into eternity by skeletal or *transi* versions of themselves, was less popular in Italy than north of the Alps, but an Italian example from 1485 survives as part of an anonymous fresco on the exterior of the church of the Disciplini Friars at Clusone, near Bergamo. The Clusone fresco appears to be in Florentine style and actually includes all of the major macabre themes of the period, with the *Triumph of Death* in the center dominating the entire wall. In this *Triumph,* which in no way

113. Paoletti and Radke, *Art in Renaissance Italy,* 142.

114. Alberto Tenenti, *Il senso della morte e l'amore della vita nel Rinascimento (Francia e Italia)* (Turin: Giulio Einaudi Editore, 1957), 438.

115. Francesco Petrarca, *The Triumphs of Petrarch,* trans. Ernest Hatch Wilkins (Chicago: University of Chicago Press, 1962), 54.

116. Alison Cole, *Art of the Italian Courts: Virtue and Magnificence* (London: Everyman Art Library, 1995), 48–50, iii; Vigo, *Danze Macabre,* 67–68.

follows Petrarch, the figures are larger than life-size, but the giant skeleton representing Death towers above them all. Wearing a crown and a royal mantle, he perches on the front edge of a tomb in which the rotting corpses of a pope and an emperor swarm with serpents, toads, and a scorpion. On each side of this monster are two other skeletons, one transfixing his victims with arrows while the other dispatches people with an up-to-date arquebus.[117]

In front of the tomb on which the skeletons stand, the rich and powerful, including a pope, bishops, and other clergy, kneel and attempt to purchase their lives from Death with goblets and vases full of coins. One of them, a king, is buying a jewel from a Jew for this purpose. But all around, as if mocking the would-be bargainers, lies a carpet of corpses, all of them lords, ladies, and ecclesiastics of high rank.[118] Above the entire scene four ribbons or banderoles flutter in the air, two of them held aloft by the crowned figure of Death. They display in Gothic letters the usual terrifying threats and warnings, which are supplemented by further inscriptions above and below the fresco.[119] In a register below the *Triumph of Death* and separated from it by an inscription is the *Dance of Death*. At Clusone it takes the form of a procession issuing from a door on the left; the skeletons lead their partners by the left hand while the living figure extends his right hand back to the following figure. There are other Italian examples of the *Dance of Death* at Pisogne and Pinzolo, and similar figures once existed in Ferrara and at San Lazzaro outside Como.

At carnival in Florence in 1511, mummers riding the "Car of Death" (*Carro della morte*) designed by Piero di Cosimo acted out "The Triumph of Death." The car was painted black and decorated with skeletons and white crosses; at the top stood an enormous figure of Death armed with a scythe. Men with torches flanked the car, their heads covered in black and painted with white skulls. According to the description by Vasari, the flickering torchlight gave them "an appearance of the greatest reality, but were also horrible and terrifying to behold." Other figures of the dead rode alongside the car on horses specially chosen for bony decrepitude and led by cadaverous grooms. At intervals "certain muffled trumpets" sounded "low and mournful" notes.[120] The car would then pause,

117. Vigo, *Danze Macabre,* 28–29.

118. Ibid., 30; Clark, *Dance of Death,* 51–52.

119. Vigo, *Danze Macabre,* 29–30.

120. Georgio Vasari, *Lives of the Painters, Sculptors and Architects,* trans. Gaston du C. de Vere (New York: Knopf/Everyman, 1996), 1:253.

Figure 2.1. Anonymous Italian painter. The central portion of the *Triumph of Death* and *Dance of Death*. Frescoes on the exterior of the oratory dei Disciplini at Clusone (1485). Photograph from Erich Lessing/Art Resource, New York.

and "skeletons" would rise partway out of tombs around the edges of the car to sing a song that Vasari says was still famous in his time:

Sorrow, Tears and Penitence
That torments all life,
This dead company
We walk crying out, "Repent!"
Shades like us you see,
You too like us shall be
We are dead as you can see,
Just as dead will you soon be.
And there will be no joy;
Therefore repent.[121]

Such morbid verses were not uncommon in Italy. Castellano de' Castellani (1461–1519), a follower of Savonarola, wrote some gruesome ones as part of his *Meditation on Death:*

Stop, reader, feet cease your steps:
I am an example to wretched mortals:
Your rest is under this stone.
. . . .
Wretches look at this stone,
Come inside and smell a little,
You who take pleasure in this world.

Vermin, stench and dung is your place,
Stink! you who perhaps an hour ago tasted to the full
The sin you will be able to play at no more.

What is it, mortal, that pleases your mind?
Your body is grazed upon by all kinds of vermin:
That think you are nothing but a bad dinner.[122]

Escapist responses were as much a part of the culture as these morbid ones and will receive the bulk of our attention. From the beginning of the Black Death doctors recommended using the mind as a defense for the body by avoiding all unpleasant thoughts and distracting oneself with pleasures both mental and sensual. In the fourteenth century

121. Courtesy of Pifarro Renaissance Band, Philadelphia (Joan Kimball, director), who performed this piece in Florence in June 1999.

122. Tenenti, *Il senso della morte,* 166–67.

Tommaso del Garbo, teacher of medicine at Bologna, Florence, and Milan, advised that during a plague one should think only about the most pleasant subjects, avoiding the thought of death above all others. One should surround oneself with beautiful things—gold, silver, and gems—and put on the finest raiment. Thus equipped, one should sing and tell amusing stories and fables, even doing acts of kindness that spread happiness among others.[123] We recognize this, except for the acts of kindness, as exactly what Boccaccio's characters were doing in the *Decameron*. One of the strongest quattrocento advocates of this mental therapy was Michele Savonarola, physician to the dukes of Ferrara and grandfather of Fra Girolamo Savonarola, who counseled the Florentines in the 1490s to renounce their worldly vanities and meditate upon death.[124] When Piedmont was afflicted with plague in 1585, the university doctor Agostino Bucci expanded upon earlier recipes for mental defense:

> Arm yourself with hope and confirmation in the faith of God; seek out jolly company; treat yourself to music, honest and pleasing games, ban all lugubrious and troublesome thinking. Make every effort to stay happy; dress in silk or in cloth with light and happy colours; wear a ring with precious stones; hang out sometimes with jesters; give an ear to comedies, games, and pleasing stories; read books, tell jokes and delightful stories.[125]

Lorenzo Condivi added that, after the evening's delights were ended, one should retire to one's chamber, lock all the windows and doors, and have a stiff drink![126] People acted on this advice, not because doctors recommended it, but because people instinctively know how to protect their own sanity.

Boccaccio's *Decameron* clearly demonstrates the way that escapism arises naturally from the excess of morbidity. After his hair-raising description of the Black Death, Boccaccio introduces his readers to seven young ladies begging for divine mercy in the church of Santa Maria Novella. One of them, Pampinea, says that in her mind the faces of departed loved ones "no longer appear as I remember them but with strange and horribly twisted expressions that frighten me out of my senses." To

123. Tomasso del Garbo, *Consiglio contro la pistolenza,* 40–42, quoted in Cohn, *Black Death Transformed,* 241.

124. Michele Savonarola, *I trattati in volgare della peste e dell'acqua ardent,* ed. Liugi Beloni (Milan: 1953), 15; quoted in Cohn, *Black Death Transformed,* 241.

125. Agostino Bucci, *Regimento presservativo degli huomini, luoghi, et città dall'influsso della peste* (Turin: Apresso Martino Crauotto, 1564); quoted in Cohn, *Cultures,* 267.

126. Ibid., 274.

preserve their sanity she suggests that they leave the city, "just as many others have done before us, and as indeed they are doing still," and repair to "one of our various country estates." There, she tells them:

> We can move from place to place, spending one day here and another there, pursuing whatever pleasures and entertainments the present times will afford. In this way of life we shall continue until such time as we discover (provided we are spared from early death) the end decreed by Heaven for these terrible events.[127]

Having recruited three young gentlemen to join them, the ten young people spend ten days in the most idyllic settings, enjoying all manner of delights, each telling a story on a designated theme each day. Meanwhile, they solemnly charge their servants that, "no matter what they should hear or observe in their comings and goings, to bring us no tidings of the world outside these walls unless they are tidings of happiness."[128]

The frame-story from the *Decameron* anticipates the actual behavior of Italian elites during times of plague over the next several centuries. As popular plague tracts emphasized, flight to an isolated location was the only effective means to escape infection.[129] Eventually, flight from plague evolved into the regular custom of *villeggiatura,* spending the summer months, when plague was most common, at a country villa devoting oneself to pleasant and tranquil pursuits far from the contagion and horrifying sights of the cities. Neither the fictional young people in the *Decameron* nor the real Italians of the Renaissance confined escapism to a literally physical flight from danger; they were also very careful to crowd out repellant thoughts and memories by filling their minds and flooding their senses with delightful and engrossing images. The *Decameron* characters not only amused themselves with stories; they also immersed themselves in idyllic settings: gardens, villas, and woodland glens, each of which Boccaccio described in sensuous detail.

The Renaissance contrived countless examples of this kind of protected environment, a *hortus conclusus*—a "walled garden" that could be on the scale of a small, private room, a literal garden, a secluded villa, or even an entire city. Two factors define a *hortus conclusus* (a term that I will use throughout this book): it is a place of refuge clearly separated

127. Boccaccio, *Decameron,* 60–62.

128. Ibid., 66.

129. Cohn, *Black Death Transformed,* 118.

and set aside from ordinary environments, and it is dedicated to therapeutic pleasure. But the perfection and delight in a *hortus conclusus* always self-consciously avoids whatever is practical, whatever is here-and-now, whatever is real and pressing, seeking to replace it with what is past or timeless, abstract, or ideal. Furthermore, the pleasures of a *hortus conclusus* seek to occupy the mind, to absorb thought, to prevent an accidental slip into awareness of unpleasant reality.[130]

In the life of Aeneas Silvius/Pius II, war will be almost a constant theme and plague will be a frequent occurrence. Furthermore, we will find that the church, to which men and women might expect to turn for succor and comfort, was long in a state of nearly permanent crisis. Aeneas/Pius shows us very little of the morbid response to these disasters, but for escape he turned to humanism, to travel, to festivities, and above all to enjoyment of nature. He will encounter chivalric tournaments in Florence. His friend and ally Federico da Montefeltro created the most famous of Renaissance *studioli* as his own *hortus conclusus*. Pius frequently sought out country retreats, one of which later became the Villa d'Este, one of the most famous villa and garden complexes in Europe. Pius converted his own native village into a new city—the most ambitious kind of *hortus conclusus*. Pius will lead us, therefore, into a good sampling of both the stresses of his period and its escapist strategies.

130. When practical themes were addressed, as in Alberti's *Della Famiglia* [On the Family] or Palmieri's *Della Vita Civile* [On Civic Life], they usually described an imaginary ideal case with almost no attention to messy realities that make such ideals impossible and rarely applicable in the real world. Toward the end of the Renaissance Machiavelli and Guicciardini certainly confronted messy realities, but they attracted few contemporary imitators. Their practicality is actually a portent of the end of the Renaissance; but that topic takes us beyond the scope of this book.

3

Corsignano and Siena

At the dawn of St. Luke's day, October 18, 1405, Vittoria Piccolomini, wife of the lord of the hardscrabble Tuscan village of Corsignano in the Republic of Siena, bore a son named Aeneas Silvius, whom she would have been astonished to learn was a future pope. You will not find Corsignano on a map; its name vanished on the twelfth of February 1462, when Pope Pius II, as Aeneas Silvius had become, officially renamed it "Pienza" in his own honor—part of his intent to transform his birthplace into the summer capital of the papacy. Even today, in spite of Pius's transformations, Corsignano, the medieval Tuscan hill town, still shows through the skin of Pienza like the ribcage of an undernourished horse. Undernourished also was young Aeneas. The Piccolomini were an ancient noble house of Siena, now fallen on hard times. In the thirteenth century Siena had been one of Europe's major banking centers, and the Piccolomini had been international bankers with branches even in distant England; they also possessed castles and agricultural lands across southern Tuscany and as far south as Amalfi. Along with a few other noble families, like their cousins the Tolomei, who claimed descent from the family of Cleopatra, they had dominated the economy and government of Siena.[1] The Piccolomini's combination of feudal estates with commercial and banking interests was quite normal in medieval Italian cities, where families called nobles, magnates, *grandi,* or *gentiluomini* sought wealth wherever they could find it without regard to Marxian distinctions between feudal classes and bourgeoisie. The lifestyle of these

1. Ady, *Pius II,* 2.

families was feudalism come to town. Their town dwellings, called *castellari,* were fortified castles shoehorned into the narrow urban confines. In stone buildings tightly clustered around a courtyard, these *castellari* housed members of the clan with their retainers and servants, including soldiers. The *castellari* were defended by tall, thin towers whose proportions reflected the lack of ground space combined with the ambition to have the tallest fortress in town.[2] The resulting skyline, prickly with competing towers, was once common to most Italian cities, but exists today only in a remnant at San Gimignano.

The need for such defenses sprang from the constant feuds among noble families that enabled them to bring their favorite sport—war—into the crowded city streets. Shakespeare's fictional Montagues and Capulets were no more bloody-minded than the very real Malavolti and Piccolomini in old Siena. As late as 1334, four young blades of the Piccolomini, accompanied by retainers, strode into the Malavolti courtyard, found Niccolò Malavolti playing chess, and plunged a knife into his throat—after which they sauntered home unchallenged.[3]

By that time both Siena and her swaggering nobles were in slow but inexorable decline. Ironically, the decline began with the greatest of Sienese victories, the battle of Montaperti on September 4, 1260. Even today, good Sienese are eager to tell visitors about this victory over Siena's hated rival, Florence. The battle was part of the endless wars between Guelphs and Ghibellines. Theoretically, Guelphs supported the pope and Ghibellines supported the Holy Roman emperor; but the fact that Florence was Guelph was enough to make Siena Ghibelline. Unfortunately, the pope, by far the juiciest banking client in Europe, was not pleased to see his partisans, the Guelphs, humiliated, and after Montaperti he withdrew his business from Siena. Six years after Montaperti the Guelphs reversed its results in a decisive victory at Benevento, so that Siena was forced to turn Guelph, and its noble-dominated government fell.[4] Losing patience with the nobles' perpetual urban warfare, the new government in 1277 permanently excluded *gentiluomini* families from high offices, including membership in "The Nine," the supreme council that controlled the city.[5] The nobles never stopped trying to regain power, but their unceasing quarrels among themselves usually made them ineffective. Visits to Siena by the nobles' ally, Holy Roman emperor Charles IV, in 1355 and 1368 rallied the

2. Schevill, *Siena,* 278–79.

3. Ibid., 208–10.

4. Ibid., 186–90.

5. Ibid., 138.

nobles to unite temporarily and overthrow the existing regime. Nevertheless, the *gentiluomini* could not hold onto power and only brought on themselves yet more rigorous exclusion from government.[6]

In 1343–1345 the Florentine banking houses of the Bardi, Peruzzi, and Acciaiouli failed, bringing down with them most of the Sienese banks, including the Piccolomini. Just a few years later the Black Death hit Siena with maximum ferocity. Siena could not recover from depopulation and the ruin of her banks because, unlike Florence, she had little manufacturing capacity. Florence had the flowing waters of the Arno to drive the wheels of countless mills; Siena, located on hilltops, had no flowing water. Even the supply of water for drinking and cleaning required a remarkable network of underground aqueducts carved out of the tufa stone beneath the city. These aqueducts brought water to pools sheltered under massive arcades, two of which, the Fontebranda and Fontenuova, still survive as monuments to medieval engineering.

While Siena and her nobles lost ground rapidly, the Piccolomini fell farther still. The grandfather of the future pope, also named Aeneas Silvius, had still enjoyed a comfortable income from extensive lands, but he made the mistake of dying young, leaving his wife pregnant with Silvio, the future pope's father.[7] Silvio's guardians gave him the education and social skills befitting a gentleman, but also ran through his fortune, sold off his assets, and squandered his money. When he came of age Silvio tried to recoup his losses in a military career, but failed miserably. At length he returned to insignificant Corsignano, the last remnant of his inheritance, to become a farmer. We can gauge the character of old Corsignano from its two churches, San Francesco and the Pieve (parish church) of Saints Vito and Modesto, where Aeneas was baptized. San Francesco is thirteenth-century, and, but for its simple Gothic door and some interior frescoes in bad condition, it might be taken for a long stone barn. The Pieve, in a lonely spot outside the town, is much older than San Francesco and has an atmosphere of timeless rural isolation. The lintel over its door, carved with primitive fish-tailed creatures, and the rudimentary caryatid that divides the upper window seem to echo pre-Christian fertility cults.[8]

Silvio Piccolomini took a wife, Vittoria Forteguerri, who could sym-

6. F. Thomas Luongo, *The Saintly Politics of Catherine of Siena* (Ithaca and London: Cornell University Press, 2006), 140; Schevill, *Siena,* 218–22.

7. *Comm.,* Smith, I.11.

8. Marco Pierini, *Pienza, Guide to the Town and Surroundings: Corsignano, Spedaletto, Monticchiello, Sant'Anna in Camprena* (Siena: Nuovo Immagine, 2007), 47 and 50.

pathize with his reduced circumstances because the Forteguerri, an even more ancient family than the Piccolomini, had fallen to equal ruin.[9] Vittoria proved a miracle of fertility: she had several pairs of twins and produced no less than eighteen children in all. Yet the high infant mortality of the fifteenth century frequently culled Vittoria and Silvio's little flock so that they never had more than ten living offspring at any given time. Eventually, the plague, that supreme winnower of populations, swept away the whole brood except for Aeneas and two sisters.[10]

Although he survived so many siblings, Aeneas was never robust. All who saw him in adulthood described him as little, and he liked to pun, saying that his family name meant *piccoli uomini,* "little men."[11] During his papacy observers noted his rosy plumpness, but that could not have characterized him as a boy.[12] He would have been a wiry lad, browned by the sun, with the scrawny leanness of farm boys working unforgiving land. He went about the fields powdered by dust or caked with mud because he and his father did their own plowing not with an up-to-date moldboard plow—the technological revolution in medieval agriculture never reached this part of Italy—but with a hardwood stick tipped with iron, dragged by trudging oxen instead of horses.[13] It would be difficult today to determine exactly what lands Silvio Piccolomini farmed. They may have been in the fertile Val d'Orcia east of Corsignano or, just as likely, in the productive but hard-to-work clay called the "Crete of Siena" that lies to the north.[14] As *gentiluomini,* the Piccolomini probably owned one or two horses reserved for riding that gave Aeneas the experience to write his later treatise, "The Nature and Care of Horses."[15] In most respects Aeneas's life, mental and physical, would have been that of a Tuscan peasant boy. To the last days of his life he loved the simplest and poorest people, entered freely and naturally into their pleasures, and showed a delicate regard for their sensitivities.

9. *Comm.,* Smith, I.11.

10. Ibid., I.29.

11. Aeneas Silvius Piccolomini (hereafter, ASP), letter to Kaspar Schlick, Vienna, 1444; quoted in Ady, *Pius II,* 11.

12. Andrea Schivenoglia, "Cronaca di Mantua," in *Raccolta di cronisti e documenti storici Lombardi inediti* II.135, quoted in Ady, *Pius II,* 165.

13. William Boulting, *Aeneas Silvius (Enea Silvio de' Piccolomini): Orator, Man of Letters, Statesman, and Pope* (London: Archibald Constable, 1908), 4.

14. Siena, Province of, the Municipalities of Asciano, Buonconvento, Monteroni d'Arbia, RapolanoTerme, San Giovanni d'Asso, and the Tourist Board of Siena, *Le Crete* (Siena: APT Siena, n.d.), 18–19.

15. Ady, *Pius II,* 18.

Some edict from misty antiquity decrees that the mothers of great men are universally required to have prophetic dreams. Vittoria Piccolomini dreamed of her son Aeneas wearing a miter. Difficult circumstances apparently made her a pessimist because, instead of associating the miter with the office of bishop, she thought only of the miter placed in mockery on the heads of criminals led to execution. Until Aeneas became a bishop, his mother, then nearing the end of her life, expected him to end on the gallows. Aeneas himself later saw prophetic significance in the fact that the neighborhood boys "playing pope" had cast him in the title role.[16] But the leading role probably came his way whenever the urchins of Corsignano played "pope," "king," or "knight." Aeneas might live in little more comfort than his playmates, but his father was the landlord, and he had no brother to share the distinction. Deference to rank, which medieval people imbibed with their mother's milk, would have assured that the landlord's boy routinely took positions of honor except when honor had to be won in a fight or a competition. This automatic distinction, even in poverty, may have given Aeneas the outgoing social ease and self-confidence he exhibited all his life—and perhaps laid the foundations for his amazing vanity. It certainly inculcated his fierce loyalty to the nobility and its privileges, which later led to countless difficulties in his relations with the anti-noble Sienese government.

Corsignano indelibly marked Aeneas as a country boy. His knowledgeable descriptions of natural scenes reflect the keen eye of the countryman—he seldom speaks of trees, for example, without naming the exact species. He spent much of his adult life in sometimes harrowing travel—from Naples to Scotland, from London to Bohemia—serving the greater men who employed him. After a quarter-century on the move, it must have seemed unnatural for him to sleep continuously in the same bed. When the papacy gave him an independence he had never previously known, he spent as much time as possible out of doors and out of cities, calling himself a "lover of forests and eager sight-seer."[17] Summer *villeggiatura* was one thing, but for weeks or months at a time, not just in the milder seasons, Pope Pius lived a caravan life, dragging with him an extensive entourage of cardinals, officials, ambassadors, servants, and soldiers, most of whom did not share his bucolic tastes and his indifference to rough roads and wretched accommodations.

16. Ibid., 3–4.

17. *Comm.*, Smith, IX.570–71; here I have used Ady's translation: Ady, *Pius II*, 6.

It was in 1420, when Aeneas was about fourteen, that he first glimpsed the world beyond Corsignano. Deadly plague swept through Siena that year, causing the entire Studio, as Siena's university was called, to flee. Universities often fled *en masse* from the plague, but this was the only time the Studio took refuge in little Corsignano.[18] The scholarly refugees would certainly have imposed upon the meager hospitality of the local lord and likely stimulated the imagination and dreams of an intelligent boy ignorant of the outside world. These contacts may have influenced the family's decision three years later to send Aeneas to study in Siena.[19]

Throughout his life, Aeneas would think of Siena as his city, which, to a quatrocento Italian, meant one's homeland, even one's identity. If we wish to understand Aeneas, we need to understand his city, as well.

Today, Siena and Florence are still competitors, at least in seeking to attract tourists. Although Siena's Pinacoteca Nazionale and the Museo dell' Opera Metropolitana have superb collections of artworks that deserve to be better known, there is no question that Florence contains more and greater masterpieces. But if we compare the two cityscapes, Siena, for my taste, has the edge. The rise and fall of her hills and the winding streets curving along the ridges unfold before the pedestrian's eye a kaleidoscope of picturesque compositions—you turn a corner and find a vista over the rooftops; a Gothic palace displays itself from a variety of angles; an alley with steps plunging down toward a piazza persuades you to make a detour. The straight avenues and flat terrain of Florence do not lend themselves as often to such surprises. Siena also has an advantage in color: Florence, built of stone, is predominantly gray. In Siena, built largely of brick, a warm, peachy color prevails, set off by the stronger terra-cotta of the roof tiles, visible more often from the hilltops of Siena than they ever are in Florence.

Topographically both cities are organized around two poles, the cathedral and the municipal palace, each with its own piazza. For the exteriors of the two cathedrals and civic palaces, the Florentines take the prize. Siena's Palazzo Pubblico seems a bit rambling compared to the cubic solemnity of Florence's Palazzo Vecchio, while the east end of Florence's cathedral, its semi-octagonal choir and transepts with buttresses

18. Rosamund Joscelyne Mitchell, *The Laurels and the Tiara: Pope Pius II, 1458–1464* (Garden City, N.Y.: Doubleday, 1962), 30.

19. Mitchell, *Laurels,* 33.

of the same shape, building up to Brunelleschi's octagonal dome, is a masterpiece of architectural geometry. In comparison, Siena's cathedral seems haphazard, and its gorgeously decorated west front is all too obviously a stage set pasted on the front of the building without regard to the shapes behind it.

South of Siena's cathedral stands Europe's most conspicuous monument to the Black Death, the uncompleted Duomo Nuovo or "new cathedral." In 1339 the Sienese decided to build a gigantic new cathedral, with the existing cathedral serving as mere transepts to the new one. The artisans worked speedily, building a towering new façade, the piers, arches, and outer walls of the new nave and aisles, even much of the vaulting.[20] But the Black Death mowed down the swarming workmen, and the busy site fell silent. Although some work resumed, it halted when the government of the Nine was overthrown in 1355.[21] Some of the hastily constructed piers were left inadequately buttressed and began to buckle. In 1357 the vaults and much of the new building were ordered to be demolished.[22] What remains today is still impressive. The space that would have been the nave and western aisle is now a spacious piazza. The Museo dell'opera fits within three of the five bays of the eastern aisle. From the museum one can reach the towering entrance façade, *il facciatone*, which offers magnificent vistas of the city. The Duomo Nuovo simultaneously represents Siena's high water mark and the disaster that blasted its dreams.

In a comparison of the interiors of Florence and Siena cathedrals, Siena wins another "Battle of Montaperti" over Florence. Once, when I was on the steps of Siena Cathedral, an American woman came up to me and asked if it was worth her while to go in. She had been in other cathedrals and wasn't sure she needed to see another one. Enthusiastically, I told her that if she saw the inside of just one cathedral in all Italy it should be this one. Her expression and rapid retreat told me that I had muffed my lines—that I was supposed to say, "One cathedral is much like another; why don't you go buy yourself a purse?" My advice was rejected, but I stick by it. Personal taste might dictate other preferences—Milan, Pisa, Monreale, St. Peter's, and San Marco are justifiable

20. Tim Benton, "The Design of Siena and Florence Duomos," in *Siena, Florence and Padua: Art, Society and Religion, 1280–1400,* vol. 2, *Case Studies,* edited by Diana Norman (New Haven and London: Yale University Press, in association with the Open University, 1995), 135.

21. Benton, "Design of Siena," 2:136.

22. Ibid., 2:136 and 2:143.

Figure 3.1. Siena Cathedral viewed from inside the nave of the "new cathedral." Photograph from Luke Ashworth-Sides.

choices—but it is Siena whose interior moves me most. In spite of housing some individual masterpieces, the interior of the Florentine duomo, dominated by great expanses of white plaster, is a clear disappointment after the brilliance of the exterior, while the interior of Siena's cathedral is the city's greatest glory.

The Counter-Reformation, Baroque intrusions, and rearrangements from Vatican II have made medieval church interiors accessible only to the imagination. We are missing a riot of tombs, shrines, chantries, altars, memorials, banners, heraldic emblems, and votive figures that sprouted in the shade of the towering piers like mushrooms on the forest floor. Individually, many of these are no great loss. Wax *ex voto* images given in gratitude for answered prayer might be executed by the finest artists, but hundreds of life-sized wax figures—so numerous at Santissima Annunziata in Florence that they filled the atrium and hung from the rafters—sound almost ghoulish to us.[23] But portraits of donors and ancestors, family crests, guild emblems, patron saints, the altars of confraternities, fresco cycles

23. Glenn M. Andres, John M. Hunisak, and A. Richard Turner, *The Art of Florence* (New York: Artabras; London: Abbeville, 1994), 1:504.

with personal or family significance brought the vibrancy of a thriving, diverse community inside the church. We might find this invasion of the secular into the sacred space inappropriate—that is how the Council of Trent saw it in the later sixteenth century, when they banished all this and replaced it with dull but theologically correct altarpieces in orderly rows down the side aisles. Those who chide the Middle Ages for a lack of secularism should remember that secular concerns washed like tides through the churches themselves. To medieval and Renaissance minds our separation of sacred and secular would be incomprehensible. "The earth is the Lord's and the fullness thereof"; therefore, each individual's life, family, ancestors, guild or confraternity memberships, and, above all, his or her wealth, all needed to be presented before God in his church.

Siena Cathedral preserves at least some sense of this disordered profusion, not because it escaped Counter-Reformation purification (it didn't), but because the architecture itself conveys a sense of allover exuberance akin to what overstuffed medieval churches must have produced. Much of this vitality derives from the daring use of colorful patterns on almost every surface. The original thirteenth-century architect was a brave man to cover his church, inside and out, with horizontal zebra stripes of black and white marble. The expansion of the church in the early fourteenth century used only a few narrow black stripes separated by broad bands of white. The modification maintains unity but dilutes the zebra effect enough to avoid a sense of frenzy. Unique to Siena is the decoration of the cathedral floor—fifty-six panels of marble mosaic filled with sibyls, virtues, allegories, and biblical narratives. So much decorative exuberance might be garish if it were not for the softened light from the stained-glass windows. That slight dimness yields glowing, fragmented, highlights—here a gleam from polished marble, there a glint of gold, someplace else light and shadow playing across a curved surface. Together they glimmer like moonlight on still water, evoking a sense of the divine mysteries performed at the altars.

One area of the north aisle is particularly enriched with carved marble and fresco. In it is a small door that feels constricted as you pass through it. Then, as though someone had turned on klieg lights, you emerge suddenly into a bright world of brilliant color. You have entered the Piccolomini Library, a memorial to Pius II built by his nephew, Cardinal Francesco Piccolomini-Todeschini, who in 1502 commissioned Pinturicchio, an artist famous for his lush decorative effects, to cover the ceiling with "fantasies, colors, and compartments" and the walls with ten scenes from his uncle's life, both before and during his papacy.[24] This is not the time to dwell on the glories (and flaws) of the Piccolomini Library. It is, after all, a memorial, a retrospective on Pius's life, and we will treat it as such, returning to it after we have surveyed the events it depicts.

When Aeneas attended it, the Studio of Siena was neither distinguished nor forward-looking. Like the city itself, it had peaked in the late thirteenth and early fourteenth centuries. It had reached a low point at the beginning of the quattrocento—even closing for two years in 1402–1404; but the communal government had founded a residence for foreign students in 1416 and found the funds to support a limited revival.[25] Nominally, the Studio taught the medieval curriculum of the Seven Liberal Arts and the advanced sciences of theology, medicine, and law. But by the time Aeneas arrived, the city subsidized only the teaching of law, useful for business and bureaucracy.[26] Throughout the Renaissance Siena's Studio remained loyal to medieval scholastic traditions and never entirely embraced humanism; Francesco Filelfo, who taught Greek and Latin there in 1435–1439, was the only humanist of the front rank to grace its faculty. Even in the humanist subjects of grammar and rhetoric the teachers were trained in the medieval scholastic tradition.[27] But the lines between "medieval" scholastic subjects and "Renaissance" humanist ones were not as firmly drawn in the early quattrocento as they were in the minds of later historians. Andrea Biglia, who taught Aeneas during the winter of 1431–1432, was one of many who straddled the two currents with no particular sense of contradiction. He studied philosophy (a scholastic subject) at Padua, taught ethics, poetics, and rhetoric (humanist subjects) in Florence, and was appointed professor of natural and moral philosophy (the first scholastic, the second humanist) at Bologna in 1436.[28] It was another such "straddler," the canon lawyer Mariano de' Sozzini, who passed on his personal interest in the new humanist trends to young Aeneas Silvius.[29] Sozzini was a prime example of

24. Francesco Federico Mancini, *Pintoricchio* (Milano: Silvano, 2007), 209; Enzo Carli, *Il Pintoricchio* (Milano: Electra, 1960), 66.

25. Paul F. Grendler, *The Universities of the Italian Renaissance* (Baltimore and London: Johns Hopkins University Press, 2002), 45 and 47–48.

26. Boulting, *Aeneas Silvius,* 5–6; Ady, *Pius II,* 10.

27. Grendler, *Universities,* 49.

28. Margaret Meserve, *Empires of Islam in Renaissance Historical Thought* (Cambridge, Mass.: Harvard University Press, 2008), 171.

29. ASP to Kaspar Schlick, Vienna, 1444; quoted in Ady, *Pius II,* 12.

the intellectual versatility of the Middle Ages and Renaissance—Aeneas said that he "knows as much philosophy as Plato, as much geometry as Boethius, as much arithmetic as Macrobius; there was no musical instrument he does not know how to play; he knows agriculture like Virgil . . . he paints like a new Apelles, sculpts like Praxiteles, nor is ignorant of medicine." Sozzini was not many years older than his pupil, so that his affability, generosity, and humor could reinforce those same qualities in Aeneas through the powerful influence of genuine friendship.[30] Although still young, Sozzini was already widely respected as a canon lawyer whose opinions were sought after during the prolonged struggle between pope and councils for control of the church.[31] This struggle, which would dominate Aeneas's life after he completed his studies and was about to intrude briefly on life in Siena, requires some explanation.

As a child in Corsignano, Aeneas would have heard relatively little about the great affairs of the European world, which were the stuff of daily conversation in Siena. Even before Dante's time, such conversations had often turned upon the disgraceful state of the papacy. For seventy-two years, beginning in 1309, the popes had abandoned Rome and headquartered themselves at Avignon, a city in southern France that provided a safer environment than ever-rebellious Rome, with its powerful and fractious nobles. It was scandalous for the pope to break canon law by establishing himself so far from Rome, the city of which he was bishop; but to Italians it was an outrage, deeply offensive to their pride and damaging to their economy and their influence in Europe. Although Gregory XI returned the papacy to Rome in 1377, Italians continued for generations afterward to fear anything that hinted of a new papal departure from Rome. Just a year after he returned to Rome, Pope Gregory's death plunged the church into still greater crisis. A split among the cardinals led to the election of two competing popes, one in Avignon and the other in Rome. Each pope excommunicated the other and all his followers. France supported Avignon, causing England, France's enemy, to recognize Rome; Scotland, opposing England, opted for Avignon. Most of Italy followed Rome, except for the Kingdom of Naples, which was then ruled by the French Angevin dynasty. Some rulers, such as the Holy Roman emperors in Germany and Bohemia, often shifted their allegiance. Since each pope's legal claim could be convinc-

30. Gioacchino Paparelli, *Enea Silvio Piccolomini: L'umanessimo sul soglio di Pietro* (Ravenna: Longo Editore, 1978), 23–24.

31. Grendler, *Universities,* 461.

ingly argued, no one could be sure that the pope their rulers had chosen was the right one—and a wrong choice meant excommunication by the real pope and eternal damnation at a time when plague made the fear of death particularly acute.

To solve this papal schism required invoking a higher authority than the pope—reversing four centuries of vigorous efforts by successive popes to concentrate authority in their own hands. The only power in the church that could potentially outrank the pope was a general council of all the bishops of Christendom. Such councils were rare and, since the Council of Constantinople in 870, those in the West had met only at the call and under the leadership of the pope. The Council of Pisa in 1409 made the first attempt to use a council to solve the papal schism. The fathers in Pisa sought a fresh start by deposing both popes and electing a new one. The result was not religious peace but three popes excommunicating each other—increasing each individual's statistical odds of eternal torment to 67 percent. A second effort, the Council of Constance, guided by its sponsor, the Holy Roman emperor Sigismund, handled itself with greater care. They first persuaded the Pisan and Roman popes to resign, then excommunicated the Avignon pope, whose support melted once he became the only obstacle to reconciliation. Not until 1417 did the council successfully elect a single pope, Martin V, who made his seat in Rome.

Encouraged by its success in ending the schism, the Council of Constance decreed that the authority of a council was higher than the pope's and required that general councils be called at least every seven years. Martin V complied with this decree by calling a council at Pavia in 1427. Predictably, the council and the pope fell into conflict over both political and ecclesiastical issues. Plague in Pavia forced the bishops to leave, and Martin transferred the council to Siena, where Aeneas was then studying. Aeneas would have watched the processions of the arriving bishops and heard the talk in the streets about conciliar versus papal power. The Council of Siena proved to be a failure. Fear of the plague kept too many bishops away, giving Martin V an excuse to declare the council dissolved.[32] All of Aeneas's biographers celebrate Sozzini's influence in bringing Aeneas to humanism, but it should not go unnoticed that the man whom Aeneas acknowledged as the greatest influence in molding his mind was professionally involved in the ecclesiastical struggle, and

32. Boulting, *Aeneas Silvius,* 33.

that the two of them together, witnessing a council in action, must have discussed the issues it raised exhaustively.

Aeneas stands in the long tradition of poverty-stricken students. He skipped supper three days a week and could study only from borrowed books, copying out long extracts for future use.[33] He saved on lodging by staying with his father's half-sister Bartolomea, who had married a Sienese, Niccolò Lolli, and apparently took in students as boarders.[34] There he began a lifelong friendship with Bartolomea's son, Gregorio Lolli (usually called "Goro"), whose bedroom he probably shared. Goro later wrote that Aeneas had studied "with such diligence that he hardly allowed himself food or sleep." He took his books to bed at night and read until his eyelids closed, taking them up again before dawn. On one such occasion his candle set the bed on fire, so that Goro and other student-boarders had to beat out the flames to save him.[35]

However dedicated Aeneas was to his studies, Cicero was not his only bedfellow. Siena in the 1420s offered many amusements, among which her "pleasant ladies" were particularly celebrated.[36] Aeneas tells how he paid court to a married lady named Angela, who disdained his poverty and mocked his threadbare clothes, thus providing him with the material for *Cinthia,* his first book of poetry. Goro Lolli claimed to have possessed "innumerable examples" of Aeneas's love poetry from student days. As a favor for a friend from Ferrara, Aeneas wrote a two-thousand-line poem entitled *Nymphilexis* in honor of the friend's mistress, whom he may never have seen.[37] The great Petrarch had gained his first fame from courtly-love poems in Italian addressed to a lady named Laura. His example made the writing of love poems a necessity for generations of literary youths who succeeded him. The resulting verses, imitating Ovid, Horace, and Petrarch, were admired for technical obstacles all-too-cleverly overcome rather than for their endlessly repetitive content. Aeneas won his share of that kind of admiration, but we need not lament too much that Goro's "innumerable examples" have all disappeared.

Because Aeneas was a humanist, a writer of love poems, and, later on, father of a couple of bastard children, some writers, imbued with the modern sense of opposition between sacred and secular, have implied that he could not have been sincerely religious at the same time. But

33. Ady, *Pius II,* 14.
34. Ibid., 7.
35. Ibid., 14.
36. Ibid., 15.
37. Mitchell, *Laurels,* 48.

an incident in his student years is one of many showing that religious devotion was part of his makeup from the beginning. In May of 1425, Aeneas's second year of studies, a Franciscan friar, Bernardino degli Albizzeschi, electrified Siena with his preaching. Like Aeneas, Bernardino was from a noble Sienese family and had studied at the Siena Studio. He had joined the friars minor after "a great fear fell upon him" so that "he came to hate the pomps and vanities of the world."[38] Thereafter, he traveled about Italy drawing crowds of thousands to his sermons. Although learned himself, he kept his sermons simple and studded with homely stories. But Bernardino reinforced his message with the austerities of his own life. Aeneas says that Bernardino "lived in poverty, going about with bare feet, clad only in his woolen tunic; and because he persevered in fasts and prayers, he drew the people marvelously."[39] The severity of Bernardino's teaching matched the asceticism of his life. In 1427, when the plague was approaching, Bernardino preached on the fourteenth chapter of the Apocalypse. He conjured up before his listeners' eyes the familiar image of Death armed with a scythe. "Have you thought what the scythe might be?" he asked.

> The scythe takes part and leaves part. It happens the same when a pestilence comes: not everyone is killed.... He has the scythe in his hand. What is the hand? What is the scythe? It is your death.... He rests the scythe on the ground and holds the handle in his hand. Remaining in this position, he warns, "Where do I wish to harvest with my scythe?" And as he deliberates, he raises his scythe and waves it overhead.[40]

At San Bernardino's prompting, the ladies of Siena threw their jewels, false hair, elaborate clothes, and costly adornments into a great bonfire on the Campo. Into the flames the men cast the badges and emblems of the political factions dividing the city. In place of these symbols of division, San Bernardino commanded them to adopt the monogram of Christ (IHS) surrounded by the sun's rays. We still can see the IHS emblem today, gleaming from the highest point on the façade of the Palazzo Pubblico and in other prominent places around the city.[41]

38. Vespasiano da Bisticci, *Renaissance Princes, Popes, and Prelates: The Vespasiano Memoirs; Lives of the Illustrious Men of the XVth Century,* trans. William George and Emily Waters (New York: Harper Torchbooks, 1963), 164.

39. Pius II, *Enee Silvii Piccolominei, postea Pii PP II, De viris illustribus,* ed. Adrianus Van Heck (Vatican City: Biblioteca Apostolica Vaticana, 1991), 38.

40. Tenenti, *Il senso della morte,* 74; my translation.

41. Piccolomini, *De Viris* 38.

Bernardino enacted similar scenes in Florence and elsewhere, setting the precedent for Savonarola's more famous "bonfires of the vanities" in Florence many decades later.[42] Savonarola, who presided over a virtual theocracy in Florence in the 1490s, is sometimes portrayed as a bizarre medieval "throw-back," but he actually stands in a clear succession following (among others) San Bernardino (1380–1444) and Sant'Antoninus, archbishop of Florence (1389–1459).

Aeneas himself was deeply affected by the preacher's words. Thirty-five years later he still described Bernardino as "another Saint Paul."[43] Inspired by Bernardino, Aeneas resolved to join the Franciscans himself. His horrified friends, who perhaps knew his nature better than he did, eventually talked him out of it. But one of Bernardino's disciples told Aeneas that it was sinful to resolve on such a good deed and then not to carry it through. This idea so troubled Aeneas that he walked all the way to Rome to seek San Bernardino's personal guidance. Bernardino could be a harsh and fiery preacher, but he had a gentle heart and, having some insight into human nature, he saw no potential friar in the diminutive youth who had come all that way to see him; he assured Aeneas that he committed no sin in repenting of his momentary resolution.[44]

Renaissance religion often had the spasmodic character exemplified by Aeneas's sincere but fleeting desire to become a friar. Aeneas never doubted the truths of Christianity; he consistently said his prayers, observed the feasts and fasts, and called upon the saints for their intercession when he was in trouble. He could not control his sexual appetite, but recognized it as sinful and repented with as much sincerity as he could manage, given his realization that he would inevitably fall again. But plague-era Christianity offered much more fear than comfort. How could it be otherwise when the divine wrath regularly visited a wretched death upon whole communities, falling equally upon the just and the unjust? Thus fear seized the heart whenever there was a plague, or a storm at sea, or merely a preacher like San Bernardino, who could drive home the image of sin's vileness and God's fury. No one doubted that God's vengeance upon sinners was just. When a preacher like San Bernardino inflamed the conscience, sins that had seemed merely natural

42. Vespasiano da Bisticci, *Renaissance Princes,* 165.

43. Pius II, *Epistola ad Mahomatem II [Epistle to Mohammed II],* trans. Albert R. Baca (New York: Peter Lang, 1990), 99.

44. Piccolomini, *De Viris* 38.

the day before suddenly became demons dragging the soul to Hell. "Repent!" the fearful heart responded. The trembling conscience insisted that everything must change: "Devote everything to God," it demanded; "Cast away the world and its works, cling to the skirts of the Madonna for protection from her avenging Son!" But when the danger passed or the preacher moved on to another town, the soul fell back exhausted, burned by the white heat of its recent fervor, a fervor few people could sustain. "Well," a person might sigh, "I can keep the fasts, go to Mass, and donate to the poor. Perhaps it will be enough. Anyway, it's all I can manage."

Even after the fainthearted soul fell back from its fervor, the sinner still knew the unbearable truth: God was justly vengeful. This was the horrible reality that people had to escape, because they could only bear it for short periods of time. But between these spasms of terror, the mind could never truly relax; rather, preserving oneself from fear, not only of plague and war, but of God himself, required the perpetual vigilance of a prey animal, expressed in continual stratagems of distraction. People sought distraction in literature, in festivals, in villas, in gardens, in travel, in nature, in works of art. God was often absent in these distractions, not because of disbelief or indifference, but *because God was part of the fearful reality that people were trying to escape.* What we have taken for secularism is often a by-product of faith, symptomatic of the fear of God.

In 1429 Aeneas left Siena without taking a degree.[45] There would have been no disgrace in this; it was a common practice in an age that attached less importance to formal credentials than we do. It is likely that, after eight years of study, Aeneas felt that he had learned all that Siena could teach him; apparently he thought this was not sufficient, because he went elsewhere to expand his knowledge. His passion was ancient literature, a subject in which Siena lagged behind many other cities. If Aeneas had exhausted the humanism Sozzini could teach, there was no one else in Siena to turn to. Having come to Siena with only as much Latin as the parish priest in Corsignano could teach him, Aeneas was never able to write Latin with complete technical perfection, and learned next to nothing of Greek. That his writing gains freshness and directness from avoiding grammatical and etymological pyrotechnics would not have been evident yet. We have no accurate picture of his

45. Grendler, *Universities,* 49.

movements and activities in 1429–1432, but it appears that he visited more advanced humanist centers seeking to remedy his deficiencies. He certainly spent time in Florence, where he met some of the leading humanists of the age, among them Francesco Filelfo, who was then lecturing at the Studio in Florence. The extent to which Aeneas may have sat at Filelfo's feet as a student is disputed. Filelfo, an ill-tempered, quarrelsome man, later resented what he regarded as the pope's ingratitude. After Pius died, Filelfo claimed that he had received the young Aeneas in his own house, found him employment, and arranged a position for him in Milan that launched his subsequent career.[46] Filelfo was an infamous liar, and the last of these claims is certainly untrue. Aeneas probably spent these undocumented years sojourning in various humanist centers (we know he visited Giovanni Aurispa in Ferrara), establishing contact with famous humanists wherever he could. He returned to Siena in 1431, probably because his funds had run out. There he tried to set himself up as a teacher. But a dangerous war with Florence made wealthy Sienese reluctant to splurge on extra lessons, and Aeneas had no reputation except for love poetry. He needed a job, almost any job. The one that he happened to find at the beginning of 1432 would launch him on a tumultuous career at the heart of European affairs, full of risks and opportunities, but with only the slimmest financial rewards.

46. Ady, *Pius II,* 22.

4

The Exile

As AENEAS struggled to survive on the proceeds of his teaching, a man passed through Siena, only five years older than Aeneas but already a cardinal—or at least he claimed to be. He was Domenico Capranica, from a family allied to the powerful Colonna dynasty in Rome, the family of Pope Martin V. Capranica had been secretary to Pope Martin, who made him bishop of Fermo and a cardinal. As it happened, the ceremony installing him as cardinal was delayed, and, in the interval, Martin V died. The conclave of 1431 that elected Eugenius IV as Martin's successor refused to admit Capranica as a member. Eugenius also refused to recognize Capranica because, like the conclave, he wished to break the stranglehold over the Papal States that Martin had established for the Colonna family. In spite of the failure of the Council of Pavia/Siena, the next general council of the church at Basel in what is now Switzerland had convened in 1431. Capranica was now on his way there to seek recognition as a cardinal from the council. He needed a secretary, and Aeneas took the job. Taking this somewhat precarious employment proved to be the most fateful decision of Aeneas's life, removing him at once from provincial stagnation into the swirl of international and ecclesiastical politics.

Aeneas's journey to Basel quickly initiated him into the dangers of his new course of life. In the current war Florence was allied with Pope Eugenius, thus shutting Capranica off from the land route north to Switzerland. The little port of Piombino, on the Tuscan coast, facing the island of Elba, was an independent principality from which Capranica and his party could hope to slip out unnoticed on a ship bound for Genoa, which was then under the rule of Filippo Maria Visconti, Duke of Milan, enemy both to Florence and the pope. The local lordling in Piombino was welcoming, but secretly ordered that Capranica and his party be prevented from boarding ship. Once this pattern of obstruction became evident, Capranica and one companion rowed out from the beach to their ship and immediately departed. Aeneas and another secretary, Piero di Noceto, along with some servants, were left stranded. Once Capranica was gone, however, the lord of Piombino, "not thinking it worthwhile to chase the feathers when he had lost the flesh" (as Aeneas put it in his *Commentaries*), allowed Capranica's secretaries and servants to depart for Elba, where they slept outdoors in bitter cold before catching up with their employer. Once they were reunited with Capranica, their ship turned toward Genoa but was immediately caught in a terrible storm. Aeneas claims that "in one day and night after leaving Italy they were driven between Elba and Corsica to Africa," where the sailors, he said, feared that pirates from the Barbary Coast would enslave them. But the wind changed; they "drifted rather than sailed back again between Corsica and Sardinia" to land at last at Porto Venere, just down the coast of the Italian mainland from Genoa. Aeneas said this storm "sounds marvelous and almost incredible."[1] Indeed, no sailing vessel could ever have completed the itinerary he describes in a day and a night.[2] From this journey Aeneas acquired a terror of the sea that only intensified with later experience. "Alas!" he later wrote, "You do not know what danger is if you have never gone to sea."[3]

The Genoese received Capranica and his party at Porto Venere in a style that gave Aeneas his first participation in the splendor that accompanies great men. Filippo Maria had sent an armed galley loaded with Genoese officials and prominent citizens to meet them. As the ship approached, trumpets blared, instruments played, and "the clamor of the sailors rose up to the sky."[4] The city of Genoa staggered Aeneas's imagination. It was, he said, "as superior to Florence as Florence is to Arezzo.... Every day you see different races of men, with strange and uncivi-

1. *Comm.,* Smith, I.12–13.

2. The letter that Aeneas wrote to the *podestà* at Piombino when he arrived in Genoa makes no mention of the night on Elba or of Africa. It claims only that they "went around Corsica and part of Sardinia for most of a night"; ASP to Tommaso della Gazaia, Genoa, February 28, 1432, Wolkan I, Epistle 4, in Pius II, *Reject Aeneas, Accept Pius: Selected Letters of Aeneas Silvius Piccolomini (Pope Pius II),* trans. Thomas M. Izbicki, Gerald Christianson, and Philip Krey (Washington, D.C.: The Catholic University of America Press, 2006), 61.

3. Piccolomini, *De rebus basiliae,* in Pius II, *Reject/Accept,* 331.

4. ASP to Tommaso della Gazaia, Wolkan I, Epistle 4, in Pius II, *Reject/Accept,* 62.

lized manners, and merchants arriving with every kind of wares." As for the women, Aeneas declared that Genoa should be Venus's modern capital.[5] Capranica's party enjoyed themselves at Genoa for some days before making the difficult crossing of the Alps to Basel. The Council of Basel was already quarreling with Pope Eugenius IV and was happy to flout him by recognizing Capranica. Eugenius, however, retained possession of all of Capranica's property and benefices, forcing him before long to dismiss his secretaries and household and return to Italy, where he submitted to the pope.

After a brief employment with the bishop of Freising, who took him as his secretary to the German diet at Frankfurt, Aeneas found work as secretary to Bartolomeo Visconti, bishop of Novara, who served as agent in ecclesiastical affairs for his cousin, Duke Filippo Maria. In November 1433 the bishop's service brought Aeneas to the court of Milan. He was probably still there when Filippo Maria, at war with the pope, incited such a rebellion in Rome that Pope Eugenius fled the city by boat, pelted by stones from both banks of the Tiber. Eugenius took refuge in Florence, remaining in exile for ten years while the Colonna controlled Rome. The papacy had clung to its perch in the Eternal City for only thirteen years.[6]

Aeneas's employer, Bishop Bartolomeo, and a Florentine named Riccio were engaged in a plot to kidnap the pope. The bishop went to Florence in the spring of 1435 to meet Eugenius and speak sweet words to his intended victim. Meanwhile, he sent Aeneas to Siena to convey messages concerning the plot to Filippo Maria's *condottiere,* Niccolò Piccinino. But in Florence, the pope uncovered Bishop Bartolomeo's plot. The bishop escaped, while Piccinino, possessor of an army, begged the pope's pardon and got it. Riccio, however, was arrested, tortured, and hanged. Aeneas feared a similar fate and prayed fervently for deliverance, even though he had probably known nothing about the conspiracy himself.[7] Rescue came from Piero di Noceto, his recent companion on the stormy seas, who got him a job with Cardinal Niccolò Albergati, a man powerful enough to protect him.[8] Albergati, immensely respected in the church

5. ASP to Andeozio Petrucci, Milan, March 24, 1432, Wolkan I, Epistle 6; quoted in Ady, *Pius II,* 29–30.

6. That is, thirteen years since Martin V arrived in Rome after his election at Constance in 1420.

7. Paparelli, *Enea Silvio Piccolomini,* 40–41.

8. Mitchell, *Laurels,* 54–55; Paparelli, *Enea Silvio Piccolomini,* 41.

and later beatified, would be Aeneas's first long-term employer. Albergati was a Carthusian and, as he rose to power, he continued to follow the strict rules of that order, abstaining from meat, wearing a hair shirt, and sleeping on straw.[9] Another austere individual was the director of Albergati's household, Tommaso Parentucelli, whose encyclopedic knowledge won Aeneas's admiration—"What is unknown to Parentucelli," Aeneas wrote, "lies beyond the sphere of human learning."[10] The stern tone set by these men was not entirely congenial for an admirer of ladies like Aeneas. Parentucelli, who would reappear later in Aeneas's life, seems to have looked with a jaundiced eye upon his youthful frivolity.

Aeneas was soon on the road again; Eugenius was sending Albergati to Arras in Flanders to represent the papacy at a congress that was supposed to end the Hundred Years' War between England and France. The real purpose of the congress was quite different: it was to arrange for Philip the Good, Duke of Burgundy, ruler of the Netherlands, a prince wealthier than the kings of England and France and almost their equal in power, to switch alliances from the English side to the French. If that forced the English to make peace, well and good—but the French and Burgundians were not counting on it. The pope instructed Albergati to make a number of diplomatic calls on his way to Arras, first at Filippo Maria's court in Milan and then at Ripaille on the shores of Lake Geneva, where Amadeus, Duke of Savoy, was living in a luxurious monastic hermitage at a château built for this purpose. After his wife died in 1422, Amadeus, who had enlarged his domains by conquest and acquired the title of duke, had passed the burdens of government to his son. Amadeus then took six companions and retired to a life of holy contemplation in the comfort and scenic grandeur of his château. Each of the Knights of St. Martin, as Amadeus and his companions called themselves, had his own tower, his own suite of rooms, and his own garden at Ripaille, where the park was well stocked with game.[11] This show of piety by a prince of proven political ability greatly impressed the duke's contemporaries, some of whom hailed him as a "new Solomon" and asked him to arbitrate their disputes; some even touted him as a future pope.[12] The duke's comfortable piety did not impress Aeneas, who wrote

9. Paparelli, *Enea Silvio Piccolomini,* 41.

10. Boulting, *Aeneas Silvius,* 52–53.

11. Paparelli, *Enea Silvio Piccolomini,* 42; Richard Vaughan, *Philip the Good: The Apogee of Burgundy* (London: Longmans, Green, 1970), 212.

12. Paparelli, *Enea Silvio Piccolomini,* 42–43.

that Amadeus "was living a life of pleasure rather than penitence."[13] From this scene of devout *villeggiatura,* Albergati's party went on to Basel and eventually to Arras. Aeneas would have relished the excitement and intrigue at Arras, where Albergati was acting as midwife to the new Franco-Burgundian alliance; but while the grandees deliberated, Albergati had a riskier assignment for Aeneas: to go to Scotland to persuade King James I to distract the English with attacks across the border.

Aeneas was probably naïve to embark from Calais, the fortress town held by the English on the Flanders coast. His cover story was unconvincing, and when the English discovered that he served Albergati, who was doing them so much damage at Arras, they immediately arrested him. Cardinal Henry Beaufort, bishop of Winchester, one of the most powerful Englishmen of the day, secured his release. Beaufort was seeking to end England's continental wars and was consequently inclined to show good faith by rescuing Albergati's envoy. Under Beaufort's protection Aeneas crossed the channel, but soon found that no one would issue papers permitting him to go to Scotland. Consequently, he took in the sights of London and Canterbury and then returned to Flanders to try again.

His efforts turned up a ship captain in the Burgundian-controlled port of Sluys who was willing to take him to Scotland. Two days out, the ship encountered stormy weather that continued for fourteen hours, blowing them (according to the *Commentaries*) almost to Norway while Aeneas trembled in terror. This gale had barely subsided when a second, even more violent storm overwhelmed them, lasting two nights and a day. The ship sprang a leak, and the sailors abandoned hope when they realized they were so far north that they could no longer read the constellations. Their panic-stricken Italian passenger was on his knees imploring the Trinity and the Mother of God to save him. He swore to the Blessed Virgin that, if they ever made landfall, he would embark immediately upon a barefoot pilgrimage to her nearest shrine. At length the divine powers sent a wind out of the north to blow the ship back toward Scotland, which they sighted after twelve days of heaving seas and roaring winds.

Disembarking, probably at Dunbar, Aeneas set out at once for the shrine of Our Lady at Whitekirk, about ten miles distant. Tuscany had not prepared him for a Scottish November and its unsuitability for bare-

13. *Comm.,* Smith, I.15.

foot pilgrimages. It would not have made any difference; he had made his vow, and all his life Aeneas was immovably stubborn about fulfilling obligations of honor. His bare toes crunched step by step through the long miles of snow to Whitekirk, where he knelt before the Virgin for two hours, impeding the flow of blood to his frozen feet. When he attempted to rise, he found that he could not stand. His servants (no one lacked servants in the fifteenth century, whatever the circumstances) hitched his arms over their shoulders and carried him to the next village. As they struggled along, Aeneas repeatedly struck his dangling feet on the ground to stimulate circulation. He credited this with restoring his ability to walk.[14] But the cure was not complete. Rheumatic pain in his feet tortured him for the rest of his life, becoming more severe with age. For most of his papacy he had to be carried in a chair wherever he went. He always refers to his affliction as "gout," but it is likely to have been rheumatoid arthritis resulting from frostbite. In any case, before leaving Scotland he revived sufficiently to father the first of his two known illegitimate children, a boy born the following year who did not survive.[15]

Aeneas considered Scotland to be "outside the civilized world."[16] Years later he wrote, "If only the king of Scotland could be as well-housed as a modest citizen of Nuremberg."[17] It must have been easy to persuade King James, who had spent eighteen years in English captivity, to raid across the border, a favorite sport for his subjects even without royal encouragement. His mission fulfilled, Aeneas now had to get home without falling into English hands. The captain of the ship that had brought him offered to take him back, but Aeneas declined, saying, "I prefer to trust to the mercy of men rather than of the sea." On the return voyage, the unfortunate captain, venturing again into stormy waters, had his ship break up under his feet while still in sight of shore: he drowned along with most of those on board. Meanwhile, Aeneas took the frosty road for England disguised as a merchant, and, after adventures that included huddling in a stable for fear of a Scottish raid of the very type he had come to encourage; he bribed a boatman to take him across the channel without a royal passport.[18]

14. *Comm.,* Smith, I.17.

15. Mitchell, *Laurels,* 83.

16. ASP to Priors of Siena, April 9, 1436, in Pius II, *Reject/Accept,* 83–84.

17. Quoted in Ruth Olitsky Rubenstein, "Pius II as a Patron of Art with Special Reference to the History of the Vatican" (PhD. diss., Courtauld Institute of Art, University of London, 1957), 21.

18. *Comm.,* Smith, I.19–21.

After the Scottish mission, Aeneas did not remain long in Albergati's service. The cardinal returned to Pope Eugenius in Italy, and Aeneas, hearing that the pope was still vindictive toward participants in the kidnapping plot, decided it was safer to stay in Basel. This prudent choice began the period of Aeneas's close connection with the council he had first stumbled across when he arrived in Basel with Cardinal Capranica. Pope Eugenius had appointed Cardinal Giuliano de' Cesarini, a learned and upright man whom Aeneas unabashedly admired, to serve as the council's president. Yet Cesarini had barely arrived in Basel in September 1431 when Eugenius issued a bull dissolving the council. Cesarini had sent the pope a polite protest and persisted in his task. At that point the council had backing from Emperor Sigismund, the kings of France, England, Scotland, and Castile, and the dukes of Burgundy and Milan. Eugenius could rely only on Venice and Florence. In May 1433 Sigismund visited Rome, where Eugenius crowned him as Holy Roman emperor (officially, he was only "king of the Romans" until then). Sigismund declared himself "protector" of the Council of Basel, leaving Eugenius little choice but to withdraw his previous decree and to recognize the council once more.[19]

Cesarini, a moderate who did his best to restrain the radicals in the council, had wanted to keep the council in session partly so that it could settle the conflict then raging in Bohemia over the Hussite heresy. John Hus (1369–1415), rector of the University of Prague, had defended some of the ideas of the English reformer John Wycliff (c. 1320–1384). Wycliff's views, which often anticipated the ideas of the later Protestant reformers, had been condemned as early as 1377. By speaking in Wycliff's defense, Hus also ran afoul of the church authorities. The feeble King Wenceslaus generally supported Hus, permitting him to gain a wide following in Bohemia. In 1402 Wenceslaus's brother, Emperor Sigismund, removed Wenceslaus from power and gave support to the Council of Constance. Sigismund gave Hus a safe-conduct to present his ideas before the council; but when the council condemned Hus, Sigismund stood aside and allowed Hus to burn as a heretic. The fire that consumed Hus ignited the Hussite Wars (1419–1434), a series of civil conflicts in Bohemia. Only a month before arriving in Basel, Cesarini had been present as papal

19. Morimichi Watanabe, "Pope Eugenius IV, the Conciliar Movement, and the Primacy of Rome," in *The Church, the Councils, and Reform: The Legacy of the Fifteenth Century,* edited by Gerald Christianson, Thomas M. Izbicki, and Christopher M. Bellitto (Washington, D.C.: The Catholic University of America Press, 2008), 180–81.

legate at the Battle of Domazlice (August 14, 1431), in which the Hussites routed the Catholic crusaders who had been sent against them. In 1433 Cesarini persuaded the Hussites to send a delegation to Basel. Both sides negotiated in an unusually conciliatory spirit and eventually agreed that the Bohemians would have the special privilege of receiving wine as well as bread at communion, but in other respects would conform to the laws, customs, and authority of the Catholic Church. These terms were written into the compacts signed at Iglau in 1436. Most Hussites accepted the compacts, although some, called Taborites, demanded increasingly radical changes.

When Aeneas threw in his lot with the council of Basel, it was just about to take a fateful turn from being a potential instrument for peaceful reform to being the spearhead of a rebellion that threatened to renew the schism healed at Constance. Freeing itself from Cesarini's moderating control, the council threw down a gauntlet in front of the pope in 1435 when it abolished annates, the church tax that formed the papacy's largest source of revenue.[20] Yet, the "wedge issue" that split the council and left it in the hands of a radical rump came from a wholly unexpected source. The Eastern Roman Empire—the Byzantine Empire, as modern historians call it—had been in decline for centuries, and by the 1430s it was reduced to Constantinople, its ancient capital, and a scattering of fragile outposts around the margins of the Aegean, of which the most important was the Morea in the Peloponnesian peninsula, with its capital at Mistra, near ancient Sparta. The Byzantine emperor, John VIII, faced with the rising power of the Ottoman Turks, who had already seized most of his former territories, could see no hope for his realm without aid from his fellow Christians in the West. Fellow Christians they were, but the Orthodox Church of the Byzantines and the Roman Catholic Church of the West had diverged in theology and customs since at least the fourth century and had split officially in 1054. The Byzantine view of the Westerners soured irretrievably in 1204 when Pope Innocent III's Fourth Crusade used the schism between the churches as an excuse for a brutal sack of Constantinople and the temporary conquest of most of the Byzantine Empire. Venice had benefitted substantially from the 1204 crusade, acquiring ports and islands throughout Greece and the Aegean that gave the "Most Serene Republic" dominance over trade in the East. When the Byzantines drove the

20. Ady, *Pius II,* 55–56. Annates were the first year's revenue for any church official receiving a new benefice, paid not to the new appointee but to the pope.

Westerners out of Constantinople and partially restored their empire, they proved completely unable to dislodge the Venetians. After these embittering experiences, only extreme desperation could have driven John VIII and the Eastern bishops to seek a council with the Westerners to unite the churches. Negotiations for a future council of reunion began during the Council of Constance.[21] John VIII preferred for the union council to meet in Constantinople; he specifically ruled out Basel or anyplace else across the Alps, since he needed to be able to return quickly to Constantinople in case of Turkish or other threats. If the council were held in the West the Byzantines would come only as far as Italy or, at the most, to Buda, Vienna, or Savoy.[22] The location of this new council was the rock on which the Council of Basel foundered. The radicals at Basel, led by the French delegation, feared that the pope would dominate a council in Italy and advocated Avignon instead.

When the topic of a host city arose at Basel, Aeneas worked to procure the honor for his beloved Siena. The Sienese, however, flatly refused to put up the necessary money, and Aeneas had no choice but to drop the matter.[23] The competing cities, including several in Italy, sent delegations to Basel to plead their cases. These emissaries presented showpiece orations that brought prestige to the speaker and to the city that employed him, but had little influence in actually deciding where the council would meet.[24] Filippo Maria of Milan had sent an envoy to speak for Pavia, but his emissary's performance was so feeble that the council dismissed him. Aeneas volunteered to take his place, burning his candles all night to write his presentation. This was the first occasion in Aeneas's career in which he had the opportunity to display his humanist skills in a grand oratorical performance. He tells us in the *Commentaries* that "he spoke for two hours to a most attentive and admiring audience, and afterward everyone present had a copy of the speech made for himself."[25] Two-hour speeches are not much appreciated nowadays, but Aeneas's performance was so admired that it jolted his career to a higher plane. Up until then he had been lost in the anonymous mass of

21. J. M. Hussey, *The Orthodox Church in the Byzantine Empire* (Oxford: Oxford University Press, 1986), 269–70.

22. Joseph Gill, *The Council of Florence* (Cambridge: Cambridge University Press, 1959), 55.

23. ASP to Priors of Siena, April 9, 1436, August 6, 1436, October 25, 1436; Wolkan I, Epistle 20, 21, 22, in Pius II, *Reject/Accept,* 85–93.

24. Paparelli, *Enea Silvio Piccolomini,* 53.

25. *Comm.,* Smith, I.23.

Latinists-for-hire that great men picked up and discarded at will. Overnight, he became a recognized talent.[26] Although he was still a layman, the archbishop of Milan rewarded him for his speech by making him provost of the church of San Lorenzo, his first ecclesiastical appointment and his first independent income. Yet when he went to Milan to claim his post, he found that the local chapter had elected someone else. Duke Filippo Maria, grateful for Aeneas's service, ordered the other man to make way. When Aeneas fell ill in Milan, the duke sent his personal physician to attend him. It was a serious illness that kept him in bed for seventy-five days; but after he recovered, he returned to Basel. No one was expected actually to stick around to perform the duties of these minor church offices. He arrived in Basel in time to witness one of the more absurd moments of ecclesiastical history.

The ceremony for naming the city that would host the council with the Easterners was set for May 7, 1437, but the faction supporting a city in Italy had come to no agreement with the faction favoring Avignon or someplace else distant from Rome. Rather than yield to each other or cancel the ceremony, two rival ceremonies went ahead simultaneously in different parts of Basel Cathedral, the majority supporting Avignon, but almost as many declaring for Italy. Loudly they proclaimed rival decrees while warring choirs broke into competing *Te deums.* Aeneas wrote in disgust to Piero de' Noceto, "the wise, when they go insane, excel in every form of folly."[27]

Eugenius quickly endorsed the minority decree in favor of a city in Italy and transferred the existing council from Basel to Ferrara.[28] Cesarini, who had never ceased to work for unity, mournfully left Basel for Rome in the first weeks of 1438.[29] The comedy of the double decree in the cathedral at Basel was played out again on a larger scale when the Byzantine emperor, the patriarch of Constantinople, and other Eastern prelates and dignitaries found two rival fleets in the harbor at Constantinople, each armed for battle. One fleet, sent by the fathers at Basel, stood ready to convey them to Avignon, Basel, or Savoy; the other, sent by the pope, had orders to bring them to Ferrara.[30] John VIII chose Ferrara. There, on January 8, 1438, the council for union opened with

26. Paparelli, *Enea Silvio Piccolomini,* 53.

27. ASP to Piero de' Noceto, May, 21, 1437, Wolkan I, Epistle 24, in Pius II, *Reject/Accept,* 115.

28. Gill, *Council of Florence,* 91–92.

29. Ibid., 96–97.

30. Ibid., 79–81.

Aeneas's former employer, Cardinal Albergati, presiding.[31] At the first session Eugenius nullified in advance any further actions taken by the council members remaining at Basel. Over the ensuing summer the plague, with a nice impartiality, struck both at Basel and Ferrara. Several Russian prelates died of plague as soon as they arrived in Italy.[32] The disease gave Eugenius an excuse to move the council from Ferrara to Florence in January 1439, though the menace of Filippo Maria's army near Ferrara and Cosimo de' Medici's offer to pay the council's expenses in Florence were probably his real reasons.[33]

In Florence discussions between the Eastern and Western churches intensified. Byzantine theology rested upon the writings of recognized church fathers, but the Westerners deployed all the syllogisms and specialized techniques of scholastic philosophy. There was nothing comparable to these in the Byzantine culture of the time. By the end of the formal public debates in April, the Greeks, finding themselves always outplayed at a game they did not understand, were unconvinced but determined to endure no more.[34] Their exhaustion was not merely intellectual; they had not received a penny of the money they were supposed to receive for their maintenance and were reduced to pawning their vestments and other valuables. Rumors of a forthcoming Turkish attack on Constantinople further frayed their nerves.[35] Regarding themselves almost as prisoners, they were ready to accept any resolution that would permit them to go home.[36] Two parties were emerging among them. One, led by Mark Eugenicus, bishop of Ephesus, would not compromise the Eastern traditions; the other, led by John Bessarion, bishop of Nicaea, were persuaded that certain passages in the writings of the church fathers supported the Western positions.[37]

The turning point came with a speech by Pope Eugenius on May 27 in which he promised generous military help from the Western powers in exchange for union. Bessarion and two others told the emperor that, whatever the others might do, they were determined to unite themselves to the West. A relentless round of exhausting meetings and repeated voting wore down the resistance of all the Eastern delegates except Mark Eugenicus.[38] On July 5 the representatives of both churches

31. Ibid., 95.
32. Ibid., 127–28n3.
33. Ibid., 176–78.
34. Ibid., 232.
35. Ibid., 238–40 and 252.
36. Ibid., 409.
37. Ibid., 234.
38. Ibid., 254–55.

signed the council's final decree, which conceded every point completely to the Western Church, including both doctrinal issues such as Purgatory and the *filioque* in the Creed and the authority of the pope over the entire church. Mark Eugenicus refused to sign, and another delegate slipped out of town to avoid doing so.[39]

From this point on the West considered the matter of church union to be settled, and the popes, including Pius II, regarded the Christians of the East as part of their own flock. In December 1439 Eugenius sought to consolidate the union by raising Bessarion and Isidore, the Greek archbishop of Kiev, to the rank of cardinal.[40] All the great dignitaries, Eastern and Western, celebrated the union of the churches with great pomp in Florence on July 6, 1439. To heal a division that had lasted for four centuries and, at least theoretically, bring millions of Christians within the papal embrace was an immense boost to the pope's prestige and, by the same measure, a blow to the credibility of the rebellious council in Basel. Until this point most European states had kept all their options open in the dispute between pope and council.[41] In Germany the emperor had declared neutrality, forcing each side to compete for his favor. In July 1438 Charles VII of France had issued the Pragmatic Sanction of Bourges, which affirmed the supreme authority of general councils without specifically endorsing the authority of Basel. Since it also abolished the pope's right to fill benefices in France, ended the payment of annates, and eliminated appeals to the pope, the Pragmatic Sanction effectively made the church in France independent of the papacy.

The departure of Cesarini and the moderates left the rump of the council in Basel severely understaffed. After his celebrated speech on behalf of Padua, Aeneas, though still a layman, found himself in demand for service on the council's various committees, including (he later claimed) the Committee of Twelve that directed the whole. He gradually became something equivalent to a chancellor in an Italian state—supervising all the secretarial work and drafting the documents and correspondence that flowed incessantly from the council. It would be decades before Aeneas became an independent actor in politics, but his name was now familiar in all the chanceries of Europe.

39. Ibid., 292.

40. Kenneth Meyer Setton, *The Papacy and the Levant (1204–1571)*, vol. 2, *The Fifteenth Century* (Philadelphia: American Philosophical Society, 1978), 65.

41. Charles L. Stinger, *The Renaissance in Rome* (Bloomington: Indiana University Press, 1985), 159.

Just as Aeneas's career took this upward turn, plague struck Basel in 1439. It originated in Germany, following, as it often did, on the heels of a famine. Returning from one of his many diplomatic journeys, Aeneas saw children in Bavaria fighting over a crust of bread "as dogs fight for bones."[42] When plague reached Basel, five thousand deaths were officially recorded between Easter and Martinmas, November 11; Aeneas says they were burying three hundred a day. In his *History of the Council of Basel* Aeneas paints a familiar scene of streets filled with funeral processions and priests hurrying to bring the sacrament to the dying. He reports that one could meet a man who seemed in perfect health and learn ten hours later that he was already buried. As was often the case, the young were most heavily afflicted; Aeneas said they fell "like leaves before the first frost of autumn." Distinguished members of the council, such as the patriarch of Aquileia, fell victim, as well. Safety required moving the council elsewhere, but the Frenchman Louis d'Allemand, Cardinal of Arles, the radical leader who now dominated the council, was afraid that if the council interrupted its meetings it might never reassemble. Consequently, he resolved to stay in Basel and keep as many others there as he could. D'Allemand's own secretary, Jean Pinan, a dear friend of Aeneas, died as a result of his master's intransigence. Aeneas declared that his friend's death felt as though his own soul had been taken from him. "Alas for the uncertainty of earthly things!" he cried, "Alas for the vain promises of the world! Aeneas, who in his own person could not die, died in that of his friend."[43] Equally devastating was the death of Lodovico Pontano, one of the leading legal scholars at the council and another admired personal friend.[44] Aeneas sat up with the dying Pontano, offering what comfort he could, bidding him to maintain his courage. Later that night Aeneas himself felt ill. He examined his own body for the fatal swellings and found one on his left thigh.[45]

He dismissed his servants, telling them not to risk infection by staying with him. His prominence in the council gave him access to physicians, of which there were only two worthy of consideration: one a learned man from Paris, the other unlearned but lucky. Aeneas "preferred luck

42. *Comm.*, Smith, I.26.

43. *Commentariorum Aeneas Sylvii de Gestis Basiliensis Councilii* (*Opera quae extant omnia*, [Basel: 1551], 46–47); quoted in Ady, *Pius II*, 64–65.

44. Lodovico should not be confused with Giovanni Pontano, the great humanist of Naples, who died in 1503.

45. Boulting, *Aeneas Silvius*, 98.

to learning—reflecting that no one really knew the proper treatment for plague." He briefly describes his treatment and the course of his illness.

> Since his left thigh was infected, they opened a vein in his left foot. Then, after being kept awake all that day and part of the night, he was made to drink a powder, the nature of which the physician would not tell. Sometimes chopped-up pieces of green, juicy radish and sometimes bits of moist clay were applied to the sore and to the infected place. Under this treatment the fever increased, accompanied by a violent headache, and his life was despaired of. Therefore, he had a priest summoned, made his confession, and received Communion and Extreme Unction. Soon after, he began to wander in his mind and give meaningless answers to questions.[46]

Nevertheless, after six days, Aeneas recovered. He offered to pay his doctor the generous sum of six florins, since his "kindness and faithfulness had been remarkable and perhaps unprecedented in a physician." The good doctor accepted the money only because it would enable him to treat six paupers free of charge.[47] Meanwhile, Filippo Maria, whose support for the council was rapidly cooling, heard that Aeneas was dead and gave his provostship in Milan to someone else. The council saved him from penury by giving him a canonry at Trent.[48]

On June 25, 1439, the fathers in Basel officially deposed Eugenius from the papacy, but the plague delayed the election of a successor. In October, when the council finally designated the electors who would choose a new pope, many urged Aeneas, still a layman, to take holy orders in order to qualify as an elector. As advantageous as this might have seemed, Aeneas refused. Instead, he served as clerk and master of ceremonies at the rebel conclave. That conclave elected as pope the princely hermit, Duke Amadeus of Savoy, whom Aeneas had previously judged to be a hypocrite. Whatever his personal views, Aeneas was appointed one of the delegation sent to Ripaille to give Amadeus the news of his election and to hear the duke announce his papal name, "Felix V." Thus, only weeks after declaring an end to the centuries-old schism between East and West, the Western church itself split into schism with two competing popes.

After the election of Felix, Aeneas wrote his *Dialogues on the Authority of a General Council,* a thorough, closely argued defense of the superiority of councils to popes and defending the Council of Basel in particu-

46. *Comm.*, Smith, I.27.
47. *Comm.*, Smith, I.28.
48. Ady, *Pius II,* 65.

lar. In the same year he brought forth the *Commentaries on the History of the Council of Basel,* extolling the glorious new age now being ushered in by the council's reforms.[49] Yet, even as his writings linked his name more closely than ever to the conciliar cause, questions about the council's eventual success were giving him the queasy sensation that he had backed the wrong horse.[50]

Aeneas was in Basel for the coronation of Felix V and shortly thereafter found himself appointed chief secretary to the new pope. Normally, this would have been the juiciest of plums, a powerful and lucrative position at the very pinnacle of humanist success. But few Europeans felt any nostalgia for the spectacle of rival popes hurling excommunications at each other. The election of Felix undermined support for Basel: little business and less money flowed to the antipope's court. Felix dragged his disappointed secretary with him between Basel and the lovely but boring shores of Lake Geneva. Aeneas, who had considered Amadeus/Felix a pious humbug from their first meeting five years ago, could not have been happy serving him and sharing his lakeside isolation. He was probably glad that the council and Felix sent him on frequent diplomatic missions, including trips to Frankfurt, Savoy, and Vienna, two excursions to Constance, and three journeys to Strasburg.[51]

On one of these Strasburg visits Aeneas found a Breton woman named Elizabeth who spoke Tuscan. Her husband, away on mercantile business, had left her at an inn. There Aeneas bedded her on Valentine's Day, 1442. Their son was born in November in Florence.[52] Aeneas was pleased to be a father again and wrote to his own father, asking that his parents bring up the boy in Corsignano. He felt, nevertheless, that he owed his parents some defense of his own behavior. He told his father:

> Certainly you, who are flesh, did not beget a son of stone or iron. You know what a cock you were, and I am no eunuch nor to be put in the category of the cold-blooded, nor yet am I a hypocrite who wants to seem better than he is. I frankly confess my error, for I am no holier than David the king nor wiser than Solomon.[53]

Unfortunately, the boy lived only fourteen months and never reached Corsignano.[54]

49. Ibid., 68–69.
50. Mitchell, *Laurels,* 74–75.
51. Boulting, *Aeneas Silvius,* 94.
52. Mitchell, *Laurels,* 81–83.
53. ASP to Silvio Piccolomini, Wolkan, Epistle 78; quoted in Mitchell, *Laurels,* 82.
54. Mitchell, *Laurels,* 83.

The Holy Roman emperor Sigismund had died in December 1437. He was the last of his line and left the thrones of Bohemia and Hungary and the likelihood of election as emperor to his son-in-law, Albert von Habsburg, Duke of Austria. Albert, however, ruled only briefly, dying in October 1439, leaving a pregnant wife, Elizabeth, but no children. None of Albert's realms relished the idea of an infant king: in Bohemia control fell into the hands of George Podebrady, leader of the moderate Hussites; Hungary, seeking help against the Turks, elected the Polish king, Wladysław III; the German electors chose Albert's brother, Frederick, as king of the Romans (i.e., "emperor-elect"). Four months after her husband died, Empress Elizabeth gave birth to a boy, Ladislas (Ladislas Posthumous), and made his uncle Frederick his guardian.

Once Frederick III was elected emperor, Aeneas got Felix V to appoint him as ambassador to convey the antipope's official congratulations. Realizing that Felix's papacy was eroding beneath his feet, Aeneas dedicated himself to cultivating allies at the imperial court who might be able to get him a position in the new emperor's service. Whenever Aeneas chose to mount a charm offensive, few except outright enemies could withstand it. In this case newly won friends persuaded Frederick to crown Aeneas as "poet laureate" at Frankfurt on July 27, 1442. It was an honor dating back to antiquity, now enjoying a revival due to the humanist passion for anything connected to ancient literature. In antiquity, competitions among poets had culminated in the winner receiving a crown woven from laurel leaves. Petrarch was the most famous of the new crop of poets laureate; but there was little justification for placing Aeneas, whose poetry was undistinguished both in quality and quantity, in his company. Frederick III would not have cared; a dull, phlegmatic man, it was easier for him to grant a meaningless request than to resist it.[55] The laureate ceremony did not disturb the imperial torpor, but Aeneas was exhilarated; he wrote to the archbishop of Milan, "Do not be surprised at seeing me sign myself, 'Poet,' for thus Caesar willed me to be."[56] Not until he took holy orders did Aeneas cease writing "Poet" after his name. The imperial diploma recording the event implies that poet laureate was a kind of order or rank, carrying such purely decorative privileges as wearing gold embroidery on one's academic gown.[57]

55. Boulting, *Aeneas Silvius,* 111.

56. ASP to Francesco Pizzolpasso, December 5, 1442, Wolkan 41; quoted in Ady, *Pius II,* 74.

57. *Comm.,* Smith, 40n.

When Frederick III departed after a visit to Basel in November of 1442, Aeneas accompanied him as a newly appointed imperial secretary.

In many ways the new employment was a downward step. Aeneas was not *the* secretary to Frederick as he had been to Felix; that position belonged to the chancellor, Kaspar Schlick.[58] With the council and with Felix, Aeneas had been a big fish—even though their pond was small and drying up. The emperor's pond was no ocean, either. The imperial title made Frederick the theoretical successor of the Roman Caesars, but he had little revenue and power with which to support such a dignity. His "empire," centered on Germany, consisted of over three hundred virtually independent states whose support the emperor must woo in order to achieve anything. Even Frederick's personal hereditary lands in Austria were difficult to control, and his writ hardly ran at all in the kingdoms of Bohemia and Hungary. Yet, in Basel, as Aeneas explained in a letter to Giovanni Campisio, "I found myself stranded and I knew not how to escape save by burrowing yet deeper into German earth."[59] The secretaries under Chancellor Schlick were not even paid, only housed and fed. Their income came as "gifts" (bribes) from those whose business passed through their hands—gifts they were allowed to accept but not to solicit.[60] Although he spent day and night in their company, Aeneas could expect no camaraderie from his fellow secretaries: they resented him as a foreigner, a rival for favor, and a competitor for the all-important "gifts." His conditions of life provoked Aeneas to compose a rant in the form of a letter, *On the Miseries of Courtiers,* which became one of his most popular works.[61] Describing the dinner hour, he says that the tablecloth, sticky, filthy, and full of holes, was enough to kill any appetite. Nor would many palates be tempted by "twice-cooked joints" of meat, "rancid butter," "cheese alive with vermin," or eggs on the verge of hatching. These delicacies were cooked in the oil left over from the lamps and washed down with bad wine passed from mouth to mouth in a greasy wooden bowl. To his horror, the Germans did not eat black bread because it was cheap—they actually preferred it! As for sleep, it had to be snatched when possible in a room full of ten to twenty

58. Technically, Schlick was the vice chancellor, as the higher title nominally belonged to the archbishop of Mainz.

59. ASP to Giovanni Campisio, 1445; quoted in Boulting, *Aeneas Silvius,* 115.

60. Boulting, *Aeneas Silvius,* 116.

61. Piccolomini, *De curialium miseriis,* ASP to Johann von Euch, November 30, 1444, Wolkan, Epistle 166.

other functionaries, some drunk, some snoring, some never quiet before midnight, in a damp and filthy bed shared with whatever boorish lout plopped into it.[62] He wrote to a friend that "one cannot even spit comfortably, but one needs must soil the clothes of a neighbor."[63]

No one at Frederick's court shared Aeneas's humanist interests. There was no appreciation for the niceties of ciceronian Latin or elegant metaphor, no enthusiasm for antiquity. His companions viewed poetry as useless if not immoral.[64] The partial exception to this ignorant indifference was Chancellor Schlick, whose friendship Aeneas was predictably able to cultivate. Schlick's mother was Italian, and the chancellor had lodged with Aeneas's relatives in Siena when he had accompanied the emperor Sigismund there. For Schlick Aeneas composed poems and panegyrics and set his most popular work, a novella, *De Duobus Amantibus* ("Tale of Two Lovers," 1444) in Siena during the time that Schlick was there. It has been traditional since the eighteenth century to see Eurialis, the male lover of the tale, as a pseudonym for Schlick and to interpret the story as a *roman à clef* describing a dalliance Schlick supposedly conducted with a Sienese lady. Recent scholarship challenges this interpretation, partly because the identification with Eurialis would have been more embarrassing than flattering to Schlick.[65] In spite of Aeneas's efforts during his papacy to suppress this little fable, thirty-five editions appeared by 1500.[66] It is a harmless bit of literary fluff—a tale of seduction concocted from conventional ingredients: the lover hidden in a chest under the bed when the husband appears; the husband's separation of the lovers, but then—just when we expect love to triumph over all—it doesn't. Once separated, the lovers get on with their lives with minimal regret. Schlick probably enjoyed a light, popular tale like this, but he was not an appreciative audience for humanist literary sophistication. He was a practical man of affairs, whose only real interest in literary style was its usefulness to the imperial chancery.[67] Aeneas may have thought of Schlick when he wrote about the Germans, "Good men and true are indeed to be found here, but they are not lovers of letters, they do not delight in the things that delight me."[68]

62. Ady, *Pius II,* 76–77.

63. Quoted in Boulting, *Aeneas Silvius,* 116.

64. Ady, *Pius II,* 78.

65. Emily O'Brien, introduction to *The Two Lovers: The Goodly History of Lady Lucrece and her Lover Eurialus,* ed. Emily O'Brien and Kenneth Bartlett (Ottawa: Dovehouse, 1999), 21–22n9.

66. Mitchell, *Laurels,* 46.

67. Ady, *Pius II,* 79.

68. ASP to Giovanni Campisio, September 1445, Wolkan, Epistle 185; quoted in Ady, *Pius II,* 80.

Distasteful as his circumstances were, Aeneas had advantages over his boorish companions and found the means to lift himself above them. He had, of course, the natural charm that never failed him and that he knew how to deploy for strategic ends. He had the increasing friendship and respect of the chancellor. But, above all, he had contacts. His countless journeys on behalf of the Council of Basel continued at the same pace for Frederick III. Wherever he went, he made friends and established contacts, assiduously maintaining them afterward by correspondence.[69] He had not alienated his friends on the conciliar side of the church schism, but his departure from Basel reopened at least a few doors on the papal side. The archbishop of Milan wrote to congratulate him on his new post and offered to try to reinstate him as provost of San Lorenzo. His old mentor Cardinal Cesarini also wrote to reaffirm "the friendship and goodwill that ever existed between us."[70] His portfolio of diplomatically useful contacts made Aeneas an asset that the astute Schlick and even the bovine Frederick could appreciate. Through his many contacts in Rome, Aeneas was able to secure the appointment of Schlick's brother as bishop of Freising. This success immediately promoted him from the slovenly mess hall to Schlick's "well-appointed table." From now on he received a dependable salary and became supervisor over his former companions. He was not above gloating: "he who had once trampled upon Aeneas," he wrote, "was now obliged to reverence him."[71]

Aeneas was keenly aware that his contacts in Rome had benefitted him more than those in Basel; moreover, both Schlick and Frederick were now inclining toward the papacy.[72] Aeneas always deplored his exile in Germany, and he increasingly regretted his commitment to Basel. In September, 1445 he wrote to Giovanni Campisio in Rome:

> Would that I had never seen Basel! Then I might have died in my own country. I might have lain in the bosom of my parents.... If the fates had not led me to Basel, I might have obtained some honorable post in the Roman Curia, where I should be living in the midst of my friends.[73]

69. Ady, *Pius II,* 80.

70. Ibid., 75.

71. *Comm.,* Smith, I.31; I have preferred Ady's translation: Ady, *Pius II,* 82.

72. Ady, *Pius II,* 80 and 85–86.

73. ASP to Giovanni Campisio, September 1445, Wolkan, Epistle 185; quoted in Ady, *Pius II,* 80.

In Rome Pope Eugenius was seeking some way of fulfilling his promises to provide military relief for the Byzantines. His options in this respect were very limited: the English and French continued their interminable wars with each other, and Germany's neutrality placed it virtually beyond his power.[74] Only the continuous war in the Balkans between the Ottoman Turks and Hungary offered a foundation upon which to build. A Hungarian noble, John Hunyadi, voivode of Transylvania, won some victories in 1442 that encouraged Eugenius to declare a crusade on January 1, 1443, and to charge a tenth of the income of the entire church as a crusade tax.[75] To this the pope added a fifth of his own much reduced income from annates. Giuliano Cesarini, who seemed to get all the most difficult assignments, went to Hungary as papal legate for the crusade to draw together and organize the forces of King Wladisław of Hungary and Poland, John Hunyadi, voivode of Transylvania, and Durad Brankovic, the exiled despot of Serbia.[76] The pope's strategy was to draw all the enemies of the Turks into a coordinated effort. In this venture even the Karamanids, a rival dynasty of Muslim Turks in southeastern Anatolia, were willing to participate. The Karamanids were to attack first to draw the Sultan and his armies into what is now southeastern Turkey. Then, while a Venetian and papal fleet blocked the straits of the Dardenelles and Bosphorus to prevent the sultan from returning to the Balkans, the Hungarians would invade from the north. This strategy proved impossible to implement in 1443; the fleet was not ready, and Sutan Murad II easily defeated the Karamanids in the spring and devastated their territories. When the Hungarians finally attacked in October, they won a few easy victories until Sultan Murad himself arrived and defeated them soundly at the Zlatitsa Pass in Bulgaria. When the retreating crusaders managed to defeat a small pursuing force at another pass. Cesarini gave such publicity to this minor success that this inflated "victory" masked the reality of failure.[77]

Much of the money that the pope had raised went to equipping ten galleys being built in Venice. They were to be the core of the fleet that was to block the straits and keep Murad and his army bottled up in Anatolia. Venice itself, the Adriatic city of Ragusa, whose hinterlands lay in the path of the invading Turks, and the Byzantines contributed another

74. Gill, *Council of Florence,* 344–45.

75. Colin Imber, *The Crusade of Varna,* 1443–45 (Aldershot, UK: Ashgate, 2006), 13–14.

76. Gill, *Council of Florence,* 328–29.

77. Imber, *Crusade,* 15–17.

dozen galleys. Unlike these states, all of which lay under direct Turkish threat, Burgundy and its duke, Philip the Good, had no vital interests in the East. It was pure thirst for chivalric glory that impelled him to add ten galleys to the crusading fleet.[78] In August 1444 all these vessels assembled at Constantinople; in September they were in position, controlling the Bosphorus and Dardenelles.

As in the previous year, it proved impossible to coordinate distant campaigns in southeastern Anatolia, the straits, and the northern Balkans. Murad only had to appear in Anatolia at the head of his army for the Karamanids to surrender without a fight. But this left the Sultan far away, at the opposite end of his empire, when King Wladisław, with about sixteen thousand men, crossed the frontier.[79] Burning towns and devastating the countryside, the crusaders headed southeast toward the Black Sea coast of Bulgaria. Any hope of success depended on the fleet's ability to prevent Murad from crossing the Bosphorus. The sultan demanded cannon and ships from the Genoese at Pera, their colony across the Golden Horn from Constantinople. Since Genoese trade in the East and their possession of Pera depended entirely on the sultan's goodwill, they dared not disappoint him. With the help of a storm that kept the Christian fleet at a distance, Murad ferried his army across the Bosphorus on Genoese ships.[80]

On November 10 Murad's host of about sixty thousand men faced the sixteen thousand Christian knights at Varna on the Black Sea coast.[81] Amazingly, the Christians achieved initial success; but King Wladisław spotted the sultan surrounded by his janissaries and, in pursuit of personal glory, he charged directly at them. One of the janissaries neatly unhorsed the king and lopped off his head. Without their leader the Hungarians fell into disorder; the battle became a rout and then a massacre. Christian corpses carpeted the battlefield. Somewhere among them lay Aeneas's revered friend Cardinal Cesarini, whose exact fate was never learned.[82] The Western help on which the Byzantines were counting had failed.

Among the Byzantines themselves, the union proclaimed in Florence had already withered. John VIII observed the union personally but did little to implement it. His brother, Constantine XI, who succeeded him in 1449, supported the union more vigorously. Many among

78. Gill, *Council of Florence*, 329–30.
79. Ibid., 332.
80. Imber, *Crusade*, 30.
81. Setton, *Papacy*, 2:88–90.
82. Imber, *Crusade*, 30–31.

the Byzantine ruling classes, who stood to lose everything in a Turkish conquest, were also unionists.[83] The bulk of the population, along with most of the monks, instinctively repudiated the union. The Byzantines preferred what they saw in Turkish territories, where there was little interference in Christian religious life, to the Western-dominated churches in Venetian and Genoese colonies.[84] By the beginning of 1441 many delegates who had signed the decree of union formally repudiated their action. Mark Eugenicus poured forth writings that gave definition, focus, and intellectual substance to the resistance of the monks and the populace.[85] When Eugenicus lay dying in 1445, he deputized his former pupil, George Scholarius, to continue the opposition. Constantine XI, prodded by Isidore of Kiev, now papal legate in Constantinople, formally proclaimed the union on December 12, 1452. But only a year and a half later the Turks captured Constantinople and the sultan installed Scholarius as patriarch of Constantinople.[86] Placing the leading anti-unionist at the head of the Eastern Church extinguished all hope of implementing the union proclaimed in Florence.

The death of Wladisław enabled Frederick III to reassert the claim of his four-year-old nephew Ladislas to be king of Hungary with himself as regent, but the Hungarian nobles soon rallied around Hunyadi as regent instead. Frederick needed papal support, which coincided neatly with Aeneas's personal need to reconcile with Eugenius IV.[87] It served both purposes when Frederick appointed Aeneas to head an imperial embassy to Rome. In Rome, old friends, including Piero da Noceto and Giovanni Campisio, rushed to greet Aeneas. Before admitting him into the papal presence, Eugenius sent two cardinals to absolve him from the dire penalties prescribed for the adherents of Basel.[88] Standing before his old enemy Eugenius, Aeneas made his excuses for supporting the council as elegantly as he could. Eugenius was terse, cool, but not ungracious in accepting them.[89] The only person who pointedly snubbed Aeneas was the bishop of Bologna, Tommaso Parentucelli, under whom Aeneas had served in Cardinal Albergati's household. It may have been

83. Deno John Geanakoplos, *Constantinople and the West: Essays on the Late Byzantine (Paleologian) and Italian Renaissances and the Byzantine and Roman Churches* (Madison: University of Wisconsin Press, 1989), 261.

84. Ibid., 244–47.

85. Gill, *Council of Florence,* 355–56.

86. Ibid., 366–67.

87. Boulting, *Aeneas Silvius,* 154.

88. Ady, *Pius II,* 88.

89. *Comm.,* Smith, I.33–34.

slightly awkward, therefore, that Eugenius sent Parentucelli and Aeneas together as his envoys to Germany to try to bring reluctant German princes and prelates into line with the newly reconciled pope and emperor. This was no simple task; but, by achieving it, Parentucelli and Aeneas both gained repute as statesmen of the first order. Aeneas participated in the ceremonial submission of the German electors at the bedside of the dying Eugenius, just before his turbulent papacy ended on February 23, 1447.[90]

Aeneas was now forty-one years old but had aged far beyond his years. Travel in the fifteenth century was physically brutal except for those in the most luxurious circumstances. Since leaving Siena thirteen years before, Aeneas had known little rest, working and worrying constantly without sufficient rest or sleep, with meals (when he got any) varying from sumptuous to revolting. The pains in his feet and legs increasingly tortured him. Bald and wrinkled, he already appeared to people as an old man.[91] The embers of sexual desire were rapidly cooling; two years after the birth of his second son and the cheeky letter he had written to his father, he admitted that he was now able to "praise chastity."[92] Two years further on, in 1446, he wrote to John Freund, another imperial secretary, that "Venus avoids me now quite as much as I turn my back on her. But I thank God that my temptation is lessened, so that I can overcome it." In the same letter he takes up the theme once advocated by Petrarch, preached again by San Bernardino, and half a century later by Savonarola, that one must meditate on death.

> I do not deny my past, dearest John, but we are older, nearer to death, and it behooves us to think less about life and more about the grave. Wretched is that man, and devoid of the grace of God, whose soul is never touched, who never examines his own heart, nor seeks to amend his ways, nor thinks of Eternity.[93]

Two days before writing this letter, Aeneas had been ordained a deacon at Vienna (March 1446). He became a priest within the year, though we do not know the place or the date. He visited a parish given to him

90. Boulting, *Aeneas Silvius,* 90–91; Ady, *Pius II,* 90–95.

91. Boulting, *Aeneas Silvius,* 145.

92. Ibid., 147.

93. ASP to John Freund, March 8, 1446; *Opera,* Epistle 92; quoted in Boulting, *Aeneas Silvius,* 148–50.

in a remote Alpine fastness in Tyrol; but its possession was disputed, and he traded it for clear title to a parish in Anspach. The dying Eugenius IV rewarded Aeneas for his German diplomacy by making him an apostolic subdeacon; his companion, Parentucelli, whose papal allegiance had never been in question, became a cardinal.

Many writers have charged Aeneas with hypocrisy and opportunism, both for his switch from the conciliar to the papal side in the church schism and for turning to the priesthood only when it seemed an avenue of advancement and after the fires of sexual desire had died down. Yet, at his lustiest, Aeneas had never sought to cover up or excuse his behavior. A clerical career had been his obvious path for advancement even before 1439, when he was urged to take orders so that he might help to elect a pope. Always scrupulous about vows, Aeneas probably made a deliberate decision to delay ordination until he could be reasonably certain of upholding an oath of celibacy.

The charge of opportunism in changing his support from council to pope has somewhat more traction. We may be sure that both his initial embrace of the council and his later rejection of it were motivated in part by employment opportunities. In his letter to Campisio expressing regrets about Basel, he raised no issue of principle but only of worldly position—he might be sitting pretty in Rome now if he had not taken the seductive chances offered across the Alps. But Aeneas had to make his own way in the world, and, although he was past forty and prematurely old at the time he submitted to Eugenius, he had not yet found much security or income. He was a man of principle when it came to personal honor, but a man could change opinions without being morally compromised. Aeneas was probably sincere in the views he expressed when he was chief spokesman for the conciliar cause. But events seemed to demonstrate to him and to others that God was on the pope's side, eventually forcing even the most intransigent conciliarists to reexamine their positions.

Sincerity is a delicate question in the case of any humanist. A humanist, like an attorney, was hired to be persuasive, not sincere. Humanists reveled in their ability to make a persuasive argument even for the weakest cause, and eloquence always took precedence over accuracy. The great breakthrough in Aeneas's career had been his speech in support of Pavia as the site for a council. Yet he had no personal attachments to Pavia and only embraced her cause when he got the opportunity to make the speech. People praised and rewarded him for his speech, but no one voted to send the council to Pavia. This is not to say that Aeneas did not support the Council of Basel—he certainly did—but, in writing polemics on its behalf, personal commitment was irrelevant. The eloquence and persuasiveness of such polemics was a matter of professional pride and reputation. Whatever causes he embraced, no one ever had reason to charge Aeneas with a tepid advocacy. Professionally as well as personally, he was never lukewarm: his commitments, once made, were total.

5

The Cleric

BEFORE THE RED DYE on his cardinal's vestments had time to set, Tommaso Parentucelli was elected to succeed Eugenius as Pope Nicholas V. Aeneas served as one of the two doorkeepers of the conclave, a role similar to the one he had played at the election of the antipope Felix V.[1] Frederick III was lobbying the new pope to raise Aeneas to the rank of bishop, and the convenient death of the bishop of Trieste enabled Nicholas to oblige only three weeks into his papacy.[2] Aeneas's new diocese was far removed from the centers of political action, and it was from there that Aeneas learned of the signing of the treaty between pope and emperor and of the final dissolution of the Council of Basel. Two months later, in April 1449, he learned that "Felix V" had renounced his papal pretensions in return for a cardinal's hat.[3]

Before Aeneas saw his diocese, however, he had carried out another diplomatic mission for Frederick III. The Milanese tyrant Filippo Maria Visconti died in August 1447, leaving no male heir. He did, however, have an illegitimate daughter, Bianca Maria, whom he had been forced to give in marriage to his ambitious *condottiere,* Francesco Sforza. Using his military skill, his willingness to betray his employers, and the backing of Cosimo de' Medici, Francesco (1401–1466), the illegitimate offspring of a line of *condottieri* ("Sforza," appropriately, means "force"), had made himself a major player in Italian politics. By his marriage to Bianca Maria, he had positioned himself to claim the Visconti inheritance. The citizens of Milan, however, had other ideas and had

1. Ady, *Pius II,* 101.
2. Ibid., 93.
3. Ibid., 104.

proclaimed a republic dedicated to St. Ambrose, their fourth-century bishop and patron saint. Since Sforza had no intention of missing the opportunity he had worked so hard to create, he besieged the city and, by his stranglehold on the all the country round about, soon reduced it to famine. Legally Milan was a fief of the Holy Roman Empire; Filippo Maria's death without a legitimate heir enabled Frederick III to claim that Milan had reverted to him. Frederick knew that he had no means to enforce this legal right, but he sent Aeneas to Milan to see what leverage could be gotten out of it. Aeneas's first mission there, in 1447, produced nothing, because the colleagues whom the emperor sent with him made extortionate demands that alienated the Milanese.[4] Two years later, hoping that Sforza's siege and the famine it had created might make the Milanese receptive to his proposals, Frederick sent Aeneas to negotiate with them again. Sforza heard that ambassadors were on their way to the city and put all approaches under heavy guard. Nonetheless, Aeneas, by a combination of stealth and "God's goodness," was able to penetrate this cordon.[5] Once inside the city his intrigues with the desperate republic persuaded its leaders to offer to yield their city to Frederick.[6] Even so, Aeneas realized that it was too late for anyone, least of all the distant and penniless Frederick, to deliver the city from the grasp of Francesco Sforza. He therefore obtained a safe-conduct to call upon Sforza at his camp to test his attitude to the emperor in the likely event that Sforza became ruler of Milan. Sforza asked Aeneas how he had slipped through the besieging army and listened with admiration to Aeneas's explanations. Sforza impressed Aeneas with his energy, competence, and good sense. Thus began a long and productive relationship between the future pope and the soon-to-be Duke of Milan.[7]

In other ways Aeneas's life as bishop of Trieste was disappointing, even depressing. Tommaso Parentucelli, now Nicholas V, was one of the few people whom Aeneas never charmed. Nicholas looked back at the young man he had known in Albergati's household as a frivolous lightweight, and he had shown himself reluctant to accept the sincerity of Aeneas's conversion from conciliarist to papalist principles. Though he made Aeneas a bishop, he nevertheless gave him an out-of-the-way diocese and never consulted him on high affairs. Furthermore, the death of Chancellor Schlick in January 1449 greatly weakened Aeneas's position

4. Ibid., 105.

5. *Comm.*, Smith, I.48.

6. Ibid., I.48–51.

7. Ady, *Pius II,* 105–6; *Comm.,* Smith, I.52.

at the imperial court, where a hostile faction was now in charge. Left to cool his heels, Aeneas filled his time with writing. He dedicated much of this writing to projects conceived years earlier but never completed. The most important was a new history of the Council of Basel, *De rebus basileae gestis commentarius* ("Commentary on the Proceedings of Basel"), which was highly critical of the council and designed to counteract the favorable history, *De gestis Basiliensis Concilii* ("On the Deeds of the Council of Basel") that he had written in 1440 when he was the council's leading apologist.[8] To emphasize his rejection of the council he framed this new history as a letter to the Spanish cardinal, Juan de Carvajal, who had been a prominent papal spokesman against the council. In the new history Aeneas carefully omits most of the role that he himself had played in the council's leadership.[9] In these years he also worked on a decade-long project that he never completed: a book of biographies of famous contemporaries, *De viris aetate sua claris* ("On Famous Men of his Own Time"). Such biographical collections had been a standard type of humanist work since Boccaccio, but Aeneas was the first to concentrate exclusively on his own contemporaries.

Kaspar Wendal, tutor to Frederick III's nephew and ward Ladislas Posthumous, the ten-year-old king of Hungary and Bohemia, asked Aeneas to write something for his pupil's educational guidance.[10] Aeneas mentions this boy often and affectionately in his writings and took the opportunity to write *The Education of Boys* addressed directly to the young king himself. Ladislas probably welcomed Aeneas's counsel on balancing study with relaxation, but might have been disappointed that most of the treatise focuses closely on the study of Latin letters.[11] Aeneas asks rhetorically, "Who would not be willing to toil over literature when such wonderful fruit is plucked from it? When it holds the knowledge of good and evil? When it tells us our past, controls the present, and foretells the future? . . . The greatest attention and zeal must be devoted to literature."[12] Nevertheless, the primary purpose of reading the classics, Aeneas tells the king, is to learn how to speak and write in imitation of the ancients. "Indeed, no one possesses the art of correct speaking who

8. Emily O'Brien, "Aeneas Sylvius Piccolomini and the Histories of the Council of Basel," in Christianson, Gerald, Izbicki, and Bellitto, *The Church, the Councils, and Reform,* 75.

9. Ibid., 79.

10. Piccolomini, "The Education of Boys," in *Humanist Educational Treatises,* trans. Craig W. Kallendorf (Cambridge Mass.: Harvard University Press, 2008), 67.

11. Piccolomini, "Education," 73.

12. Piccolomini, "Education," 82–83.

has not looked at the poets and read the historians and orators. Where else may one learn whatever there is of logic, antiquity, authority and custom in the art of grammar?"[13] Aeneas devotes about a fifth of the treatise exclusively to grammar, pages of impenetrable pedantry that their author, nevertheless, seems to enjoy.

At times in this treatise we catch a whiff of Aeneas's disdain for the central European peoples among whom he had lived for so long. He speaks from experience when he defends himself against those Germans who say, "Why do you bring poets to us from Italy, and why do you corrupt the holy morals of Germany with the effeminate licentiousness of the poets?"[14] Aeneas urges the young king of Bohemia and Hungary not to read the histories of those countries, "For they are written by ignorant people, and contain much silliness, many lies, no maxims, and no elegance of style."[15]

The depressing effects of life in Trieste appear in *De Somnio,* a dialogue between Aeneas and the departed soul of Kaspar Schlick. He wrote it in November of 1449 and, like the history of Basel, sent it to Cardinal Juan de Carvajal, who was rapidly becoming a good friend and confidant. It is cast as a vision of Purgatory in which Aeneas and his departed friend trade gloomy assessments of human life and their own times. This is one of Aeneas's closest approaches to the morbid side of quattrocento culture. Much like Petrarch, Aeneas presents love of life and fear of death as moral failings, but failings that he is not strong enough to overcome.

> Bitter death has already stolen many friends. . . . Indeed, many philosophers have considered death scarcely an evil, in fact, even something to choose. I, if it could be avoided, never would choose it. But necessity dictates that what we cannot flee we must not fear. Consequently, this presses hard upon our necks: no day, no hour is sure; the final end can come at any moment. What is our life but smoke? I am not yet fifty, and yet I know more people among the dead than the living. It is pleasant, nevertheless, to be alive, and we believe it is nicer to linger among strangers than to pass to our friends.[16]

While Nicholas V kept Aeneas at arm's length, he offered a warm welcome to many other humanists. Later dubbed "the First Renaissance Pope," Nicholas founded the Vatican Library and was the first pope to subsidize lavishly not only humanists, but artists and architects who

13. Ibid., 105.
14. Ibid., 106–7.
15. Ibid., 114.
16. Ibid.; *Reject/Accept,* 295.

practiced the new, classically inspired styles. His liberality to humanists inflated the scope of every literary man's dreams. The prominent humanist Lorenzo Valla had been out of favor in Rome for anti-papal polemics and for demonstrating that the "Donation of Constantine," the document justifying papal rule in central Italy, was a forgery. But Nicholas gave him a five-hundred-florin reward for translating Thucydides and a desirable appointment at the curia. Another five hundred florins went to Niccolò Perotti for the translation of Polybius, while Filelfo got the same amount for his lifetime of services to the classics. Nicholas was so extravagant in his purchases for the new Vatican Library that even Decembrio, one of the eminent humanists employed by Nicholas and a bibliophile himself, described it as an "incomprehensible thirst for books."[17]

Giannozzo Manetti, Nicholas's contemporary biographer, tells us that, once he was elected pope, Nicholas conceived the idea that reviving the glory of Rome was the mission of the papacy, bringing glory to himself and honor to the church and even increasing the devotion of the people.[18] That reviving Roman glory was the mission of the Vicar of Christ was indeed an original idea! The funds that Nicholas spent freely for this purpose came from the thousands of pilgrims descending upon Rome in celebration of the Jubilee Year in 1450. One writer claimed that "a greater crowd of Christians was never known to hasten to any Jubilee: kings, dukes, marquesses, counts, knights, and people of every rank came there daily in such multitudes that there were millions in the city." Aeneas asserted that forty thousand arrived every day.[19] Along with their money, the jubilee pilgrims brought plague to Rome, and some members of the curia succumbed. Pope Nicholas, who had lost his father to the plague, was more than normally terrified of it.[20] He fled from Rome to Fabriano in the Apennines, bringing artists and humanists with him. It was there, according to Manetti, that he conceived his great building plans to transform the shabby muddle of medieval Rome into the imperial capital of Christendom.[21]

Rome had never been an economic center in the sense that Venice, Milan, and Florence were; from antiquity to modern times its fortunes

17. George A. Holmes, *The Florentine Enlightenment* (Oxford: Clarendon, 1969), 250–51.

18. Ibid., 250.

19. Boulting, *Aeneas Silvius,* 185–86.

20. David R. Coffin, *The Villa in the Life of Renaissance Rome* (Princeton: Princeton University Press, 1979), 25.

21. Torgil Magnuson, "The Project of Nicholas V for Rebuilding the Borgo Leonino in Rome," *Art Bulletin* 36, no. 2 (June 1954): 108; Goldthwaite, *Wealth,* 185.

have risen and fallen with its political status. Even in the High Middle Ages no merchant fleets lined the quays along the Tiber, no bustling workshops produced for world markets as in so many other Italian cities. When the papacy moved to Avignon, Rome shriveled like a severed branch. Most of the territory inside the third-century Aurelian walls was a rural landscape of vineyards, orchards, and vegetable gardens, even patches of wilderness. Wolves had recently infested the Vatican gardens, and several decades later the former quarters of the Praetorian Guards became a hunting preserve.[22] Other than pilgrims to its churches, Rome's chief industry was stock farming. Each winter flocks of cattle, sheep, and goats were brought to pasture inside the walls.[23] Thus, the ancient forum became the Campo Vaccino, or "Field of Cows," and the Tarpeian Rock on the Capitoline was Monte Caprino, or "Goat Hill." Most of the fifteenth-century population of twenty-five to thirty thousand clustered near the river on the former Campus Martius. Separate villages huddled around the Lateran and Santa Maria Maggiore. Of the eleven ancient aqueducts, only one still functioned, though not very reliably.[24]

The keystone of Nicholas's planning was to fix the headquarters of the papacy at the Vatican instead of at San Giovanni Laterano, where it had been since Constantine's time. Nicholas wanted to emphasize the papacy's link with St. Peter, but, for a pope keenly aware that his predecessor had been driven out of Rome, the Vatican's defensive advantages were probably most crucial. The fickle Roman mob would have to cross the Tiber to reach the Vatican, and the Castel Sant'Angelo commanded the bridge. Nicholas rebuilt the Castel Sant'Angelo, adding a fortified gate at the end of the bridge and a splendid papal apartment for refuge in times of trouble.[25] In addition, Nicholas rebuilt the defenses surrounding the Vatican quarter, encircling St. Peter's basilica and the palace so that, anchored by the Castel Sant'Angelo, the Vatican formed a walled city of its own, protected as much from the Romans as from foreign enemies.[26] Within the protection of these defenses, Nicholas greatly enlarged the Vatican Palace and made it his permanent residence.

22. Stinger, *Renaissance,* 21 and 24.

23. Peter Partner, *The Lands of Saint Peter: The Papal State in the Middle Ages and Early Renaissance* (Berkeley and Los Angeles: University of California Press, 1972), 420.

24. Stinger, *Renaissance,* 21 and 24.

25. Anthony Grafton, *Leon Battista Alberti: Master Builder of the Renaissance* (New York: Hill and Wang, 2000), 300.

26. Magnuson, "Project," 94–95.

Nicholas did not neglect the rest of Rome; he improved its defenses and its appalling sanitation, restored forty of its principal churches, and renovated the old palace of the senator on the Capitoline Hill.[27] Nicholas was the first to think of demolishing and replacing Constantine's Basilica of St. Peter.[28] He got as far as beginning a new choir in the classical style with an apse whose curved wall formed a tower in the Vatican defenses.[29] But it is Nicholas's plans for rebuilding the Borgo Leonino, the urban area between St. Peter's and the Castel Sant'Angelo, that made him a pioneer of that characteristic Renaissance gesture, creating an "ideal city." We will consider his plans in more detail in a later chapter devoted to such urban dreams.

The jubilee year saw the end of Aeneas's boredom in Trieste when Frederick III summoned him to a new mission. Aeneas's continued poverty made Frederick as much the master of the impecunious bishop as he had been of the indigent secretary. The emperor wanted Aeneas to go to Naples to negotiate with King Alfonso for the hand of his niece, Eleonora, princess of Portugal, whom Frederick had decided to wed. Aeneas was also to prepare the way for Frederick to come to Italy to collect his bride and proceed to Rome, where the pope would crown him Holy Roman emperor. As he traveled south to begin this mission, Aeneas heard rumors in Ferrara that Pope Nicholas had just appointed him bishop of Siena. The news must have delighted him, but when he arrived in Siena he did nothing toward claiming this new dignity, since he had not received official notice from the pope.

His sojourn in Naples was as pleasant as it was successful; Aeneas and King Alfonso took to each other at once, and word came from Portugal that Eleonora would be delighted to become an empress.[30] By the time of these negotiations Alfonso, a Spaniard and hereditary king of Aragon, had reigned successfully in Naples for seven years; but before that came twenty-two years of bitter warfare against King René, a member of the French Angevin dynasty that had ruled in Naples since conquering it in 1266. Succession disputes in Naples had a long history and were to become a major burden for Aeneas during his reign as pope. Before the Angevin conquest of 1266, Naples and Sicily had belonged to the German Hohenstaufen dynasty, who were then Holy Roman emperors and bitter enemies of the popes. Finally, in 1262, Pope Urban

27. Ibid., 89 and 92; Grafton, *Leon Battista Alberti,* 300.
28. Magnuson, "Project," 92.
29. Ibid., 96.
30. Ady, *Pius II,* 112–13.

IV, acting as overlord of these kingdoms, had invited Charles of Anjou, brother of Louis IX of France, to shatter Hohenstaufen power by conquering Naples and Sicily. Charles's successful conquest in 1266 replaced the Hohenstaufen with the Angevins; but in 1282 the Sicilians expelled the unpopular French in a gory massacre called the Sicilian Vespers and summoned the king of Aragon to support them against Charles. Thereafter, the Aragonese holding Sicily and the Angevins, who retained the mainland territories, remained irreconcilable enemies, always alert for opportunities to harm one another.

The papacy, overlord of both Naples and Sicily, consistently supported the Angevins. The Angevin dynasty undermined itself with its own disputes over succession that generated civil wars in Naples involving outside powers. The Angevin heritage eventually came into the hands of a childless woman, Joanna II, who at different times designated both Alfonso of Aragon and René of Anjou as her heir, making a war of succession almost inevitable. Alfonso's victory in that war and his benevolent rule had provided a welcome breathing space in these unending conflicts. Now Aeneas, as Alfonso's guest, enjoyed the atmosphere of humanist cultivation with which the conqueror-king surrounded himself. Even during military campaigns Alfonso took along his most eminent humanist, Panormita, to read aloud from Livy during intervals of leisure.[31] Aeneas must have agonized over the contrast between the cultivated Alfonso and his own boorish Frederick. The favorable impression King Alfonso made on Aeneas probably paved the way to his later, fateful decision to switch the papal alliance from the Angevins to the Aragonese.

In January of 1451 the Sienese enthusiastically received Aeneas as their bishop, rejoicing to welcome a native son to an office usually held by foreigners. But when he returned in October, they and all Italy were fearful and hostile to Frederick's impending visit. Holy Roman emperors were, at least in theory, overlords of all Italy north of the Neapolitan kingdom, but any interference by their German suzerain was obnoxious to the Italians. Pope Nicholas, like his predecessors, supported the Angevins and worried about Frederick's impending marriage to King Alfonso's niece. Aeneas waited to greet Eleonora at the Sienese port of Talamone, but the Portuguese fleet escorting her took 104 days to reach Italy and went to Livorno instead of Talamone. It took another two weeks for the Portuguese to agree to turn their princess over to Aeneas

31. Vespasiano Da Bisticci, *Renaissance Princes,* 70.

instead of to Frederick, who was waiting for her in Siena near the place where she had been expected.[32] Frustrated, Aeneas killed time visiting the archeological sites in the region. Eventually, Aeneas got the girl to Siena, where she met her imperial fiancé outside the Porta Camollia, where a memorial column was erected to commemorate the occasion.

After celebrations in Siena, Aeneas accompanied the betrothed couple to Rome, where their wedding took place three days before Frederick's coronation. The tradition that only the pope could crown a Holy Roman emperor stretched back to Charlemagne's revival of the imperial title in 800; but, although the succession of emperors in Frederick's Habsburg dynasty would last until 1806, only one of his descendents (Charles V, 1530) considered it worthwhile to observe this ancient ritual.[33] After the ceremony, Aeneas gave an oration before the emperor, the pope, and all the assembled dignitaries. In it Aeneas, for the first time, called upon the leaders of Europe to launch a new crusade against the Turks—a theme that would eventually come to dominate his life. He went so far as to claim that Frederick wanted to lead this venture himself. According to Aeneas, Frederick looked with horror upon the enemies of Christendom pressing in from every side in Poland, Hungary, Spain, and the Mediterranean—the result, Aeneas said, of generations of negligent Christian princes. Aeneas announced that Frederick was cut from a different cloth. Inspired by the sufferings of the Eastern Christians, the newly crowned emperor was chomping at the bit to be off on crusade. Once he embarked, Aeneas declared, he would begin with liberating Hungary and Greece, then reclaim the Holy Land, and finish by wiping Islam "from the face of the earth."[34] This prediction was absurd, and Frederick never considered the possibility of crusading in the East; but it was a rare humanist who let reality restrain his rhetoric.

Five days after the coronation the newlyweds departed for Naples, attended by an entourage of about two thousand persons. Aeneas was not with them. He had been left behind to guard young Ladislas Posthumous against the many Hungarians who sought to liberate their king from Frederick's control. In Naples King Alfonso spent 100,000 ducats

32. Boulting, *Aeneas Silvius,* 190–91; Ady, *Pius II,* 121.

33. The Habsburg succession as Holy Roman emperors was broken briefly in 1742–1745 by the reign of Charles VII of the Wittelsbach family. Frederick's descendents continued to be emperors until 1918, but the title "Emperor of Austria," adopted in 1804, was the one used after 1806.

34. Margaret Meserve, *Empires of Islam in Renaissance Historical Thought* (Cambridge, Mass., and London: Harvard University Press, 2008), 96–98.

on the festivities and assured public cheer by fountains flowing with wine. Alfonso paid for anything Frederick wanted to purchase and entertained him with a ceremonial hunt that slaughtered stags, deer, boar, and even porcupines.[35] Frederick's parade around Italy was a wonderful froth of feudal, imperial, medieval, and classical ceremonies and symbols, signifying almost nothing. Italian anxieties subsided when the emperor only asserted his authority in such welcome ways as dubbing three hundred knights in Rome.[36] When it all ended, Aeneas must have been very sorry to accompany Frederick across the Alps and out of Italy. To Aeneas's relief Frederick soon sent him on new travels, this time to Bohemia to try to pacify the unending Hussite wars. Such lengthy, often dangerous journeys were almost beyond Aeneas's capacity now as the agony in his limbs fastened itself upon him more relentlessly. He wrote to Goro Lolli in 1453 that he kept up his courage by thinking "that my pains must soon be ended by recovery or death."[37] Nevertheless, he looked with longing on the hardships of travel once he was back in the boredom of Frederick's somnolent court, which spent the whole summer of 1453 in the provincial torpor of Graz. Aeneas wrote to Goro explaining why he stayed there: "While I remain with the Emperor, the Pope and Cardinals still value me a little. If I were in Siena they would cease to remember me.... If I left the Imperial court I should be dropped, for I should be of no further use."[38]

That summer, word came to Graz of a distant event that changed the course of Aeneas's remaining years, giving him, as never before, a sense of mission that made him drive his aching body beyond the limits of its strength. On May 29, 1453, the Turkish sultan, Mehmet II, captured Constantinople from the last Byzantine emperor, Constantine XI, who died fighting on the walls. The Western help that Constantine's brother, John VIII, had hoped to purchase by submitting to the papacy at the Council of Florence had ended in disaster at the battle of Varna. The thousand-year-old Byzantine Empire faced its final agony alone. The speech he had given at Frederick's coronation reflected Aeneas's growing concern over the Turkish menace, a concern that probably originated with the Christian defeat at Varna where his friend Cesarini had

35. Mary Hollingsworth, *Patronage in Renaissance Italy* (Baltimore: Johns Hopkins University Press, 1994), 184.

36. Ady, *Pius II,* 117.

37. ASP to Goro Lolli, September 3, 1453; *Opera,* Epistle 146; quoted in Ady, *Pius II,* 121.

38. ASP to Goro Lolli; Graz, July, 1, 1453; Weiss, Epistle 48; quoted in Ady, *Pius II,* 122.

died.[39] From now on he considered rolling back the Turkish advance and recapturing Constantinople to be the most urgent duty facing all Christians. The need to save the priceless ancient manuscripts of Constantinople from alien hands was among the spurs to his resolve. He wrote to his fellow humanist, Nicholas V, "What can I say of the countless books which are yet unknown to the Latin world? ... Alas! How many names of famous men will perish? It is a second death to Homer and to Plato. Where shall we find our poets and our philosophers? The fount of the Muses is stopped." He went on to outline for Nicholas the program he would follow himself as pope. "It is for you, Holy Father, to arise, to address kings, to send legations, to exhort princes.... Now, while the evil is recent, let Christian states hasten to take counsel, to make peace with their co-religionists, and to move with united forces against the enemies of the saving cross."[40]

On the surface Nicholas seemed to comply with Aeneas's demands; he issued a papal bull proclaiming a crusade on September 30. Fra Giovanni Capistrano, a follower of San Bernardino who had continued his mentor's preaching, turned his attention to proclaiming the crusade. Even the phlegmatic Frederick had wept at the news from the East and bestirred himself to call a congress of Christian rulers at Regensburg to plan the expedition. It was, as one of Aeneas's biographers aptly put it, "a respectable appearance of activity." But the undertow began to pull against this merely respectable tide almost immediately. The pope, seeing Frederick's congress as a potential revival of conciliarism, did not support the imperial summons.[41] The indolent Frederick found that, after all, he could not bother to go personally to Regensburg. Only one ruler of European stature publically committed himself to go on the crusade, and his manner of doing so speaks volumes about the priorities of the age.

Philip the Good, Duke of Burgundy, was as eager as ever to appear before Europe as the gallant crusader. At the very least, he could seize this opportunity to burnish the image of his court as a second Camelot by an extravagant display of chivalric pageantry. It began with a tournament at Lille on February 16, 1454, followed the next day by a banquet, long renowned in courtly circles as the "Feast of the Pheasant." Three tables were set up in the hall, each serving as a platform for a series of in-

39. Meserve, *Empires,* 95–96.
40. ASP to Nicholas V; Graz, July 12, 1453; quoted in Ady, *Pius II,* 125.
41. Ady, *Pius II,* 126–27.

tricate displays with live or clockwork figures. The duke's own table had four of these *entremets*: in one, musicians played inside a church, complete with belfry and stained glass windows; in another was a ship with clockwork sailors who climbed the rigging and moved casks around the decks; in a third was a lead-and-glass fountain placed in a meadow of glass and jeweled flowers; in the fourth a naked boy stood upon a rock urinating rose water. The other tables carried another dozen *entremets,* including one in which twenty-eight musicians played from inside a giant pastry.[42] Food arrived at the tables on carriages or on litters let down from the ceiling. Each such litter carried eighty-two pieces of meat prepared in forty different varieties.[43]

Eight times during the evening, the feasting paused for music and pageantry, which included a horse walking backwards; a flying, fire-breathing dragon; a hunt by real falcons who brought down a heron released in the hall; and a play in three acts on "The Adventures of Jason at Colchis."[44] The climax came as musicians played and sang "The Lament of the Church." A giant dressed as a Saracen entered, leading an elephant with a castle on its back in which sat the imprisoned "Holy Mother Church." At the conclusion of "The Lament of the Church," the Golden Fleece king-at-arms brought in a live pheasant wearing a collar of gold and jewels, which he offered to the company as the occasion for oaths to go on crusade. The duke set the example with an elaborate oath sworn "before God my creator, the glorious Virgin Mary, the ladies, and the Pheasant." Philip vowed that, subject to the approval of his lord the king of France and provided that the crusade was led by a prince of such high rank that he would not lower himself to follow him, Philip would go in person on the crusade.[45] Vows by Philip's courtiers followed.

> Philippe Pot vowed to keep his right arm uncovered and not to sit at table on Tuesdays until he had fought successfully against the Unbelievers.... Louis de Chevalart [declared] that as soon as the army reached a distance of only four days march from the enemy, he would wear no covering on his head and would bare his right arm to the glove until he had faced an Unbeliever.... the esquire Guillaume de Martigny, who had formerly undertaken to wear a piece of his armor day and night until he had met a Turk, now vowed in addition that he would wear a hair shirt from the day of departure onward, that he would not sit at table on Saturdays, nor drink wine

42. Cartellieri, *Dukes of Burgundy,* 143.
43. Ibid., 145.
44. Ibid., 145–46.
45. Ibid., 147–49.

> nor sleep in a bed. Jean de Rebremettes, another esquire, pledged himself that if before the Crusade his mistress had not granted him her favors, then on his return he would marry at random the first lady he met who had twenty thousand shillings, provided she was agreeable to the match.[46]

Over a hundred such oaths were made. After a final enactment of an allegory and awards for the previous day's jousting, the feast ended at three in the morning.[47]

The Feast of the Pheasant features in Huizinga's work and elsewhere as one of the prime examples of the extravagant, over-elaborate—not to say manic—lengths to which northern Europeans during the "Autumn of the Middle Ages" would go in order to drug themselves with splendor and thereby escape from the grim realities of their time.[48] We cannot miss the almost lunatic disproportion between the wealth and trouble expended and the practical value of anything that was achieved. Not only was all this hoopla largely irrelevant to the crusade, but the crusade itself was quite irrelevant to the real interests and circumstances of the Burgundian state. As we proceed, we will find Italians engaging in equally overblown escapist behaviors equally disconnected from reality.

When Aeneas, burning with enthusiasm for the crusade, went to Regensburg for the princely congress that was to organize it, he found that Philip of Burgundy was the only notable ruler who bothered to attend. Aeneas sang his praises: "One prince seems to me, above all others, worthy of praise—Philip, Duke of Burgundy, who when he was bidden to a Congress summoned for the salvation of Christian peoples, refused to desert the common cause by sending an excuse."[49] The congress adopted an outline of how an army might be raised—a piece of paper used as a fig leaf to cover the congress's substantial failure. The death of Nicholas V on March 24, 1455, suspended all further action on the crusade. After Regensburg, Aeneas had no illusions about the obstacles to a unified Christian crusade. He wrote to an Italian friend:

> What ground do you find for hope? Christendom has no head that all men will obey. Neither Pope nor Emperor receives what is due to him.... Each state has its own ruler; each ruler is dominated by his own particular inter-

46. Ibid., 91–92.
47. Ibid., 149.
48. Huizinga, *Autumn,* 101–2; Cartellieri, 143–49.
49. ASP to Leonardo Benvoglienti, July 5, 1454; *Opera,* Epistle 127; quoted in Ady, *Pius II,* 128.

> est. What eloquence could draw such dissentient antagonistic powers together in battle-array, who would have such temerity as to take the chief command? What common plan of action could be devised? What discipline could be enforced? . . . Where is the mortal man that could bring England into accord with France, or Genoa with Aragon, or conciliate Germans, Hungarians, and Bohemians in their disputes? Let some small army embark in the sacred cause and it will be annihilated by [the infidels]; let a great host set forth and its internal enmities will destroy its organization, and its end will be general ruin. . . . Behold a true picture of Christendom as it stands.[50]

In spite of this all-too-perceptive assessment, Aeneas would devote the final decade of his life to the crusade. We can admire his dedication; yet, having made this assessment at the outset and finding its accuracy continually reinforced as he proceeded, Aeneas did not sit down and say, "Given these facts, what realistic steps can we take that will blunt the Turkish advance?" Rather, he kept his eyes on the chimera of the grand crusade—united Christendom in arms against the infidel—even though there was hardly a man in Europe with more experience than he of the inertia, irresponsibility, indifference, and selfishness that prevailed in the highest circles, nor anyone who knew better that, apart from Venice and Burgundy, the states of Europe barely had the funding to meet their most urgent responsibilities, much less distant and risky adventures. Perhaps he bridged this chasm between reality and aspiration with religious faith, like the commander of the Spanish Armada in the following century who admitted that "we are sailing in the confident expectation of a miracle." Aeneas was capable, intermittently, of that kind of faith; but he was more consistently capable of distracting himself from unpleasant realities—of knowing but ignoring them. It was the golden age of the unacknowledged elephant in the room.

Aeneas had certainly hoped that Nicholas, his old colleague, would make him a cardinal, but since he had not, Aeneas missed his chance to attend the conclave that elected the elderly Spaniard Alfonso de Borja (Borgia in Italian and English) as Pope Callixtus III. The cardinals probably expected the frail seventy-seven-year-old to provide them with a tractable, somnolent papacy. But the old man, knowing that his days and his energies must be few, focused them with indomitable will upon

50. ASP to Leonardo Benvoglienti, July 5, 1454; *Opera,* Epistle 127; quoted in Boulting, *Aeneas Silvius,* 207–8.

the two objects he wished to achieve: the crusade and the greatness of the House of Borgia. Instantly, he expelled the flocks of humanists and artists roosting in the Vatican. Whenever possible, artworks and books were sold for ready cash to fund the crusade. Gold and silver were sent to the mint, not only from the papal dinner service but from the altars of Rome. "Away with it," Callixtus exclaimed when he got to his last silver saltcellar, "earthenware will do for me." Most of the money went to building ships, rushed to completion within the year. The pope sent out a phalanx of friars who crisscrossed Europe selling indulgences, collecting tithes, and recruiting soldiers for the crusade. Personally, he wrote out an oath vowing destruction to the Turk and posted it in his bedchamber, where it was always before his eyes.[51]

Aeneas did not have to wait long to greet the new pope; Frederick sent him to Rome to renew the imperial submission to the papacy. Because of Aeneas's enthusiastic support of the crusade, many observers (probably including Aeneas himself) expected him to be among the first new cardinals created by this pope. That creation, however, was dedicated to Callixtus's other passionate cause, the advancement of his family: the beneficiaries were a Portuguese prince and two papal nephews, Luis Juan del Mila and Rodrigo Borgia. Cardinal Mila never played an important role, and the Cardinal of Portugal soon died; but Rodrigo Borgia, a vigorous youth in his mid-twenties, made himself prominent in the curia, especially after his uncle promoted him to the powerful office of vice chancellor during the final year of his papacy. Eventually, in 1492, Rodrigo would become Pope Alexander VI and would be responsible for much of the ill repute of the Renaissance papacy. He and his son Cesare would render the name of Borgia infamous for decadence, treachery, and murder through the ages.

Meanwhile, Siena faced a crisis that required its bishop's immediate attention. The *condottiere* Jacopo Piccinino, acting independently of King Alfonso, his employer, had invaded Sienese lands intent upon conquering all or part of Siena's territory for himself. The desperate Sienese called upon their bishop, renowned for diplomacy, to intercede with King Alfonso. Alfonso, deaf to previous appeals, had become fond of this intelligent and engaging envoy but agreed to withdraw Piccinino only for the extortionate sum of 40,000 ducats. Their business concluded, Alfonso kept Aeneas in Naples for four months, taking him along on his hunting

51. Boulting, *Aeneas Silvius,* 212.

trips. Whenever the king was busy with hunting or his mistress, Aeneas made side trips to visit ancient ruins at Baiae, Cumae, and Nola and to Salerno and Amalfi. Aeneas, busy with historical writing of his own, was nonetheless happy to assist the Neapolitan humanist Panormita in his laudatory biography of Alfonso. Back in Naples the king turned to the courtiers around him, asking if they wanted him to show them the future pope. "There he is," Alfonso declared, pointing to Aeneas. "The Bishop of Siena, who is just entering the gate, is destined by God to be pope and he is the man whom the cardinals will elect to succeed Callixtus when he dies. There is no one they could justly prefer to him."[52] When the courtiers congratulated him, Aeneas objected that he was not even yet a cardinal. This was the last time Aeneas saw this congenial king. Alfonso died in June of 1458, leaving Naples in his will to his illegitimate son Ferrante. Pope Callixtus, however, refused to recognize Ferrante's succession and declared Naples forfeited to the papacy.

These years in high clerical office, from 1449 until his election as pope at the end of 1458, provided Aeneas with more leisure for writing than he had enjoyed since his student days. It was in this period that he wrote most of his works of history and geography. No other Italian humanist was as well placed as he to write a geographical description of Germany (*Germania,* 1457),[53] a country he had crisscrossed continually since 1435, or the *History of Bohemia* finished the next year. He was also uniquely qualified to write the *History of Frederick III* (written in 1452–1458), since he was the only person with intimate knowledge of the men and events who also had the necessary literary skill. His ambitions as a geographer went further when he wrote *De Europa* and *De Asia.* He finished *De Europa* before his papacy, but *De Asia,* his only description of a region he had never visited, was cut short when he became pope. Based on firsthand knowledge (except for *De Asia*), these works had some practical usefulness that sets them apart from the many humanist treatises and dialogues on abstract moral topics or on the "misery" or "dignity" of man.[54]

52. *Comm.,* Smith, I.83–84.

53. The full title is *De ritu, situ, moribus et conditione Germaniae descripto.*

54. It is worth noting in passing that Pico della Mirandola's famous "Oration on the Dignity of Man," often cited as evidence of the high opinion of mankind entertained by humanists, was originally entitled only "Oration." Mankind's greatest quality, according to Pico, is his ability to reject the physical world for a higher, spiritual one—something far removed from the secularism often imputed to this composition on no basis other than the title later imposed on it. In fact, treatises on the misery and dignity of man were

On December 18, 1456, Aeneas realized his fondest ambition when Callixtus III finally made him a cardinal. Even so, Aeneas was still too poor to maintain the dignity of the office. The bishopric of Siena, he complained, was "as unfruitful as an elm tree."[55] "My honor has increased," he wrote, "but not so my riches."[56] He was now decidedly crippled by his gout. The only available treatment was to soak himself at mineral baths near Viterbo. This gave him an excuse to linger in the countryside and leisure to begin writing his *History of Bohemia.*[57] While he was taking his restorative baths, he learned of the death of Pope Callixtus on August 6, 1458. Cardinal Calandrini, a nephew of Nicholas V, was also taking the baths near Viterbo, and they traveled to Rome together. In Rome mobs rioted against the Spaniards whom Callixtus had installed in positions of authority, but Aeneas and Calandrini, as Italians and potential popes, received a thunderous welcome.[58] On August 16 the seventeen cardinals attending the conclave were sealed into their quarters in the Vatican, which consisted of a large chapel subdivided into individual cells and the Chapel of St. Nicholas, recently frescoed by Fra Angelico, where the formal meetings took place; two more adjoining halls were for walking about and conversation.[59]

Most observers had long expected Aeneas's first employer, Cardinal Capranica, to succeed Callixtus; but Capranica died just a month too early, leaving the field more than usually open. In his *Commentaries* Aeneas recorded his own maneuvers to win the papacy. The "scrutiny," as the voting procedure was called, required each cardinal to write the name of his chosen candidate on a slip of paper and deposit it in a chalice on the altar under the eyes of three cardinals stationed as guardians. The first scrutiny, usually nothing more than a testing of the waters,

---

longstanding medieval and Renaissance topos going back to the fourth century. Pope Innocent III (r. 1198–1216) intended to write on both topics but completed only the "misery," thus giving specious credibility to an unjustified contrast between the supposedly negative medieval view of man and the supposedly positive renaissance one; Giovanni Pico della Mirandolla, *Oration on the Dignity of Man,* trans. A. Robert Caponigri (Washington, D.C.: Renery Gateway, 1956); Charles Edward Trinkhaus, *The Scope of Renaissance Humanism* (Ann Arbor: University of Michigan Press, 1983).

55. ASP to Domenico Capranica, January 22, 1454; Weiss, Epistle 130; quoted in Ady, *Pius II,* 136.

56. *Opera,* Epistle 352, 830; quoted in Ady, *Pius II,* 136.

57. *Comm.,* Smith, I.91.

58. Ady, *Pius II,* 141.

59. *Comm.,* Smith, I.93–94. The Sistine Chapel, where conclaves have been held for the last four centuries, was not built yet.

gave five votes each to Aeneas and Calandrini; no one else received more than three.[60] Afterward, Aeneas tells us, the Frenchman Guillaume d'Estouteville, Cardinal of Rouen, launched an intensive campaign against Aeneas and Calandrini. D'Estouteville claimed that Aeneas was too poor and too lame. Aeneas depicts him as saying, "How can a destitute pope restore a destitute church, or an ailing pope an ailing church?" D'Estouteville dismissed Calandrini as "thick-headed." For himself, d'Estouteville pointed out that he was the senior cardinal and descended from royal blood. "I am rich in friends and resources with which I can succor the impoverished Church." Appealing to the cardinals' greed, he added, "I hold also not a few ecclesiastical benefices, which I shall distribute among you and the others, when I resign them."[61] By nightfall the conclave knew that eleven cardinals out of the twelve needed for election had pledged their votes to d'Estouteville. Traditionally it brought great rewards to a cardinal if he were the one to cast the deciding vote by rising from his chair and declaring, "I make you pope." Therefore, the Cardinal of Rouen's twelfth vote seemed assured.

In the dead of night Calandrini came to Aeneas, urging him to gain rewards from the new pope by going at once to pledge his vote to d'Estouteville. Aeneas gives us his reply to this temptation in high-minded humanist eloquence, no doubt considerably polished up for posterity.

> No one shall persuade me to vote for a man I think utterly unworthy to be the successor of St. Peter. . . . You say it is hard not to have the pope well-disposed to you. I have no fear on that score. I know he will not murder me because I have not voted for him. "But," you say, "he will not love you, will not make you presents, will not help you. . . ." Poverty is not hard for one accustomed to it. I have led a life of indigence heretofore; what matter if I die indigent? He will not take from me the Muses, who are all the sweeter in humble fortunes.[62]

He continues in even loftier tones to declare his faith that God will not let the papacy fall to a man he describes as "a limb of the devil." At daybreak Aeneas went to young Rodrigo Borgia to ask if he were committed to d'Estouteville. "What would you have me do?" Borgia replied. "The thing is settled. Many of the cardinals have met in the privies and decided to elect him." Furthermore, he told Aeneas, he had a note from

60. Ibid., I.94.
61. Ibid., I.95.
62. Ibid., I.97.

d'Estouteville promising that he could retain his vice chancellorship. Aeneas made no appeal to Borgia's nonexistent idealism, but emphasized that a Frenchman would be prejudiced against a Spaniard. Both of them were probably thinking of the coming French and Aragonese struggle for control of Naples. Perhaps because of Rodrigo's youth, Aeneas took a bullying tone with him.

> You young fool! Will you then put an enemy of your nation in the Apostle's chair? And will you put faith in the note of a man who is faithless? ... Take care, you inexperienced boy! Take care, you fool! And if you have no thought for the Church of Rome, ... at least take thought for yourself, for you will find yourself among the hindmost, if a Frenchman is pope.[63]

With a similar blend of threats, blandishments, and slurs against his opponent, Aeneas pried more votes away from the Frenchman. His greatest weapon was the Italian fear that a French pope might once more abandon Rome for Avignon. These speeches to his fellow cardinals, couched in rolling humanist periods to be recorded in the *Commentaries,* are baldly political intrigues mixed with appeals to self-interest. Far from apologizing for his tactics, Aeneas clearly expects the reader to admire his skill and enterprise. But Aeneas gives himself too much credit; he omits the efforts of others on his behalf, which were probably more influential than his own. Ambassadors were admitted to the conclave as observers, and it is certain that those from Francesco Sforza in Milan and King Ferrante in Naples were working assiduously for Aeneas. The Venetian Cardinal Barbo, determined to prevent the election of a foreigner, assembled all the Italian cardinals except Colonna to propose that they vote in a body for Aeneas.[64]

D'Estouteville himself was among the three guardians when the second scrutiny was taken in the morning. When Aeneas came up to deposit his ballot, d'Estouteville could not resist whispering, "Look, Aeneas! I commend myself to you!" "A rash thing to say," Aeneas mutters to his readers in the *Commentaries,* "but ambition overcame prudence." The three guardians each counted and recorded the votes. Speaking for them, d'Estouteville announced that Aeneas had eight. Stunned by disappointment, the Frenchman had miscounted. "Look more carefully at

63. Ibid., I.97–98.

64. Ibid., I.100; Ludwig Freiherr von Pastor, *The History of the Popes from the Close of the Middle Ages, Drawn from the Secret Archives of the Vatican and Other Original Sources,* trans. Frederick Ignatius Antrobus (St. Louis: B. Herder, 1898), 3:12–13.

the ballots," Aeneas called out, "for I have nine votes." The other two guardians confirmed that he was correct. D'Estouteville had only six.[65]

They decided to proceed by another method called "accession," whereby all the cardinals sat silently in their chairs waiting to see if anyone would stand up and announce a change of vote. "It was a strange silence and a strange sight," Aeneas says, "men sitting there like their own statues." Borgia broke the silence, standing to declare, "I accede to the Cardinal of Siena." This, Aeneas says spitefully, "was like a dagger in Rouen's heart, so pale did he turn."[66] The silence resumed, and, after a bit, two cardinals went to the privy, but by their return nothing had changed. Jacopo, Cardinal of Sant'Anastasia, then gave his vote to Aeneas. It was the eleventh; one more would make a pope. With great dignity, Prospero Colonna rose to perform this office. But immediately d'Estouteville grabbed him and was joined by the Greek cardinal, Bessarion. Together, they tried to drag Colonna out of the room. Colonna resisted and managed to call out from the midst of his assailants, "I too accede to the Cardinal of Siena and I make him pope!"[67]

Once this was heard, all the cardinals fell at Aeneas's feet, hailing their new pope. Then they returned to their seats to make the vote unanimous. Bessarion, who was soon to become one of the new pope's most loyal allies, spoke for the outvoted minority, saying that it was only Aeneas's gout that made them vote against him.[68] As Aeneas assumed the white papal tunic for the first time, the cardinals asked by what name they should call him. His answer, "Pius," was a typically humanist allusion to Virgil's *Aeneid,* where Virgil calls his hero "pious Aeneas."[69] It had long been a joking nickname among Aeneas's friends.[70] Meanwhile, the servants who had attended the needs of the conclave helped themselves to the contents of his cell, including his clothes and books. Custom allowed the Roman mob to break into a newly elected pope's house and run off with its contents; Pius certainly exaggerates when he says they demolished the building and carried away the stones.[71] Other mobs sacked several other cardinals' homes because they were rumored to have been elected or because the crowd mistook Aeneas's name for

65. *Comm.,* Smith, I.101.

66. Ibid., I.102.

67. Ibid., I.103.

68. Ibid.

69. *Aeneid* I.378, *Sum pius Aeneas, fame super aethera notus;* "I am pious Aeneas, in fame extolled above the stars."

70. Letter of Campisio, May 8, 1445; quoted in Boulting, *Aeneas Silvius,* 245.

71. *Comm.,* Smith, I.104.

theirs—or so they claimed. Siena had been bracing for a new attack from the *condottiere,* Piccinino, now released from King Alfonso's restraining hand; but, at the news that for the first time a Sienese citizen had been elected pope, joy at their city's honor overwhelmed all fears. Agostino Dati, secretary to the republic, tells us that the whole population rejoiced together amidst the pealing of bells. That night the city was illuminated while her citizens sang and danced in the streets with olive wreaths around their heads.[72] In rival Florence the mood was glum: people answered the polite greeting of "God bless you," by saying, "He is occupied with the Sienese, and reserves all blessings for them."[73]

At the new pope's coronation procession on September 3, gallant banners painted by Benozzo Gozzoli snapped in the breeze overhead, but witnesses noticed that Pius looked tired and sad.[74] Perhaps the responsibilities he had assumed were already weighing on him, or perhaps he was merely shaken by the voracious Romans. The crowd was entitled to steal the pope's coronation horse; but they had seized the poor animal before Pius could get off of it. That evening Pius hosted the cardinals, the ambassadors, the court, the officials, and the nobles and leading citizens of Rome at a banquet. Not until the small hours of morning did he retire to the papal apartment for the first time.[75]

72. Agostino Dati, *Opera* (Siena: 1503), 84–85; quoted in Ady, *Pius II,* 152–53.
73. *Comm.,* Smith, I.106–7.
74. Rubenstein, "Pius II," ix; Ady, *Pius II,* 156.
75. Boulting, *Aeneas Silvius,* 247.

6

The Road to Mantua

ON THE VERY DAY after his election Pius summoned the cardinals to discuss the crusade. Within three months, on October 12, 1458, Pius announced to the entire papal court and the foreign ambassadors that he would summon a congress of all Christian princes to organize the crusade; the next day he promulgated his first papal bull, summoning this congress to meet at Mantua on June 1 of the next year.[1] The congress was an expression of Pius's universalism: the idea, central to medieval political thought, that Christendom was a single entity, headed by pope and emperor, and not, as it had actually become in practice, a patchwork of rival states with conflicting interests. Pius regarded the crusades of the twelfth and thirteenth centuries as the highest expression of this unity and had often remarked that "the conquest of the Turks was not the concern of this or that nation but rather of all Christians."[2] The congress, as he visualized it, was a harmonious concert of Christians, gathered under pope and emperor to plan, prepare, and launch the holy war that would reclaim Europe from the Turks and cement Eastern Christendom into the Roman Church.[3] This bold action by a newly elected pope caught everyone by surprise. New popes generally proceeded with caution, carefully nurturing the support of the College of Cardinals. The Congress

1. Von Pastor, *History of the Popes,* 3:23–25.

2. John Gordon Rowe, "The Tragedy of Aeneas Sylvius Piccolomini (Pope Pius II): An Interpretation," *Church History* 30, no. 3 (1961): 293.

3. Marco Pellegrini, "Pio II, il Collegio cardinalizio e la Dieta di Mantova," in *Il Sogno di Pio II e il vaiggio da Roma a Mantova: Atti del convegno internazionale, Mantova, 13–15 aprile 2000,* edited by Arturo Calzona, Francesco Paolo Fiore, Alberto Tenenti, and Cesare Vasoli, 43 (Mantova: Leo S. Olschki, 2000).

of Mantua, however, was Pius's personal brainchild, sprung on the unsuspecting cardinals on the first full day of his reign and put into execution almost before the cardinals could digest the idea. A decision to take the Curia out of Rome without prior discussion by the Sacred College violated the consultative nature of church government dear to the cardinals and embodied in the election capitulations agreed upon in the conclave.[4]

Pius probably enjoyed stunning everyone. He had had his fill of dilatory leadership under Frederick III, and he had constantly urged Nicholas V to act more decisively for the crusade. To Pius, ardent for a crusade that he believed was politically, religiously, and morally urgent, his action, though dramatic, must have seemed logical, even inevitable. Among the few cardinals who shared this view was the Greek Bessarion, who had opposed Pius's election but immediately became the new pope's most ardent supporter. In reality the sudden summoning of the congress was a blunder that turned many of the cardinals and the princes of Europe against their new pope. It is not that Pius failed to understand either the need for support from many sources or that the planning and the control of the crusade would have to be shared among various states and princes—the very purpose of the congress was to marshal and coordinate such widespread support.[5] Nevertheless, the speed and scale of his action caught the European powers off guard, sending each of them into quivering protectiveness regarding their own interests and prestige. The French party and their allies, already disappointed in the outcome of the papal election, were instinctively hostile to enterprises that placed pope and emperor at the head of united Christendom, since that ruled out any special prominence for the king of France. Frederick III, who had always regarded Aeneas as a creature of his own, did not fancy himself in the role of loyal supporter of a papal initiative—not that Frederick was keen to take initiative himself. Other German princes would back Frederick in resenting anything that seemed to cast the pope as the active leader of Christendom. Like the French, they would notice the lack of a special position for Germans, who thought it was their ancient prerogative to be the "sword of Christendom."[6] A similar lack of recognition for the unique role that Venetian sea power must play in any ex-

4. Ibid., 51.

5. Nancy Bisaha, "Pope Pius II and the Crusade," in *Crusading in the Fifteenth Century: Message and Impact,* edited by Norman Housley, 42 (London: Palgrave Macmillan, 2004).

6. Pellegrini, "Pio II," 43.

pedition to the East cost Pius the support of Cardinal Barbo, who had been such a crucial promoter of his election.[7]

Most of the cardinals, offended by the scope and suddenness of Pius's decision, taken without their prior endorsement, sank into a mood of sullen distrust. The curia had been settled in Rome for only fifteen years since Eugenius's exile. This pope, whom they had elected to ensure that the papacy stayed in Rome, had now launched the curia on a prolonged stay in distant Mantua.[8] Moreover, any gathering of European potentates raised fears of a church council—especially when promulgated by a former spokesman for conciliar authority. On the personal level hardly any of the cardinals would have relished a difficult journey and an indefinite sojourn far from their comfortable palaces and villas in Rome. Among the most powerful disaffected cardinals was Ludovico Trevisan, whose first loyalty was always to his native Venice.[9] He had not participated in the election because he had been serving as papal legate with the fleet fighting the Turks in the Aegean and Black Seas. He considered Pius's election a mistake, for which he blamed his Venetian colleague, Cardinal Barbo.[10]

It was inevitable that Pius would bend all his energies toward the crusade from the first moment of his papacy; but, after his bitter disappointment at Regensburg and his own scathing assessment of the prospects for a unified crusade, summoning another European congress of princes might seem an odd decision. Nothing in Aeneas's all-too-extensive experience of German diets while serving Frederick III could justify any faith in the deliberations of independent-minded princes. But faith was, in fact, at the heart of Pius's dedication to the crusade. From the moment of his election, Pius showed a consistent faith that God would act through the Vicar of Christ; that what was impossible to men was not only possible to God, but obligatory for a pope if he were not to shirk his sacred responsibility. Nicholas V had neither attended nor supported the Diet at Regensburg; therefore, Regensburg failed. Pius II would preside in person at Mantua and devote all his energies to the cause; therefore, with divine aid, Mantua and the crusade stemming from it would succeed. Without this element of faith, Pius's actions would be incomprehensible.

7. Ibid., 41.

8. Ibid., 48–50.

9. Trevisan is sometimes mistakenly called "Scarampo."

10. Pellegrini, "Pio II," 60–61.

A description of Pius about a year after his election shows how overtaxed his body already was when he began his reign. "The Holy Father is a little, rosy man, with red rims to his eyes, about sixty years of age [he was fifty-four].... He is gouty and cannot walk, so that he is obliged to be carried."[11] Bartolomeo Platina, a humanist in papal service, comments on Pius's "delicate hands and rather small feet," adding that he suffered from gout, kidney stones, and a chronic cough, but that he made himself freely accessible to all. Platina describes his habitual expression as "kindly but grave" and says that his clothes avoided the extremes of both "negligence and elegance."[12] Contemporary portraits of Pius, painted, sculpted, cast, or engraved, are too inconsistent with each other to leave us a sharp image of his face. Yet, a recent historian has pointed out that the most convincing ones "are double-chinned and irritable looking."[13] Platina confirms the abundant evidence of Pius's kind consideration for those of lowly rank. Once, when an attendant tried to cut short an old man's long, rambling talk, Pius scolded him: "Do you not know that as pope I have to live not for myself, but for others?" His manner was normally kindly, genial, and enlivened by wit. His anger could flare quickly but just as quickly subside. He cared little about personal criticism but would not tolerate any challenge to the sacred office he held. He was deeply devoted to the church and its sacraments and insisted on fasting even when he was ill.[14] As an outgrowth of the ingrained modern prejudice that humanists were necessarily secularists, it was long customary to refer to the "humanist pope" as if the term were contradictory and his election were a kind of practical joke played on the church. Nothing supports that interpretation.

Pius seems to have decided at the very start of his pontificate that he would record his experiences as pope in the manner of Julius Caesar's *Commentaries on the Gallic Wars.* From Caesar he borrowed the title *Commentaries,* and he imitates Caesar in always referring to himself in the third person as "the pope." He worked on *The Commentaries* in snippets whenever he could snatch the time, sometimes dictating, sometimes writing in his own hand. His friend and biographer Gian-

11. Schivenogli, *Cronica di Mantova,* in *Raccolta di cronisti e documenti storici Lombardi inediti* (Milan: 1857), 2:135; quoted in Ady, *Pius II,* 165.

12. Von Pastor, *History of the Popes,* 3:32–33; David S. Chambers, *Popes, Cardinals and War: The Military Church in Renaissance and Early Modern Europe* (London: I. B. Tauris, 2006), 58.

13. Chambers, *Popes, Cardinals and War,* 53.

14. Von Pastor, *History of the Popes,* 3:33.

antonio Campano tells us that he seldom found as much as two uninterrupted hours to write, hours he could often gain only by depriving himself of sleep. As a result, the *Commentaries* are uneven in pace and quality. Some events he summarizes quickly; some he omits; some he dwells upon in loving detail. Connections between parts are often weak or nonexistent. The most detailed, moment-by-moment treatment usually goes to some diversion he had particularly enjoyed, almost always when he was traveling outside of Rome. In the *Commentaries* Pius crams everything in the life of Aeneas Silvius before his papacy into Book I of the thirteen books that he eventually wrote (the thirteenth was left unfinished at his death). Consequently, although Aeneas crisscrossed Europe before he was pope, the *Commentaries* rarely describe the places he visited before his papacy. In any case, he had already done that in his geographical treatise *De Europa,* completed the year of his election. But with his five-month journey to the Congress of Mantua the *Commentaries* take on the detail and liveliness of fresh observations.

The distance from Rome to Mantua hardly required a January departure for a congress in June. The pope's traveling entourage objected that the dead of winter was unsuited for travel, while the Romans howled at the loss of income and the potential breakdown of public order that a lengthy papal absence would bring. The economy of Rome depended upon the spending of the papal court and its visitors. It is easy to imagine the shock and resentment among the Romans at first news of the proposed congress. Rumors flew that Pius might move the papacy to Siena or Germany.[15] Nevertheless, Pius had political business on the way and could hardly wait to parade around Italy in his new status. Pius was addicted to the pleasures of travel and indifferent or inured to its hardships, however much these might afflict his entourage. He might have left Rome even sooner if the region around the city had been safe.

It was unsafe because of the *condottiere,* Jacopo Piccinino, employed by Ferrante, illegitimate son of King Alfonso of Naples. Alfonso had left his Iberian kingdoms to his brother, Juan, but had declared Ferrante his heir in Naples.[16] Since Alfonso's rule had itself been imposed by conquest, René of Anjou, the French Angevin king Alfonso had ousted, was reasserting his claim against the bastard Ferrante. Fighting had already begun. Eugenius and Alfonso had recognized each other as king

15. Ibid., 3:29.
16. Ryder, *Kingdom of Naples,* 42.

and pope in 1443; Eugenius had even legitimized Ferrante and recognized him as heir. Oddly, it was Callixtus, who was Aragonese himself, who scuttled this papal-Aragonese reconciliation out of fear of an overly powerful neighbor south of the Papal States. Naples was technically a papal fief and, after the reconciliation of 1443, Eugenius and Nicholas had made no difficulty over investing Alfonso with the kingdom. Callixtus, however, refused to do this, hoping to delay it until Alfonso died so that the papacy could claim Naples as a lapsed fief. His hopes seemed vindicated when Alfonso died and Callixtus issued a bull on July 14, 1458, asserting this claim. Ferrante tried to negotiate with Callixtus while simultaneously appealing to a new pope or a new church council. To lend force to his persuasions, his *condottiere,* Piccinino, invaded the Papal States, occupying Assisi, Nocero, Gualdo, and other places.[17]

When Callixtus died in August Piccinino remained in place to influence the election and frighten the cardinals out of electing a French pope.[18] Pius, however, had been fond of Alfonso and was aware of the help Ferrante had given toward his election. After the election, when Ferrante's congratulatory ambassadors arrived, Pius offered to recognize their king, but only if Ferrante ceded some strategic border towns and paid an annual tribute. Ferrante balked at first, but soon accepted the terms.[19] Pius protected his options by including a clause that his recognition of Ferrante would not prejudice legitimate claims others might have to Naples. Thus a switch to King René's side was always a possibility. Even with this escape clause, the recognition of Ferrante, alongside the calling of the congress, established the new pope as a man of surprises. At least it got Piccinino out of the way of the pope's travels.

Pius departed from Rome on January 22, 1459, accompanied by cardinals Calandrini, Alain, d'Estouteville, Borgia, Barbo, and Colonna and an entourage of well over two hundred officials, soldiers, and attendants; the remaining cardinals were given until spring to come to Mantua.[20] Pius left his trusted friend Cardinal Nicholas of Cusa in charge of Rome, while his nephew Antonio Piccolomini held the Castel Sant'Angelo.[21] On the first night Pius stopped at Campagnano as a guest of the Orsini family, deadly rivals of the Colonna for dominance in Rome. He then worked his way up the Tiber valley into Umbria. It

17. Ibid., 38–41.

18. Von Pastor, *History of the Popes,* 3:5.

19. *Comm.,* Smith, II.123.

20. Von Pastor, *History of the Popes,* 3:47; Paparelli, *Enea Silvio Piccolomini,* 149.

21. Paparelli, *Enea Silvio Piccolomini,* 148.

was a triumphal procession, extremely gratifying to the bottomless vanity that the papacy brought out in Aeneas. Even in rural areas he tells us:

> The people poured out to greet him; the priests bearing holy relics offered prayers for his happiness as he passed; boys and girls wearing wreaths of laurel and carrying olive branches wished the great Bishop long life and felicity. Those who could touch the edge of his garment thought themselves blessed. Everywhere the road was thronged with people and strewn with fresh grasses; the squares in the towns and cities were carpeted with precious fabrics; the houses of the citizens and the churches of God were splendidly decorated.[22]

Nevertheless there was no repressing the disorder of the age. At Narni the locals brandished swords while trying to seize the pope's horse.[23] After that he gave up riding and traveled henceforth by litter; in any case, his pain-racked body could no longer endure jarring hours on horseback.[24] He proceeded on to Terni and to Spoleto, where he spent four days with his sister Caterina. There Pius received the discouraging news that Frederick III, on flimsy pretexts, had decided not to come to Mantua. This was a serious blow, destroying at once the image of united Christendom acting together under its spiritual and temporal heads. No doubt this bad example would influence other invited participants. The real reason for Frederick's defection was a war brewing in Hungary. Frederick's young nephew, King Ladislas of Hungary, had died in 1457; the Hungarian nobles, ignoring Frederick's claim as the boy-king's uncle, had elected Matthias Corvinus, one of the sons of John Hunyadi, as their king.[25] In spite of the need to strengthen Hungary as much as possible as the main bulwark against the Turks, Frederick was preparing to claim the kingship and plunge this vulnerable country into civil war.

Pius continued on his way through Foligno; on the way to Assisi he met a messenger with Piccinino's announcement that his army had evacuated Assisi, Gualdo, and Nocera—the first fruits of Pius's recognition of Ferrante.[26] From Assisi Pius continued on to a gratifying reception at Perugia on February 1. The local magistrates presented the keys of the city to the pope, who politely returned them; the citizens decked their houses and churches with flowers, tapestries, and heraldry. Pius

22. *Comm.*, Smith, II.138.
23. Ibid., II.138.
24. Boulting, *Aeneas Silvius*, 253.
25. Paparelli, *Enea Silvio Piccolomini*, 149–50.
26. Ibid., 149.

wore his pontifical vestments and his papal miter as he rode through the streets in a litter decorated in purple and gold. He stayed at the governor's palace for three weeks, during which he consecrated the church of San Domenico and tried in vain to reconcile the city's bitter factions.[27] In Perugia he met, perhaps for the first time, the famed *condottiere,* Federico da Montefeltro, Count of Urbino (Duke after 1474), a man who shared Pius's humanist tastes. Remembered today for his art patronage, Federico, who was to become a firm ally to Pius, was coming to consult him about a war he was then waging against his neighbor Sigismondo Malatesta, Lord of Rimini. Both Federico and Sigismondo held their tiny statelets as vassals of the pope in the Marche region near the Adriatic in the northern part of the Papal States. The attitude of their overlord in their local dispute could be crucial, and Federico proved wise to hasten to the pope's side.

Ambassadors from Siena also met the pope at Perugia. The Sienese were much less enthralled with "their" pope than they had been at his election. In their initial celebration the city had restored the Piccolomini to full citizenship rights. But Pius demanded that these be extended to all *gentiluomini* and other disenfranchised factions. Sienese reluctance to comply is understandable. The nobles never ceased in their efforts to overthrow the regime; just a few years earlier Pius's cousin and friend, Goro Lolli, had been among those exiled for such an attempt.[28] When the Sienese balked at Pius's demands, Pius said that, although he would not punish them, he would withhold the benefits he had meant to confer and would bypass Siena on his way to Mantua. The city's rulers, knowing the economic value of a prolonged papal visit, moderated their restrictions on the nobles and sent a delegation to urge the pope to bless them with his presence. Pius relented, knowing that he could achieve more for the disenfranchised factions if he were personally in the city. He also could not resist savoring his return home as pope.[29] Turning west, Pius crossed Lake Trasimeno in a season when storms frequently churned its waters. When his passage proved tranquil, Pius attributed it to the divine protection that must by right accompany the pope.[30]

How eagerly he must have anticipated his stop at Corsignano! His mother had now been dead for four years and his father for eight, but

27. Von Pastor, *History of the Popes,* 3:49.
28. Rubenstein, "Pius II," 49.
29. Von Pastor, *History of the Popes,* 3:50–51.
30. *Comm.,* Smith, II.145.

he "hoped to have some pleasure in talking with those with whom he had grown up." The aged parish priest who first taught him his letters was there to kneel before him. Otherwise, "those of his own generation had died and those who were left kept to their houses, bowed down by old age and illness, or, if they showed themselves, were so changed as to be hardly recognizable, for they were feeble and crippled and like harbingers of death." Aeneas was worn from travels and discomforts, but these men, his old playmates, had been ground almost into the grave by unceasing agricultural toil. Pius reflected, "At every step the Pope met with proofs of his own age and could not fail to realize that he was an old man who would soon drop." Just a few lines later he seems to pull himself together, and almost in a spirit of defiance says, "He decided to build there [in Corsignano] a new church and a palace and he hired architects and workmen at no small expense, that he might leave as lasting as possible a memorial of his birth."[31] This was the genesis of Pienza, the grander reincarnation of Corsignano, which has, indeed, done more than anything except Pinturicchio's paintings to keep Pius's memory alive with the general public.

After three days in Corsignano, Pius arrived in Siena on February 24. His reception was suitably magnificent, but noticeably cooler than the enthusiasm at Perugia. He stayed two months there, struggling with the city fathers, but reaching only an uneasy compromise on the status of the *gentiluomini.* In fact Pius had to discourage the *gentiloumini* themselves from trying to seize the city by force. Nevertheless, he granted a border fortress to the Sienese, ordered a splendid new tomb for his parents, and raised the see of Siena to a metropolitan archbishopric. The Sienese must have profited handsomely from the papal visit and from the delegations from kings and princes that attended the pope there.[32] Warmer weather brought a spring crop of embassies from all the Iberian kingdoms and from Burgundy, Austria, and Brandenburg. Pius received emissaries from George Podiebrad, the Hussite king of Bohemia, and from Matthias Corvinus, whom he recognized as king of Hungary. It is a speculation, though not a wild one, that this recognition of Frederick III's rival for the Hungarian throne was, in part, revenge for Frederick's refusal to come to Mantua. In any case, Frederick's ambassadors were so outraged that they stayed in Florence and refused to meet the pope.[33]

31. Ibid., II.146–47.
32. Von Pastor, *History of the Popes,* 3:52–54.
33. Paparelli, *Enea Silvio Piccolomini,* 153.

The disaffected Cardinal Trevisan also rejoined the curia in Siena after his naval ventures in the East and set to work immediately undermining the pope's projects. Among the cardinals and his numerous correspondents and connections all over Europe Trevisan spread the word that Pius was delusional, divorced from reality, incapable of understanding political complexities, with a childish, impulsive character given to such naïve "leaps" as the approaching congress. A crusade, he asserted, could only prove a disastrous humiliation, since the Turks were invincible.[34] Trevisan is probably the author of a letter to Charles VII of France urging him to boycott the congress, in which, the letter said, Pius only sought to promote his old master Frederick III at the expense of the French.[35]

It was April when Pius finally left Siena for a ten-day stay at Florence. There the harvest of embassies was even richer. Francesco Sforza sent his fifteen-year-old son, Galeazzo Maria, escorted by 350 horsemen, to attend the pope. Galeazzo Maria leaped from his horse when the pope arrived, kissed his feet, and delivered an oration composed by court humanists in Milan.[36] Sigismondo Malatesta, now defeated by Federico of Urbino, hurried to his overlord to seek redress. He, along with the lords of Forli, Faenza, and Carpi, was assigned the honor of carrying the pope's chair.[37] The proud Sigismondo was anything but gratified; as he took his place, Pius heard him grumble, "See to what we lords of cities have been brought!"[38] Sigismondo's indignity was brief; the priors who constituted the Signoria, the government of Florence, bore the chair once it passed the city gates.

After blessing the crowds at the church of the Reparata and at the famous twelfth-century baptistery in front of the cathedral, Pius took up residence in the apartments at Santa Maria Novella, where Eugenius IV had lived during his exile from Rome. The festivities proper began on April 29 with a tournament, a form of celebration with which the Florentines marked almost all special occasions, in the Piazza di Santa Croce.[39] Tournaments originated as full-fledged battles, but courtly love changed these *mêlées* into occasions for knights to win the admiration of their ladies. This female audience transformed tournaments into relatively orderly spectator entertainments. Injuries still occurred; in 1450

34. Pellegrini, "Pio II," 62.

35. Ibid., 64.

36. Von Pastor, *History of the Popes,* 3:55.

37. Ibid.

38. *Comm.,* Smith, II.160.

39. Ivan Cloulas, *Lorenzo, il Magnifico,* trans. Cesare Scarton (Rome: Salerno Editrice, 1986), 89.

Federico da Montefeltro had lost his right eye and the bridge of his nose in a tournament.

What kind of tournament would Renaissance Florence have staged for a visiting pope? We have no details of the tournament presented to honor Pius, but it certainly would have been an extravagant production, unmarked by sobriety and restraint. In Florence the festivities usually began with a herald and a troop of followers, sometimes including ladies, who visited the homes of the participating knights, summoning them to prove their valor. The combatants sallied forth to the sound of drum and trumpet with horses, escorts, companions, and attendants riding behind their banners in the growing parade.[40] Along the sides of the Piazza di Santa Croce, the usual site of Florentine tournaments, there would have been reviewing stands crowded with spectators squirming in anticipation. Each knight entered the square to a trumpet blast. A page preceded him, holding his banner aloft, while numerous companions escorted him.[41] We can form an idea of what Pius saw in 1459 from the ample descriptions of a tournament staged ten years later for Lorenzo de' Medici's twentieth birthday. At Lorenzo's tournament each of the sixteen participating knights had a dozen companions. Cries of admiration burst from the crowd at the sight of the magnificent clothing and jewels worn during the entrance ceremonies by the knights, their companions, and their horses. Lorenzo de' Medici rode a warhorse caparisoned in velvet, a gift from King Ferrante. His costume was red and white silk, the colors of Florence, and a cape draped from his shoulders was spotted with roses embroidered with pearls and bore the motto *le temps revient*.[42] On his head Lorenzo wore a black velvet cap decorated with pearls and crowned with a fan-shaped ornament of diamonds and rubies.[43] His blue shield carried the lilies of France arranged around the famous diamond, "*il libro,*" a prized possession of the Medici. His younger brother Giuliano wore gold cloth embroidered with pearls. Coluccio Salutati's nephew Benedetto wore a helmet made by Antonio Pollaiuolo, who also made and engraved a solid gold cuirass for another participant.[44] Poggio Bracciolini's son rode a horse caparisoned in black velvet, embroidered with

40. Cesare Molinari, *Spettacoli fiorentini del Quattrocento: Contribute allo studio delle sacre Rappresentazioni* (Venice: Neri Pozza Editore, 1961), 18–19.

41. Cloulas, *Lorenzo,* 114.

42. "The times return," signifying return to a past "golden age."

43. Cloulas, *Lorenzo,* 114–15; Andres, Hunisak, and Turner, *Art of Florence,* 2:715.

44. Cloulas, *Lorenzo,* 115.

five hydras made of pearls. None of this magnificent raiment was soiled in combat. Each participant changed into splendid but more protective armor for the actual joust. For combat Lorenzo wore armor given to him by the Duke of Milan and rode a fresh horse given by Borso d'Este, Duke of Ferrara. Combat lasted from noon to sunset. Lorenzo, the inevitable victor of "his" tournament, won a silver helmet surmounted by a statue of Mars made by Pollaiuolo.[45] Pius complained about the lack of actual bloodshed in the tournament he saw in 1459.[46] The events he saw were probably jousts between individual knights with a low wall between them, using lances fitted with a trio of wooden prongs on the tip, called "coronels," which diffused the impact; swords would have had sharp edges but no points. In the evening, after Pius's tournament, the Florentines staged a banquet for the pope in the Loggia del Mercato Nuovo, which was hung all around with rich tapestries. As the pope dined, seventy splendidly costumed youths danced for his entertainment.[47]

The next day's festivities were at the Piazza della Signoria, converted for the occasion into an arena. Two lions were turned loose in the enclosure—then two horses, four oxen, two bulls, a cow with her calf, a wild bear, some wolves, and finally, a creature hardly anyone had seen before—a giraffe! Like their Roman ancestors, the Florentine crowd eagerly anticipated bloody mayhem among the various species here assembled. The animals, however, had not been starved for the occasion according to Roman practice. Terrified by the noise of the crowd, the unfortunate creatures cowered quietly in corners of the arena, leaving each other alone. Even twenty men who entered the piazza to provoke the beasts failed to elicit the expected carnage. That evening the Florentine welcome to the Sienese pope concluded with a military parade down the Via Larga led by Cosimo de' Medici's young grandson, the future Lorenzo il Magnifico, mounted on a great white horse caparisoned in purple and gold. Twenty musicians followed him, escorting his standard. Next came twelve knights in lavish costumes, each accompanied by liveried pages and servants. A hundred men dressed as Turks brought up the rear.[48]

One thing was conspicuously lacking in Pius's Florentine reception—the city's leading citizen and virtual ruler, Cosimo de' Medici,

45. Ibid.

46. *Comm.*, Smith, II.166.

47. Cloulas, *Lorenzo,* 89.

48. Ibid., 89–90.

made no public appearance and did not even meet privately with the pope. His excuse was illness, yet he did meet with Galeazzo Maria Sforza, the fifteen-year-old son of his staunchest ally, and private discussions within the Florentine government indicate that the city's hospitality was intended more to delight the teenager than the pope.[49] Florence, like Venice and Genoa, had extensive trade in the East; this inevitably produced conflicted attitudes toward the crusade. Florentine trade with Constantinople had recently increased; but the sultan was unlikely to let that continue if Florence was supporting a war against him.[50] On the other hand, Florentines and other Italians knew that Venice had gained her Eastern empire from the Fourth Crusade and that a successful crusade would only bring them similar benefits if they had actively supported it. As Christians the Florentines felt as keenly as anyone the shame of Christian defeat and the obligation to defend the faith. Cosimo, who had paid for the repair and renovation of churches in Jerusalem, was not deaf to the call for Christian defense; but he was one of many who thought the sudden summoning of a European congress was excessive and premature. He would not stand in the pope's way, but he was not ready to come out in support.[51]

Florentines could never generate warm feelings in any Sienese heart; but Pius left Florence in an unusually sour mood, complaining that "They spent very little on entertaining the Pope nor did they lay out much on lavish spectacles, though they brought lions into the piazza to fight with horses and other animals and arranged tournaments in which more wine was drunk than blood spilled." To this he added a more general complaint against Florence for its mercantile traditions.

> They [the Florentines] most excel at trade, which philosophers think sordid. They seem too bent on making money, and therefore when the chief men of the city had collected 14,000 ducats from the people to honor the Pope, they kept the greater part for the city and used part to support Galeazzo [Sforza] and his retinue.[52]

Pius harbored a bitter contempt for all mercantile republics, including the existing government of Siena. It was, after all, the coming to power of merchants that had ruined the families of his parents. Under

49. Robert Black, *Benedetto Accolti and the Florentine Renaissance* (New York: Cambridge University Press, 1985), 249.

50. Ibid., 246.

51. Ibid., 279.

52. *Comm.,* Smith, II.166.

the influence of Roman and Greek writers, whose pages bristle with contempt for moneymaking, Pius, like most humanists, despised all mercantile activity. Petrarch, for example often railed against the desire for wealth. "Let us ... overcome that avarice which dangles great riches before us as necessary for our leisure," he wrote in a treatise.

> For in truth, cupidity, while it is injurious to all who aim at virtue, is particularly hostile to our purpose, for it has no end, and by heaping up superfluities burdens with a handicap the life to which it promises support.... Surely it is well known that many who seemed capable of everything have been hindered in achieving this by the greatness of their wealth and power.[53]

Leon Battista Alberti, whose treatise *Della famiglia* ("On the Family") wrestles with the gulf between the humanist ideal and the mercantile base of Florentine wealth, is no less disdainful.

> No occupation seems less attractive to a man of large and liberal spirit than the kind of labor by which wealth is in fact gathered.... Having neither petty nor vulgar minds, I imagine you probably find these activities, which are solely directed to making a profit, somewhat below you. They seem entirely to lack honor and distinction.[54]

Yet, Alberti knew that distinguished Florentine families needed to constantly replenish their fortunes through commerce. His solution to that dilemma speaks volumes about the humanist view of the mercantile life. Recognizing that even the best of families may produce the occasional dullard, he advises that the family's least talented youths be set to moneymaking. "If they are useless for anything else, let the father do like those gymnosophists [who advocated downing worthless children], let him drown these children in greed. Let him make them into moneygrubbers, let him kindle in them the desire not for honor and glory, but for gold, riches, cash."[55] Although excuses for moneymaking and even some real defenses of it can be found in Italian writings, including sections of Alberti's *Della famiglia,* they are not nearly as common as this humanist disdain, which is repeated far too often and emphatically

53. Francesco Petrarca, *De vita solitaria* II.5, in *The Life of Solitude, by Francis Petrarch,* trans. J. Zeitlin (Urbana: University of Illinois Press, 1924), 306.

54. Leon Battista Alberti, *I libri della famiglia* II, in *The Family in Renaissance Florence: A Translation by Renee Neu Watkins of "I libri della famiglia," by Leon Battista Alberti* (Columbia: University of South Carolina Press, 1969), 141–42.

55. Alberti, *Della famiglia* I, in *Family,* 59.

to permit us to associate humanist culture with bourgeois capitalism.[56]

From Florence Pius made his way, "with considerable toil and difficulty,"[57] across the Apennines to Bologna, once more within the borders of the Papal States. The turbulent politics of Bologna were shocking even to Italians—and the dominant party was hostile to papal authority.[58] To insure the pope's safety there, Francesco Sforza lent Pius a cavalry unit.[59] The next stop was Ferrara, ruled by Borso d'Este, who had entertained Frederick III so lavishly on his coronation trip that the emperor rewarded him with the title "Duke of Modena and Reggio." Aeneas had been present on that occasion and gave a speech on "the glories of the house of Este, the ability of Borso, and the exalted rank conferred upon him."[60] Borso's vanity was insatiable; he liked to be called "glorious," "heavenly," and "divine." A modern writer says that "his vanity was so shameless, so obviously a source of pleasure that it almost becomes a cause of admiration."[61] Borso deeply craved the additional title "Duke of Ferrara," which he could obtain only from Ferrara's overlord, the pope. Borso had been softening up Pius for some time, lighting bonfires throughout his lands to celebrate Pius's election, and claiming kinship to the pope because his mother was a Tolomei.[62] Continuing this courtship, Borso personally greeted the pope at the city gate, handed him the keys to the city, and walked humbly among the bearers of the papal chair until Pius bade him mount his horse. Pius rode in his litter under a *baldacchino* covered with gold embroidery. "All the road to the cathedral was covered with carpets and strewn with flowers," he tells us; "the houses were decorated; there was singing and cheering everywhere and the people kept up a continuous cry of 'Long live Pope Pius!'"[63] Borso provided all the meals for the whole papal entourage and housed Pius in his own palace while the local nobility took in the cardinals. At

56. Alberti's *Della famiglia* is the favorite authority for those who equate the Renaissance with capitalism. But this dialogue actually presents conflicting viewpoints. The material that supports a mercantile outlook comes from the speeches of Giannozzo Alberti in Book III. Giannozzo is clearly intended to represent the outlook of an older generation. Alberti respects this view but does not endorse it.

57. *Comm.*, Smith, II.174.

58. Von Pastor, *History of the Popes,* 3:57.

59. Ady, *Pius II,* 163; *Comm.*, Smith, II.177.

60. *Comm.,* Smith, I.66; Werner L. Gundersheimer, *Ferrara: The Style of a Renaissance Despotism* (Princeton: Princeton University Press, 1973), 129.

61. Ibid., 127.

62. *Comm.,* Smith, II.182.

63. Ibid., II.182–83; Von Pastor, *History of the Popes,* 3:58.

Borso's expense the neighboring lords of the Romagna region came to Ferrara as his guests during the papal visit.[64] Nevertheless, though he bestowed other favors, Pius withheld the coveted ducal title and would not remit the tribute that Ferrara paid to the papacy.

Pius stayed a week in Ferrara before embarking up the Po River in a flotilla of boats with the still-hopeful Borso at his side. At the Mantuan border the flotilla of Lodovico Gonzaga, Marquess of Mantua, met them. Pius says that trumpeters in both fleets "filled all the surrounding valley with an extraordinary din," while above them, "a whole forest of banners" snapped in the wind. On the riverbanks, crowds of people shouted "Viva!" as the pope blessed them.[65] Borso then took his leave, and Pius spent the night with Lodovico in the Marquess's half-finished palace at Revere.

The next day the flotilla turned off the Po onto the Mincio and arrived at Mantua on May 27, five months and seven days after Pius left Rome. At the city gate the Marquess dismounted and presented Pius with the keys to the city. In the long procession of cardinals, princes, ambassadors, functionaries, clergy, and holy relics that wound its way through Mantua toward the cathedral, Pius rode in his litter on the shoulders of nobles behind three banners, one displaying the cross, one the papal keys, and one the Piccolomini arms.[66] Along the way, Pius says:

> Not a foot of ground but was covered with carpets and the walls on both sides were adorned with flowers and tapestries. Women, boys and girls crowded the windows and roofs, but still there was a great press and all the approaches were thronged with people. In many places were altars smoking with incense. No voice was heard except the shouts of the populace crying, "Long live Pope Pius."[67]

The day of his entrance into the city was probably the only time that Pius was entirely pleased with what he found at Mantua.

64. Ady, *Pius II,* 163–64.
65. *Comm.,* Smith, II.182–84.
66. Von Pastor, *History of the Popes,* 3:59.
67. *Comm.,* Smith, II.187.

7

Renaissance Chivalry

ONE FAMILIAR INTERPRETATION of the Renaissance contrasts the supposed bourgeois, mercantile, practical world of Florence with the feudalism of northern Europe. Those acquainted with this view may be a little surprised to find the Florentines staging a tournament, a celebration of knighthood, as their welcome to a visiting pope. In fact, tournaments were a favorite form of public celebration, both in Florence and in the rest of Italy. When Florence conquered Pisa in 1406, the Parte Guelfa sponsored a tournament in celebration that was repeated annually thereafter.[1] It was an established custom for the Florentine signoria to order tournaments to celebrate public occasions and give a subsidy to pay for it to the Parte Guelfa, which made all the arrangements. Individuals and families in Florence also put on jousts at their own expense.[2] Elites of every European country loved to display themselves as knights in tournaments, providing the lesser classes with a much-enjoyed spectacle. Even though Italians had added a second dream world, the idealized version of ancient Rome, alongside the more widespread chivalric ideal, Italians were just as enthralled with Camelot as everyone else.

In Italy chivalric romance was not a just medieval survival; it grew *alongside* the classical ideal as *part* of the Renaissance. Introduced to Italy in the thirteenth century, the chivalric ideal followed the same trajectory as the classical one, gathering strength in the fourteenth cen-

1. Frederick Antal, *Florentine Painting and Its Social Background: The Bourgeoise Republic before Cosimo de' Medici's Advent to Power; XIV and Early XV Centuries* (1948; repr. London: Routledge and Kegan Paul, 1965), 29.

2. Wackernagel, *Florentine Renaissance Artists,* 199n13.

tury, expanding during the quattrocento, and reaching its peak in the cinquecento.[3] The psychological and emotional operations of the classical and chivalric themes were identical. Functionally interchangeable, each served as a mental alternative to intolerable reality. Renaissance Italians moved as effortlessly between classical, chivalric, and pastoral themes as Disney's tourists move from Frontierland to Tomorrowland. As often as not, the two themes were fused together, used simultaneously in the same poem, artwork, or tournament. Such themes were much more than passing diversions—each was also an ideal, a model of a better world than this one. The mind of the age could only imagine improving this present world by imitating these better worlds. Being held up as models for real-life imitation is the most significant difference between the fantasy themes of the Renaissance and those of today.

In the thirteenth century Charles of Anjou (d. 1285), the first Angevin king of Naples, had introduced tournaments in Naples, where they continued under his successors. Charles's grandson, King Robert, Petrarch's patron, personally participated in six tournaments in the first five months of 1343.[4] Boccaccio's description of a Neapolitan joust in *Fiammetta* reveals his obvious enthusiasm for what was still, in his time, a form of real combat.

> When the gay group had shown themselves to the onlookers as their mounts caracoled around the lists with short, prancing steps, the tilts began: erect in their stirrups, protected beneath their shields and holding their light lances so that the tips almost grazed the ground, they spurred their steeds to run faster than the wind; the air, resounding with the voices of the spectators, with the many harness-bells, with the many musical instruments, with the shock of the clanging armor of horses and riders, urged them on to still greater speed. And as the watchers saw them thus, not once but many times, right worthily they made themselves laudable in the hearts of the beholders.[5]

As we have already seen, the influence of courtly love had turned tournaments from bloody battles into entertaining spectacles for the enjoyment of all classes. Italian cities were already presenting them for this purpose in the thirteenth century.[6] By 1400 five forms of combat

3. Mallett, *Mercenaries,* 205.

4. Branca, *Boccaccio: The Man and His Works,* trans. Richard Monges and Dennis J. McAuliffe (New York: Harvester Press, 1976), 21.

5. Boccaccio, *Fiammetta* V.27.1–6; V.29.1–3, in Branca, *Boccaccio,* 20–21.

6. Molinari, *Spettacoli,* 15.

were customary: (1) the *mêlée,* which was still a pitched battle; (2) foot combat; (3) the joust, the most popular form, in which two knights on horseback charged at each other with lances, each hoping to strike his opponent with enough force to break his own lance; (4) two teams of knights fighting for possession of a mock castle; and (5) very rarely a *naumachia,* a mock naval battle.[7] A series of several of these types over several days constituted a *pas d'armes.*[8] Allegorical fables, ceremony, music, and pageantry accumulated like barnacles on the tournaments of Europe as early as the thirteenth century. An elaborate etiquette evolved, codified by King René of Anjou, Ferrante's rival for the throne of Naples, in his *Traité de la forme e devis d'un tournois.* One of the tournaments King René staged in his French exile, the *Chasteau de la Joyeuse Garde* of 1448, lasted forty days, featuring such embellishments as lions led in procession on silver chains.[9]

A Neapolitan tournament of 1423 shows how tournaments had evolved into choreographed spectacle during the eighty years since Boccaccio's account.[10] The centerpiece of the 1423 tournament was a wooden elephant on wheels, escorted by men dressed as Turks, armed with clubs, led by a sorcerer. The Turks fought with angels; Catalan knights fought Neapolitan ones; and the Grand Seneschal led the attack against thirty mounted devils and a car full of fire and explosives.[11] By 1469 the gulf between jousting and real warfare had become so great that when Lorenzo de' Medici asked Federico da Montefeltro to lend him fighters to participate in a Florentine tournament, Federico answered that his army had no men proficient in that kind of fighting.[12] In 1518 Cardinal Antonio de Beatis echoed Pius's complaint in Florence when he scoffed that a tournament in Milan had not produced a single wound or even an "honorable thrust."[13]

Medici propagandists saw to it that the jousts best remembered in

7. Roy Strong, *Art and Power: Renaissance Festivals, 1450–1650* (Berkeley: University of California Press, 1984), 12; Mallett, *Mercenaries,* 213.

8. Strong, *Art and Power,* 12.

9. Ibid., 12–14.

10. Boccaccio, *I diurnali del duce di Monteleone,* ed. M. Manfredi, in *Rerum italicarum scriptores* (hereafter *R.I.S.*) XXI.6, edited by Lodovico Antonio Muratori, 109 (Milan: typographis Societatis Palatinae, 1723–51), 109, excerpted in "'Uno elefante grandissimo con lo castello di sopra': Il trionfo Aragonese del 1423," by Hope Maxwell, *Archivio storico italiano* 150, no. 3 (1992): 847–49.

11. Maxwell, "'Elefante grandissimo,'" 848–49.

12. Goldthwaite, *Wealth,* 163.

13. Ibid., 164.

future generations were those staged for the young Lorenzo de' Medici in 1469 and for his brother Giuliano in 1475. In the previous chapter we borrowed details from Lorenzo's tournament as examples of the kinds of things Pius might have seen a decade earlier. Six years after Lorenzo's tournament another such show celebrated Guiliano de' Medici's twenty-first birthday and the peace recently made between Florence and Venice.[14] Knights came from all the courts of Italy—Naples, Milan, Mantua, Urbino, and Rimini—and rode to the Piazza di Santa Croce through streets hung with banners and tapestries. Giuliano's outfit, reputed to have cost a thousand florins, was made of gold and silver, studded all over with gems.[15] The harness of his horse had a gold lion's face on the breast and figures of dragons on the throat guards and sidepieces. Verrocchio designed Giuliano's helmet, which sported a statuette of a lady on the crest.[16] Botticelli painted Giuliano's banner with a portrait of Simonetta Vespucci, Giuliano's current amorous interest. When Giuliano and Jacopo Pitti won the tournament they received engraved helmets as prizes, after which the festivities concluded with feasting and dancing.[17]

By the fifteenth century tournaments were organized around a "legend" or myth.[18] Poliziano, the humanist who educated Lorenzo and Giuliano de' Medici, hoped to immortalize Giuliano's tournament with his *Verses for the Joust of the Magnifico Giuliano de' Medici,* which allegorized the event in pseudo-classical fable. In Poliziano's version Giuliano is an innocent huntsman living peacefully in an idyllic landscape until Cupid shows him the nymph Simonetta, whom he cannot resist. This leads into a word picture describing the garden and palace of Venus on Cyprus, which Poliziano derived from Claudian's *Epithalamium.*[19] In Book II Venus sends out cupids to wound other young men who will fight Giuliano for the love of Simonetta and sends Giuliano a dream based upon Petrarch's *Triumph of Chastity,* in which Simonetta defeats Cupid and ties him to Minerva's olive tree—the scene Botticelli painted on Giuliano's banner. We are spared the rest of Poliziano's elaborations

14. Cloulas, *Lorenzo,* 154–55.

15. Ibid., 158–59.

16. Wackernagel, *Florentine Renaissance Artists,* 201n16.

17. Cloulas, *Lorenzo,* 159.

18. Molinari, *Spettacoli,* 15; Strong, *Art and Power,* 43.

19. Angelo Poliziano, *The Stanze of Angelo Poliziano [Stanze Cominciate per la Giostra del Magnifico Giuliano de' Medici],* trans. David Quint (Amherst: University of Massachusetts Press, 1979), ix.

because he left the work unfinished when young Giuliano was murdered in the Pazzi conspiracy in 1478.[20]

Venice, arguably the most mercantile place in Europe, also held spectacular tournaments in the quattrocento to celebrate victories, the election of a new Doge, or other state occasions. Unlike the Florentines, the Venetian patricians did not participate themselves; the purpose was to demonstrate the might of the *Serenissima*'s arms and reward her most skilled champions. Consequently, Venetian tournaments kept a genuinely military flavor, and the individual joust did not so completely displace the general *mêlée.* Francesco Sforza, still a mere *condottiere* then, competed in 1441 on the occasion of the marriage of the Doge's son. Colleoni, another *condottiere,* presided over a tournament in 1458 that culminated in a battle between two teams of seventy men fighting for possession of a wooden castle outside the Doge's Palace. Nevertheless, after 1480, when Venice outlawed horses on the streets, mock naval battles replaced tournaments.[21]

The most enthusiastic sponsor of tournaments in cinquecento Italy was Alfonso II d'Este, Duke of Ferrara from 1559 to 1597. The five tournaments he staged in 1561–1570 represent the final evolution of the genre. All were accompanied by music and had themes and stories laden with symbolism, spectacular stage machinery, and declamations of verse written by leading poets. *Il tempio d'amore,* staged in 1565 to honor Alfonso's marriage to Barbara of Austria, was much more opera than combat. It took place in a courtyard of the palace, with a great hemicycle of seats for the spectators at one end and a stage set of towering mountains at the other. At the beginning of the performance the "Temple of Love" appeared among the mountains; but when six old sorceresses tried to enter it, the temple disappeared behind clouds. In revenge, the witches swore to keep any knights from approaching it. To achieve this they turned themselves into seductive young women and conjured up the palaces of Pride and Voluptuousness to distract their victims. These enchantresses turned the "Knights of Glory" into rocks, releasing them only when the knights agreed to defend their new mistresses. A series of paladins came to challenge them, each making an elaborate triumphal entry, heavy with symbolism. A variety of combats ensued, with staged allegorical incidents, music, and drama, each ending with the victory

20. Ibid., xi.

21. Mallett, *Mercenaries,* 214–15.

of the sorceresses, who consigned the defeated warriors to a forest or a labyrinth. At length the "Knights of Honor and Virtue" arrived, defeating evil spells by moral superiority as well as triumphing by arms. When their victory was complete, the clouds parted and the Temple of Love reappeared, more glorious than ever. From it the Graces emerged and made a speech to the bride about the power of Virtuous Love.[22] All the incidents of combat fitted into this pageantry must necessarily have been carefully scripted.

The enormous expenditure of wealth and artistry lavished on these tournaments—comparable in disproportion to the extravagance of Philip the Good's "Feast of the Pheasant"—has left little trace behind it. The 1492 inventory of the Medici Palace lists several splendid pieces of armor made from costly materials, but these were probably dismembered when the family was driven out of Florence two years later. Objects made from precious metals and jewels fell prey to greed, and rot overtook even the costliest fabric. The prize helmets, made of silver by artists such as Verrocchio and Pollaiuolo, have all disappeared.[23] A *David* painted by Castagno hangs as an artwork in the National Gallery in Washington, but it is actually a shield, probably from a forgotten Florentine tournament. The Uffizi has a drawing by either Verrocchio or the young Leonardo for a tournament banner showing Venus and Cupid.[24] Botticelli's well-known *Birth of Venus,* painted on canvas, may have been a banner of some kind.[25] We have lost an entire genre of work by Renaissance artists that, had it survived, might have made it easier to see the strong parallels between Italian and northern culture in the fifteenth century and the importance that Italians gave to feudal and chivalric themes.

The ethos of chivalry and courtly love reflected the solidly aristocratic values of Italian ruling classes, whether they lived in one of the many despotisms or in a commercial city-republic. Whatever pragmatic, materialist, bourgeois capitalist outlook may have existed in Italy had peaked in the twelfth and early thirteenth centuries. In the previous chapter we saw Petrarch, Boccaccio, Alberti, and Pius II pouring contempt upon mercantile activity. By the quattrocento the Florentine elite, especially

22. Strong, *Art and Power,* 53–54.

23. Wackernagel, *Florentine Renaissance Artists,* 110.

24. Ibid., 201.

25. Frederick Hartt, *History of Italian Renaissance Art: Painting, Sculpture, Architecture* (New York: Abrams, 1969), 291; Lopez, *Three Ages,* 26.

that part of it influenced by humanists, shared this disdain for commerce and distanced themselves from its taint as much as they could.

The days of the Piccolomini's prosperity in the twelfth and early thirteenth centuries had been the "heroic age" of Italian and Florentine capitalism. In that age of opportunity, a determined, energetic, ruthless, and lucky man could rise to riches as a result of his own commercial endeavors.[26] It is not surprising that the artistic productivity of the Italian cities in that period lagged behind their economic expansion; these single-minded entrepreneurs were unlikely to distract themselves from profits for the sake of painting and poetry. As John Larner pointed out in one example, "The Frescobaldi family became poets shortly before they became bankrupts."[27]

Even then, these high-medieval self-made men were not bourgeois or "middle class." After the end of Roman rule, when urban populations shriveled in the sixth and seventh centuries, cities, like the countryside around them, fell under the dominance of a warrior nobility. The only real distinction between urban nobles and rural nobles (many, like the Piccolomini, were both) was the kind of economic opportunity they exploited.[28] The mentality of a "merchant adventurer" in a time when commerce was truly adventurous was not so very different from that of the military adventurer who might be his brother or cousin or, at times, himself. When new men made new fortunes, they adopted the behaviors of the ruling class they aspired to join. That meant that old and new families alike often conducted feudal warfare within the narrow limits of the medieval streets. As we saw in Siena, this led to the reaction against nobles or "magnates" who refused to restrain their violence.

During the mid- to late thirteenth century this "heroic" age of commerce settled down to something more regular and dependable. Business partnerships were commonly among brothers or other close relatives, with directors of the enterprise staying at home and managing their agents in the field through regular correspondence and meticulous recordkeeping.[29] In the fourteenth century these resident agents abroad were often younger members of the clan. This tribal approach to busi-

26. Benjamin Z. Kedar, *Merchants in Crisis: Genoese and Venetian Men of Affairs and the Fourteenth Century Depression* (New Haven and London: Yale University Press, 1976), 43.

27. John Larner, *Culture and Society in Italy, 1290–1420* (New York: Scribner's, 1971), 32.

28. George A. Holmes, *Florence, Rome and the Origins of the Renaissance* (Oxford: Clarendon, 1986), 5.

29. Kedar, *Merchants in Crisis,* 24, 26–27.

ness, reflecting the family-oriented ethos of the aristocracy, produced a notable concentration of wealth among a few families.[30] The extreme case was Venice, Europe's largest and most economically dynamic city. Virtually all Venetian fortunes had commercial foundations; nevertheless, at the early date of 1297, membership in the Great Council was closed and the names of the eligible, now considered to be a hereditary nobility, were inscribed in the "Golden Book."[31] By 1379 the noble families held 69 percent of the wealth in Venice, with the top 10 percent of them holding half of it.[32] In Florence the patriciate was never legally delimited and endowed with formal nobility as in Venice, but Florentines clearly understood who was included, designating them by such terms as *ricchi, nobili, grandi, savi* ("the wise") or, perhaps most eloquently, as *le case,* "The Houses."[33] By the time of the *catasto* (tax declarations) of 1427, which gives a household-by-household snapshot of Florentine assets and incomes, about a hundred families controlled a quarter of the wealth of Florence—more than was owned by the poorest 87 percent of the households.

The republican institutions of Florence, Siena, and Venice were designed to maintain the power of a small oligarchy over the vast majority while at the same time keeping any one individual, family, or faction from dominating their peers. Throughout Italy the family never lost domination over its individual members. The status of a man's family determined whether he could participate in the government and, if so, at what level; it determined whom he could marry and conditioned or mediated almost every individual interaction.[34] Individualism in our sense of the term would therefore have been incomprehensible. This also explains why Pius II and Callixtus III, among others, worked so hard to elevate their kinfolk once they had reached a pinnacle of power themselves. Many prominent members of originally mercantile clans had little to do with commerce, passively drawing their income from landed estates or shares in businesses managed by others—exactly the role that Alberti envisioned for the more worthy and intelligent members of the tribe.[35] The elites in commercial cities like Florence, Venice,

30. David Nicholas, *The Later Medieval City, 1300–1500* (London: Longman, 1997), 155.

31. Ibid., 21.

32. Kedar, *Merchants in Crisis,* 53–54.

33. Felix Gilbert, *Machiavelli and Guicciardini: Politics and History in Sixteenth Century Florence* (Princeton: Princeton University Press, 1965), 49.

34. Lauro Martines, *Social World,* 50.

35. Gene Brucker, *Florentine Politics and Society 1343–1378* (Princeton: Princeton University Press, 1962), 35.

Siena, and Genoa, who held both political and economic control of the state, whose wealth flowed from rural estates as well as urban businesses, who lived in luxury upon the sweat of others, saw no reason to distinguish themselves from the feudal nobility, who were similarly situated in other parts of Europe—they certainly did not think of themselves as "middle class."

The memoirs of Buonaccorso Pitti, written in 1412, might go a long way to purge our minds from Marxian assumptions about social classes. A member of a prominent Florentine mercantile family, Buonaccorso went in his youth to the Low Countries, where he associated freely with the Duke of Brabant, the Count of Holland, and their courtiers—not with the burghers of Bruges or Ghent. Buonaccorso was accepted easily in the courts of England, France, and Burgundy, participated in tournaments, and even fought in their armies as a knight. At the same time he was amassing a fortune from gambling and commerce in wool.[36] Eventually, after Buonaccorso had returned to Florence and become influential there, the Holy Roman emperor gave Buonaccorso patents of nobility for himself, his brothers, and their descendents and the right to display a golden lion on his arms.[37] Buonaccorso seems entirely unaware of any social distinction between himself and nobles whose income derived solely from land. Boccaccio, a banker's son who grew up among the nobles of Naples, insisted upon his essential equality with them. Unlike Buonaccorso, Boccaccio's defensive tone shows that he was well aware that bankers would have been excluded from noble status in Naples. But nobility was defined in countless ways in the various states of Europe, and Boccaccio clearly intended to overcome this minor technicality:

> I have lived from my childhood to man's estate, nourished in Naples and amongst noble youth of my own age who, although noblemen, were not ashamed to enter my house nor to visit me. They saw me ... living in a very refined way, the way Florentines live; in addition they saw my house, its furnishings and fittings, very splendid, within the measure of my means. Many of those friends are still living, and having grown old along with me, they have attained dignity and high office.[38]

36. Buonaccorso Pitti, "Memoirs," in *Two Memoirs of Renaissance Florence: The Diaries of Buonaccorso Pitti and Gregario Dati,* by Buonaccorso Pitti and Gregorio Dati, edited by Gene Brucker, translated by Julia Martines (New York: Harper Torchbooks, 1967), 29–45.

37. Ibid., 71.

38. Boccaccio, *Epistles* xii; quoted in Branca, *Boccaccio,* 19.

Like any ruling class at any time or place, the Italian urban patriciates needed a code of behavior recognized among themselves and by other elites that differentiated them from their inferiors. The two ideals, chivalry and classicism, each performed this function. Until the quattrocento the only available aristocratic code was chivalry supplemented by courtly love. Later, when the humanists made Roman models of aristocracy available and the expense of a humanist education ensured that only the elite could acquire it, the two models of aristocratic behavior, chivalric and classical, coexisted without conflict. Castiglione's melding of the two in the *Courtier* was so welcome in the cinquecento that the emperor Charles V kept a copy by his bedside.[39]

The Florentine Signoria reinforced the chivalric code by bestowing knighthoods upon its leading citizens and reserved the right to confirm foreign knighthoods received by Florentines.[40] Florentine knighthood began in the thirteenth century when Charles of Anjou, the first Angevin king of Naples, knighted Florentines for their service to the Guelph cause.[41] The short-lived Ciompi regime of 1378 rewarded its followers with sixty-seven knighthoods, of which the succeeding regime confirmed thirty-one. When conservatives ended the guild regime in 1382, they celebrated with twenty new knighthoods.[42] Boccaccio and Sacchetti scorned these political "carpet knights," but the glut abated in the quattrocento, when the honor was more closely guarded and usually bestowed upon citizens who had some connection with the commune's war efforts.[43] The ceremonial investiture of Florentine knights took place in the Piazza della Signoria until 1418, when it moved to the cathedral or the baptistery.[44] At this ceremony the knights received swords and spurs, shields, banners, and—under humanist influence—a laurel wreath and a Latin oration—one of many examples of cross-fertilization between the two aristocratic codes.

Some Florentines, such as Donato Velluti (1313–1370) and Giovanni Morelli (1371–1444), were single-mindedly dedicated to the pursuit of

39. John Robert Woodhouse, *Baldesar Castiglione: A Reassessment of "The Courtier"* (Edinburgh: Edinburgh University Press, 1978), 4.

40. Sharon T. Strocchia, *Death and Ritual in Renaissance Florence* (Baltimore: Johns Hopkins University Press, 1992), 78.

41. Leonardo Bruni, *The Humanism of Leonardo Bruni: Selected Texts,* ed. Gordon Griffiths, James Hankins, and David Thompson (Binghamton, N.Y.: Renaissance Society of America, 1987), 108.

42. Strocchia, *Death and Ritual,* 78.

43. Mallett, *Mercenaries,* 211–12.

44. Strocchia, *Death and Ritual,* 78–79.

profit without much regard to aristocratic pretensions, but they became much rarer at the highest level of society during the quattrocento. To a Florentine humanist like Alberti, such men were respectable but old-fashioned. He portrays them that way in *Della famiglia* in the person of Giannozzo Alberti.[45]

Giovanni Rucellai (1403–1481), who amassed one of the greatest Florentine fortunes of the century, declared, "I think I've done myself more honor by having spent money well than by having earned it." This indicates the replacement of the capitalist urge to amass money by the aristocratic desire to be honored for liberality. An important distinction is necessary here. Capitalists may spend lavishly to exhibit their wealth, as the residences of the nineteenth-century American Vanderbilt clan so ponderously demonstrated; but there is a crucial difference between their expenditures and those of earlier European aristocrats. The capitalist wishes to be valued for what he has amassed; the aristocrat, for what he has dispensed. One values money, the other shows contempt for it. The aristocrat spends himself into penury if necessary to show his liberality and even his prodigality. The Vanderbilts would never have done that. An exchange in Alberti's dialogue *Della famiglia* establishes the distinction quite clearly:

> ADOVARDO: I don't know about other people, but I myself would certainly risk much wealth in the hope of gaining honor.
>
> LIONARDO: And we, like you, I assure you, are of the number that thirsts eagerly for praise.
>
> ADOVARDO: And what do you think about other men?
>
> LIONARDO: I think hardly anyone not altogether barbarous would hesitate to be prodigal for the sake of praise and honor.
>
> ADOVARDO: If that is our opinion, we shall say that, in the hope of praise and fame, we do not care much for money.[46]

It is important to note that patronage of art and letters—that is, patronage of the Renaissance itself—sprang from this aristocratic notion of liberality, not from capitalism. The banker Cosimo de' Medici was an exemplar who helped confirm public expenditure as an inescapable component of an aristocrat's prestige. He did this primarily through architecture, beginning with the rebuilding of the convent of San Marco

45. Alberti, *Della famiglia* III, in *Family,* 155–245.

46. Ibid., IV, in *Family,* 293.

in Florence in 1436 and later by the church of San Lorenzo, the Badia at Fiesole, and his palazzo and villas, as well as shared projects at Santa Croce and Santissima Annunziata, all of which earned him credit for liberality.[47] Lorenzo de' Medici claimed that his father and grandfather had spent 663,755 florins on their buildings and other patronage, but that he did not begrudge the loss to his purse, since it had conferred such benefit on the Florentine state.[48] Princes such as Lodovico Gonzaga, Francesco Sforza, Federico da Montefeltro, Pius II, and Alfonso V soon followed in the banker's footsteps.[49] The Medici family ultimately followed Alberti's advice in *Della famiglia* by squandering their banking wealth for the sake of political power and the fame of their magnificence. Since they rose to be hereditary grand dukes of Tuscany, it is hard to fault their strategy.

Traditionally, we are taught that secularism grew out of humanism and the down-to-earth bourgeois mentality of Florentine merchants. But all over Europe the first widespread theme of purely secular art and literature was chivalry and courtly love—an aristocratic expression if ever there was one. As literature it originated in the eleventh and twelfth centuries, but in visual art its great expansion comes after the Black Death.[50] If any sizeable percentage of this art had come down to us, it would be visibly evident that secular art was originally a medieval and aristocratic expression that had little to do with either commerce or the classics. The Florentine patricians, who played at knighthood in the Piazza della Santa Croce, brought chivalric themes into their houses, as well. Decorative household objects such as marriage plates and *cassoni* (wedding chests) typically displayed scenes of courtly love and chivalric romance.[51] Frescoes and tapestries were the wall decorations of choice, and each lent itself to narratives of battles, tournaments, hunting scenes, cavalcades, games, dances, portraits of heroes, and allegories, particularly allegories of love. Dino Compagni (d. 1324) describes a palace with frescoes of Tristan, Isolde, and Lancelot.[52] We also have accounts of chivalric decorations at the Cangrande castle in Verona and the Carrara

47. A. D. Fraser Jenkins, "Cosimo de' Medici's Patronage of Architecture and the Theory of Magnificence," *Journal of the Warburg and Courtauld Institutes* 33 (1970):164.

48. Lauro Martines, *Social World,* 23.

49. Jenkins, "Cosimo," 167–68.

50. Paoletti and Radke, *Art in Renaissance Italy,* 124.

51. Antal, *Florentine Painting,* 366–67.

52. Ibid., 272n15.

castle at Padua. Examples still exist at the castle of La Manta in Saluzzo and the Palazzo Borromeo in Milan.[53]

In Florence we have no evidence of depictions of commerce in wealthy homes; if they ever existed, they yielded very early to scenes of aristocratic pursuits such as hunting, music, dancing, tournaments, chivalry, and courtly love. The Museo di San Marco preserves fragments of frescoes from a fourteenth-century Florentine house illustrating the story of Tristan and Isolde; the Davizzi (Davanzati) Palace displayed scenes from the romances of Chastelaine de Vergi around the walls of the principal bed chamber.[54] Even a specifically commercial institution, the Arte della Lana, decorated its guildhall with scenes of a tournament, while the processes of its woolen-cloth business were discreetly tucked into quatrefoils underneath.[55] The most important surviving quattrocento chivalric frescoes, though they were never completed and are badly damaged, are the cycle from the legends of Lancelot that Pisanello painted for Lodovico Gonzaga in Mantua in 1447–1448. These were still fresh when Pius II was at Mantua and must have been familiar to him. The subject is a tournament in which Lancelot's cousin Bohort defeats sixty challengers in order to win the hand of a princess, while gorgeously attired ladies watch from a reviewing stand. Above the scene are heraldic emblems, including the imperial Order of the Swan, which the emperor had bestowed on Lodovico Gonzaga and his wife.[56]

We should probably see Uccello's three large panel paintings of the *Battle of San Romano* (c. 1445) as part of this chivalric genre. They once decorated the walls of Lorenzo de' Medici's bedroom in the Medici Palace, but are now divided between the Uffizi, the Louvre, and the National Gallery in London. Art historians have usually emphasized Uccello's interest in perspective but have said much less about the subject and its treatment. Nonetheless, observers cannot fail to notice an odd paradox: for all its rearing horses, swinging swords, and lances cutting through the scene like lightning strokes, there is little sense of violence or even of movement in these scenes. Men and horses seem like waxworks.[57] No one is really hurt: the one corpse on the ground could be

53. Arnold Hauser, *The Social History of Art,* trans. Stanley Goodman (New York: Knopf, 1951), 1:291.

54. Antal, *Florentine Painting,* 264–65.

55. Ibid., 363.

56. Paoletti and Radke, *Art in Renaissance Italy,* 249–50.

57. Hartt, *Italian Renaissance,* 215.

Figure 7.1. Paolo Uccello. *Battle of San Romano* (1456?). Tempura on wood. Uffizi, Florence. Photograph from Scala/Art Resource, New York.

sunning himself on the beach if it were not for his armor. This stasis must be a deliberate choice by Uccello or his patron, since his contemporary fresco of the *Deluge* at Santa Maria Novella is tumultuous, with drowning people clinging desperately to the side of the ark and a raven plucking out the eyes of a dead baby.[58] Why, then, is the battle so placid? The usual subject for such a room would have been a tournament—a game of war with all the pageantry and no pain. This seems to be what Uccello provided: a battle domesticated for interior use. In their original place, the effect of the three panels (thirty-four feet long) must have been spectacular, but, with their action frozen and stylized, they would not have been disturbing. The Magnifico would probably have objected to the raven-and-baby vignette in his bedroom.[59]

In the late fifteenth and sixteenth centuries, when Italy was dotted with an archipelago of despotic courts, chivalry provided themes for an Italian vernacular literature reemerging from its humanist tutelage to Latin.[60] Lorenzo de' Medici's mother commissioned Luigi Pulci, bosom

58. Paoletti and Radke, *Art in Renaissance Italy,* 700.
59. Hartt, *Italian Renaissance,* 214.
60. Hauser, *Social History,* 61–62.

friend and court buffoon to her son, to write the epic poem that became *Morgante* (1478 and 1483).[61] Pulci used the Carolingian epic of Roland (Orlando) as a template, just as humanists used classical works.[62] Pulci turned his Carolingian heroes into comic fools and made the giant Morgante the central figure of the poem.[63] Comedy prevails, yet death, combat, and loss of friends evoke pathos.[64] For Pulci, whose profession was to be amusing, chivalry served more as entertainment than ideal.

The ever-chivalric Este court at Ferrara was the origin of three of the more enduring works of Italian literature, Boiardo's *Orlando innamorato,* Ariosto's *Orlando furioso,* and Tasso's *Gerusalemme liberata.* Boiardo recasts the Carolingian warrior Orlando as a heartbroken lover and sends him on a series of Arthurian-type adventures in the Orient. Boiardo holds up chivalric virtues as an ideal, not to be ridiculed, but retains a certain detachment and humor, even if it seems mild beside Pulci's buffoonery.[65] Boiardo left his poem unfinished, which tempted Lodovico Ariosto (1474–1533) to write a sequel, *Orlando furioso,* one of the liveliest literary works produced in the Renaissance. Ariosto wrote three versions, one each in 1516, 1521, and 1532.[66] Ariosto's intent, as one of his modern editors has said, was "the desire to escape reality and to create a world which is all magic and fantasy."[67] One delightful landscape succeeds another, each peopled with knights, fair maidens, giants, sorcerers, hermits, and magical beasts.[68] Ariosto weaves the classical among the chivalric, including bits from Dante and Petrarch, and large doses of the supernatural, demonstrating that all sources were fair game for fantasy. A bewildering thicket of overlying plots intertwine and entangle each other. The name of the poem derives from Orlando's insanity, caused when his lady, Angelica, marries a Saracen. In his madness

61. Lorenzo de' Medici, *The Autobiography of Lorenzo de' Medici,* trans. James Wyatt Cook, Medieval and Renaissance Texts and Studies 129 (Binghamton: State University of New York at Binghamton, 1995), 16.

62. Ernest Hatch Wilkins, *A History of Italian Literature* (Cambridge, Mass.: Harvard University Press, 1966), 159.

63. Cloulas, *Lorenzo,* 108.

64. Wilkins, *History of Italian Literature,* 159.

65. Ibid., 172–73.

66. Ibid., 192.

67. Ludovico Ariosto, *Orlando Furioso,* ed. Bruno Maier (Turin: UTET, 1964), introduction, 10; quoted in Lauro Martines, "The Gentleman in Renaissance Italy," in *The Darker Vision of the Renaissance: Beyond the Fields of Reason,* edited by Robert S. Kinsman, 86 (Berkeley: University of California Press, 1974).

68. Lopez, *Three Ages,* 44–46.

Orlando uproots forests and slaughters men and beasts until his friend Astolfo goes to the moon on a flying horse to retrieve Orlando's wits and return them to him. Meanwhile, there are three Saracen attacks on Paris, a Christian invasion of Africa, aided by Ethiopian Christians with magical weapons, and a naval battle in which the Christian fleet springs into existence by magic. The poem ends when the chivalric hero Roger finally defeats Rodomonte, the last Saracen champion, in single combat. Along the way, Roger rescues Angelica from a sea monster (based on Perseus and Andromeda), and the sorceress Alcina lures men to her enchanted island, where (*à la* Circe) she turns them into beasts, trees, and rocks.[69]

The third chivalric writer at the Este court, Torquato Tasso (1544–1595), was eighteen and studying in Padua when he wrote his first chivalric epic, *Rinaldo.*[70] It is not *Rinaldo* but *Gerusalemme liberate* on which Tasso's fame rests. Writing under the patronage of Cardinal Ippolito d'Este, builder of the famous villa at Tivoli, Tasso himself was suffering from intense anxiety and bouts of depression.[71] By the time *Gerusalemme* was published in 1581, its author, after several violent outbursts, was in a mental asylum. Whereas Pulci had been comic, Boiardo gently humorous, and Ariosto clearly enjoyed himself, the tormented soul of Tasso throws a mantle of solemn gloom over his tale. Tasso attaches all the fantastic paraphernalia of Boiardo and Ariosto's epics to an actual historical event, the capture of Jerusalem by the First Crusade in 1099. As in the *Iliad,* human combats invite the constant intervention of supernatural forces.[72] Nevertheless, love and its mental states are Tasso's real interest.[73] The central love story concerns Tasso's old hero Rinaldo, this time smitten by a Saracen enchantress, Armida. She entices him, then falls in love with him herself and transports him to a "bower of bliss" located in the Fortunate Isles. Eventually Christian knights arrive to recall Rinaldo to his duty. The infuriated Armida goes to lend magical aid to the Saracens, but when the infidels are defeated, Rinaldo rescues her and they return to love's joys. Another Christian/Saracen duo is Tancred and the Saracen maid Clorinda who, not recognizing each

69. Wilkins, *History of Italian Literature,* 187–88.

70. Ibid., 269.

71. Hauser, *Mannerism: The Crisis of the Renaissance and the Origin of Modern Art* (NewYork: Knopf, 1965), 306.

72. Wilkins, *History of Italian Literature,* 273.

73. Hauser, *Mannerism,* 306.

other in the dark of night, engage in furious combat. When Tancred fells Clorinda with a mortal wound they discover their identities, and Tancred baptizes her before her death.[74] Along the way the protagonists meet with enchanted forests, nymphs, and hundred-armed giants.[75] Tasso's style is full of conceits, literary ornaments, and technical displays, which Galileo, among others, found insufferable.[76]

The real historical incident at the foundation of his story did nothing to inhibit Tasso's unlimited fantasy. In fact, Tasso deliberately subordinated reality to fantasy because, Tasso declares, untruth is more poetic than truth and the poet's domain is the marvelous, which is, by definition, untrue.[77] This frank disdain for reality reflects late-sixteenth-century mannerism and contrasts markedly with Alberti's belief that the "Ideal" is not only better than reality but also *more* true and, therefore, more beautiful. What is common to both is repugnance toward the world of the here and now. Alberti looks to the "Ideal" (a kind of higher reality), but Ariosto and Tasso, disillusioned with reality and ideal alike, look to the unashamedly imaginary.

74. Wilkins, *History of Italian Literature,* 274.

75. Ibid., 276.

76. Hauser, *Mannerism,* 305.

77. Hauser, *Mannerism,* 306.

8

Mantua and After

PIUS MUST HAVE BEEN disappointed but hardly surprised to find that not one of the rulers he had summoned to meet him in Mantua had arrived or sent representatives. The European princes did not oppose a crusade against the Turks, but they shunned binding commitments and had little stomach for inconveniencing themselves; consequently, they certainly had no intention of going to Mantua or sending an expensive embassy unless failing to do so became positively embarrassing. Records from Florence show great uncertainly and division among the Florentine leadership about their attitude to the crusade. The Florentines appointed ambassadors, deliberately delayed their departure, replaced the men appointed with others, then delayed some more, even though Pius II was prodding them with letters of increasingly testy tone. The envoys they eventually sent carried secret instructions forbidding them to commit the republic to anything at all without specific consent from the Signoria.[1]

The cardinals, most of them compelled to go against their will, rumbled with discontent, saying that Mantua "was a swamp and a hazard to health; it was too hot; the wine was terrible and so was the food; everyone was getting sick and many were catching their death of fever; all you could hear was the frogs."[2] A delegation of them came to Pius, saying, "It is no use to keep us here unless you mean to kill us with this pestilential climate.... You were here on the appointed day; you have

1. Black, *Benedetto Accolti,* 248–51.

2. Pius II, *Commentaries,* ed. Margaret Meserve and Marcello Simonetta, I Tatti Renaissance Library (Cambridge, Mass.: Harvard University Press, 2007), 2:7.

remained a sufficient time. The princes stay at home and insult you and us."[3] Privately, some cardinals were spreading the word that the pope was a dreamer and that his crusade was a disastrous folly.[4] D'Estouteville used the heat as an excuse to get Pius to let him withdraw from the congress, which he privately called "the craziest enterprise I've ever seen or heard of."[5] Pius ignored their pleas and busied himself writing urgent letters to the rulers of Europe, no less than fifty-two of which survive.[6] For their part the cardinals scattered to various hill towns in search of cooler weather.[7] In spite of that, Mantua teemed with foreign emissaries—most of them from places threatened by the Turks who were seeking help, not offering it.[8] Week after week Pius stayed in Mantua, playing a risky waiting game. The longer he waited for the European princes to appear or send emissaries, the more embarrassing it was for them to stay away. But if they boycotted the congress and *never* came, the shame would recoil on the pope and could haunt the papacy for decades. On June 1, the proclaimed opening date of the congress, Pius spoke to those attending, most of them members of his own entourage. "With misery in his eyes," according to one witness, he lamented that, while the Turks willingly gave their blood for a "vile faith," Christians seemed unwilling to inconvenience themselves for the gospel.[9]

Meanwhile, at Mantua, he established friendships with men who would become essential supports to his papacy. One of these, Jacopo Ammanati, was a Tuscan humanist of humble background who had benefited from the patronage of Nicholas V. Callixtus had promoted him to papal secretary, and Pius kept him at his post. There was little self-seeking in Ammanati's genuine admiration for Pius, who eventually made him bishop of Pavia and a cardinal. The second of these friends, Gianantonio Campano, was introduced to Pius by Ammanati. His origins were lowly indeed; he had been a shepherd boy, an orphan who lacked even a surname until he adopted one based upon the name of the region, "Campagna," where apparently he was born. Taken in and educated by a priest, his intellect enabled him to study under Lorenzo Valla in Naples and to begin lecturing at Perugia by age twenty. Perugia sent him to Rome to offer congratulations to Pius after his election. There Ammanati noticed his talents and brought him into the

3. *Comm.,* Smith, II.194.
4. Pellegrini, "Pio II," 55–56.
5. Ibid., 65.
6. Mitchell, *Laurels,* 139.
7. *Comm.,* I Tatti, III.3.1, II.7.
8. *Comm.,* Smith, III.200.
9. Setton, *Papacy,* 2:24.

papal service.[10] Shepherd boys might acquire education, but Campano never acquired polish. This may have been one of the principal reasons that Pius, once the playmate of the urchins of Corsignano, found him such a comfortable companion. Since sophistication eluded him, Campano was not above playing the buffoon, as we see in his description of himself:

> What is Campano like? Well, he snores all the night through, a-bed and naked he is a more appalling sight than any wild beast of the forest. His feet are like hooks, his hands are gnarled and hairy, his nose is flat, with great gaping nostrils, his brow overhangs his eyes, his belly is swollen with food and wind, he is short of limb, fat and round as a ball.[11]

One day in the long summer of waiting at Mantua, Pius went boating on the Mincio with these new friends and his oldest friend, Goro Lolli, along with Lorenzo Roverella, whom Pius would make bishop of Ferrara in 1460, and the Roman poet Agapito di Conci de' Rustici. This congenial group sought to raise the weary pope's sinking spirits.[12] Ammanati had brought a stack of the congratulatory verses that had rained down upon the newly elected pope from needy humanists who hoped that Pius would restore Nicholas V's largesse. The friends waxed hilarious making up couplets deriding these versifiers.[13] Some of the couplets have survived, but, like many jokes that are side-splitting when concocted at a party, they are embarrassingly limp to those who were not there to share the fun. When a few of these gems leaked out in public, they enraged aspiring humanists whose talents were going unrewarded. Among those offended was Filelfo. At Pius's election Filelfo had written to him, "In the eyes of all distinguished and cultured men, you have arisen like a sun, dispersing the mists of darkness."[14] Out of respect for Filelfo's reputation, Pius allowed him an annual pension of two hundred ducats; but Filelfo demanded more, even coming to Rome with his sons to push his claims. Relations soured when Filelfo tactlessly pointed out a grammatical error by the pope. Pius thanked him for the correction but supposed that it was easy for the idle to find errors in the work of a man as busy as himself. After Pius died, Filelfo celebrated his demise in an insulting poem and published anonymous libels against his memory.[15]

10. Boulting, *Aeneas Silvius,* 280–81.
11. Quoted in ibid., 281.
12. Paparelli, *Enea Silvio Piccolomini,* 211.
13. Boulting, *Aeneas Silvius,* 281–82.
14. Filelfo to Pius, November 1, 1458; quoted in Ady, *Pius II,* 247.
15. Ady, *Pius II,* 249.

It was probably during the months of waiting in Mantua that Pius wrote what strikes modern minds as one of his oddest compositions, the *Epistola ad Mahomatem II,* supposedly a letter to Mehmet II, the Turkish sultan, intended to convert him to Christianity and thus make a crusade unnecessary. This fantasy probably originated with the German cardinal Nicholas of Cusa, a friend from Aeneas's early days in Basel. In Nicholas's treatise *De pace fidei* (c. 1453) he advanced the idea, still encountered at times today, that all of mankind's religions were fundamentally the same, differing only in form and observance. Therefore, he proposed that "spiritual leaders" armed with "plenipotentiary powers" should congregate at Jerusalem, proclaim the common faith, and thereby establish universal peace. By 1460 or 1461 Nicholas had completed his *Cribratio Alchorani* ("The Sifting of the Koran"), in which he scrutinized the text of the Koran to "sift out" the good from the bad. Nicholas and others, probably including Pius, believed, erroneously, that Islam had grown out of the Christian heresy of Nestorius (an idea Pius mentions in the *Epistola*) and that Mehmet II himself had formerly been a Christian who required only an intellectual nudge to revert to his old faith. Nicholas even persuaded himself that most educated Muslims were secretly Christians who laughed at the Koran behind closed doors.[16] It would have been quite easy for Nicholas, Pius, or any highly placed individual in quattrocento Italy to disabuse himself of such fantasies by inquiring among the many people familiar with Islamic societies and the few acquainted with Mehmet himself. The actual arguments Pius uses in the *Epistola* to convince Mehmet came mainly from another cardinal, Juan de Torquemada, a Spaniard, who was writing his *Contra principales errores perfidi Machometi* ("Against the Principal Errors of the Wicked Mohammedans") at this time.[17] Pius would borrow the same arguments for his principal speech at the Congress.[18] We do not know if Pius sent, or Mehmet II ever saw, the *Epistola.* He would not have enjoyed such lines as "If we had to mention all the errors of your religion, we would not have the time to write about them" or "Besides, you realize yourself, since you are intelligent, that many of these things are so stupid that there is no way to defend them."[19] Nor would Mehmet

16. Baca, introduction to Pius II, *Epistola,* 5–6.

17. Juan de Torquemada should not be confused with his nephew Tomás, the infamous Grand Inquisitor.

18. Baca, introduction to Pius II, *Epistola,* 7.

19. Pius II, *Epistola,* 70.

have succumbed to Pius's assurance that the Turks and all the peoples of the East would follow his example if he converted or that his conversion would bring all peoples voluntarily flocking to his rule.[20] Could Pius have seriously hoped to convert the Ottoman sultan with his eloquence? Like other humanists, his faith in word-spinning was nearly boundless, but, on the whole, I think it is unlikely that he expected any such result. To a humanist, beautiful words were never wasted. Pius's mind was full of these Eastern issues, and he had time to write that summer. An eloquent discourse with plenty of classical references was an *objet d'art,* needing no practical justification. It turned out, in fact, to be one of his most popular works—but only in the West.[21]

In that long, torrid summer, as he waited for embassies that never seemed to come, Pius also turned his thoughts to architecture, the transformation of Corsignano, and his other ambitious building schemes in Rome. It is very likely that Leon Battista Alberti was there and joined in discussions of Pius's architectural projects. Alberti's influence on early Renaissance architecture, painting, and sculpture was enormous. Although he is considered the architect of important buildings in Florence, Mantua, and Rimini, Alberti was primarily a humanist rather than an architect or artist, and his impact was diffused through his books more than his buildings. Alberti never supervised the construction of his designs; he saw himself as an aesthetic advisor to the patron and preferred to withdraw from the construction lest he sully his reputation with imperfections in execution.[22] He would have functioned in this advisory role with Pius II. Although Pius often seems to have ignored his advice, Alberti's influence is unmistakable throughout Pius's architectural undertakings. We know very little about Alberti's movements during the Congress of Mantua, but he probably made his first contacts with his future patron, Ludovico Gonzaga, at this time.[23] Alberti's architecture and Mantegna's paintings, both produced for Ludovico, would later make Mantua one of the centers of the Renaissance.

Another likely participant in architectural discussions at Mantua was Flavio Biondo, the leading archeologist of the quattrocento, who also wrote in support of papal supremacy and the crusade. Biondo, a native of Forli in the Romagna, had written his three-volume *Roma In-*

20. Ibid., 18–21, 27.

21. Baca, introduction to Pius II, *Epistola,* 8.

22. Andres, Hunisak, and Turner, *Art of Florence,* 1:508.

23. Rubenstein, "Pius II," 39.

staurata ("Rome Restored") in 1446 while serving Eugenius IV. By examining the ruins of ancient Rome and comparing what he found with descriptions in Livy, Pliny, and Varro, among others, Biondo was able to identify and describe not only the monuments of the ancient city but also its shops and apartments and the lives people lived in them.[24] Oddly enough, Biondo was out of favor at the court of Nicholas V, usually so generous to classicists; but he used his time to travel around Italy compiling his next major work, *Italia Illustrata* (1453), a book that combined geography, history, and antiquarian studies with contemporary observation.[25] This was a book that Pius knew intimately and drew upon constantly in the *Commentaries* and elsewhere for the vignettes of history and topography with which he peppers his narratives.[26] During the same period, Biondo worked on what is considered the first history of the Middle Ages, the *Historiarum ab inclinatio Romanorum imperii decades* ("Decades of History since the Decline of the Roman Empire" or simply "The Decades").[27] Biondo returned to papal favor and employment by dedicating his fourth major work, *Roma triumphans,* to Pius II and presenting it to him at Mantua.

Like many early humanists, Biondo did not merely linger nostalgically over Rome but hoped to recreate it. Already in the preface to *Roma instaurata,* Biondo hailed Rome as "the progenitor of genius, student of virtues, model of renown, acme of praise and glory, seedbed of good things for the whole world."[28] Biondo opined that Rome's later wealth and luxury had led to the decline of the old republican *virtus,* which, had it been maintained, could have ruled the world forever. For Biondo the fall of Rome had humbled classical civilization and its *virtus* but not erased them; they were incarnate today in the Roman Church. Rome was still the "head of the world" by virtue of its relics, its sacred sites, and the residence of the popes. Instead of the tribute of provinces, there were the donations of the faithful; where there had been consuls there was now the pope; the senators had become cardinals; bishops replaced provincial governors; kings and princes functioned as legates, quaestors, and military tribunes. Why then is Christendom weak and trembling

24. Stinger, *Renaissance in Rome,* 62–63.

25. Charles R. Mack, *Pienza: The Creation of a Renaissance City* (Ithaca: Cornell University Press, 1987), 225; Denys Hay, *Flavio Biondo and the Middle Ages* (Oxford: Oxford University Press, 1960), 102.

26. Rinaldo Rinaldi, "L'Italia 'romana,'" 109–28, and in passing.

27. Hay, *Flavio Biondo,* 116–17.

28. Stinger, *Renaissance in Rome,* 62.

before its enemies? It is because the kings and princes do not follow the pope and his cardinals as their classical predecessors once obeyed the consuls and the senate. Biondo tells us in the introduction to the *Triumphans* that he hopes that his book will inspire a return to classical *virtus* and classical civilization. Were that to happen, he says, victory over the Turks and the restoration of Roman rule over the world would follow automatically.[29] The starring role in this pipe dream went to the pope. Biondo specifically cast Pius himself as the restorer of Rome, reviver of ancient institutions and *virtus,* liberator of the East and scourge of the Turks.[30] As delusional as all this is, it was a phantasm Biondo shared with Petrarch, Cola di Rienzo, and (to a considerable extent) Pius II, among others. It is a mistake to see classical movements in art and literature as mere fashions; they were never entirely separable from delusions of Roman revival that now seem to border on lunacy. The fact that such ideas were completely out of touch with reality was no handicap—escape from reality was precisely what people hungered for.

In the real world Frederick III's refusal to attend the Congress of Mantua had all but doomed it to failure. When Frederick's envoys finally arrived, they were men of insultingly low rank: Pius's successor as bishop of Trieste and two court officials who were personal friends of the pope but of very minor stature. Pius flatly refused to receive them; accepting such men as imperial representatives would have signaled to all Europe that the Congress of Mantua was not to be taken seriously. Pius sent Frederick a scolding letter, but it was five months before better envoys, the Margrave of Baden and two bishops, arrived in Mantua.[31]

The pope's patience finally produced a reward when a splendid embassy arrived from Philip the Good of Burgundy on August 18. The duke sent four hundred horsemen to escort his nephew, Jean, Duke of Cleves, accompanied by Jean de Croy, Comte de Chimay, a member of the duke's inner circle.[32] There were disadvantages to such high-ranking potentates, as well; the duke of Cleves would discuss nothing

29. Angelo Mazzocco, "Rome and the Humanists: The Case of Flavio Biondo," in *Rome in the Renaissance: The City and the Myth,* edited by P. A. Ramsey (Binghamton: State University of New York at Binghamton Center for Medieval and Renaissance Studies, 1982), 189–92.

30. Meserve, "Italian Humanists and the Problem of the Crusade," in *Documents on the Later Crusades, 1274–1580,* edited and translated by Norman Housley, 25 (New York: St. Martin's Press, 1996).

31. Ady, *Pius II,* 167–68.

32. Von Pastor, *History of the Popes,* 3:71.

until the pope ceded him the town of Soest, which he was disputing with the archbishop of Cologne.[33] After the great Feast and Oath of the Pheasant, it was disappointing that Philip had not come in person. His envoys pointed out the escape clause in his oath, which said that he only had to participate if other princes of appropriate rank also joined. Pius had difficulty extracting a promise that Philip would recruit a contingent of two thousand horses and four thousand infantry to serve for the duration of the crusade. The Comte de Chimay fell sick in the Mantuan heat, and the Duke of Cleves was eager to depart. Both refused to linger in Mantua until more ambassadors arrived.[34]

If the Burgundians had waited another week they could have witnessed the arrival of Francesco Sforza, the first potentate to come in person. He came sailing up the Mincio on September 17 with a flotilla of forty-seven magnificently decorated ships. The Marquess of Mantua and his wife went forth to greet them with their own escort of twenty-two vessels, which combined with the Milanese ships to make a stirring sight as they approached the city. Sforza's arrival prompted most of the other Italian powers to send envoys. But neither Sforza nor the other Italians were attracted to Mantua by crusading zeal; they were much more concerned with the emerging war in Naples between Ferrante of Aragon and the French candidate, René of Anjou. In August the Prince of Taranto, the most powerful Neapolitan noble, had risen in open rebellion against Ferrante in favor of King René.[35] The French duc d'Orleans had a strong claim on the Visconti inheritance in Milan, so, from Sforza's point of view, keeping the French out of Italy was a matter of prime importance.[36]

This purely Italian affair induced even the reluctant Venetians to send an embassy with five hundred mounted nobles and two hundred lesser men-at-arms, which all the dignitaries in Mantua rode out to meet.[37] Among all the Western powers, Venetian policy toward the Turks was the most delicately balanced—like a sensitive needle on a dial, it quivered nervously between peace and war. The Venetians knew far better than Pius what a daunting task it would be to inflict a meaningful defeat on the Turks and what overwhelming forces would be needed to

33. *Comm.*, Smith, III.211.

34. Ibid., III.217; Von Pastor, *History of the Popes*, 3:72–73.

35. Von Pastor, *History of the Popes*, 3:73–74.

36. Ady, *Pius II*, 171–72.

37. Michael Mallett, "Venezia, i Turchi e il Papato dopo la pace di Lodi," 237.

guarantee success.[38] The Venetian colonial empire in the East—Negroponte, Lepanto, Nauplia, Modron, Codron, Crete, and the Aegean Isles, not to mention their ships, merchants, and goods—were continually exposed to potential Turkish attack. While the Venetians had to stand in defense at all these places, the Turks could select vulnerable points at their leisure, concentrate their forces, and reduce the Venetian posts one at a time. The Venetians knew that defending their possessions under those circumstances was beyond their capability, which meant that their empire, their trade, and their prosperity depended on Turkish forbearance. A war with the Turks was, therefore, an "all or nothing" affair. Either an overwhelming European coalition would crush the Turks with irresistible power, or Venice stood to lose everything while others took little risk. On the other hand, if the Turks seemed bent on nibbling Venice away to nothing bit by bit, resistance could become unavoidable.[39] For Venice merely sending a delegation to Mantua risked offending the Turks. It is not surprising that the Venetian ambassadors made it clear to the pope that Venice would join the crusade only if *all* other Christian powers did so—a nearly impossible condition, as the Venetians well knew, but necessary for an assured victory. Other mercantile states such as Genoa and Florence were in similar positions to the Venetians, but with less to lose.

By September 26 enough envoys had arrived for Pius to formally convene the congress originally summoned for June 1. This he did with a Mass (at which the ambassadors quarreled over precedence), followed by a three-hour speech by the pope, followed by another speech by Bessarion and one from the Hungarians in which they complained more about Frederick III's attempt to seize their throne than about the invading Turks.[40] Pius's speech was at least a personal success; over 120 manuscripts of it survive, and there were at least sixteen printed versions, making it, according to one historian, "the most widely distributed oration of all European humanism."[41] After excoriating Islam in various ways ("a sect of pleasure and violence founded by a charlatan") and telling atrocity tales to emphasize its threat to Christianity, Pius concluded with a reference to the speech by Pope Urban II that had launched the First Crusade.

38. Ibid., 239.

39. Setton, *Papacy,* 2:237.

40. *Comm.,* Smith, III.252–53.

41. Johannes Helmrath, "The German *Reichstage* and the Crusade," 63.

> Oh if Godfrey, Baldwin, Eustace, Hugh the Great, Bohemund, Tancred [heroes of the First Crusade] and other great men were here who once penetrated Turkish battle lines and recovered Jerusalem by force, they would not allow us to speak at such length, but rising up, as in the presence of Urban II our predecessor, they would cry out passionately, "God wills it!"[42]

The next day saw the *only* high-level working session of the congress. In attendance were Francesco Sforza, Ludovico Gonzaga, the Marchese of Montferrat, Sigismondo Malatesta, and envoys from Ferrante of Naples and his uncle the King of Aragon, along with the cities of Venice, Florence, Siena, Lucca, Bologna, and Ferrara.[43] Sforza suggested that the soldiers for the crusade should come from Hungary and other territories under direct threat, with the rest of Europe supplying the money. The Venetians (who insisted that they were only observers) said that the naval aspect of the expedition must be under their exclusive control. It would require, they estimated, thirty triremes (though Pius demanded forty) and eight other ships to attack the coasts of Greece and Asia Minor, carrying eight thousand soldiers in addition to the rowers and sailors. Venice would provide the ships and their equipment; others would have to pay for the rest. For their pains, the Venetians expected to receive all the spoils of war. The arrogance of their requirements and the limitations on their contribution inspired Pius to write a lengthy diatribe in the *Commentaries* venting his loathing against this (to him) detestable mercantile republic.[44] To cover expenses for the naval forces and a projected army of fifty thousand men, the envoys agreed that over the next three years all the clergy of Europe would be taxed a tenth of their revenues, the laity would pay a thirtieth, and the Jews would pay a twentieth. On October 1 the princes and envoys, except for the Venetians and Florentines, who held back, signed a solemn *Instrument for the Defense of the Faith* that poured on the pathos in describing Christ's sufferings in his Passion and then listed the promised commitments of each party.[45] The Florentine envoys gave the pope private assurances that Florence would accept the crusade taxes, but the Signoria explicitly warned them

42. Bisaha, "Pope Pius II and the Crusade," 43–44.

43. Paparelli, *Enea Silvio Piccolomini,* 164.

44. *Comm.,* Smith, III.257–59; Paparelli, *Enea Silvio Piccolomini,* 164–65.

45. Marcello Simonetta, "Pius II and Francesco Sforza: The History of Two Allies," in *Pius II "el più expeditivo pontifice": Selected Studies on Aeneas Silvius Piccolomini (1404–1464),* edited by Zweder Von Martels and Arjo Vanderjagt, 158 (Brill, Leiden, and Boston: Brill's Studies in Intellectual History, 2003).

against signing anything publicly because of the five hundred Florentine citizens and a hundred thousand florins worth of goods now in the sultan's domains.[46] The fact that Venice, provider of sea power, abstained, along with the various conditions required by other parties, rendered the *Instrument* little more than a goodwill gesture. Having signed it, princes and envoys hastened to depart. How much goodwill there really was can be seen in an ugly little quarrel between the cardinals and Sforza over whether the duke or the clergy should receive the taxes in his territory. The duke commented acidly that "We do not want cardinals to fatten up personal friends, who are very often our mortal enemies, in our own household."[47]

The French arrived only on November 24, after everyone else had left.[48] Their relations with the pope had already soured. Pius's election had disappointed French hopes for d'Estouteville to become pope, while Pius's support of the Aragonese in Naples had utterly stunned them. On his side Pius keenly resented the restrictions on papal authority embodied in the Pragmatic Sanction of Bourges which had been promulgated during the schism between Eugenius IV and the Council of Basel. In their first audience on November 14, the French made the case for King René with words that Pius considered "bombastic and pretentious" and full of "characteristic French threats and boasts."[49] Pius told them that he must consult the cardinals before making his reply. Pius had been sick with a cough for some time and considered it no less than divine intervention that he had not coughed during his three-hour speech before the congress. Now, once he turned his back on the French emissaries, he had severe stomach pain and the cough became worse, so that "both he and his physicians had doubts whether he would live." The French let it be known that they considered this illness a mere excuse for delaying his reply to their unanswerable arguments. Hearing this, Pius steamed with fury, exclaiming, "Even if I must die in the midst of the assembly, I will answer this insolent embassy and pain shall not conquer my spirit nor shall sickness make me appear a coward."[50] The French were summoned to hear a seething Pius declare that they had no business meddling in the affairs of Naples and treat them to an excoriating condemnation of the Pragmatic Sanction. The offended ambassadors protested that the

46. Black, *Benedetto Accolti,* 251–52.
47. Simonetta, "Pius II and Francesco Sforza," 158.
48. Paparelli, *Enea Silvio Piccolomini,* 167.
49. *Comm.,* Smith, III.264.
50. Ibid., III.265.

pope had insulted their king and demanded to be heard in his defense. Pius spit out his reply: "I will hear you when and as often as you please, but understand that I shall have the last word and do not be surprised if you who have stung me are stung yourselves. This See does not yield to any, even the mightiest king."[51] Pius asked directly what help the French king meant to provide for the crusade, but the envoys said they could not discuss any such a thing while the war with England persisted.[52] Pius had rejected the credentials of the two low-ranking clergymen sent by England, so no discussion with them was possible.[53]

In December there was an even more unpleasant interview with representatives of King René, along with the king's son, Jean, Duke of Calabria, who had come in person to protest against Pius's recognition of Ferrante. Pius sought no conciliation with the House of Anjou. His hostility glowered in his face from the moment they entered the room, and he barely troubled to listen to them. He directed his greatest fury against Duke Jean, who had seized twenty-four galleys at Marseilles to carry his forces to Naples, even though they had been built and prepared for war against the Turks. For this Pius threatened that he might proceed against René and his son as heretics![54] Thus began the breach between Pius and France and his involvement in the Neapolitan war, which would drain away a great proportion of the energy and resources needed for the crusade.

The German envoys, representing numerous states with divergent interests, quarreled among themselves, particularly over Frederick III's efforts to seize the Hungarian throne. In the end the Germans renewed their earlier promise to Nicholas V of 32,000 infantry and 10,000 horses but postponed any action to future diets.[55] Even then, nothing could be done without peace in the war between Frederick III and Matthias Corvinus in Hungary so that German troops could pass safely to the Balkan front.[56] In January Pius declared Frederick III the supreme commander of the crusade, a purely honorary gesture, but made Albert, Margrave of Brandenburg, whom he called "the German Achilles," the commander of the theoretical German forces.[57]

The Congress of Mantua had only accomplished what its attending

51. Ibid., III.266.
52. Von Pastor, *History of the Popes,* 3:94.
53. Paparelli, *Enea Silvio Piccolomini,* 169.
54. Von Pastor, *History of the Popes,* 3:93–94.
55. Ibid., 3:95.
56. Setton, *Papacy,* 2:213.
57. Paparelli, *Enea Silvio Piccolomini,* 170–71.

envoys intended—placing a fresh fig leaf over the lack of any meaningful preparation for a crusade. All that Pius could accomplish on his own was to issue a bull imposing the agreed-upon tax payments.[58] Pius addressed the failure of this first ambitious initiative of his papacy with as much optimism as possible when he greeted envoys from Rome on his return.

> If we have not succeeded as we hoped, still we do not regret the intention and the effort. The whole world understands that it is our strength not our courage that has failed us.... Very few came; fewer still put their faith before their pleasure. But who can blame us for any of it ... ? And so we return in victory—not over the Turks perhaps, but at least over the whole of Christendom. Even if no crusade is launched against the Turks, as we had wished, still we hope that a seed has been sown from which we shall someday reap a reward.[59]

Such a pallid hope could not disguise Pius's bitter disillusionment at the failure of the Congress of Mantua. With the utmost effort, employing all his political resources, he had wrenched out of the princes and republics only the most meaningless promises. Of the spontaneous enthusiasm that had greeted Urban II at Clermont—and that was essential if the crusade were to succeed—he had seen no trace. He had no more illusions, either, about the strength of his opposition. There were murmurings among the French and others offended by papal policy that they might summon a council. A quarrel over the succession to the archbishopric of Mainz, the highest church post in Germany, alerted him to the danger that everything he did could be nullified or at least suspended by appealing his acts to some future council. Diether von Isenberg, the successful candidate for the see of Mainz, turned against Pius because of what he thought was an exorbitant payment that Pius demanded for recognizing him. Gregor Heimburg, writing as a polemicist on Isenberg's behalf, called Pius's decrees mere "cobwebs" and their author "a chattering magpie," and he appealed his case to a future general council of the church.[60] This appeal prompted Pius to issue the bull *Execrabilis* on January 18, 1460, that categorically forbade and condemned any appeal from the authority of a pope to a future general council. By this decree Pius condemned in advance appeals to this nonexistent council, which

58. Von Pastor, *History of the Popes,* 3:98.
59. *Comm.,* I Tatti, II; IV.39.6–39.8.351–53.
60. Baca, introduction to Pius II, *Reject/Accept,* 3, and editor's note, 391.

never, in fact, materialized.[61] Popes very rarely invoked *Execrabilis* before the Protestant Reformation, but its existence was a fundamental safeguard against the revival of conciliarism.

On January 19, the day after signing *Execrabilis,* Pius left Mantua in spite of the bitter weather. Many of the cardinals had refused to make the trip at this season and had scattered to comfortable sites in northern Italy to wait out the winter. Borso d'Este, who had not attended the congress and whose promise of 300,000 ducats for the cause was understood to be meaningless, nonetheless staged a spectacular water pageant for Pius's return to his city, wafting him down the Po on a magnificent barge, escorted by so many other galleys "that there was no part of the river that was not churned by their oars." "Trumpets, pipes, and all sorts of instruments made sweet music from the lofty sterns." There were impersonations of various gods and goddesses, giants and virtues, "while the river banks resounded with shouts of "Viva!"[62] Borso's substitution of show for substance could stand as a symbol of the entire Mantuan enterprise. Pius demonstrated his displeasure by remaining only one night in Ferrara.

Pius's route took him from Ferrara by boat, threading through the marshes that lie between the mouth of the Po and that of the Reno. Here he encountered some of the perils that made other men so reluctant to travel in winter; the shallow waters were locked in ice, and the boatmen had to chop their way with axes through the frozen swamp. The ice on the Reno was too thick for the axes, so they had to leave the boats and carry the pope over the frozen surface while the others walked. Reaching no shelter by nightfall, they scouted out a country house for the pope, but most of the party endured a freezing night in peasant huts. After only one night in Bologna, where Pius again refused invitations to stay longer, the grueling rigors resumed as they mounted the Apennines for the crossing into Tuscany.[63] Even today the roads in this region are harrowing, coiling like a slinky-toy up and down giddy, precipitous slopes; the idea of traveling there by donkey through snow and ice, or on foot while carrying a litter, is spine-chilling, to say the least.

In Florence Pius says that "he was loaded with extraordinary honors by the state," but describes no entertainments or tapestry-draped streets. Instead, his three days there were devoted to hard bargaining with the republic, which had already repudiated the agreement about

61. Boulting, *Aeneas Silvius,* 278–79.

62. *Comm.,* Smith, IV.298.

63. Ibid., IV.299.

crusade taxes that their representatives in Mantua had accepted only informally and privately. Cosimo de' Medici was on hand this time for what seems to have been earnest late-night discussions of the Neapolitan succession. Apparently, it was all quite friendly, with both of them joking about their gout. Cosimo was willing to agree to any argument Pius presented about the righteousness of Ferrante's cause but stuck to his neutrality, saying that the Florentine populace could only be persuaded to act "when forced by self-interest or fear"—a view that so closely matches Pius's own low opinion of republics that we cannot tell whether Cosimo was playing to his guest's prejudices or Pius heard only what he wished.[64] Perhaps Pius simply falsified the record in the *Commentaries*. Later that year Francesco Sforza prodded Cosimo into ignoring Florentine objections and taxing the clergy for the crusade.[65]

On the last day of January Pius returned to Siena to the wild rejoicing (he tells us) of the inhabitants. He spent the next seven months in the city or at baths nearby, doing everything he could to secure full rights for the Sienese nobility and encountering the most dogged and determined resistance.[66] During his first visit Pius had decided to build a great palace for his family in Siena and a lesser one for his sister Caterina. The palace that Pius built for his sister on the Via di Città, the most prominent street in Siena, still stands. Its design is clearly derived from Cosimo de' Medici's palace in Florence, yet the window arches are pointed, perhaps a concession to Siena's conservative taste.[67] Also on the first visit he had ordered a new white marble tomb for his parents in the church of San Francesco that may have been completed by the time he returned. We know little about the tomb, because a fire in 1655 destroyed it. What survives are two portrait medallions of Pius's parents, wearing quattrocento clothing, against a scallop-shell background.[68]

In their former days of greatness the Piccolomini had dominated the neighborhood in Siena around the church of San Martino just off the southeastern corner of the Campo. Pius planned to rebuild this whole precinct around a giant palace that would assert the glory of the Piccolomini for ages to come. The palace itself was to be a great square with a nine-bay façade on each side, including, probably, a side facing the Campo itself. Between the palace and the church of San Martino Pius planned a great piazza where the Piccolomini Loggia would stand. The

64. Ibid., IV.300–301.

65. Black, *Benedetto Accolti,* 280.

66. Rubenstein, "Pius II," 50.

67. Ibid., 64–65.

68. Ibid., 56–58.

scale of the scheme was its undoing. It took Pius so long to procure the various properties and prepare the site that he was never able to lay the first stone of his palace.[69] A stubborn grammarian who refused to sell his house forced Pius to change the location of his planned loggia.[70] Pius's nephew Giacomo eventually did built a splendid Renaissance palazzo on the site; however, its one architecturally developed façade does not face the modest triangular piazza, but towers over the narrow Via Banchi di Sotto, where it is difficult to see it to good effect.[71] Nevertheless, Pius did finish the Piccolomini Loggia, or Logge del Papa, a graceful structure consisting of three cross vaults supported on monolithic columns.

Lent was coming, at which time Pius was expected to appoint new cardinals. The rulers of Europe each had candidates for these appointments, while the existing cardinals were always reluctant to dilute their individual honor and emoluments by adding to their numbers. Pius appointed six cardinals that year, five of them Italian. All of the appointments, including the one German, had some sort of personal link to the pope. One was his twenty-three-year-old nephew, Francesco, whom he had just made archbishop of Siena two months previously. In the *Commentaries* Pius, blatantly contradicting the truth, claims that this appointment was forced on a reluctant pope by the cardinals![72] He also appointed Niccolò Forteguerra, a distant kinsman of his mother, whom he had befriended when Niccolò had been in Siena studying law.[73] In an age in which every individual put family loyalty first, such nepotism, which Pius deplored in theory, was almost the only way that a reigning pope could hold onto the reins of the church and the Papal States.[74] With all the opposition he had encountered among the cardinals, Pius needed reliable supporters too desperately to be squeamish about how he acquired them.

When the weather warmed sufficiently, Pius left Siena for the mineral baths at Macereto, some miles south of the city. His happiness at this retreat into the countryside leaps from his pages in the earliest of the lyrical descriptions of natural landscape that hereafter become such a feature of the *Commentaries.*

69. Ibid., 66–68.
70. Ibid., Rubenstein, 71.
71. Ibid., 68.
72. *Comm.,* Smith, IV.304–5.
73. Chambers, *Popes, Cardinals and War,* 61.
74. *Comm.,* Smith, I.79.

> All the hills about Siena were smiling in their vesture of foliage and flowers, and the luxuriant crops were growing up in the fields. The Sienese country immediately around the city is indescribably lovely with its gently sloping hills planted with cultivated trees and vines or plowed for grain, overlooking delightful valleys green with pasture or sown fields, and watered by never-failing streams. There are also thick forests planted by nature or man where birds sing most sweetly.... Through this region the pope traveled in a happy mood nor did he find the baths less pleasant. They lie ten miles from the city in a valley.... [That] at its entrance is highly cultivated and thickly dotted with castles and villas; near the baths where it ends, it is wilder. It is closed by a substantial stone bridge and by dark wooded cliffs. The mountains which ring the valley on the right are almost all covered with the evergreen ilex; those on the left with the acorn-bearing oak and the cork tree. Around the baths are simple houses used as inns. Here the pope passed a month and though he bathed twice every day, he never omitted the *signatura* or other state business. About the twenty-second hour he was accustomed to go into the meadows and, sitting on the riverbank where it was greenest and grassiest, he heard embassies and petitioners. Every day the wives of the peasants brought flowers and strewed the path by which the pope went to the baths; and the only reward they expected was permission to kiss his feet.[75]

In this passage the boy of Corsignano peeks out from under the stiff brocades of the papal vestments. It may be questioned whether cardinals and great ambassadors appreciated putting up in "simple houses used as inns" and having to attend the pope on grassy riverbanks. Ammanati and Campano would not have minded, which may explain their intimacy with the pope.

Pius returned to Siena to celebrate Pentecost with great splendor. But these exertions canceled out the physical benefits of the healing waters, forcing him, he says, to stay at Siena longer than intended. Pius is at pains to portray his Sienese sojourn as a medical necessity, since many, especially at Rome, criticized it and begged him to hasten his return. He was certainly ill: his doctor prescribed more visits to the baths for arthritis, bronchitis, gastric flu, and kidney stones.[76] But he was also still at loggerheads with the Sienese government, which would yield only trivial concessions to the nobility. After Pentecost, Pius went not

75. Ibid., IV.311–12.
76. Rubenstein, "Pius II," 52.

to Macereto, but four or five miles farther south to Petriolo, where the baths "are believed to contain more sulphur and to be more efficacious."[77] Petriolo was destined to be Pius's favorite country retreat. As he aged he became increasingly dependent on mineral baths for relief from the pains in his feet and legs. The spring of Petriolo lies in the deep valley of the Farna River, where the hills form steep walls, locking in the smell of sulphur that hangs heavily in the air above the spring. From this gorge the pope could look up at the rising mountains, with grassy patches on the uplifted rocky shelves. Pius reports that the teeming papal court lived in a number of houses scattered about. Some of these houses remain today, as does a fine arcaded building rising from the riverbank that may date from Pius's time. Petriolo in the quattrocento was the most fashionable watering place in Tuscany; princes and prelates came there from all over Italy and enjoyed each other's society as much as the sulphurous waters.[78] The doctors had decided that Pius's joints were aching because his brain was too wet! Their prescription was to have the warm waters poured through a pipe onto the top of Pius's head twice a day so that he would sweat out the excess moisture.[79] Today, as it comes fresh from the rock, the water is almost scalding; but as it overflows from one small pool to the next it cools in stages to milder temperatures. When it reaches the cool waters of the shallow Farna, the sulphur collects in little white beards around every rock and pebble that breaks the surface. Today Macerata and Petriolo are as wild and wooded as Pius described them, frequented only by families from nearby towns, whose Fiats parked alongside the narrow roads are the only sight that would be foreign to Pius.

In 1460 Pius was still learning how to be pope, and it appears that Macerata and Petriolo taught him the need and the possibility of escaping to nature for relief from tension. Once he learned this lesson the *Commentaries* reflect a regular psychological rhythm in his life. Many pages go by filled with diplomacy and war, the constant struggle for advantage over adversaries in and out of the church, marked now with disaster, now with victory. Then he goes to some remote monastery, to a mountaintop, a wooded glen, or placid lake. His pen becomes lyrical; his joy and relief still sing from his pages. Pius took delight in many things: architecture, festivals, archeology, and simple country people, but the

77. *Comm.*, Smith, IV.312–13.

78. Rubenstein, "Pius II," 53.

79. *Comm.*, Smith, IV.312–13, fn. 38.

dependable well from which he could always draw healing for his soul was natural scenery. As time goes on he would develop a certain connoisseurship in such matters. In 1461 at Tivoli he will "go with the cardinals for refreshment of mind, sometimes sitting in a grassy nook under the olives, sometimes in a green meadow on the edge of the Aniene where they could look down into the translucent waters."[80] A year later, on Mt. Amiata, his selectivity becomes even more explicit. There cardinals and other officials "came to the signature, which Pius held in the woods under one tree or another by the sweet murmur of the stream. Every day he changed the place, finding new springs in the valleys and new patches of shade among which it was hard to choose." In this selectivity we see that his enjoyment of nature was not passive; it was an activity—one to which he set his intellect as he "rode daily through the woods."[81] He had definite criteria: shade, running water, views; and he searched diligently for his specimens and compared them to one another. He mentally enjoyed them all over again as he wrote them out in the *Commentaries.* These descriptions show Pius using nature, like the idealized worlds of classicism and chivalry, as another alternative world to the one he was usually forced to occupy.

It was not uncommon for people in the Renaissance to use nature for mental escape; Petrarch had used the natural beauties of his homes at Vaucluse and Arca that way. More commonly, however, those who used nature as escape idealized it as Virgil and Horace had done in antiquity, thus turning it from direct enjoyment of nature into the conventions of the pastoral theme. Although the pastoral was usually a literary theme, King René staged a tournament in 1449, *La pas de la bergière,* in which the knights dressed as shepherds and contended for the hand of a shepherdess who awaited the victor among her lambs.[82] Pastoral narratives were invariably located in an idyllic setting of natural beauty. The characters were nymphs and shepherds as noble in character and as mellifluous in speech as the denizens of Camelot or the Capitoline. Lorenzo il Magnifico loved pastoral themes and, by his own writing, brought them to the forefront in Italy. Like other Renaissance writers, Lorenzo often contrasted nature favorably with the busy urban world.

> Seek who will pomp and other honors,
> The squares, temples, and great buildings,

80. Ibid., V.396.
81. Ibid., IX.571.
82. Strong, *Art and Power,* 14.

The delights and treasure accompanied by
A thousand hard thoughts, a thousand sorrows.
A green meadow full of fair flowers
A pool embowered with fresh leaves,
A little bird that sighs for love
Better deserves our worship.[83]

Pius's responsibilities could chase him down even at Petriolo, where he had to deal with a scandal involving Cardinal Rodrigo Borgia, who had invited some of the ladies of Siena to a garden party without their husbands or male relations. There, according to the scolding letter Pius wrote to him, he spent five hours dancing and flirting, "toying" with the women and pelting them with fruit. The young Aeneas Silvius would hardly have been shocked by such behavior, but then he had not been made a cardinal at age twenty-four as Borgia was. Pius threatened the young cardinal with public shame if he repeated such behavior, but Pius always found it difficult to be severe with the young, and concludes his letter, "We have always loved you and regarded you as a model of gravity and decorum [!]. . . . Your years, which give hope of reformation, lead us to admonish you as a father."[84]

More urgent matters than Borgia's peccadilloes were soon to flush the pope out of his rural covert. While Pius pursued his architectural dreams, wrestled with the local authorities in Siena, and bathed in the waters at Petriolo, the kingdom of Naples was descending into chaos. We have seen that Jean of Calabria, King René's son, had seized twenty-four ships at Marseilles that had been built for the crusade and used them to transport an army to Naples. Rebellious nobles, many from families of longstanding pro-Angevin traditions, immediately rushed to his support.[85] The states of the church were quickly sucked into this vortex. In this and other wars Pius took a keen and detailed interest, constantly corresponding with his commanders in the field, exhorting them, encouraging them, and often intervening directly in their military decisions. That summer Pius was particularly concerned with defending Benevento, a strategically valuable papal enclave embedded

83. Lorenzo de' Medici, *Opere* I.83 (Bari, Italy: G. Laterza e figli, 1913); quoted in Eugenio Battisti, *L'antirinascimento, con una appendice di manoscritti inediti* (Milan: Feltranelli, 1962), 186.

84. Pius II to Cardinal Borgia, Petriolo, June 11, 1460, in "Raynaldus, 1460," *Annales ecclesiastici,* by Odorico Raynaldus (Lucca: 1747–56), 31 and 32; quoted in Ady, *Pius II,* 238.

85. Von Pastor, *History of the Popes,* 3:102–3; Ady, *Pius II,* 183–84.

in the kingdom of Naples. He sent Bartolomeo Roverella, archbishop of Ravenna, to defend the city and ordered the papal *condottiere,* Simonetto, to reinforce Roverella with infantry and horse. Roverella received a stream of papal letters both instructing him and urging on his efforts.[86]

On July 7, at the Battle of Sarno, Ferrante of Naples, by a rash, premature attack, converted what should have been a victory into a crushing defeat; most of his soldiers were captured, and Ferrante himself escaped to Naples with only twenty horsemen. Jacopo Piccinino, Ferrante's *condottiere,* had declared for King René, and Milanese and papal forces commanded by Federico da Montefeltro were trying to intercept him before he reached the theater of war. Federico had rushed to Siena to make military plans with the pope. But before the end of July, Piccinino defeated Alessandro Sforza and Federico da Montefeltro, drove them across the border, and invaded the Papal States. In the Romagna, Sigismondo Malatesta of Rimini was in full rebellion against papal rule. Pius went into an orgy of letter-writing—twenty letters in November and December to Cardinal Forteguerri, who was leading the fight against Sigismondo, some with very specific instructions. Pius sent orders for troop movements on October 22; on December 12 he ordered Forteguerri to pursue the enemy, even though his horses were exhausted. At war, Pius was not a gentle man. Papal armies had committed outrages against civilians, but Pius excused Forteguerri: "not even Alexander, Hannibal, or Julius Caesar could always restrain their troops." As winter approached Pius insisted that Forteguerri devastate the lands of the rebel Jacopo Savelli with "fire and sword" before retiring from the field.[87]

In the midst of all these crises the eggshell fragility of papal rule in Rome itself was revealed for all to see—the pope was losing Rome, not to Piccinino's invading army, but to an adolescent street gang. Back in 1347, the year before the Black Death, Cola di Rienzo, an innkeeper's son, motivated by fantasies not unlike Biondo's, had inflamed many imaginations (including Petrarch's) by proclaiming the restoration of the Roman Republic with himself as tribune. The pope, then in Avignon, was irrelevant, but when the Roman nobles realized that fine rhetoric was the strongest weapon in Cola's armory, they easily suppressed him. Eight years later Cola's second attempt to restore the republic ended with a mob dragging his corpse through the streets. A

86. Chambers, *Popes, Cardinals and War,* 59.
87. Ibid., 61–62 and note 28, 198.

century later, under Nicholas V, Stefano Porcaro, a man of high rank and ability, inspired by Cola's example and intoxicated with dreams of antiquity, again plotted the revival of the ancient republic. Cardinal Bessarion tipped off the pope and entrapped the conspirators before they had time to act. Nicholas, remembering Eugenius IV's long exile from Rome, took ruthless action, executing Porcaro and all his associates, even leveling the Porcaro house.[88]

Among those executed were Angelo de' Maso and his eldest son; but his younger sons, Tiburzio and Valeriano, nephews of Porcaro on their mother's side, were too young to have been involved, understanding only that the pope had killed their father and brother.[89] By the summer of 1460, however, these youths had fashioned a gang of other boys, about three hundred in all, with which they terrorized the city. Unable to maintain order, Nicholas of Cusa, Pius's governor in Rome, withdrew to the safety of Nicholas V's Vatican fortifications.[90] The city magistrates took no action, because they hoped the disorders would force Pius to return to Rome with his lucrative court. The noble families of Savelli, Colonna, and Anguillara took advantage of the breakdown of authority to declare for the Angevins and form an alliance with Piccinino's invading army, now headquartered at Jacopo Savelli's town of Palombara. Tiburzio's gang avoided attacking rich citizens who might offer resistance and whose sons were often gang members, but they terrorized the poor, whom they robbed of both their goods and their daughters. On May 16 a gang member appropriately called "Inamorato" ("the lover," or "lovesick") kidnapped a bride on the way to her wedding. This at last produced popular protests strong enough to force the embarrassed authorities to restore order and arrest Inamorato.[91] For nine days the gang holed up in the Pantheon while supporters in the neighborhood kept them supplied.[92] After killing some officers with impunity, they broke out of the Pantheon, liberated Inamorato, and openly took control of the city.[93] It was the nobles, always the real power in Rome—and also the fathers and uncles of the gangsters—who negotiated with Tiburzio for his tactical withdrawal to Palombara, where he would be welcomed

88. Mitchell, *Laurels,* 157.

89. Anthony F. D'Elia, *A Sudden Terror: The Plot to Murder the Pope in Renaissance Rome* (Cambridge, Mass.: Harvard University Press, 2009), 63.

90. *Comm.,* Smith, IV.327.

91. Von Pastor, *History of the Popes,* 3:106–8.

92. D'Elia, *Sudden Terror,* 64.

93. *Comm.,* Smith, IV.327–28; Von Pastor, *History of the Popes,* 3:108.

by Piccinino's army. Tiburzio's departure from Rome was as public and festive as one of Pius's triumphal entries into welcoming towns.

Piccinino seemed irresistible. In Tivoli, the anti-papal party almost succeeded in delivering the town to him, and from the walls of Rome, the citizens could see blazing castles and villages torched by his troops.[94] In Palombara Savelli conspired with Tiburzio to open the gates of Rome to Piccinino.[95] When the interception of a messenger revealed this plot, word was sent to Pius, still soaking himself in the warm pools of Petriolo. On its heels came further news that Tiburzio's gang had sacked a convent and raped the nuns.[96] Realizing at last the extent of the danger, Pius finally embarked on his return.

When Pius left Siena on September 10, his conflict with the city fathers over noble rights had become so bitter that he stayed away from Siena until a few months before his death.[97] He got only as far as Corsignano, where he lay prostrated for twelve days by an illness he describes as "moisture spreading downward from his head and so weakening his chest, arms, and entire body that he could not stir without assistance and seemed on the point of death."[98] When he recovered, he took time to admire the progress that his architect, Rossellino, was making toward transforming Corsignano with "buildings which seemed likely to equal any in Italy."[99] When he finally crossed into the Papal States he was met by gratifying cheers, rejoicing, and banqueting.

The "Papal States" were named in the plural because they consisted of sixty-four separate entities—duchies, counties, lordships, and cities, each virtually independent in its own internal affairs, offering to their overlord, the pope, only token obedience and tribute. Each of these "states" wished both to honor its overlord and show its own importance by giving its citizens the exclusive right to carry the papal litter within its borders. The proud city of Orvieto had disputes with its neighbors about where, precisely, those borders lay. As the pope approached from Bolsena, the Orvietans arrived at the spot they claimed as the border and demanded the Bolsenians turn over the pope to their care. The Bolsenians resisted; swords flashed, men cried out, and blood flowed. The pope's horse guards, parading somewhere ahead or behind, heard the shouts, hastened to the fray, and subdued the men of both towns with

94. *Comm.*, Smith, IV.329; Von Pastor, *History of the Popes*, 3:109.

95. Ady, *Pius II*, 194.

96. *Comm.*, Smith, IV.329.

97. Rubenstein, "Pius II," 50.

98. *Comm.*, Smith. IV.335–36.

99. Ibid., IV.336.

lances and arrows.[100] When he left Orvietan territory toward Bagnoregio, the same kind of fracas erupted once more, and again the pope's bodyguards had to whisk him out of danger.[101] No wonder he sought peace in places like Petriolo!

Orvieto, which had lost half its population in the Black Death, had never fully recovered. Representatives of the city met Pius outside the gates and told him that they blamed their misfortunes on the curse of a previous pope (left unnamed) and asked Pius for his blessing to lift the curse. Pius made the sign of the cross over the city and entered amidst popular rejoicing. As a lover of scenic views, Pius commented on Orvieto's spectacular site: the flat top of a plateau rising vertically from a verdant valley. He particularly admired the great cathedral and the realism of its Gothic sculpture.[102] When he reached Viterbo, two days after leaving Orvieto, Roman envoys arrived to welcome him and urge him to hasten to their city, and Pius greeted them with a long, highly decorated oration that he records in the *Commentaries.* Six miles from Rome, more officials arrived to escort the pope. Among the youths sent to carry his litter were associates of Tiburzio's. Warned of this, Pius nevertheless called them to him and made them a pretty speech that he ended by saying, "These youths were ready, if they had been able, to despoil us of our city and our life. They were not able. They have realized their error. Now grown gentle they will carry on their shoulders him whom they wished to trample under foot."[103] When Pius entered their city on October 7, the Romans went wild with rejoicing, since they could now expect some slight protection of life and property as well as the resumption of their economic life.

The bizarre career of Tiburzio de' Maso ended soon after. A turncoat betrayed his brother Valeriano and another gang member to the authorities. Valeriano escaped, but Tiburzio, not knowing this, made a daring if foolish rescue attempt. This time no one answered Tiburzio's call to rebellion, and papal soldiers captured him along with five of his minions.[104] Torture, as usual, secured full confessions. The gangsters were turned over to the papal executioners, who were devising ingenious torments until Pius intervened to say that hanging was enough. As their corpses swung, Pius tells us that he wept for Tiburzio and his companions, prayed for them, and absolved them of their sins.[105] They were, after all, young.

100. Ibid., IV.335–37.
101. Ibid., IV.345.
102. Ibid., IV.337.
103. Ibid., IV.346.
104. Von Pastor, *History of the Popes,* 3:111.
105. *Comm.*, Smith, IV.350–56.

In the twenty-one months that Pius was absent from Rome, two themes are inescapable. One is the dizzying array of hypocrisy, intrigue, self-seeking, and violence running through society from heads of state to children. We have been taught to associate such unbridled mayhem with the Middle Ages. While the medieval centuries fully deserve their reputation for chronic violence, there was little or no improvement in this respect during the Renaissance. On the other hand, it is more characteristic of the Renaissance than of the Middle Ages to make a display of respect for rank and authority in exaggerated public celebration and ceremonial, such as the welcomes Pius received in Perugia, Ferrara, and Mantua. The incidents on the borders of Orvieto demonstrate as clearly as anything that the *show* of deference to the pope was as remarkable as the *actual* defiance of his authority—or any authority. It is easy to condemn Pius for basking at Petriolo and decreeing a new city to commemorate himself at Corsignano while Rome trembled before invading armies and street gangs. But placing these self-indulgences and the endless ceremonies that almost seem to mock reality next to the torrents of anxiety generated by violence, deceit, and war reveals a hidden logic. The two extremes, deferential magnificence and mayhem, each so unbalanced and almost manic by itself, acquire a bizarre equilibrium if we see them together as people actually experienced them. The consciousness of constant insecurity elicited the most bombastic celebrations of hierarchy, authority, and deference, all in the fond hope that these might provide some degree of security. When Pius bathed in the peace of Petriolo he could imagine that he was not beset by enemies on every side. When he watched Corsignano transforming at his order into a splendid new city, he could almost fancy that he controlled the streets of Rome.

9

The Political Pope

FOR THREE-AND-A-HALF YEARS after Pius left Mantua in January 1460, it appeared to anyone outside the pope's inner circle that he had lost interest in the crusade. He had more than enough to occupy his attention in the affairs of Italy, and, aside from that, he seemed thoroughly enmeshed in his own diversions and pleasures. This appearance was at least partly misleading; as early as March 1462 he revealed to a trusted few his intention to go on crusade himself. But at that time he himself lamented that "since our return from Mantua we have neither done nor said anything toward repulsing the Turks and protecting religion."[1] In the aftermath of the Mantuan conference Pius sent Bessarion to Germany to try to wheedle substantive commitments out of the imperial diet.[2] Cardinal Juan de Carvajal went to Hungary to sort out that kingdom's tangled affairs, but aside from these missions, Pius took no new initiatives toward the crusade.[3]

Pius was both discouraged and distracted. When he eventually turned his attention back to the crusade, he would claim that the urgency of Italian affairs had forced him to give them priority—a claim with considerable merit. In late 1460 not only was the succession war in Naples going badly and overflowing into papal territories, but Sigismondo Malatesta was seizing towns in Le Marche from the pope and the pope's ally Federico da Montefeltro. Sigismondo felt he had every right to do so. He had always known that a Sienese pope would have a grudge against him. In 1454 Sigismondo had been Siena's *condottiere*

1. *Comm.*, Smith, VII.515.

2. Setton, *Papacy,* 2:216–18.

3. Pellegrini, "Pio II," 73.

Figure 9.1 Piero della Francesca. *Sigismondo Malatesta*. Musée du Louvre, Paris. Photograph from Gianni Dagli Orti/Art Archive at Art Resource, New York.

but had betrayed his employers by making peace with the enemy behind the city's back. This treason may have originated Pius's visceral hatred for Sigismondo, which was of an altogether different order from his dislike of anyone else. Sigismondo had gone to meet Pius in Florence, seeking the protection of his overlord the pope in his war against Federico. Pius kept him waiting for an answer to his plea for some time; then, in Mantua, Pius imposed a humiliating settlement. Sigismondo not only had to concede the disputed towns to Federico, but had to turn over two

Figure 9.2 Piero della Francesca. *Federico da Montefeltro* (c. 1465). Uffizi, Florence. Federico lost his right eye and the bridge of his nose in a tournament. Photograph from Alfredo Dagli Orti/Art Archive at Art Resource, New York.

more towns, Sinigaglia and Mondavio, to the pope as security for debts he owed to Ferrante. Sigismondo considered himself robbed and vowed revenge; Piccinino's victory over Ferrante's forces gave him the opportunity to retaliate.[4] In November 1460 Pius summoned Francesco Sforza to put down Sigismondo's rebellion; on Christmas day Pius excommunicated the rebel and confiscated all his property.[5] Sigismondo scoffed that

4. Ady, *Pius II,* 192.
5. Von Pastor, *History of the Popes,* 3:117.

excommunication would not spoil the flavor of his wine.[6] Sigismondo was certainly cruel, rapacious, and duplicitous, and led an openly immoral life—none of which were rare among Italian despots. Ferrante of Naples, whom Pius defended so tenaciously, had nine illegitimate children and collected the mummies of slain enemies and displayed them to his guests.[7] It may have been the Lord of Rimini's contempt for the spiritual weapon of the holy church that finally pushed Pius to declare that "of all men who have ever lived or ever will live he was the worst scoundrel, the disgrace of Italy and the infamy of our times."[8]

Pius therefore had two wars on his hands in 1460: one in Naples, the other against Sigismondo in Le Marche (and briefly, a third if we count Tiburzio's cheeky usurpation in Rome). Does that mean that he had no choice but to shelve the crusade while he tended to these urgent challenges? To combat Sigismondo and the Angevins and to put the crusade aside while he did so was the commonsense, prudent choice. Just like other rulers, Pius was reluctant to gamble the immediate interests of his own state for the sake of a more remote, if nobler cause. But the papacy was supposed to be more than just a political dominion, and there were other options that Pius might have pursued if his *primary* commitment was to wage war on the Turks at all costs. If he expected other rulers to make peace with their enemies to free their hands for crusading, he would certainly have to set them an example. It should have been possible, for example, to grant Sinigaglia and Mondavio to Sigismondo on condition that he go on crusade. He was untrustworthy, of course, but a fierce fighter, and the possibility of conquering a Malatesta principality across the Adriatic would have made his mouth water. Naples, in theory, was also simple: Pius had only to recognize King René and his son Jean of Calabria, a man as gallant and chivalrous as Ferrante was vicious and cruel. It is true that this would have brought the French into Italy, but they were no more foreign than the Aragonese and much more able to contribute substantially to the crusade as the price of papal recognition. After Ferrante's defeat at Sarno, Pius did, indeed, toy with the idea of abandoning him and backing the Angevins. Since whoever triumphed in Naples would become the most powerful neighbor of the Papal States, the vital interest of the papacy was to be allied with the winner rather than to champion either cause.

6. Boulting, *Aeneas Silvius,* 303.
7. Burckhardt, *Civilization,* 41.
8. *Comm.,* Smith, II.168; Chambers, *Popes, Cardinals and War,* 67.

If the papacy switched sides, the biggest loser other than Ferrante himself would be Francesco Sforza, whose title to Milan was subject to French challenge. Thus Sforza sent envoys to Pius who stoked his fears that, if the French achieved dominance in Italy, it would lead to the election of a French pope. That fear, which implied the dread name of Avignon, was persuasive to most Italians. But Ferrante could not afford to rely on merely theoretical fears. He responded to papal hesitation by ceding the Tuscan town of Castiglione della Pescaia and the island of Giglio to Pius's nephew Andrea. The strategic town of Terracina on the coastal border between Neapolitan and papal territory went to another nephew, Antonio.[9] These gifts to his nephews were not the deciding factor in Pius's decision to stick by Ferrante, but they did allow others to raise embarrassing questions about the purity of the pope's motives. Pius made his choices, not as an idealist sacrificing everything to the cause of the crusade, but as a politician intent on outwitting his opponents—which was what his life experience had made him. Secular rulers followed his example by putting their political interests ahead of the crusade, as well. By the time Pius finally realized that only a *sacrificial* example from the pope could inspire other princes to make sacrifices, it was too late to change the perceptions that other rulers had formed about him.

The pope's personal behavior, though morally blameless, also undermined the image of a holy pontiff sacrificing himself to lead Europe in a sacred cause. As rulers in fifteenth-century Europe go, Pius was neither extravagant nor given to luxury. His personal desires were simple; his meals consisted of plain, homely food and little wine. His daily personal expenses were lower than those of any other pope of the period. After sleeping only five or six hours, he awoke at dawn, recited the daily office, then attended Mass or celebrated it himself. After that he began work at once, not waiting for the cardinals or the officials of the *segnatura* to join him. Before dinner he allowed himself a walk in the garden and took a nap after eating. When he awoke he attended to paperwork or gave audiences until supper. After that he conducted business with Ammanati or Goro Lolli. He recited another office before going to bed, but continued to read or dictate until he drifted off to sleep.[10]

Pius always retained a thoroughly rustic concept of comfort. All he

9. Boulting, *Aeneas Silvius,* 287–88.

10. Von Pastor, *History of the Popes,* 3:30–32.

needed for luxury was a shady spot beside a sparkling spring. His comforts may have been simple, but he set a pattern on his return from Mantua in 1460 that indicated a reluctance to sacrifice them. No one forgot the image of Pius bathing in the waters at Petriolo while Ferrante lost a kingdom and a gang of adolescents seized Rome. After that his month-long progress from Siena to Rome (even allowing for twelve sick days in Corsignano) was hardly the lightning stroke of a ruler racing to snatch his state from the teeth of its enemies. We must recognize as we chronicle the stretches of time that Pius devoted to his travels that, although he received ambassadors and conducted state business wherever he was, his wanderings presented an image of self-indulgence and leisurely pace to secular rulers who would only confront the Turks if they believed it was an urgent matter of survival that could not be delayed.

In spite of his bucolic personal tastes, Pius understood that magnificence in housing was a measure of status and power among European potentates from which the popes were not exempt. Even before he left for Mantua he had ordered new work on the ceremonial rooms on the first floor of the east wing of the Vatican. These included the room now called the Camera del Pappagallo and the now unidentified *Camera Nova* or "New Room" that served as Pius's personal audience chamber.[11] While Pius was in Mantua, Piero della Francesca, a celebrated painter whose portraits of Sigismondo Malatesta and Federico da Montefeltro adorn this book, was apparently at work decorating one of these rooms.[12] If Piero's work at the Vatican had survived, Pius might figure more prominently today as a patron of painting. In 1460, while Pius was in Siena, Piero's work appears to have perished in a fire. Pietro Giovenale replaced the lost décor in a conservative Gothic style. In 1925 a narrow band of quattrocento Gothic fresco that may be Giovenale's work was discovered above a lowered ceiling in the Camera del Pappagallo, and similar bits turned up in another room in 1940.[13] These fragments, a doorframe, and a marble portrait bust of Pius are all we have left of Pius's work in the Vatican Palace.[14]

Nicholas V had conceived ambitious plans for the Vatican gardens, including numerous fountains, a theater, an assembly hall, and a loggia of benediction—but he built none of them.[15] Up the hillside toward the future site of the Villa Belvedere, where Bramante would later build his

11. Rubenstein, "Pius II," 124.
12. Ibid., 116 and 123–24.
13. Ibid., 126–32.
14. Ibid., 116.
15. Ibid., 139.

terraces, there was already an informal garden with trees that Urban V had imported from Provence, along with orchards, vineyards, and enclosures for a leopard and possibly other exotic beasts. At a lower level, on the east side of the palace, between it and the fortifications, was a formal garden of the traditional medieval type, featuring a fishpond and probably cages for singing birds and exotic animals. Apparently Pius kept a monkey there.[16] When weather permitted Pius ate and gave his audiences in this garden.[17] To this garden Pius added a stone and wood pavilion, probably a vine-covered pergola, along with ornamental covers for the fountains made by a goldsmith.[18]

When spring reopened the military season in 1461, Pius kept his *condottieri,* Federico da Montefeltro and Alessandro Sforza, brother of the Duke of Milan, close to home subduing rebels in the Papal States—especially Jacopo Savelli, who had plotted with Tiburzio to open the gates of Rome to Piccinino. Once Savelli made his submission, the church armies invaded the area around L'Aquila, a strategic Neapolitan city built by the Hohenstaufen in the thirteenth century as a military post against their papal enemies. Those who accept at face value Machiavelli's charge that the wars of the Italian Renaissance were mere parades should read Pius's description of what his forces did to the country around L'Aquila.

> In one onslaught they laid waste all the plain below the city, drove off more than two hundred captives as well as oxen, beasts of burden, mules, and almost innumerable flocks and herds of all kinds (for it is a great grazing country), and carried off all the corn that was lying already threshed on the threshing floors as well as what had just been cut or was still standing in the fields. They carried off also more than 20,000 hens. When the booty had been collected and heaped together, they encamped at San Vittorino, a village four miles from Aquila, but near enough for their banners and tents to be seen from the city.

Pius tells us that the people of L'Aquila deserved all this for having turned against the pope. Later, when an earthquake leveled L'Aquila, it confirmed his opinion. "It may be that God will exact still heavier penalties," he mused.[19] Although such depredations fell most directly and

16. Ibid., 138–39; *Comm., Smith,* XI.767; approximately where the Cortile San Damaso now is.

17. Rubenstein, "Pius II," 142–43.

18. Ibid., 140.

19. *Comm.,* Smith, V.398.

heavily on the peasantry, those same fertile fields, oxen, herds, and hens were the source of elite incomes, as well. The endemic and brutal warfare of the quattrocento made itself felt at every socioeconomic level.

In 1461 Federico da Montefeltro's military campaign, trying to suppress rebellion and pacify the countryside around Rome, delayed Pius II's summer *villeggiatura* until July. By that time many cardinals had already left on their own, since, as Pius says, "everyone was afraid of the summer climate" (i.e., plague or malaria, not mere discomfort).[20] Even in July the military situation kept Pius close to Rome. When Pius finally departed for *villeggiatura* in Tivoli on July 21, the infuriated Romans, who lost business whenever the pope left town, broke into riots bordering on open rebellion. Authorities even discovered and thwarted a plot to blow up the Castel Sant'Angelo. The Mantuan ambassador wrote home that Rome was ungovernable, since mildness and severity were equally ineffective.[21]

Pius chose Tivoli as his summer headquarters for strategic reasons. This restive, disaffected town had been eager to open its gates to Piccininio's troops the previous summer. Before Pius arrived the most prominent of his local opponents fled. Pius urged the remainder "to submit calmly to the building of a fortress" in their midst. He built on the site of previous citadels, using stone obtained by demolishing an ancient amphitheater.[22] This massive castle, the Rocca Pia, with two large round towers and two smaller ones added later by Alexander VI, still seems like a hostile presence looming oppressively over the heart of the town.[23]

In spite of the necessity of building a fortress to secure the town, Pius found everything he enjoyed most at Tivoli. Flavio Biondo was there to lead him around to archeological sites—not only the famous villa of the emperor Hadrian, but ruined churches with intricate floor mosaics in the Cosmatesque style of the early thirteenth century.[24] In response to conversations he had had with Federico da Montefeltro, Pius wrote his *De Asia* in Tivoli that summer.[25] The chief attraction for Pius was always natural beauty. Around Tivoli he found "the most delightful green fields," into which he dragged his cardinals to conduct their business. Pius searched out places along the River Aniene, "where they could look down into the translucent water."[26] In the *Commentaries* he describes

20. Ibid., V.392.
21. Von Pastor, *History of the Popes,* 3:115.
22. *Comm.,* Smith, V.394.
23. Rubenstein, "Pius II," 108–9.
24. Ibid., 43.
25. *Comm.,* Smith, V.393.
26. Ibid., V.396.

the whole course of the Aniene as it almost encircles Tivoli, with special attention to gorges and cataracts such as the one at the lower edge of Tivoli, where the water "hurls itself headlong into the deep valley below with increased noise and uproar—and that not with a single leap, but rent and torn by numerous cataracts before it reaches the bottom and rushes on its foaming and complaining course with a din that drowns the human voice."[27]

There was no papal palace in Tivoli, so the pope lodged with the Franciscan friars in their monastery on a high point "where there was a view of Rome, the plain below, the Aniene, and beautiful green orchards, but no other attraction." In fact, he found his accommodations unacceptable. "The house was old and tumble-down, full of rats as big as rabbits, which disturbed the night with their scuttling up and down. The winds too ... were annoying and it was impossible to keep the rain out of the leaky old building which the careless monks had not taken the trouble to repair." In fact, the place was so neglected that Pius took it away from these improvident brothers and gave it to the stricter Observant Franciscans.[28] After Pius's description it is surprising to learn that this tumbledown monastery is the very building that is now renowned as the Villa d'Este. We will return to consider this villa in a later chapter.

If there is a sacred city of *villeggiatura,* it is Tivoli. In antiquity it attracted the Roman emperor Hadrian, who built there the most elaborate villa the Roman world had ever seen. That Hadrian used this enormous complex of buildings, gardens, pools, fountains, and art works for escapist purposes goes without saying, since that is the only function this enormous extravagance, isolated in the countryside, could serve. Pius describes the ruins as more like a "big town" than a residence. Among these broken walls and marbles Pius wrote a meditation on the transience of earthly grandeur that has an inescapable resemblance to the many contemporary meditations on the decay of corpses and the evanescence of human beauty.

> Time has marred everything. The walls once covered with embroidered tapestries and hangings threaded with gold are now clothed with ivy. Briers and brambles have sprung up where purple-robed tribunes sat and queens' chambers are the lairs of serpents. So fleeting are mortal things![29]

27. Ibid., V.395.
28. Ibid., V.397.
29. Ibid., V.396.

Pius's experience of these impressive ruins was quite different from any available today. Gone are the ivy, the briers, and the brambles; today we see partial reconstructions, explanatory signs, special exhibitions, and our fellow tourists. In his day much that we now see was under ground; on the other hand, much more remained in place than exists today. In the sixteenth century, when Pirro Ligorio began systematic excavations on the site, one of his major purposes was to cart away the sculptures and other artistic treasures to the Villa d'Este. Once begun, these depredations continued to the point that there are now over five hundred bits of sculpture from the villa scattered among the museums and collections of Europe.[30]

After Pius had stayed about two months at Tivoli the heat abated, but the trees were still green. Pius then took four cardinals with him and went "for pleasure and refreshment" from Tivoli to the famous monastery of Subiaco.[31] On the first night of this expedition Pius stayed at Vicovaro, where he comments on the Roman ruins and the dramatic site above the gorge of the Aniene. The next day he followed the river to the monastery of San Clemente, where he paused for prayer before lunching at his favorite kind of location, a sparkling spring by the river with the town of Agosta silhouetted against a blue sky on the high cliff above.

> Under the town of Agosta such a head of water bursts forth from the living rock that it furnishes enough power to keep four mills or even more going all the time.... The bottom is covered with shining gravel which in many places is spattered up with a pleasant sound by the bubbling water. The water itself is cold, sweet, and so crystal clear that you can see the very bottom. By this spring the Pope lunched with the cardinals. He took long draughts of the fresh water and the cardinals did the same, enjoying the cold water more than sweet wine.[32]

All the populace of the neighborhood turned out to see the pope, who rewarded them by ordering that all should be fed. After lunch, as the papal caravan continued along the riverbank through level meadowland, peasant boys jumped into the river to catch trout with their bare hands. With every fish retrieved they shouted excitedly, brandished their tro-

30. Benedetta Adembri, *Hadrian's Villa,* trans. Eric De Sena (2000; repr. Milan: Ministero per i Beni e le Attività Culturali, Superintendenza per i Beni Archeologici del Lazio and Electa, 2011), 28 and 48.

31. *Comm.,* Smith, VI.461.

32. Ibid., VI.461–62.

phy aloft, and presented it to the pope's attendants.[33] I was able to find the spring along the Aniene below Agosta; it no longer "bursts forth from the living rock," but flows sedately and unattractively from four pipes at the base of a control structure. It is still a shady, natural place, protected as a small provincial park. Trees overhang the still-crystalline water through which you can see the sparkling pebbles on the bottom. There was not a trout to be seen, or I would have had to round up some local boys to see if they could catch them with their bare hands.

The Romans had also been impressed by the sparkling waters of the Aniene, and, in 272 B.C., shortly after conquering the region, they built the first of four aqueducts that would bring its waters to Rome. To make a pleasure villa for himself Nero dammed the river and turned its natural gorge into three deep lakes, rising like steps one above the other, high into the Simbruini mountains. To provide access to the villa he built a road, the Via Sublacense (from *sub lacus,* "beneath the lakes"), the origin of the name "Subiaco."[34] Pius followed Nero's road, but the dams, lakes, and villa were long vanished. Pius's goal was the monastery built around the "Sacro Speco," the "Holy Cave" where St. Benedict had lived as a hermit for three years shortly after 500 A.D. Benedict's cave pierced the almost perpendicular flank of Mont Taleo, five hundred feet above what was then the surface of Nero's highest lake.[35] Since it was virtually inaccessible, a monk from a monastery a few miles away brought food for the hermit and lowered it to him on a rope. After Benedict ended his solitary meditations and became a leader of monks and nuns, he founded twelve monasteries in the region of the lakes, of which only one, St. Scholastica, named for Benedict's sister and located further down the mountain from the cave, still exists. No one in his right mind would found a monastery on a sheer rock face, but the fame of Benedict's sanctity brought a steady trickle of monks seeking out the holy cave. Finally, in the eleventh century, the abbot of St. Scholastica began to raise buildings for them. Most of the structures we see clinging to the rock today date from the thirteenth and fourteenth centuries; the frescoes that cover almost every inch of the interior except where the bare rock has been preserved were completed by the time of Pius's visit.

The site of the monastery (if we can call it a site) is partly hacked

33. Ibid., VI.462.

34. Ibid., V.395.

35. Benedictine Monks of Subiaco, *The Sanctuary of the Sacred Cave, Subiaco* (Subiaco, Italy: Monastery of St. Benedict, n.d.), 55.

out of the mountain and partly supported upon massive Gothic arches whose foundations reach far down the precipice. It all looks somewhat like a Native American cliff dwelling, though located at a more vertiginous height. The labyrinthine interior, arranged in a series of chapels on many levels connected by staircases, is stuffed with treasures both religious and artistic. There is a portrait of St. Francis of Assisi possibly painted during his life, presumably during a visit he made here for the dedication of the Chapel of St. Gregory.[36] The "Cave of the Shepherds" at the lowest level takes its name from a sermon that Benedict preached there to the rough herdsmen who pastured their animals among the peaks and cliffs. In this cave is a fragment of a fresco showing the Madonna attended by saints dating back to the sixth century in a style echoing mummy portraits from Roman Egypt.[37] Most holy and most moving is the holy cave itself, an irregular cavity of natural stone little bigger than a monk's cell and used by St. Benedict for that purpose. Even the intrusion of an effeminate baroque statue of Benedict rapt before a marble cross cannot erase the sense of holiness in a place that Petrarch called "the threshold of Paradise."[38]

Surprisingly, Pius, usually inspired to eloquence by natural scenery, says almost nothing about the dramatic site at Subiaco. Instead, he writes at length about something rarer—lives of great sanctity. One of the monks was a Portuguese bishop who had resigned his position "to exchange the things of this world for those of Heaven." Aside from this hermit, there were about twenty other monks whose austerity inspired the pope. They slept little, spending the hours stolen from sleep at prayer; they never ate meat and heavily diluted their wine, subsisting only on cabbage, bread, and beans, with eggs as a rare luxury. On this diet, Pius says, they "lived in perfect health to eighty." Furthermore, "their faces are animated; their conversation worthy of reverence. Their one desire is to be dissolved and be with Christ."[39] Pius was not capable of living this kind of life, but he venerated those who could.

The monastery at Subiaco possesses one of the best-preserved of the surviving *Triumphs of Death,* painted on a wall along the "Holy Staircase" leading down from the Chapel of St. Gregory to Our Lady's Chapel. It is fourteenth-century, probably painted not long after the Black Death, since the iconography was still evolving. Death is a female *transi*

36. Ibid., 41.

37. Ibid., 52–53.

38. Ibid., 55.

39. *Comm.,* Smith, VI.462–64.

Figure 9.3. The Monastery of the Holy Cave (Sacro Speco) at Subiaco. Photograph from Luke Ashworth-Sides.

Figure 9.4. Sienese School. Fresco, fourteenth century. *The Triumph of Death* at the Monastery of the Holy Cave, Subiaco. Photograph from Alfredo Dagli Orti/Art Archive at Art Resource, New York.

with long hair and black pupils who rides an all-too-lively horse galloping across a ground paved with the corpses. Death is doubly armed: in her left hand she wields her scythe over the corpses trampled under her horse's hoofs; with the right, she plunges her sword into the neck of an elegantly dressed courtier. The artist is skilled; the eyes of the victim, who does not yet realize what has happened to him, have just gone slightly heavy-lidded and will soon glaze over. A companion speaking with him shows the first hint of concern for his doomed friend. The Subiaco artist was probably Sienese; a similar scene once existed near Siena itself in the Church of San Francesco at Lucignano.[40] On the opposite wall of the holy stair is another morbid theme, the Three Living and the Three Dead. St. Macarius the Hermit displays to three splendidly dressed youths three corpses, one fresh, one burst open revealing the rotting intestines, and the third a skeleton barely covered with skin. Lower down is a *Slaughter of the Innocents,* hardly more cheerful than its companions. After the visit to Subiaco, Pius returned to Tivoli (not without another luncheon beside "a copious and very clear spring") and only made it back to Rome in early October.[41]

Ferrante was still hanging on in Naples, but the war was, as Pius said, "a seven-headed monster." "If Ferrante succeeds in winning one battle," Pius wrote, "the enemy are seven times victorious."[42] Jean of Calabria's successes had brought Calabria, Apulia, and Abruzzi into open revolt. Worse still for Pius were the successes of Sigismondo Malatesta, who had captured the papal city of Mondavio and was besieging Sinigaglia. Pius had sent an army of five thousand under Bartolomeo Vitelleschi, bishop of Corneto, but Sigismondo marched by night and caught the papal forces unaware at sunrise, utterly defeating them and capturing most of their baggage and three hundred horsemen.[43] In frustration, Pius turned from temporal weapons to spiritual ones. He had already excommunicated Sigismondo, but now Pius took a step unique in papal history. If canonization by the pope could enroll saints in the ranks of the blessed, could he not also send the likes of Sigismondo to hell—even while he still lived? Shortly after Christmas Pius issued this remarkable decree:

> No mortal heretofore has descended into hell with the ceremony of canonization. Sigismondo shall be the first deemed worthy of such honor. By an

40. Tenenti, *Il senso della morte,* 438.
41. *Comm.,* Smith, VI.465.
42. Quoted in Ady, *Pius II,* 187.
43. *Comm.,* Smith, V.403–4.

> edict of the pope, he shall be enrolled in the company of hell as a comrade of the devils and the damned. Nor shall we wait for his death ... since he has left no hope of his conversion. While still living he shall be condemned to Orcus and perhaps while still living he shall be hurled into the flames.[44]

No pope has ever followed this precedent of formal damnation of the living—though not for lack of well-qualified candidates. We get a queasy feeling that Pius was stepping across a boundary here, motivated more by personal vendetta than by sober ecclesiastical judgment.

As events in Italy seemed to be sliding into an abyss, Pius nevertheless achieved one of his major objectives in France: the repeal of the Pragmatic Sanction of Bourges. In July 1461 Charles VII of France died and was succeeded by his shrewd and ruthless son, Louis XI, whose skillful practice of *realpolitik* would earn him the nickname of "the Spider King." In order to pry Pius away from Ferrante and attach him to King René, Louis was ready to sacrifice the Pragmatic Sanction. In return, Pius created a new cardinal in December, Jean de Jouffroy, bishop of Arras, the chief negotiator of the repeal. Jouffroy had been a close associate of Louis' before he became king, and Louis had requested his elevation. In spite of warnings from the other cardinals, Pius felt that his promotion was a political necessity. As it turned out, Jouffroy had played his cards deviously. During all the negotiation over the Pragmatic Sanction, Jouffroy never revealed to Pius that Louis expected the pope to abandon Ferrante as part of the deal. Only after his cardinal's hat was firmly on his brow did he disclose this royal assumption. His revelation put Pius in a most awkward position. A few months earlier, in order to secure the pope's wavering support, Ferrante had bestowed his illegitimate daughter as a bride for the pope's nephew Antonio and set him up as Duke of Amalfi. After that it was all but impossible for Pius to yield to Louis' demands; he could only delay his definitive refusal for a few months on the excuse that he was waiting for an official French embassy to deliver a formal request.

Meanwhile, on April 12, 1462, the day after Palm Sunday, Pius staged a great pageant in Rome to receive the reputed head of the Apostle Andrew and install it in St. Peter's. This precious relic was a gift from Thomas Paleologus, Despot of Morea and brother of the last Byzantine emperor, Constantine XI. In 1460 the Turks had overrun Thomas's little state in the Peleponnesus, the last bit of independent Byzantine ter-

44. Ibid., V.375–76.

ritory. In escaping from the Turkish tide, Thomas paused long enough at Patras to grab the sacred head of St Andrew, who had been martyred there, to save it from the infidel.[45] Pius wrote to Thomas at once, insisting that such an important relic must be at Rome with the bones of Andrew's brother Peter and in the custody of the pope. If Thomas brought it to Rome he could expect to live in exile as befitted a prince. Thomas obeyed this summons and arrived at Ancona with the relic in 1461. It was not until the following year that political conditions in Rome were stable enough for the kind of ceremony Pius envisaged; in the interim the relic stayed in the citadel at Narni.[46] Pius conceived of the ceremony as a great act of propaganda for the crusade. The Congress at Mantua had conspicuously failed to elicit any groundswell of crusading fervor. Now Pius planned a paroxysm of pageantry to work up religious devotion combined with fear and hatred against the Turks.[47] To maximize the crowd, Pius offered plenary remission of sins to everyone who attended the festivities.[48]

For the reception of the relic Pius had a platform built in the meadows across the Milvian Bridge from the city, in the fields where Constantine had been victorious in 312 with the initials of Christ on his men's shields, thus convincing him to legalize Christianity. Here, Cardinal Bessarion, who had fetched the relic from Narni, brought it to the pope. An immense crowd watched in silence as the head was lifted from its reliquary. Then, "Bessarion in tears, taking the sacred head of the Apostle, offered it to the weeping Pope." Pius, kneeling—which must have been difficult and painful, as he had suffered a violent attack of gout over the winter—said a prayer of welcome that he said "drew tears from all eyes."[49] Pius then carried the head in his own hands into the city, escorted by cardinals, bishops, and other clergy, all carrying palm branches. They went only as far as the church of Santa Maria del Popolo, where the pope spent the night with the relic. On both that night and the previous one there had been torrential rains, but the weather miraculously (so Pius believed) cleared for each day's ceremonies.

The next day pope, cardinals, bishops, abbots, the Senate of Rome, ambassadors, and anyone else of importance who could be found were to walk in procession for two miles on a circuitous route through the city from Santa Maria del Popolo to St. Peter's. Everyone naturally as-

45. Von Pastor, *History of the Popes,* 3:249.
46. *Comm.*, Smith, VIII.524.
47. Rubenstein, "Pius II," 232–33.
48. Ibid., 232–33.
49. *Comm.*, Smith, VIII.527–28.

sumed that the ecclesiastical dignitaries would ride in this procession. "This however did not please the Pope," since he did not want it to appear "as if the priests failed in devotion or paid less reverence to the divine Apostle. He therefore ordered that all should go on foot and do honor to the sacred head by their own exertions and earn indulgences." Those who were physically incapable of making the trek could ride by the back ways but should not be seen in the procession. A few took advantage of this alternative, but most, even those who were old and ill, found strength to make the journey. The pope, however, was carried in his litter. Pius greatly praised the piety of these frail, elderly men who walked the muddy streets.

> It was a fine and impressive sight to see those aged men walking through the slippery mud with palms in their hands and mitres on their white hair, robed in priestly vestments, never lifting their eyes from the ground but praying and invoking the Divine Mercy upon the people. Some who had been reared in luxury and had scarcely been able to go a hundred feet except on horseback, on that day, weighed down as they were with their sacred robes, easily accomplished two miles through mud and water.[50]

These tributes strike a somewhat sour note, since Pius did not imitate these other lame and elderly men. In mitigation, we should remember that Pius's infirmities had originated with his ten-mile walk through snow in fulfillment of a pious vow.

According to Pius, the procession was so long that the front of it had reached St. Peter's before he himself had started out. Then, carried in his golden chair and holding the sacred head, Pius passed among crowds so dense that soldiers had to use cudgels to clear the way. The route wound through the city to allow as many people as possible to see the relic and admire the procession. From Santa Maria del Popolo at the northern edge of the city the procession plunged southward, "through the narrow streets and high buildings" to the Pantheon in the center of the inhabited core of Rome; then, turning northwest, it wound its way past San Eustachio, the Campo de' Fiori, and San Lorenzo in Damaso to the Ponte Sant'Angelo, where it crossed the Tiber and passed through the Borgo to St. Peter's.[51] Along the way canopies and branches hung across the streets to shade them. Tapestries and lavishly embroidered

50. Ibid., VIII.531–32.

51. Ibid., VIII.534; Rubenstein, "Pius II," 238–39.

cloths smothered the house fronts, and everyone who had fine paintings or statues displayed them outdoors. In the windows women wearing their finest clothes held candles and prayed. Bonfires of fragrant herbs and branches supplemented the scent of incense rising from the many altars. Children dressed as angels sang, and "there was no instrument that might not be heard." The cardinals had decorated their own residences with all the magnificence they could muster. Alain de Coëtivy, Cardinal of Avignon, hung the square in front of his house with tapestries imported from Arras. In the center of the square under a canopy of cloth of gold, he erected an altar on which were burning varied perfumes. Rodrigo Borgia, always excelling at display, had hung tapestries on all sides of the piazza next to his "huge, towering house" and roofed it over with "a lofty canopy from which were suspended many and various marvels"—which, unfortunately, Pius does not describe. The effect, he tells us, was that of "a kind of park full of sweet songs and sounds, or a great palace gleaming with gold such as they say Nero's palace was." Among the tapestries, the buildings displayed the texts of "many poems recently composed by great geniuses, which set forth ... praises of the divine Apostle and eulogies of Pope Pius."[52]

Pius himself had worked to transform the great piazza in front of St. Peter's not merely with the temporary trappings of the festival, but with permanent constructions. The reception of St. Andrew's head gave Pius the original impetus, but his ambitious architectural projects in and around the basilica and piazza of St. Peter's continued for the rest of his reign. Compared to the audacious but unrealized plans of Nicholas V, Pius's projects were merely repairs and replacements of existing pieces of the Vatican's architectural puzzle. Replacing Constantine's ruinous steps leading to the atrium through which visitors entered St. Peter's, Pius built new steps of gleaming marble, broader and more numerous than Constantine's, with colossal statues of St. Peter and St. Paul flanking them.[53] In time for the reception of St. Andrew's head he had cleared the piazza of booths, houses, and other obstructions. To the right of the atrium was the entrance to the Vatican Palace, which Pius was rebuilding with a new tower and staircase.[54] On the left of the atrium Pius had begun a benediction loggia from which the pope would be able to bless the crowds in the square. When the bearers of his chair brought Pius

52. *Comm.*, Smith, VIII.534–36.
53. Rubenstein, "Pius II," 165–67 and 169–70.
54. Ibid., 116.

to the top of his new staircase, Pius displayed the head of the apostle and blessed the crowd. His eyes lighted upon the colossal new statue of St. Peter, probably still unfinished. The thought of bringing the brothers Peter and Andrew together after fourteen centuries of separation brought tears to the pope's eyes.[55]

As was common in medieval churches, St. Peter's had gradually filled with tombs, monuments, and small chapels, proliferating in the nave and aisles during the 1132 years since Constantine had built the basilica. In compliance with Alberti's opinion that the centers of churches should be free of encumbrances, Pius had ordered them all swept away.[56] In theory, they were placed along the walls, but at least some must have been lost in the process. In spite of this drastic clearing, the immense church could hardly contain the dense crowd of worshippers, bearing lighted candles, who crammed inside. It took soldiers brandishing their swords to force a way for the pope's chair through the devout mob. Overhead, the flickering lights of great candelabra and innumerable lesser lamps made darkness retreat into the ancient beams and rafters above. The thick air must have been misty with smoke, incense, and human breath. "All this," Pius tells us, "was made still more marvelous by the music of the organ and the singing of the clergy." When the precious head was placed under the altar with the bodies of Andrew's fellow apostles, Peter and Paul, all the prelates and distinguished persons passed by and kissed it. After that came a series of orations, climaxed by Bessarion calling for a crusade. There was then a Mass and another papal blessing of the crowds. Finally, the pope took up the holy relic once more and brought it to the Castel Sant'Angelo for safekeeping until a permanent chapel could be built for it.[57] Pius built this chapel in the first bay of the far left aisle of St. Peter's at a cost of 1,651 florins.[58] From a drawing and descriptions we know that it had a two-tiered tabernacle of simple early Renaissance design, with an altar at the lower level and above it the chamber displaying the head.[59]

The later history of the head of St. Andrew is an anticlimax after the fervor of the throngs in 1462. The chapel of St. Andrew disappeared along with the rest of Constantine's ancient basilica, demolished in stages during the sixteenth century to make way for the gargantuan structure we know today. In the new St. Peter's the head of St. Andrew

55. Ibid., 160; *Comm.*, Smith, VIII.536.
56. Rubenstein, "Pius II," 240.
57. *Comm.*, Smith, VIII.536–42.
58. Rubenstein, "Pius II," 244.
59. For a complete description see ibid., 241–42 and fig. 56.

was enshrined in one of the four central piers supporting the enormous dome. In 1629–1633 the sculptor François Duquesnoy filled the niche in this pier with a baroque statue of St. Andrew embracing the diagonally oriented cross on which tradition says he was martyred. The head, however, is no longer there. In an ecumenical gesture Pope Paul VI in 1964 returned it to the Greek town of Patras, site of Andrew's martyrdom, from which Thomas Paleologus had rescued it five centuries before.

10

A Room of One's Own

IN JUNE OF 1461, while warfare in the surrounding districts kept Pius locked inside Rome, he took the action that has probably affected ordinary Catholics more than anything else he did—he raised a maiden from Siena, Catherine Benincasa, to the rank of sainthood. Today prayers arise to her every day, and, along with St. Francis of Assisi, she is the patron saint of Italy. In the short term Pius not only honored his beloved Siena and inaugurated a stream of pilgrim-tourists that still flows today, he also scored a public relations triumph for all his favorite causes: the crusade, papal authority, church reform, keeping the papacy in Rome, even the status of nobles in Siena—all causes that Catherine had conspicuously supported. He also gave his blessing to the extreme forms of piety that Catherine practiced and that, like most of his contemporaries, he respected deeply, even though he never contemplated adopting them personally.

Palm Sunday coincided with the Feast of the Annunciation on the day when Catherine and her short-lived twin sister were born in 1347, five months before the Black Death attacked Siena and probably (though it is undocumented) winnowed out some of her twenty-three brothers and sisters.[1] Her father, Jacopo, was a prosperous dyer with a home and shop on the steep street that leads from the enormous hilltop church of San Domenico down to the Fontebranda, one of Siena's largest water sources.[2] Her family belonged to the Dodici faction and class, a group of prosperous but non-noble merchants that held power in Siena between the noble revolts of 1355 and 1368. Her brothers flourished and even

1. Her parents had one more child after her—a total of twenty-five; Lodovico Ferretti, *Saint Catherine of Siena* (Siena: Edizioni Cantagalli, 1996), 7.

2. Schevill, *Siena,* 259.

opened a branch of their business in Florence before another Sienese revolution in 1371 led to attacks on Dodici properties, exclusion from office, and bankruptcy—such was security in trecento Italy.[3]

But Catherine always sought her security in another world. When she was six she had a vision of Christ blessing her from his heavenly throne.[4] After that, nothing her family could do would dissuade her from devoting herself entirely to Christ, excluding all earthly ties and finding a secret place in the house in which to scourge herself.[5] Her father gave in to her practices only after he saw a dove hovering over her head while she prayed.[6] For the next six or seven years she made her little room in her parent's house a monastic cell, where she slept on wooden planks, and which she left only to climb the hill for Mass at San Domenico.[7] Sometime during this period she joined a group of pious women, mostly widows, whom the Sienese called *mantellate* because of the black mantles they wore. The *mantellate* led a monastic life in their own homes under the direction of the friars at San Domenico. It was controversial for Catherine to join them, since she was a young virgin, not a widow.[8] "She's a woman," her critics carped; "Why doesn't she stay in her cell if it's God she wants to serve?"[9]

Catherine's asceticism has a manic quality, repellent to modern tastes but typical of the plague era and certainly respected by Pius II. When she was a teenager, her mother, trying to "cure" her of her piety, took her to hot springs at Vignone, where Catherine scalded herself in steaming waters while contemplating the pains of purgatory.[10] She had a "holy hatred" for her body and an insatiable appetite for pain. "O Eternal Trinity!" she begged, "furnace and abyss of Charity! Dispel on the instant this cloud, my body!"[11] To be free of the body's yoke, she beat herself, first with ropes and later with chains, three times a day, once for the living, once for the dead, and once for herself.[12] Each of these beatings lasted

3. Luongo, *Saintly Politics,* 31, 45–48.

4. Raymond of Capua, *The Life of Catherine of Siena,* ed., trans. Conleth Kearns (Wilmington, Del.: Michael Glazer, 1980), 29; Ferretti, *Saint Catherine of Siena,* 8.

5. Raymond, *Life of Catherine,* 30 and 34–35.

6. Raymond, *Life of Catherine,* 49; Luongo, *Saintly Politics,* 33.

7. Raymond, *Life of Catherine,* 61 and 76; Luongo, *Saintly Politics,* 33.

8. Luongo, *Saintly Politics,* 38–39.

9. Raymond, *Life of Catherine,* 339 and 365.

10. Ibid., 64; Ferretti, *Saint Catherine of Siena,* 16.

11. Raymond, *Life of Catherine,* 330.

12. Richard Kieckhefer, *Unquiet Souls: Fourteenth Century Saints and their Religious Milieu* (Chicago: University of Chicago Press, 1984), 139 and 148.

well over an hour and left blood streaming down to her feet.[13] She often asserted that suffering refreshed and strengthened her. Were it not for pain and suffering, she said, "she would have found it well nigh unbearable to remain on here in the body; but when she had these to bear, she was more than willing to wait longer for her crown in heaven."[14] Food disgusted her. She subsisted most of her adult life on nothing but uncooked vegetables and water, but the legend that she lived only on wafers consumed at Holy Communion is unfounded.[15]

Dominican piety, like that of all the mendicant orders, required service to the community; Catherine busied herself at Siena's hospitals and among the lepers at San Lazaro outside the city.[16] When plagues visited Siena, Catherine tended the sick abandoned by others. In the plague of 1374 she cured, among others, the rector of a hospital, a saintly hermit, and Raymond of Capua, her confessor and biographer. In that plague she herself lost two brothers, a sister, and eight nieces and nephews, whom she buried with her own hands.[17] Once, when tending a patient, she became nauseated by the stench of a festering cancer, but she overcame this revulsion by drinking the fluid from the sore. She told Raymond of Capua that Christ rewarded her by allowing her to drink also from the wound in his side.[18]

Visions of Christ were not unusual for Catherine, who often went into trance-like ecstasy during her prayers and after taking Communion. She could barely get through a Pater Noster before she went rigid, remaining immobile and insensible for hours.[19] Once in a while she spoke during such an ecstasy, murmuring things like "O love, O love, You are the sweetest thing there is, you allow us to have a foretaste of the good and joyous things that we hope to enjoy more fully without ever being satiated in eternal life."[20] For a period near the end of her life she dictated the book known as her *Dialogue* while she was in such states of ecstasy.[21] A defining moment for Catherine came at age twenty, when, like her name-saint, Catherine of Alexandria, she contracted a mystical marriage with Christ himself. David played the harp

13. Raymond, *Life of Catherine,* 58.

14. Ibid., 97.

15. Ibid., 43 and 55.

16. Ferretti, *Saint Catherine of Siena,* 23.

17. Raymond, *Life of Catherine,* 238–39, 240, 245, 232–33, 252; Luongo, *Saintly Politics,* 102–3.

18. Raymond, *Life of Catherine,* 162–63, 155; Luongo, *Saintly Politics,* 102–3.

19. Raymond, *Life of Catherine,* 105.

20. Ferretti, *Saint Catherine of Siena,* 97–98.

21. Raymond, *Life of Catherine,* 309.

and saints John, Paul, and Dominic were witnesses as the Blessed Virgin placed Catherine's hand in Christ's and he slipped a golden, jeweled ring on her finger.[22] She asked "one little request of Christ: that she be allowed to share in all his sufferings, and that she be united with him on earth through his passion since she could not yet be united with him in heaven."[23] Raymond of Capua later witnessed Christ's answer to her prayer when the stigmata came to her from a crucifix in Pisa as rays of light, etching the five wounds of Christ into Catherine's body, causing such pain that she said it was another miracle that she survived.[24] Catherine's visions and asceticism made her an authoritative figure in Siena and beyond, attracting around her a hundred or more devoted followers, whom she called her "family." Most of them were Sienese youths from prominent and noble families, including Gabriele di Davino Piccolomini and others with ties to Pius's family.[25]

Although she was illiterate, Catherine dictated a prodigious correspondence—over 380 surviving letters.[26] Like Petrarch's letters, they were more public than private, and many were probably never sent to their putative addressees.[27] Even before she took an active political role, letters had made her views known throughout Italy and sometimes beyond. Today Catherine's letters are still moving to read; informal, full of affection for her correspondents (she calls the pope *babbo,* "daddy"), centered on rejection of self and love for God and neighbor.[28] For her contemporaries she set forth a clear ecclesiastical and political agenda: the clergy must reform their lives; the pope must return from Avignon to Rome and transform the mercenary soldiers devastating Italy into crusaders to win back the Holy Land. She even sent a letter to the hard-bitten English *condottiere* John Hawkwood, whom she addressed as "her sweet brother in Christ," recruiting him for the crusade, saying, "In order to serve the Devil, you have until now endured hardships and worries ... from this moment on, I want you to change your ways and take up the cause and Cross of Christ.... You who are so fond of wars and combat, stop afflicting poor Christians, for it is an offense against God, and go fight against those others!"[29]

22. Raymond, *Life of Catherine,* 107; Kieckhefer, *Unquiet Souls,* 158.
23. Raymond, *Life of Catherine,* 197; Kieckhefer, *Unquiet Souls,* 95.
24. Raymond, *Life of Catherine,* 186; Kieckhefer, *Unquiet Souls,* 95.
25. Luongo, *Saintly Politics,* 140.
26. Ibid., 2.
27. Ibid., 77.
28. Ibid., 72–73.
29. Ferretti, *Saint Catherine of Siena,* 60–63.

Although Pius certainly revered Catherine for her devotional, ascetic, and mystical practices, it was probably her political interventions that he hoped people would remember as he canonized her. Pope Gregory XI (r. 1370–1378), though a Frenchman, was determined to bring the papacy from Avignon back to Rome and had already issued bulls seeking to begin a crusade.[30] What he needed was an independent spokesman of undoubted sanctity to promote this agenda. He had been using an influential holy woman, St. Birgitta of Sweden, founder of the Bridgettine Order, who advocated clerical reform and the return to Rome. After Birgitta's death in 1373 Catherine was summoned to attend the General Chapter of the Dominican Order in Florence, where she was apparently vetted for the role of Birgitta's successor. Raymond of Capua, an important ecclesiastical statesman, later to become the head of the Dominican order, was assigned as her confessor, and she began to undertake political missions for the pope.[31]

Florence, alarmed at the prospect of a pope returning to Rome and erecting a new political power on her frontiers, was organizing a league of cities to oppose Pope Gregory in what would soon become "the War of the Eight Saints" (1375–1378). Catherine's first overtly political assignment was to go to Lucca, a city of divided loyalties, to persuade its leaders to support the pope.[32] Alongside the savage suppression of antipapal rebellions in the Papal States by Robert of Geneva, "the butcher of Cesena," the war was waged as a propaganda campaign as well as a military one. Florence's spokesman was no less than her eloquent chancellor, Coluccio Salutati. Against Salutati's brilliant Latin rhetoric the pope put forward an illiterate girl. In composing persuasive letters, the propaganda medium of the day, she would prove every bit a match for the learned chancellor.[33] Florence was disunited during this struggle; the bulk of the population supported the war, led by the committee of eight who directed the military effort (the "Eight Saints" for whom the war is named). But Gregory imposed an interdict on the city, shutting down all its churches and allowing foreign rulers to seize Florentine goods at will. The mercantile elite, now eager for peace, besought Catherine to intercede with Pope Gregory.[34] This Catherine promised to do in Avignon, where she was going to persuade Gregory that the return to Rome could no longer be delayed.

30. Ibid., 60.

31. Luongo, *Saintly Politics,* 58.

32. Ferretti, *Saint Catherine of Siena,* 51.

33. Luongo, *Saintly Politics,* 79.

34. Ibid., 173–74.

Gregory, of course, needed no convincing; what he needed was a storyline in which he responded to divine persuasions delivered by a recognized messenger of God such as Catherine. Catherine remained in Avignon until November 1376, during which time she persuaded the French king's brother, Louis of Anjou, to lead the projected crusade. The pope left Avignon in September, entering Rome on January 17, 1377. By that time Robert of Geneva, along with Hawkwood, who now served the pope, had defeated Florence and her allies (including Siena) and captured Bologna, bringing the war to an end.[35] Catherine went to Florence as a mediator, where a mob of assassins attempted to murder her.

As we have already seen, the death of Gregory XI two years after he returned to Rome was followed by the election of Urban VI, which led to schism in the church. The brutal Robert of Geneva became the antipope "Clement VII" and returned to Avignon. The schism was devastating to Catherine, who had worked so hard to get the church past the disgrace of Avignon only to see it fall into a new, even more humiliating crisis. She never doubted the legitimacy of Urban VI and threw herself into a frenzy of letter writing on his behalf. She joined him in Rome, where his enemies held the Castel Sant'Angelo. As Urban himself said, "This little lady confounds us! We are afraid and she is fearless."[36] She further intensified her fasts and rigors, which were now undermining her strength. "Normal sweat," she said, "is not enough to satisfy the holy and ardent desire I feel ... I want to sweat blood!"[37] In the months of her final illness, each new pain or stage in her decline caused her to "raise her eyes and heart to God, thanking him for the favor."[38] She died in Rome on April 29, 1380, at the age of only thirty-three. Raymond of Capua, now master general of the Dominican Order, supervised her burial in the church of Santa Maria Sopra Minerva in Rome, only blocks from the house where she died; but he detached her head (and one of her fingers, which went to a devoted follower) and sent it back to Siena, where her eighty-year-old mother watched it being installed in the church of San Domenico.[39] Visitors can see her there today, face to face, her head ensconced in a marble tabernacle. The lower part of her face is disfigured by the shrinking of the lips from around the teeth, but the upper part retains a look of youthful innocence and serenity.

35. Ibid., 171n47.

36. Ferretti, *Saint Catherine of Siena,* 110.

37. Ibid., 112.

38. Kieckhefer, *Unquiet Souls,* 63.

39. Ferretti, *Saint Catherine of Siena,* 143.

As the ceremonies of Catherine's canonization unfolded within the safety of Rome's walls, Federico da Montefeltro was leading his soldiers in a campaign to secure the surrounding country from the pope's enemies. The soldier-prince Federico seems to be a complete contrast to the ascetic Catherine; yet they have something important in common. Each of them created a tiny, protected spot from which they could escape the everyday world. Any Christian who bravely and frankly confronted a God who treated mankind the way he seemed to be treating trecento and quattrocento Italians would rationally conclude, as Catherine did, that God demanded total submission, the embrace of suffering, and the complete rejection of this world. It would be impossible to reject the world completely without some "poky little box," as Raymond of Capua described her cell, where the soul could hide from the world around it. Most people at some level recognized this bitter truth, yet recoiled at a life of self-flagellation in a barren cell. All that such people could do was to hide *both from reality and from God.* Those hiding from reality and God needed a protected refuge just as much as the ascetics who were hiding *with* God from the world. Such an asylum was Federico's tiny *studiolo* in his palace at Urbino. The cell of the fourteenth-century saint, the scene of religious ecstasy and self-inflicted pain, and the cell of the soldier-prince, where he read the ancient classics or sang and played the lute amidst priceless works of art—each served its owner as a sanctuary, whether at the religious, morbid, realistic pole of the plague-era mentality or at the escapist, idealist, fantasy pole. Each enabled its inmate to shut out a clamorous, unstable, anxiety-ridden world that sensitive minds could never embrace. We have seen that Catherine's hours of ecstasy did not prevent her from playing an active role in the sordid politics of her time. Federico's withdrawal also proved compatible with a brilliant political and military career. Occasionally the parallel between ascetic seclusion and secular *studioli* was noticed by contemporaries; a notary writing to the merchant Francesco Datini in 1395 said, "I remain alone at home, in bed and in my study, as happy as the good hermits are on the mountain, and I feel no winds either from left or right."[40]

Federico da Montefeltro, an illegitimate scion of the house that ruled the insignificant hill town of Urbino, seized power in Urbino after the particularly grizzly murder of its previous lord in 1444.[41] Sigismondo

40. Dora Thornton, *The Scholar in His Study: Ownership and Experience in Renaissance Italy* (New Haven and London: Yale University Press, 1997), 11.

41. Some accounts said that Oddantonio da Montefeltro's killers cut off his sexual

Malatesta, who coveted the territory, probably engineered the murder, but it was Federico who claimed the prize, inaugurating the long struggle between these two ambitious men.[42] Urbino, under Federico da Montefeltro and his son Guidobaldo, became one of the important artistic centers of Italy entirely because of its rulers' desire to create a protected dreamworld to enjoy between military campaigns. Federico made his palace at Urbino a walled, sheltered paradise, a *hortus conclusus* that Castiglione described as "a city in the form of a palace."[43] It was the prototype of a new kind of elite residence that not only provided comfortable accommodations and grandeur but also supplied a kaleidoscope of delights in a protected world of its own. Urbino and its Ducal Palace (Federico did not get the title of "Duke" until 1474) sit on a high hill; the gardens, terraces, and loggias of the palace open onto splendid views over the countryside. Since only a few of the earliest rooms of the building have windows facing the city streets, its inhabitants could almost forget the little town, living in a self-contained world of splendid halls and sheltered gardens with their own theater, library, and chapels. Federico and his beloved wife, Battista Sforza, lived in still more private rooms with their own *giardino segreto* ("secret garden").[44] In the midst of these private rooms Federico had his yet more secluded sanctum, his *studiolo,* sealed away even from the rest of his personal apartment.

For centuries merchants, princes, scholars, and clerics had possessed small private rooms where they kept their important papers and valuables and from which they conducted their business.[45] This business use, however, made these earlier rooms places of engagement, not retreat. In the quattrocento these rooms began to withdraw from the world; in the first phase the *studiolo* became, as its name implies, a place well stocked with books by ancient authors used for reading and study. In *Della famiglia* Alberti emphasized the privacy of the *studiolo* by having one of his speakers insist that papers kept there were "almost like sacred and re-

---

organs and stuffed them in his mouth; Robert Kirkbride, *Architecture and Memory: The Renaissance Studioli of Federico de Montefeltro* (New York: Columbia University Press, 2008), 32n9.

42. Ibid., 13 and 32n9.

43. Georgina Masson, *Italian Villas and Palaces* (New York: Harry N. Abrams, 1959), 149; Count Baldesar Castiglione, *The Book of the Courtier,* trans. Leonard Eckstein Opdycke (New York: Horace Liveright, 1929), 1:9.

44. Pasquale Rotondo, *The Ducal Palace of Urbino: Its Architecture and Decoration* (New York: Transatlantic Arts, 1969), 5–6.

45. Stephen J. Campbell, *The Cabinet of Eros: Renaissance Mythological Painting and the Studiolo of Isabella d'Este* (New Haven and London: Yale University Press, 2004), 31.

Figure 10.1. The *studiolo* of Federico da Montefeltro in the ducal palace in Urbino. Photograph from Alinari/Art Resource, New York.

ligious objects" and that his wife was not allowed to enter, even in his company.[46] In this case the "sacred" papers seem to have been business documents. But in a later writing, the *Profugiorum ab aerumna,* Alberti visualizes another stage of inwardness, almost a sensory-deprivation chamber. "So from day to day we will devote every effort to live free of every anguish, shutting out and cutting off access to the perturbations so that they will find every entrance closed and every window barred through which they might get into our minds."[47]

Federico's palace at Urbino contained one of the greatest libraries of the age, but it was on the floor below the *studiolo,* which had only enough shelf space for a few choice volumes. The *studiolo* occupies less than 160 square feet squeezed between Federico's bedchamber and his *Sala d'Udienze* (audience and council chamber), with a direct door only to the bedroom. To reach it from the *Sala d'Udienze* the few invited guests had to pass through a small vestibule that opened onto a loggia with sweeping views across the countryside. Federico could leave the door to this passage open, receiving light and fresh air (though not the view) in his *studiolo.* Since this is the way modern visitors see the room, they might not realize that, with doors closed, this tiny chamber would have the effect of a sealed capsule, with only a high window above the door providing indirect light from the loggia. In fact, when the doors are closed, they disappear, camouflaged in the continuous wooden marquetry that covers the lower half of the walls. An inmate can almost feel that there *is* no outside world! Some Renaissance *studioli* had no windows at all; we must, therefore, assume that this claustrophobic feeling was desirable.[48] Federico must have sought it: in the older wing of the palace where Federico lived before the later ducal apartments were built, his former bedroom still contains a square compartment, eleven feet on a side, more a large piece of furniture than a room (it is not attached to the walls), which served as his private alcove.[49] Such furniture-like rooms-within-rooms used as private studies are well documented throughout the Renaissance, but few examples survive.[50]

Two rows of portraits line the upper walls of the Urbino *studiolo,* one

46. Alberti, *The Family,* 209.

47. Quoted in Campbell, *Cabinet of Eros,* 37.

48. Kirkbride, *Architecture and Memory,* 11.

49. Paolo dal Pogetto, *Guide to the Galleria Nazionale delle Marche in the Ducal Palace at Urbino* (Urbino: Gebart Srl, 2007), 24–25.

50. Thornton, *Scholar,* 33ff, 53–54, 74.

depicting great minds from the past, the other portraying contemporaries, Pius II among them. But the source of the Urbino *studiolo*'s fame is the *trompe l'oeil* paneling on the lower half of the walls. Using only the inlay of variously colored natural woods, the artist gives the pictorial illusion that the room is surrounded by cabinets, some open, some closed, others merely ajar. A bench seems to run around the room, though some of the seats are raised, and there would be little room to sit among the objects that seem to litter the surfaces. Either tucked into open cabinets or strewn upon the fictional benches we see books, musical instruments, musical scores, the duke's heraldic emblems, and scientific instruments, such as an armillary sphere and an astrolabe.[51] Not only the perspective, but the "sparkling" of glass and metal objects challenges us—dares us—to deny their reality.[52] From the hourglass that will soon need turning and the burning candle's drippings, we might deduce that Federico has spent most of an hour at his desk but has just now stepped out. Perhaps there was a musical party the previous night, since ten of the fourteen instruments depicted have been casually left out on the benches. Two spoons are still in an open container of candied fruit, as if left over from the evening's refreshments.[53] To add to the confusion of the fictional and the real, five of the intarsia panels imitate paintings. One of these shows a view over the countryside seen through the arches of a loggia—echoing the real view from the real loggia just a few steps outside the room. In the foreground of this picture are a basket of fruit and a life-sized squirrel eating a nut. We do not know whether we should interpret the squirrel and basket as part of the picture of the loggia or as further examples of illusionistic "objects" like the others that we see all over the room.

Fascinated by these deceptions, the visitor is probably too preoccupied to notice the most significant illusion of all. We stand in the midst of a magnificently equipped *studiolo,* full of objects that reveal the owner's mind and interests and cater to all his needs. Yet this marvelously equipped room contains nothing for *actual* use except a fold-down desk (which we do not see) and space for a handful of books. We can only assume that there must have been chairs in the middle of the room, since the benches surrounding it are illusory. The artist was obviously engaging Federico and anyone he admitted to his sanctum in a mind game, played on several levels and designed to engross attention

51. Campbell, *Cabinet of Eros,* 42–43.
52. Kirkbride, *Architecture and Memory,* 26.
53. Ibid., 16.

for long periods. Robert Kirkbride, who has studied this room, wrote that "it is swiftly apparent that a full reading . . . , were it possible, would exhaust even the most rapacious observer. Clearly, such *studioli* were intended for slow and pleasurable digestion."[54] In fact "slow and pleasurable digestion" is the *only* activity for which Federico's *studiolo* is actually equipped—its functions are entirely mental and presumably therapeutic. It must have been effective, since Federico's son Guidobaldo had another version made for his palace at Gubbio, now installed at the Metropolitan Museum in New York.[55]

The lack of furnishings (other than fictional ones) in Federico's *studiolo* is not typical; most *studiolo* owners filled them with collections of jewels, books, and *objets d'art.* The constant addition of new decorations and collectables enhanced the pleasurable digestion of a *studiolo* and helped it to occupy the owner's leisured attention for a lifetime. When young Galeazzo Maria Sforza met Pius II in Florence on the way to the Congress of Mantua, he brought with him the architect Filarete (Antonio Averlino, c. 1400–1469). From this visit Filerete has left us a description of the way Piero de' Medici (Cosimo's son) used his *studiolo* in the Palazzo Medici, which Filarete presumably visited along with Galeazzo Maria. Filarete begins with the books: Latin, Greek, and vernacular; he says that Piero sometimes read them himself and at other times had them read to him. Such was the variety of these books, says Filarete, that "more than a month would be required to understand their dignity." So great was the beauty of their scripts, their bindings, and ornaments that on some days Piero did not read but merely looked at them. After reading one day and admiring his books on another, Piero would, on a third day, look at his collection of coins, effigies, and portraits of Roman emperors, savoring each, both for the personage depicted and for "the noble mastery of these ancient angelic spirits" [the artists], who have "made a worth greater than gold by means of their skill." On yet another day Piero would contemplate "his jewels and precious stones" and on another his vases made of gold and silver and other materials. Finally he would devote a day to exotic objects from around the world, especially "various strange arms for offense and defense."[56] What we infer from Filarete's account is that Piero had a variety of objects and a variety of ways to enjoy them and that he paced and organized his enjoyment so as to minimize repetition and avoid the exhaustion of impressions that over-familiarity might produce.

54. Ibid., 25.

55. Ibid., 2 and 23.

56. Campbell, *Cabinet of Eros,* 29–30.

In the late quattrocento books and reading gradually yielded primacy in the *studioli* of the wealthy to these collections of antiquities, paintings, *objets d'art,* medals, coins, and curiosities; but the *studiolo*'s basic function—refuge, seclusion, and serenity—continued unchanged.[57] One effect of this change of emphasis was that a *studiolo* became a source of fame and repute to its owner. The Venetian collector Giacomo Contarini went so far as to declare that his *studiolo* was the source of "all honors and esteem for my person."[58] A *studiolo* that brought "honors and esteem" must contain architectural or painted decoration, books, antiquities, medals, sculptures, fossils, minerals, and natural curiosities. In the cinquecento the Venetian noble Andrea Loredan received this letter from an admirer of his collection:

> You could never leave your sons any land, palace or treasure which could equal the value and excellence of these antiquities of yours. These are not material goods, which one may acquire with simple labor; the collection is not a gem which one may obtain at a price: these are virtuous riches, which do not fall to the lot of the uneducated, which one may collect only with judgment, with infinite knowledge over a long period of time. These antiquities of yours will bear good witness to your fine mind, and to your very noble thoughts, in future centuries. On account of them, your house, as much as the city itself, [...] will be honored by strangers, eager to see rare and excellent works.[59]

Stephen Campbell, a modern student of these *studioli,* suggested that contemplating the collected objects and paintings was a form of reading.[60] This is particularly true of the mythological paintings that became fashionable at the end of the quattrocento, which are only a jumble of meaningless figures and objects unless they are "read" with knowledge of a whole language of personages and symbols. In addition, the *acts* of collecting and arranging with discernment—activities that remained in process throughout the owner's lifetime—helped overcome an intrinsic weakness of physical possessions—that familiarity can make them boring. The decision to seek a type of object, the search, the obtaining, the selection of a means of display, the integration of the new purchase with the old ones (not so much physically as symbolically and allegorically), then inviting in some friends for their views or receiving and sending letters about all of the above—these activities kept the *stu-*

57. Ibid., 36.
58. Ibid, 40.
59. Quoted in Thornton, *Scholar,* 114.
60. Campbell, *Cabinet of Eros,* 46.

diolo and its contents alive, dynamic, and therefore effective. The *studiolo* failed, however, as a means of assuring the collector's future fame. The collector's death, leaving his collection as inert objects to be preserved forever, robbed it of the greater part of its joy and doomed it to dispersal. The heirs would have their own *studioli* to create with their own "studiousness and care."

Among the most famous creators of *studioli* was Isabella d'Este, Marchesa of Mantua (1474–1539), who assembled several of them. Isabella was the daughter of Ercole d'Este, Duke of Ferrara, and Eleonora of Aragon, daughter of King Ferrante of Naples. At the age of sixteen she married Marchese Francesco Gonzaga of Mantua. From the beginning Isabella took an active role in the management of Mantuan affairs.[61] When the Venetians captured her husband in 1509 she grabbed the helm and pursued a nimble, multifaceted diplomacy.[62] When her husband returned from captivity, his health ruined by syphilis, she continued to be the real director of the Mantuan state. At his death in 1519 Isabella became regent to her son Federico II until he came of age in 1522, after which she continued to be his principal adviser.

To art historians the importance of Isabella's *studioli* lies in their mythological paintings, a genre that emerged in the *studioli* of this period and only later expanded into other settings.[63] She commissioned pictures for her *studioli* from Mantegna, the in-house court artist at Mantua, from Perugino, Lorenzo Costa, and Correggio, but, in spite of repeated efforts, she failed to get what she wanted from Giovanni Bellini, Leonardo da Vinci, Fra Bartolomeo, Francesco Francia, and Raphael. Her effort to collect painters was a sign of the artists' rising status, the awareness of individual artistic styles, and the gradual transition from wanting "a Madonna" or "an Apollo and Daphne" to wanting "a Mantegna" or "a Raphael." That transition was not complete with Isabella; she was creating a therapeutic environment for herself, not assembling the "Isabella d'Este Gallery of Art"; uncoordinated, self-contained works would not do. Her pictures had to "go together," not only artistically, but allegorically, in their themes, subjects, and symbolism.

There was an accepted method to achieve this artistic and allegorical unity—consult a humanist. If Isabella had wanted an altarpiece or a frescoed chapel, she would have gone to a cleric to devise the program and iconography, which the painter would then execute. In the case

61. Ibid., 2–3.

62. Ibid., 221.

63. Ibid., 1.

of mythological paintings the humanist replaced the cleric. The more complex, arcane, obscure, allusive, allegorical, and stuffed with symbols a painting might be, the more the patron's delight in pondering, interpreting, and discussing it with friends. If the allegorical gymnastics of one picture interacted with those of another, delight would multiply. If there were tricks, ambiguities, and conflicting meanings, they raised the paintings to the highest level of success. The painter would not be expected to understand all that. His job was simply to paint what he was told to paint—for which he received lengthy, detailed instructions, permitting no deviation without ruining the labyrinth of implied meanings. Thus Isabella wrote to Perugino:

> Our poetic invention which we greatly desire you to paint, is a battle of chastity against lasciviousness, that is Pallas and Diana fighting manfully against Venus and Cupid. And Pallas should appear almost to have defeated Cupid, having broken the golden arrow and cast his silver bow underfoot, holding him with one hand by the band which the blind one wears over his eyes, and with the other lifting her lance which is poised to wound him. And Diana in conflict with Venus must appear [to] show herself to be equal with her in victory; Venus has only been struck by her on the surface of her body, on her crown and garland, or by some little veil she might have around her; Diana has been burned in her clothing by the torch of Venus, but in no other part will either of them have been wounded.[64]

At the end of more specifications in the same vein, Isabella concludes, "you are free to reduce the [number of the] figures, but do not add anything to them. Please be content with this arrangement." This is only one of seventy letters that passed between patron, artist, and the patron's agents concerning this one painting. At one point Perugino apparently planned to deviate from instruction by depicting Venus nude, without realizing that this would ruin the entire mythology: a clothed Venus represented carnal love, while a nude Venus represented divine love.

When art historians read this correspondence in the twentieth century, a time that defined art as the artist's individual "self-expression," it inspired indignation and revulsion. This interfering woman is asking a great artist to surrender his soul! She is crushing his genius, stifling his creativity! Obviously the resulting picture, should the artist cravenly submit to this outrage, could only be a stillborn failure. So, indeed, it

64. Quoted in ibid., 172.

has been judged. *The Battle of Chastity and Lasciviousness* (in the Louvre) is undeniably dull and lifeless. Isabella was disappointed. "If the work had been finished with more diligence," she sniffed at Perugino, "it would have brought more honor to you and more satisfaction to us."[65]

To the mythologically naïve the pictures from Isabella's *studioli* seem to be a series of inexplicable activities taking place in beautiful gardens and pleasant dales that provide an overall atmosphere of calm beauty. Nevertheless, within their atmosphere of serenity, the figures and their actions reveal all sorts of violence and grotesqueries. Satyrs and other hybrid creatures abound, as well as the arresting armless woman (representing sloth) among the *Vices.* In Isabella's pictures satyrs are dragging women by the hair; armed women prepare to skewer babies; a woman is about to shoot another at close range with an arrow, except that her victim is retaliating with a torch. In one of the Correggios nymphs blast a wind instrument into a satyr's ear, apply biting snakes to his arm, and flay the skin off his leg while a nasty-looking infant grins fiendishly at the viewer.[66] Nevertheless, a sense of agitation rarely breaks through the bucolic calm of the settings: whatever happens in the paintings, little of it disturbs the viewer. The parallel to Uccello's tranquil battle scene in Lorenzo de' Medici's bedroom is probably not a mere coincidence but the product of similar desires from the two patrons.

One key to this veneer of calm over violence lies in Isabella's instructions to Perugino about the *Battle of Chastity and Lasciviousness.* It is a battle that no one is winning. Pallas and Diana fight "manfully" against Venus and Cupid. "Pallas should appear almost to have defeated Cupid.... Diana in conflict with Venus must appear [to] show herself to be equal in victory"—hence the standoff between the archer goddess and the one with the torch. The battle is static because its antagonists are in eternal balance. Other clues—and the whole point is to use clues to decipher a mystery—appear in the decorations and inscriptions of the *studiolo.* Most significant is the Senecan motto *nec spe, nec metu* (neither hope nor fear), an exhortation to serenity that hints that Seneca is the key to the numeral "XXVII" on the ceiling, a punning way to say "*vinti i saeti*" ("overcome the arrows"). Seneca uses this phrase in *De constantia sapientis* to describe mental triumph over the wounds of fortune, calumny, and envy. The musical notation "tempi e pause" means a bar of silence, represent-

65. Ibid., 173–75.
66. Ibid., 86.

ing tranquility. The monogram YS, the first letters of Isabella's name, refers us to the Pythagorean "Y," a symbol of moral choice.[67] Finally there is Isabella's personal device of lottery tickets, alluding to the vicissitudes of fortune, and the letters "FELI" for "*felicitas*" in the intarsia, a combination that referred to happiness beyond the reach of fortune. Stephen Campbell and Peter Porçal, leading students of Isabella's *studiolo,* agree that its theme was "the freeing of the mind from disruptive passions or *perturbations* through the pursuit of study and contemplation" (Campbell's italics).[68] The paradoxically tranquil, unresolved struggle that runs through the paintings is the ongoing struggle for serenity.

The use of the pagan gods and their stories as symbols, allegories, or entertainment never died out in the Middle Ages, but usually did not, for obvious reasons, invade churches, chapels, oratories, and monastic buildings. This fact made mythology a means of marking the boundaries between sacred space and secular.[69] To fill one's *studiolo* with Madonnas and saints and biblical narratives would have seemed an egregious claim to personal sanctity, inappropriate for anyone less than a holy abbot (whose cell ought to be bare). With all the variety of objects they contained, with all the differences in their owners' personalities, and through all the changes in taste from early quattrocento to late cinquecento, all *studioli* seem to have been rigorously secular. In a religious age where every home contained devotional images, perhaps an entire chapel, devotional pictures were rare in the *studioli.* The Muses, the liberal arts, great men or scholars, the pagan deities, the passions and their control, tranquility of spirit, self-discipline, the pleasures of music and its links to the music of the spheres—all these themes are typical of *studioli,* but not the saints, the martyrs, the history of salvation; not life and death or the fate of the soul, for these themes would lead quickly to painful thoughts about the shortness and fragility of life, the vengeance of God, and the terrible uncertainty of fortune. The function of a *studiolo* was above all therapeutic; as someone in the cinquecento remarked, a well-fitted *studiolo* "will give pleasure to yourself regularly and to others on occasion, besides it serving as an antidote to all your worries."[70] Isabella d'Este wrote to a friend who was away taking the waters in Viterbo.

67. Ibid., 75–76.

68. Ibid., 75; Peter Porçal, "Le Allegorie del Correggio per lo *Studiolo* di Isabella d'Este a Mantova," *Mitteilungen des Kunsthistorischen Institutes in Florenz,* 38, no. 2 (1984): 225–76.

69. Campbell, *Cabinet of Eros,* 13.

70. Thornton, *Scholar,* 105.

> The first health-giving bath you should take is the attitude of keeping away from sad thoughts, and to live with those that bring health and sustenance.... There is no need to attend to anything other than the health of the mind, before and beyond the honor and comfort of your person, so as to hang onto something in this transitory world. The one who does not know how to measure the allotted time of their life will pass through it with much emotional suffering and little praise.[71]

To the same friend she said that, during her friend's absence, "The time that I thought to spend in joy and consolation with your ladyship, I shall now spend in solitude, remaining in my study."[72] The frank acknowledgment of one's actual and perilous situation in this world and the next was one of the principal things this therapy was meant to cure. Consequently, the paintings and objects in the *studiolo* are "protected by an insistence on their trivial, marginal, escapist, above all non-exemplary character."[73] Christians, who could never completely forget the plague and war unleashed upon them by their angry God, wanted to feed their minds upon lofty, even inspiring, topics, but without danger of crossing into existential or theological truths that were painful to contemplate. To do that threatened to turn the *studiolo* into a monastic cell and oblige its inmate to admit that Catherine of Siena's fasting and self-flagellation were the *realistic* responses to the facts of human life.

71. Campbell, *Cabinet of Eros,* 62.
72. Ibid., 38.
73. Ibid., 20.

11

Plague and Pleasure: 1462

IN MARCH 1462, when most of Europe as well as the pope seemed to have forgotten about the crusade, Pius called together six trusted cardinals and confided to them that his own inaction on the crusade privately tormented him.

> My brethren, perhaps you, like almost everyone else, think that we are neglecting the common weal because since our return from Mantua we have neither done nor said anything toward repulsing the Turks and protecting religion.... We have been silent; we do not deny it. We have done nothing against the enemies of the Cross; that is evident. But the reason for our silence was not indifference but a kind of despair.[1]

The congress in Mantua, he said, proved that councils and congresses were useless; since then, his emissaries were laughed at, and efforts to raise money for the crusade met with accusations of papal greed. "No one believes what we say. Like insolvent tradesmen, we are without credit." "Our mind has long been perplexed and sorely anxious and our soul could not be comforted." He reminded them of the oath that Philip of Burgundy had taken at the Feast of the Pheasant, swearing to go on crusade if some great prince "whom it would not be beneath him to follow" would lead it. Then Pius shocked the six cardinals by declaring that he would fulfill the condition of Philip's oath by leading the crusade in person! "We are resolved, old and ill as we are, to undertake war against the Turks in defense of the Catholic Faith. We will set out on the crusade. We will summon Burgundy to follow us who are both king and pontiff

1. *Comm.*, Smith, VII.515.

and we will claim the fulfillment of his vow and oath. No excuse will be open to him." He asserted, furthermore, that the king of France and many others would then feel compelled to contribute troops. He Pius, would declare a five-year truce throughout Europe, exhort all to support the crusade, and excommunicate those who did not.

> Unless we are mistaken, this is the one way we can rouse the sleeping Christians and stir the hearts of kings and peoples. When this resolve is spread abroad it will shatter sleep as with a thunderclap and rouse the hearts of the faithful to protect religion. Not arms or horses or men or ships will be lacking. On land and sea we shall equip the war when it once becomes known that the Pope of Rome with the holy senate [the cardinals] is marching straight on to win salvation for all.

The one essential prerequisite was the support of the Venetians, who controlled the sea.[2] To secure that support he would write secretly to the doge informing him of his intentions.[3]

The six cardinals heard this "with wonder and stupefaction." They conferred among themselves for several days before replying that "Nothing could be said against so praiseworthy and noble a plan," adding with breathtaking understatement that "there seemed to be some difficulties in the way."[4] The cardinals were precisely correct to say that "nothing could be *said* against" Pius's proposal; on the theoretical level it was immune from criticism. As the cardinals told him, one could only praise the pope if "like a shepherd [he] did not hesitate to lay down his life for his sheep." But the gulf between theory and reality was unimaginably wide: such a dangerous venture not only endangered the pope's personal safety, but even threatened the credibility of papal authority. If the pope personally led thousands of Christians to captivity or death in an act of consummate folly, would there be anyone in Christendom whose faith in the pope or in the providence of God would remain unshaken? Pius believed that his plan would both shame and inspire the rulers of Europe into participating in the crusade; but if he was wrong—if neither shame nor inspiration budged the powerful—then the authority of the papacy over princes would be exposed as so much smoke! On the other hand, the cardinals had to consider that perhaps God had planted this idea in the pope's mind to prepare the way for a miracle. Faith in God as well as obedience to the pope required them to give their support. Even

2. Ibid., VII.516–17.
3. Von Pastor, *History of the Popes,* 3:311.
4. *Comm.,* Smith, VII.518.

so, they proceeded cautiously, sending Lorenzo Roverella, bishop of Ferrara, to France and Burgundy to sound them on the pope's proposal.[5] This, of course, was another way of seeming to act while achieving delay—the standard response to the crusade.

It would still be over a year before Pius would unveil in public this shocking proposal. During 1462 only a handful knew about the idea, and nothing visible came of it. Those who were not in on the secret saw only a pope busy in war but immersing himself in pleasures. In the *Commentaries* Pius describes his diversions that year with such enthusiasm that he really does seem to have forgotten the crusade, though we know that he had not. In the midst of his delights he must have anticipated the crusade with the tension of a soldier on the eve of battle—which he alone knew himself to be. Perhaps that anticipation of the impending struggle is the reason that summer seemed more devoted to pleasure than any other. War was not the only fear haunting the pope that year; during that summer plague seemed to be stalking the pope and his entourage, hounding them from place to place, leaving no certain refuge.

The spring of 1462 was the first time that Pius could consider himself rich, perhaps stoking his summer extravagance. Ever since the return from Avignon eighty-four years ago, the papacy had been poor. The councils of Constance and Basel and princely actions like the Pragmatic Sanction of Bourges had reduced papal revenues to about a third of what the Avignon popes had enjoyed.[6] This was not, of course, poverty as peasants and wool-carders knew it, but poverty of a sort nearly universal among rulers in this period, whose incomes were woefully inadequate for their responsibilities, much less their ambitions. These responsibilities included three permanent and inescapable drains on their resources—war, patronage, and ostentation. Avoiding war by a policy of pacifism would have been incomprehensible. Rulers and people alike recognized the advantages of peace, but peace, like a warm day in December, was a thing to be enjoyed when it happened, but not to be counted on or planned for. Rulers and republics regarded war as their fundamental business and waged it whenever they saw an opportunity for aggrandizement; a strong ruler owed it to his dependents and successors to seize such opportunities. Weaker states—those that provided the opportunities for stronger ones—sought allies to defend themselves. Aggressor and defender alike considered themselves wholly justified.

5. Von Pastor, *History of the Popes,* 3:316.

6. Mitchell, *Laurels,* 171.

A second expensive obligation of every ruler, perhaps especially the pope, was to enrich supporters and associates. Indeed, this was the only way to *have* supporters and associates. A ruler neglecting this obligation was friendless, had no one to advise or assist him or carry out his orders, and was likely to be overthrown. Few thought of thrift as a virtue in princes; generosity was universally admired, and parsimony was a mean and contemptible vice. Ostentation was equally obligatory. Princes and republics had to demonstrate their status with feasts, ceremonies, clothes, and palaces of appropriate splendor. To fail in this regard disgraced one's position and disappointed one's subjects, who expected to be entertained and impressed. Ordinary folk, whose lives were difficult and drab, hungered to see the extravagance of their betters. The poor apparently regarded the magnificence purchased by their labor as a kind of return owed them on their investment. The papacy's weakness since the return from Avignon stemmed in part from its inability to embody its pretensions with appropriate panache.

In 1462, by the time he left Rome for the summer, Pius could anticipate being able to meet all these responsibilities. Giovanni da Castro, a former acquaintance of the pope's, had taken refuge from his creditors under Pius's protection. Debt, Pius implies, is exactly what Giovanni deserved for wasting his talents on commerce and prospecting for minerals instead of devoting himself to Latin letters. But in May Giovanni came to Pius, announcing, "Today I bring you victory over the Turk." Giovanni explained that Christendom spent 300,000 ducats every year importing alum from the Turks, a mineral essential for setting dyes in cloth. Wandering about papal territory in the mountains near Tolfa, Giovanni had discovered "seven mountains so rich in this material [alum] that they could supply seven worlds."[7] By early 1463 eight thousand men were employed in mining operations that were soon sending 100,000 ducats a year to the papal treasury.[8] Pius erected a statue of Giovanni da Castro at Tolfa—not a famous work of art, but one that heralds the future works of Bramante, Raphael, Michelangelo, and Bernini, all of whom were subsidized by profits from Tolfa.

Shortly after receiving this welcome news, Pius embarked upon his most extended and elaborate *villeggiatura,* one marked by an unplanned rhythm in which rounds of pleasure alternated with flights from plague. The place originally chosen for the summer's sojourn was Viterbo,

7. *Comm.,* Smith, VII.505–7.
8. Von Pastor, *History of the Popes,* 3:263.

whose mineral baths were much closer to Rome than those of Petriolo. The baths, a short way north of town, had been used for cures since Etruscan times and even had an elegant little palazzo built by Nicholas V that Pius had enlarged. There doctors supervised the pope's treatment with sulphur-laden waters that sprang from the rock at 140 degrees.[9] Viterbo's excellent food and wine soon won the court's approval. Viterbo still boasts a magnificent thirteenth-century papal palace whose loggia, adorned with delicate Gothic tracery, is the most photogenic monument in the city, but Pius lodged himself in the castle, La Rocca, at the northeastern end of town. On most mornings, before the heat of the day, attendants carried the pope out to the countryside, where he admired the sky-blue fields of blooming flax. Pius mentions no forests or fine scenery but says that he "inspected all the meadows and crops riding on different roads every day." In the midst of these agricultural tours he conducted business and received envoys and petitioners. Before lunch he would stop outside the town at an Observant Franciscan convent called "Paradise," where he held consistories with the cardinals or meetings of the *segnatura,* the highest papal court and administrative council. The affairs of Naples intruded even in "Paradise." The marshall of Toulouse, ambassador from Louis XI, presented very forceful demands that Pius repay the repeal of the Pragmatic Sanction by abandoning Ferrante and recognizing the Angevin claim to Naples. The pope's refusal was firm and uncompromising.[10] Even before this, Florentine ambassadors were reporting that Louis XI had sworn to take vengeance on the pope for not switching to the Angevin side.[11]

Early in the summer the cardinals who had stayed in Rome came hastening to Viterbo with word that the papal city was gripped by plague. Perhaps because he had so many cardinals with him to share the expense and pleasure, or perhaps because the celebrations for St. Andrew a few months earlier had whetted the pope's appetite for public displays, Pius decided that the court would observe the approaching Feast of Corpus Christi (June 17 that year) "with all possible reverence and particular honors."[12] Viterbo's location suggested a special observance of Corpus Christi because it is just a few miles from Bolsena, where a

9. Bruno Barbini, *Viterbo: History and Masterpieces* (Sesto Fiorentino, Italy: Bonechi Edizioni "Il Turismo," 2009), 60.

10. *Comm.,* Smith, VIII.549–51.

11. Von Pastor, *History of the Popes,* 3:141.

12. *Comm.,* Smith, VIII.551.

miraculous bleeding of the eucharistic host in 1263 had prompted Pope Urban IV to declare Corpus Christi a universal feast of the church. The St. Andrew celebrations were probably much larger than the Corpus Christi festivities at Viterbo, but Pius described them only in general terms. With the Viterbo festival he is more specific about many of the displays of the cardinals, including mechanical "stage effects" that may have existed but went unmentioned in Pius's account of the St. Andrew pageantry.

A great frenzy must have gripped Viterbo in the days before Corpus Christi. Anyone who has ever organized a festival, dramatic performance, or large wedding will understand the difficulty of staging such an event with only two or three weeks' notice. Pius had been in Viterbo for only a month before Corpus Christi, and his account gives the impression that the decision to stage an elaborate celebration was not made immediately upon arrival—probably not before other cardinals began to arrive from Rome.[13] We may speculate that perhaps some of the equipment for the festival was reused from the St. Andrew celebrations, but Pius never says that; in fact, he reacts to everything as if he is seeing it for the first time. He also scorns one of the cardinals for using material originally intended for another purpose, as though this were cheating. Even if platoons of skilled craftsmen were available, the design, coordination, and execution of what Pius describes remain inexplicable in the short time available.

In the days before the festival the pope ordered that all balconies, galleries, porticoes, or other encroachments on the street be cleared from the processional route so that the streets might be as wide and unobstructed as possible.[14] The cardinals chose what sections of the route they would decorate, with bishops, other officials, and local guilds filling in the rest. The pope's own contribution was a tent or "tabernacle" in the cemetery of the Church of San Francesco, which served as the setting for the vespers service on the eve of the feast.

The vespers procession led from the citadel where the pope was staying to a fountain at the bottom of a hill. "Countless arches of flowering broom and myrtle and laurel constructed with admirable skill lined both sides of the road," and the road itself was "strewn with flowers."

13. Niccolà della Tuccia, "Chronica di Viterbo et di altre città," in *Chronache e statute della città di Viterbo,* edited by Ignazio Ciampi, 84 (Bologna: A Forni, 1976). Pius arrived in Viterbo on May 17; the first of the new arrivals came on May 31; the festival was June 17.

14. *Comm.,* Smith, VIII.551–52; della Tuccia, *Chronica di Viterbo,* 84.

The buildings disappeared beneath "representations of the cardinal virtues and the fluttering banners not only of the Pope but of kings and cardinals or by embroidered hangings or flowers."[15] The Viterbo chronicler, Niccolà della Tuccia, also mentions a wooden castle covered with flowers and complete with cannon on the battlements.[16] A triumphal arch marked the end of the processional way and doubled as the entrance to a tabernacle built inside the cloister of San Francesco. Beyond the arch one passed through a vestibule hung with silk and cloth of gold into a chamber with a purple couch (presumably for the pope) and walls depicting "ancient tales woven in silk, wool, and gold, portraits of illustrious men, and representations of various beasts." Della Tuccia adds that the high altar, ornamented with silver and statues of Peter and Paul, was lit by a cardboard chandelier covered in lilies and other flowers. In this setting the pope celebrated vespers before the entire court and a throng of citizens.

> The sun was still high and its rays, penetrating the woolen walls which imitated the varied colors of the rainbow, gave the tabernacle the appearance of a celestial hall and the dwelling of the King of Kings. It seemed indeed like a kind of paradise since choristers like angels were singing sweet hymns and lights, distributed with marvelous art, imitated the stars of heaven.

Vespers, however, was only an appetizer for the main events on the next day. In our modern parades the spectacle passes through the street in front of the spectators. But in this and many other Renaissance festivals, it was the streets and squares themselves that provided the spectacle while the pope and other dignitaries, the spectators who mattered, passed by in admiration. The throngs of ordinary people lining the way, shouting, "Long live Pope Pius," could only move in the wake of the procession, missing most of the active performances that entertained the high dignitaries as they passed. Nevertheless, the sight of the pope, the cardinals, and other potentates would have been excitement enough for the crowds, most of whom had never set eyes upon such exalted persons. As at the St. Andrew celebrations, Pius inflated the size of the crowd by offering a plenary indulgence to all who attended.[17]

We do not know what time the festivities began or how long they lasted. The canopies hung over all the streets and squares along the

15. *Comm.,* Smith, VIII.552.

16. Della Tuccia, *Chronica di Viterbo,* 85.

17. *Comm.,* Smith, VIII.552.

route were meant for shade against the beating sun, but the thirty-six torchbearers that della Tuccia mentions near the end of the route imply that the long summer twilight was yielding to darkness before the procession reached its end. We may speculate that the procession departed from La Rocca sometime in mid- to late afternoon and took perhaps four hours to reach the civic plaza where della Tuccia first mentions torches. Pius, riding in the procession himself, could not see much of the parade ahead of him or behind him and does not describe it. Della Tuccia says the procession included seventeen cardinals and twenty-two bishops and other prelates. Carried in a triumphal chair, Pius wore a miter and all his pontifical regalia, sewn all over with pearls and precious stones. In his hands he carried the sacramental host, the object of the day's veneration, displayed in a gold and crystal tabernacle.[18] Pius tells us that "every square and every street [was] packed with men, women, and children so that it was difficult for the Pope and the procession to pass"; they made their way only by "much pushing and effort."[19]

The pope and other dignitaries had certain expectations for the displays and enactments they were going to see. Each cardinal was expected to deck the buildings around his presentation with tapestries, curtains, and banners carrying his coat of arms; a canopy must stretch from rooftop to rooftop fending off the summer sun; gold or silver altars, singing choirs, and fountains flowing with wine were more or less routine.[20] Between the major installations, the houses were decked in garlands, while blue canopies with golden stars hung from house to house overhead.[21] All along the route priests chanted, and incense rose from numerous altars brimming with gold and silver vessels displaying sacred relics gathered from the churches around Viterbo. At each of the seventeen major installations the papal procession halted for some sort of performance. Among the modest ones near the beginning, the *referendarii,* officials of the court of the *segnatura,* presented a nude youth representing the resurrected Christ, holding a banner of victory, who somehow simulated the sweating of blood and "filled a cup from the healing stream from a wound in his side." The pope stopped there to listen to the two sons of a local citizen sing verses in his praise.[22]

18. Della Tuccia, *Chronica di Viterbo,* 86–87.
19. *Comm.,* Smith, VIII.552.
20. Hollingsworth, *Patronage,* 276.
21. Von Pastor, *History of the Popes,* 3:289.
22. *Comm.,* Smith, VIII.553; della Tuccia, *Chronica di Viterbo,* 86.

The installations of the cardinals were, of course, the most impressive. Cardinal Torquemada presented Christ and the apostles at the institution of the Eucharist with two angels kneeling in adoration while a priest representing St. Thomas Aquinas celebrated Mass. Juan de Carvajal presented his display amidst houses covered with leather, tooled and gilded in floral designs, and crowned by a red canopy. In this opulent setting a huge and terrifying dragon awaited, accompanied by demonic spirits. When the pope arrived, St. Michael the Archangel strode forward and struck off the dragon's head. All the demons immediately fell to the ground, howling like hounds.[23] As usual, Rodrigo Borgia outdid everyone for inventive ostentation. He was in charge of the Piazza delle Erbe in the heart of the city, which he ringed with his own armorial banners and those of his uncle, Pope Callixtus III, and covered with a canopy of tapestries. Arriving there, Pius found the piazza hidden behind an enormous purple curtain, in front of which he saw statues, "representations of stories," an ornate bedchamber with a ceremonial bed, and the requisite fountain spouting water and wine. The ensuing performance was almost a parody of the Easter vigil service in which the priest, outside the church, knocks on the door, saying, "Lift up your heads O ye gates, and the King of Glory shall come in." A voice inside asks, "Who is the King of Glory?" and the priest answers, "The Lord strong and mighty, the Lord mighty in battle, He is the King of Glory." In the version that Cardinal Borgia produced for Pope Pius, two choir boys dressed as angels came forward and genuflected before joining a larger angelic choir that sang, "Lift up your gates, O princes, and King Pius, Lord of the World will come in." Five kings then appeared, each with an armed retinue, and demanded, "Who is this King Pius?" The angels answered that he was "The Lord of the World!" Then, as trumpets, organs, and other instruments blared, the gigantic curtain parted to reveal a triumphal arch, fortified like a castle and bristling with armed soldiers. The five kings, their resistance overcome, did obeisance to the pope while reciting verses in his praise. Pius reports seeing a "savage" wrestling a lion for his amusement as he passed through the square. Della Tuccia explains that there were twelve men dressed in suits of leaves like wild men and others dressed as lions and bears, who "in that place made great rejoicing." When the pope reached the fortified arch through which he was to exit, bronze "engines" sounded peals of thunder that "struck terror into the passers-by."[24]

23. *Comm.*, Smith, VIII.553; von Pastor, *History of the Popes,* 3:289.

24. *Comm.*, Smith, VIII.553–54; della Tuccia, *Chronica di Viterbo,* 85.

In the next block he passed between youths dressed as the four cardinal virtues and attended by twelve singing angels standing on columns, holding torches aloft.[25] This brought him to the civic square (today's Piazza del Plebiscito), where the palaces of the priors, the podestà, and the captain of the people were all covered with tapestries and linked by a blue and white canopy up above. Here Cardinal Angelo Capranica presented an artificial hill containing Christ's sepulcher, guarded by sleeping soldiers and a cadre of angels. We can catch Pius's excitement when he says, "Lo! of a sudden there was let down along a rope as if flying from heaven a beautiful boy with wings like an angel, the face of a seraph, and a heavenly voice," who sang a hymn announcing the resurrection. The immense crowd fell silent in expectation; Pius says, "All listened with delight as if an actual event were taking place and it was a real messenger from heaven." Suddenly gunpowder exploded in a bronze urn, waking the soldiers, who quaked in terror. A "sandy-haired" actor suddenly appeared as Christ, wearing a crown and holding the banner of the cross. After displaying his wounds to the multitude, he declaimed a poem proclaiming salvation for all Christians.[26]

Pius had now passed through the whole length of Viterbo, which stretches along a crescent of hills from La Rocca at its northeastern point to the Romanesque cathedral, with its majestic Gothic campanile at the northwest. In front of the cathedral and papal palace lies the Piazza San Lorenzo, the largest square in Viterbo. The piazza, cathedral, and palace occupy a high, isolated hill, connected to the rest of the city by a bridge. Cardinal Jouffroy, whom Pius hated for his role in the broken negotiations with Louis XI, had claimed a place of honor, the last stretch of the route from the bridge to the piazza. He had draped it with English cloth from which he had intended to make a new livery for his servants, but a high wind the night before had torn much of it, "thus depriving his servants of some of their expected dresses." Pius makes no other mention of this gale or any other damage it caused. God apparently sent the storm only to spite Cardinal Jouffroy.

The immense Piazza San Lorenzo required poles with a net of ropes between them to suspend the canopy. At the highest point of the square, Cardinal Juan del Mila y Borgia, governor of Viterbo, had erected a tomb of the Blessed Virgin "decorated lavishly with wonders." An altar stood in a chapel that replicated the one in the apostolic palace; around

25. Della Tuccia, *Chronica di Viterbo,* 86.

26. *Comm.,* Smith, VIII.554.

it were the papal throne and seats for the cardinals, bishops, protonotaries, and abbots. On the roofs of the houses around the piazza the angelic court of heaven looked down on the world below. Among the rooftop angels, amidst "burning stars and the joys of supreme glory expressed in marvelous ways," God himself presided from his throne. Before Cardinal Barbo began celebrating Mass, a chariot arrived at the cathedral from the Church of San Francesco at the other end of the city carrying Christ, portrayed by a man carrying a cross and wearing only a loincloth and crown of thorns. He "seemed to be exuding blood" from his wounds and stood "as motionless as a statue" during the Mass. At the end of the liturgy a boy angel sang of the Assumption of the Virgin. As he concluded, the Virgin's tomb opened and a beautiful young girl emerged, borne aloft by angels. She sang sweetly with an expression "rapt with joy" as she rose above the piazza, up to the rooftop heaven. There, Christ welcomed her with a kiss on the forehead, presented her to the Father, and enthroned her at his own right hand. Then all the angels on the rooftops burst into song and played musical instruments. "They rejoiced and made merry and all Heaven laughed."[27]

As angels sang from the rooftops, the procession and all the papal and city officials entered the papal palace. Behind the palace a cliff drops far below to a green valley inside the city walls that could produce food for the people in time of siege. In the valley the population of Viterbo gathered, along with pilgrims and holiday-makers from towns and villages all over the region who had come to see the pope, enjoy the spectacle, and obtain forgiveness of sins. Della Tuccia's chronicle estimates fifty thousand persons, not an impossible number.[28] Seen from the valley the papal palace appears as a towering castle atop the cliff. From one of the windows of the great hall, Pius looked out over the crowds below and gave them his blessing. When that was finished Cardinal Mila y Borgia hosted a banquet in the vast hall for the pope, the curia, and other dignitaries. At this banquet Pius said, "Nothing you could possibly desire was missing." He praises the marvelous artistry of the tapestries, the fountain decked in gold and silver cloth, and the dishes of "heavy gold and silver and most delicious and elegant food."[29] Pius gives no details, but quattrocento fashions in food presentation had been set in 1395, when the court of Milan celebrated Giangaleazzo Visconti's in-

27. Ibid., VIII.555–56.

28. Della Tuccia, *Chronica di Viterbo,* 87n1.

29. *Comm.,* Smith, VIII.556.

vestiture as duke with great silver platters carried aloft, displaying birds in their plumage or whole gilded animals. One course at Giangaleazzo's feast consisted of four chickens, four capons, six pigeons, two hares, four rabbits, four pheasants, quails, and partridges—all on an immense platter surrounding an entire roasted stag covered in gold foil. Sauces were served separately in silver bowls, and guests drank their wine in golden goblets.[30] A stuffed peacock, exotic, gorgeous, and sanctified by association with Juno, climaxed the procession of meats.[31] By 1462 peacocks and whole animals in gold foil had become standard.[32] Between courses, Pius found the singers and lyre players delightful. Aside from the decorations, food, and entertainment, Pius found that "pleasant conversation and wit seasoned with wisdom made the hours seem short." When the last performer bowed out of the hall and the last goblet was drained, Pius returned to La Rocca by the same route he had taken during the day. Back at the citadel he seems to have sat down at once to write his account of the day, concluding with words of elation.

> All those who entered Viterbo that day and beheld so many marvels and such an array and succession of sights as they walked through the city thought they had assuredly entered the dwelling of gods, not a habitation of men, and said that while living in the flesh they had beheld Heaven.[33]

But Pius's next sentence shocks us. Suddenly, he asks, "But what joys of mortals are lasting? All that pleases is too brief. Grief succeeds happiness. Lamentation follows hard on laughter." Apparently, he had no more finished his breathless account of the day's wonders when news arrived that there was plague in Viterbo. To avoid panic, the townspeople were kept ignorant of the danger, but terrified cardinals begged Pius to take them away from the stricken city. Pius himself needed another day to inspect a nearby monastery he had just given to his nephew. He kept a few officials with him and told the rest to flee wherever they wished. The next evening, returning from his inspection of the monastery, Pius found crowds of townspeople, still elated and still ignorant of the plague, flocking to meet him. Looking at the festive crowd as it shouted, "Long life and prosperity to Pius," and knowing that many of them were doomed, Pius was moved to tears. He reflected in his *Commentaries:*

30. Claudio Benporat, *Feste e banchetti: Convivialità Italiano fra tre e quattrocento* (Florence: Leo S. Olschki Editore, 2001), 27–28.

31. Ibid., 37.

32. Ibid., 69.

33. *Comm.*, Smith, VIII.556.

> Behold the hard lot of mortals! Alas for the mind that cannot know the future! Men and matrons joyfully applaud us; maids and brides exult; the most lovely people of both sexes are given over to happiness and express their gladness. The streets are gay with throngs of little children. But how many will escape that fatal summer? The plague will devastate the city; it will carry off children and youths; it will spare no age. If it is granted us to return one day, we shall find but few of those who today honor us so highly. O flesh! O life of men! How fragile and fleeting ye are![34]

Even five and a half centuries later, the contrast between "while living in the flesh they had beheld Heaven" followed by "what joys of mortals are lasting?" makes us feel the brutality of the shift from escapist delight to pitiless reality. What powerful means it needed to drive the gloomy thoughts away, to forget the divine wrath and purge from the mind the faces of loved ones frozen in death! Men must wrestle lions, dragons must lose their heads, houses must hide behind tapestries, choirs must sing, wine must flow, there must be explosions, and maidens must ascend to heaven! Then perhaps we can believe, just for a night, that we are not *here*—but carried away to the "dwellings of the gods." Then comes the word—death is stalking the streets—the illusion shatters and we are on earth after all; where "all that pleases is too brief, grief succeeds happiness. Lamentation follows hard on laughter." Momentarily, we had forgotten God's wrath, but God had not.

In the midst of fear and despair the heart craves the return to illusion, even knowing how "fragile and fleeting" it is. There is no doubt that Pius's tears and his laments over the doomed throngs at Viterbo were sincere. Nevertheless, once he reached a place of refuge, he said nothing more about plague. His *Commentaries* focus on his immediate pleasures with no further mention of the death and suffering a few miles away; this, no doubt, reflects what everyone in the plague era trained their minds to do at the end of each forced encounter with grim realities: to scuttle as quickly as possible back into the cloud of illusion. Niccolà della Tuccia, however, informs us that the plague in Viterbo lasted almost until Christmas and claimed about two thousand lives.[35]

Pius's new place of refuge was the Farnese castle at Capodimonte, a great rock forming a peninsula that jutted into the waters of Lake Bolsena about twelve miles north of Viterbo. It towers like a small Gibralter

34. Ibid., VIII.556–57.
35. Della Tuccia, *Chronica di Viterbo,* 87.

over the low, almost flat lakeshore and rises to two peaks; the lower one, flat enough to accommodate the village square, is linked by a bridge to the castle on the highest pinnacle. The castle is still a private residence whose tiny garden sports a tall date palm, rising on the skyline like a feather in a gigantic hatband. Pius's description of Capodimonte sounds wonderfully idyllic.

> Three sides are washed by the lake, the fourth is protected by a strongly fortified citadel. A rocky mound almost a stade [600 feet] high in the middle and difficult of approach rises from the water. On the top is a plateau surrounded by a wall, where are the houses of the rustics and barns of the nobles. Between the walls and the cliff they have laid out a vineyard six or eight feet wide, which bounds three sides of the town. It is level and easy to walk on and in summer affords pleasant shade.... The cliff, where there is no flintrock, is planted with vines and fruit trees. There is a path almost like steps down to the lake and here among rugged stones and jagged boulders grow many evergreen ilex trees which make a grove beloved of thrushes. Between this and the vineyard they have hewn out a path wide enough for two persons, where they often set snares for birds.

It was on this narrow path above the cliffs that Pius held the outdoor sessions of the *segnatura*. The *referendarii* who attended these sessions had to commute by boat, since Capodimonte was too small to house them.[36] Today, the houses of the village spill over the sides of the girdling cliff, but patches of vineyard remain. Pleasure craft dock in rows in the little harbor below, and swimmers crowd the beach. At the summit, however, all is as quiet and serene as Pius describes it. There is still not a single hotel on the rocky headland, whose steep slopes seem to deter everyone but its residents from making the climb.

As at Viterbo, Pius explored the neighborhood, this time by water as well as land. He describes an ingenious method for trapping eels and the way the monks on the island of Bisentina caught rabbits. There were monasteries on each of the lake's two islands, Bisentina and Martana, and Pius visited both. On Bisentina the pope celebrated Mass on the feast of St. John the Baptist (June 24). For lunch he was content with the coarse food that the friars had begged from the neighboring villages. After the pope's Spartan lunch the towns around Lake Bolsena staged a boat race. Teams of rowers from the lakeside towns of Bolsena, Clar-

36. *Comm.*, Smith, VIII.557–58.

entani, Cornetani, Crypte San Lorenzo, and Martani competed for an eight-ell length of Florentine purple cloth. The course was two miles long and ended at the harbor of Capodimonte, where the papal party must have returned after lunch.

The boatmen fired themselves up with a testosterone fest of competitive braggadocio. "All were extraordinarily confident," Pius says, "and even more boastful. Everyone despised everyone else and exalted himself and the more they had to drink the more they lauded their own exploits." Nobles and prelates on the shore joined in the bragging. Guicciardo Forteguerra, kinsman of the pope's mother and prefect of Bolsena, boasted, "I know the strength of the Bolsinians. Nowhere will you find stronger arms. Our men are made lusty by exercise and by drinking unadulterated wine"—to which Gabriele Farnese, Lord of Capodimonte, answered, "If the palm belongs to heavy drinkers I do not deny that your clients are famous for that. But it is not so easy to pull an oar as to drain a goblet." Each small skiff held a coxswain and four rowers wearing white linen cloths and wreaths of poplar leaves on their heads; otherwise, they were "naked except for loin cloths and glistening with oil."

Pius says that he conducted business with the cardinals while watching the race, but he missed nothing of the hard-fought contest. Early on the Bolsinians took the lead, and the Martani had fallen to third when their coxswain called out, "Can we who have never been conquered before endure the disgrace of being conquered today before the eyes of the Pope? Death would be better." At this, Pius says, "with mighty strokes they smote the flood and stole the ground from under their quivering boat." As a result the Martani won, and the Bolsinians, having peaked too soon, brought up the rear. Pius's kinsman, the prefect of Bolsena, "left the crowd heartbroken." Perhaps papal business distracted Pius after the race, because he teases our curiosity with his terse description of the next event.

> As all were withdrawing the referendarii who had equipped two ships, gave a realistic imitation of a naval battle after the manner of the Ethiopians fighting now with pikes and now with bows. The battle was interrupted by the gale from which at last they barely escaped after being submerged many times shaking with cold.

What on earth was the quattrocento concept of a naval battle "after the manner of the Ethiopians"? Pius reports with satisfaction that the same gale terrified Cardinal d'Estouteville, not just because of the wind and waves, but because the boatmen from Clarentani, who were rowing him home, "were so drunk that they could not steer straight nor bend well to their oars."[37]

Pius had stayed close to the southwest corner of Lake Bolsena because plague was raging on the opposite shores. Some days after the boat race, when the danger seemed to have lifted, he rewarded the town of Crypte San Lorenzo for its steadfast loyalty to himself and previous popes with a special visit. Surely he was also curious to see the place, "a rocky mound two stades high, pregnable by one approach, which is however fortified by a moat and a high wall. Everywhere else it is steep and protected by very deep valleys. The townspeople have dug out caves in which most of them live. There are also houses of hewn stone."[38] These cave dwellers were just the sort of humble people that the former lad of Corsignano loved. He and the cardinals with him ate the modest lunch the villagers provided at the home of their parish priest. Three centuries later Pope Clement XIV ordered Crypte San Lorenzo abandoned because of its unhealthy site and had it rebuilt farther from the lake, where it is now known as San Lorenzo Nuovo.

Today, the abandoned site of Crypte San Lorenzo is a steep, forested hill amid the wheat fields. At the one place where a public lane skirts it, what may have been a tower serves as a farmhouse, and what may have been a tiny shrine with a Gothic lancet is the only indication of its history. The caves, however, are still there. The ones I explored were roughly eighteen feet wide and twenty-five or thirty feet deep with manmade passages at the back leading to a room with yet more passages where I did not venture. The farmer used two larger caves for storage and for goats. One of those was barrel-vaulted and had passages leading to other rooms at what must have been its second-floor level. All of them showed very clearly where the front wall had been attached. On a day when newspapers were proclaiming record heat, the caves were wonderfully cool. Pius, who loved any cool, shady place in the midst of nature, would have delighted in them—the attending cardinals probably less so. He did not stay long; this stop was part of a leisurely journey toward the former Corsignano, now transformed by his orders into the new city of Pienza.[39]

Pius found a more prolonged escape from the heat at the monastery of Abbadia San Salvatore on the slopes of Mount Amiata, one of the

37. Ibid., VIII.560–62.
38. Ibid., VIII.562.
39. Ibid., VIII.564.

highest points in Italy, a lovely spot with cool weather and dense forests. From this refreshing height Pius could see Pienza across the Val d'Orcia and, beyond it, the towers of Siena with the coast on the hazy horizon. In the valleys, Pius says, the fields were toasted and the trees dry; but "around the monastery and the higher places everything was green; no heat was felt and a sweet breeze stirred.... You would have said that here [on the mountain] was the abode of the blest; in the valley the punishments of the damned." Pius stayed in the monastery itself; six cardinals and some of the other officials found homes in the town of Abbadia, but others had to lodge two miles away at Piano, commuting every few days for a *segnatura,* which Pius always held *al fresco* in a spot carefully chosen for the purpose.

> Every day he changed the place, finding new springs in the valleys and new patches of shade among which it was hard to choose.... Sometimes too Pius held a consistory with the cardinals under the chestnuts and heard embassies in the meadow. He rode daily through the woods accompanied by the curials and dispatched private and public business on the way. When evening came on he would go a little beyond the monastery to a place where the Paglia [a river running below the mountain] could be seen and would sit conversing delightfully with the brethren.[40]

A century ago, in 1911, a monument under a chestnut tree overlooking the valley commemorated Pius's meetings on that spot, but today, what is probably the same monument sits in the square in front of the church.[41] Pius gives Abbadia his most glowing praise: "Surely here, if anywhere in the world, sweet shade and silvery springs and green grass and smiling meadows allure poets.... And for our part we think that the slopes of Cirrha and Nysa, though they are often mentioned in literature, cannot compare with these."[42] On one of his frequent excursions, Pius indulged in an engineering daydream that he says he had often contemplated before. He would divert a stream, dam a river, and cover the Val d'Orcia with an immense lake, useful both for fishing and for defense—no more parched valleys! He admits, however, that "it would be an expensive operation and need a pope with plenty of leisure."[43] Nevertheless, this was not a passing fancy but a serious intention on Pius's part, mentioned by Gianantonio Campano and the poets Lofrisio

40. Ibid., IX.571.
41. Von Pastor, *History of the Popes,* 3:35.
42. *Comm.,* Smith, IX.570.
43. Ibid., IX.573.

Crivelli and Porcellio Pandoni. Pius himself made exploratory expeditions up the Orcia and its tributaries. A few years after his death Siena embarked on a similar project to dam the Bruno River; they spent great sums on the project for twenty years, only to fail in the end.[44]

This hydraulic fantasy was not the only one Pius entertained. Both he and Nicholas V had dreamed of making the River Aniene navigable so that marble could be shipped from mountain quarries direct to the Milvian Bridge in Rome.[45] Fantasies of hydraulic engineering fascinated Renaissance minds. Brunelleschi, the great architect-engineer who built the dome of Florence Cathedral, concocted ambitious plans to defeat Lucca in 1430 by diverting the river Serchio, but his efforts flooded the Florentine camp instead.[46] Leonardo da Vinci was a technological Don Quixote who often tilted at engineering windmills. He concocted a scheme to help the Florentines reconquer Pisa in 1503 by diverting the Arno; the project had Machiavelli's enthusiastic backing and consumed 7,000 ducats, only to flood the countryside.[47] For years Leonardo worked tirelessly on the idea of bypassing Pisa's port with a navigable canal linking Florence to the sea. For this purpose he made countless maps, designed giant excavating machines mounted on rails, and filled pages with calculations.[48] To carry the canal across the mountains he intended to use a series of tunnels and locks. Excitedly he wrote, "Thanks to the principle of the pump one can move any river to the highest mountains."[49] Leonardo, like many of his contemporaries, had little sense of practical limitations. Vasari reports that he conceived a plan for raising the entire baptistery of Florence several feet off the ground in order to build a platform with steps underneath. Leonardo's explanations of how to do this temporarily seduced his hearers, "although each man, after he had departed, would recognize for himself the impossibility of so vast an undertaking."[50]

As Pius was returning to Abbadia from one of his country expeditions, a cowherd, awed at the passing procession, thought to offer the pope a gift of milk, presenting it in the filthy bowl from which he him-

44. Mack, *Pienza,* 155.

45. Rubenstein, "Pius II," 206.

46. Holmes, *Enlightenment,* 178.

47. Serge Bramly, *Leonardo: The Artist and the Man,* trans. Sian Reynolds (London and New York: Penguin, 1991), 330–31.

48. Ibid., 336.

49. Leonardo da Vinci, Codex Atlanticus iv-a, Biblioteca Ambrosiana, Milan, Italy; quoted in ibid., 336.

50. Vasari, *Lives of the Painters,* 1:627.

self usually drank. Pius "smiled and did not disdain to touch the black and greasy bowl with his lips, pretending to drink, nor to hand it to the cardinals to taste; for he would not appear to scorn the attention and reverence of a poor peasant who had offered him his most precious possessions."[51] Few of the cardinals would have appreciated this gesture, but cowherds claimed a place in Pius's heart to which most cardinals could not aspire. Pius's affection for the peasantry is all the more notable in contrast to other views of the time. In *Della famiglia* Alberti has Giannozzo, spokesman for the old-fashioned mercantile outlook, declare that an advantage of a compact estate is that it

> reduces the number of peasant families one has to deal with: it is hard to believe how much wickedness there is among the plowmen raised up among the clods. Their one purpose is to cheat you, and they never let anyone deceive them in anything. All the errors are in their favor; they try constantly and by every means to get and obtain what is part of your property.... Even though he be richer than his master, he is always wailing about how poor he is. He forever needs something, and he never speaks to you but to bring you some expense or burden.[52]

So the rich have regarded the poor in every age!

The Sienese struck one of the few sour notes in the pope's idyllic stay at Abbadia. They were in an ugly mood as a result of Pius's continued pressure for the political rehabilitation of the nobles—so much so that the nobles themselves petitioned him to stop interfering, since it only excited resentment against them.[53] Siena had issued harsh decrees resisting the papal interventions in their politics and had not properly greeted him when he entered their territory. But now, fearing that they might miss the bonanza of a papal visit, they sent an embassy urging him to come. Pius coldly refused; he would go to Pienza but would promise nothing more.[54]

51. *Comm.,* Smith, IX.574.
52. Alberti, *Della famiglia* III, in *The Family,* 189.
53. Ady, *Pius II,* 262.
54. *Comm.,* Smith, IX.574–75.

12

The Age of Spectacle

THE GOAL of the Renaissance festival was not merely to entertain, but to overwhelm the participants, to leave them *stupiti,* to inspire wonderment—to make them say, "that while living in the flesh they had beheld Heaven."[1] The need for spectacle crossed the lines between sacred and secular as easily as it crossed those between public and private or between classic and chivalric. The cardinal's installations at Pius's Corpus Christi festival were closely related to the Italian tradition of *sacre rappresentazioni,* which had originated in the efforts of the mendicant orders to make the laity more vividly aware of the doctrines and mysteries of their faith.[2] The representations at Viterbo of the resurrection of Christ, the assumption of the Virgin, and the institution of the Eucharist were, in a sense, a series of short *sacre rappresentazioni.* In the first half of the quattrocento, most *sacre rappresentazioni* were still a humble kind of street theater that a confraternity might enact on a cart as part of the celebration of a feast day.[3] Vasari says that every quarter of Florence except San Giovanni had a larger religious spectacle of this type given annually in one of its churches. These festivals in the *quartieri* were similar to those

1. *Comm.,* Smith, VIII.556.

2. Literary historians define *sacre rappresentazione* as a type of religious play indigenous to quattrocento Florence, usually written anonymously and presented and acted by a lay confraternity. It has a particular literary form: *ottava rima,* with a rhyme scheme of ABABABCC. It is never divided into acts or scenes, even when the action shifts in time and place, and it begins with a prologue delivered by an angel. Literary form, however, is not our concern; regardless of rhyme scheme or other technicalities, we shall use "*sacre rappresentazione*" to mean any Italian Renaissance religious drama put on by the laity; Wilkins, *Italian Literature,* 133.

3. Molinari, *Spettacoli,* 33.

that the confraternities presented on other occasions, except that, with an entire church to serve as stage, there were more actors, more scenery, richer costumes, and more ambitious dramatic effects.

Oddly, the productions in the *quartieri* with the biggest churches, Santa Maria Novella and Santa Croce, have left us little record of their character.[4] The earliest stage machine for a *sacre rappresentazione* for which we have detailed knowledge is from the small church of Santa Felicità in the Oltrarno *quartiero,* which Vasari described in his biography of Brunelleschi, its designer. Vasari implies that Brunelleschi was developing an older tradition when he says that he invented it "in order to hold the Representation, or rather, the Festival of the Annunciation, in the manner wherein the Florentines were wont to hold it in that place in olden times."[5] He later adds that some people said that such machines "had been invented long before." Brunelleschi's "Paradise of Santa Felicità" consisted of an inverted bowl suspended from the roof trusses of the church. On the surface of this hemisphere, three rings of small lamps flickered as stars. At its lower edge dangled twelve adolescent boys dressed as angels, with gold wings and wigs of golden hair, all holding each other by the hand, waving arms and legs so that they seemed to be doing an aerial dance. The struts that supported them, obscured by cotton wool, appeared to be a ring of clouds. This entire hemisphere turned, giving the appearance of revolving heavens with the angels flying in a circle.[6] On the outside of this moving heaven God the Father presided, surrounded by more angels. Vasari is unclear about the structure of this part—whether God rotated with the rest of the heaven or was held stationary in the front. Possibly his place was inside the sphere, which, Vasari says, had moving doors that opened and closed, perhaps to reveal God at the proper times.[7] The dramatic performance of the Annunciation unfolded below on a stage in front of the altar. At the appropriate point in the story, the audience saw another ring of eight angels (smaller boys) who dropped down from inside the "Heaven." In the midst of this second ring of angels, Gabriel, the angel of the Annunciation, stood in front of a gleaming copper mandorla spangled with flickering stars, made by placing lamps on the back side of the mandorla behind tiny holes through which the audience saw the flame.[8] The

4. Ibid., 37–39.

5. Vasari, "Brunelleschi," *Lives of the Painters* I.355–56.

6. Ibid., I.356–58.

7. Molinari, *Spettacoli,* 50–51.

8. A "mandorla" is an almond-shaped radiance that functions as a "full-body halo," usually used only for Christ or the Trinity.

descent of the second ring of angels stopped less than halfway down, but the mandorla continued to descend until it touched the stage and was secured there by an unseen stage hand. As the mandorla descended, Gabriel (a boy of fifteen) was able to kneel to the Virgin because the iron strut that held him could shorten and lengthen like a telescope. When the mandorla was secured to the stage, the hidden stage hand unhooked Gabriel, who then walked over to the Blessed Virgin to deliver his message. When Gabriel left the mandorla, a spring closed all its openings, extinguishing the "stars." Once Gabriel delivered his message and the Virgin accepted it, he returned to the mandorla for the ride back to heaven. As soon as he took his place, all the stars reappeared. During all of this, choirs, including the angels suspended on the machine, provided "very sweet music" so that, Vasari says, the whole effect "truly represented Paradise."[9]

Abraham, bishop of Suzdal in Russia, one of the Eastern delegates to the Council of Florence, left a description of a *sacre rappresentazione* of the Annunciation that he witnessed in the large Florentine church dedicated to that feast.[10] At Santissima Annunziata there were two distinct settings at opposite ends of the church. One, at the sanctuary, was the house of the Virgin, indicated by a bed and a chair in the choir, probably in front of the altar; the other, raised over the door of the church, was a "paradise."[11] This, however, was hidden behind a curtain during the first part of the performance, which consisted of a half-hour dialogue among four prophets, enacted in one of the transepts. When the prophetic speeches concluded, a crash of thunder from behind startled the spectators, forcing them to turn around toward the entrance of the church. The curtain over the door parted and revealed God the Father, enthroned and wearing priestly vestments, surrounded by a circle of boys dressed as angels. Around God and his angels seven concentric circles revolved, representing the seven heavens of the planets. Each heaven "undulated" as it revolved and bore "hundreds" of tiny lamps representing stars. Then, from the heavenly throne, passing over the spectators' heads, the audience saw Gabriel flying—probably suspended from a ring sliding down an inclined wire. He then delivered his message to Mary at her house. Once she had given her consent, a torch, or some form of fire, also descended from the heavens, lighting all the candles in the church, filling the building with light.[12] How this was achieved without inciner-

9. Vasari, "Brunelleschi," I.357–58; I.355–56.

10. Molinari, *Spettacoli,* 148.

11. Ibid., 40.

12. Ibid., 43–44.

ating the church and all the spectators we can only speculate. In Arezzo in 1556 the use of lights set a baldacchino on fire during a religious drama; sixty-six people were trampled to death, while the unfortunate man fastened above the baldacchino to represent God the Father died horribly in the flames.[13]

Vasari and Bishop Abraham both describe machinery for the Ascension of Christ at the Church of the Carmine that by Vasari's time had been taken down because its weight was straining the timbers of the roof.[14] Here the stage was built at the level of the top of the rood-screen that separated the presbytery from the nave. In 1439 Bishop Abraham saw a "stone" castle with towers and bastions, representing the city of Jerusalem. The "Mount of Olives" was a wooden mound ten and a half feet high, draped in red cloth, with the "Heavens" above it. Two angels descended from heaven sliding down ropes, but held upright by weights on their feet. They informed Christ that he was to ascend to heaven and then went back the way they came. Christ was lifted up on "a cloud covered with angels," but Vasari does not specify if these angels were sculptures, paintings, or boys. Vasari says that the "Heaven" where Christ was received was similar to Brunelleschi's inverted bowl at Santa Felicità. But he adds that in some years another heaven was installed above this one, which, from his description, sounds similar to the one Bishop Abraham saw at Santissima Annunziata, except that it had ten revolving heavens instead of seven.[15]

While the enactments staged by the cardinals at Viterbo in 1462 derive from *sacre rappresentazioni,* the parade of the pope and other grandees conformed to another familiar model, of which we have seen several examples during Pius's journey to Mantua: the state entrance of a prestigious ruler into a city. State entries had been much simpler in the Middle Ages; town officials, the clergy, guild members, and leading citizens had met the distinguished visitor at the gate and escorted him to the town hall, the cathedral, or the place where he would be staying. During the fourteenth century and throughout the Renaissance the elaboration of these occasions escalated dramatically in every country of Europe; the *joyeaux entreés* of France and the Burgundian lands were as elaborate as those of Italy. Certain observances became standard ev-

13. T. S. R. Boase, *Giorgio Vasari: The Man and the Book,* National Gallery of Art, Bollingen Series 35 (Princeton: Princeton University Press, 1979), 182.

14. Vasari, "Brunelleschi," *Lives of the Painters* I.356.

15. Ibid., "Cecca," *Lives of the Painters* I.501–2.

erywhere: the visitor would receive the keys to the city at the gate; if he or she had any kind of jurisdiction over the town, the visitor would solemnly confirm all the rights and privileges of the town and its citizens, after which an exchange of gifts sealed friendship between hosts and guest. In the procession the honored visitor would ride or be carried under a baldacchino attended by all the high officials of his court; then would follow the nobility, gentry, and knights, all the ranks and orders of society riding or marching in strict precedence as if to graph the hierarchy of power and prestige. In urban republics officers of the city government replaced the feudal nobles, with guilds and confraternities also participating in the procession. The local clergy always marched and chanted, carrying banners, sacred pictures, or relics.[16]

In the decades after the Black Death guilds and confraternities began staging street pageants and *tableaux vivants* along the ceremonial routes of these entries.[17] During the quattrocento whole buildings arose in the streets and squares—triumphal arches, temples, colonnades, castles, even hills and mountains—turning the city itself into a giant stage set.[18] The festivities for Pius II at Viterbo in 1462 represented only the midpoint in this evolution. For the most advanced stage we must move forward about half a century to 1515 and the entry of Leo X, the first Medici pope, into his native city of Florence. It was the first time a pope had visited Florence since Pius II; but Leo's entry to Florence had much greater political significance. By then the Medici were outright rulers of the city, and Leo's entrance was intended to emphasize that. Less than two months elapsed between the announcement of the visit and its scheduled date of November 30, 1515. Florence mobilized her artists and architects, and the fevered preparations charged ahead, uninterrupted by sabbaths or holidays. Churches commandeered as workshops suspended their normal functions. Even so, Luca Landucci, whose diary is one of our important sources, says that many finishing touches were not ready in time.[19]

The composition, form, and precedence of the procession conformed to long-established traditions for papal processions, and it followed the same route used by Pius II in 1459.[20] When Pope Leo arrived, the Signoria met him, all the officers and magistrates of the city walking on foot

16. Strong, *Art and Power,* 7.

17. Ibid., 7–8.

18. Molinari, *Spettacoli,* 23.

19. Landucci, *Florentine Diary,* 280.

20. John Shearman, "The Florentine Entrata of Leo X, 1515," *Journal of the Warburg and Courtauld Institutes* 38 (1975): 143.

but decked out in more than usual splendor. The other leading citizens came on horseback, displaying their wealth in magnificent clothing. Of course, all the clergy and monastics were there to hail their pontiff. All who greeted Pope Leo also processed with him, escorted by fifty or sixty youths dressed in purple silk with miniver collars, carrying silver maces. Some members of the Signoria carried the pope in a chair, while others bore the baldacchino that shaded him. Another baldacchino carried by members of the Parte Guelfa covered the Blessed Sacrament. Three hundred guards of the Signoria escorted the parade, along with five hundred papal guards, including mounted bowmen, musketeers, and infantry bearing two-edged axes.[21] Fourteen temporary structures and one permanent one punctuated the ceremonial route. A document that appears to be an early draft of the program for these constructions specifies only eight: seven triumphal arches representing the seven cardinal virtues, with an eighth showing all the virtues together. But other constructions were added at every turning point of the route, along with a theater at the Piazza di Santa Trinità and permanent modifications at Santa Maria Novella, where popes visiting Florence traditionally resided.[22]

The pope entered Florence at the gate of San Pietro Gattolino in the Oltrarno, where he encountered the first triumphal arch, representing Prudence.[23] The outer defenses had been demolished and the remaining fortifications disguised behind classical columns over thirty feet high, painted to look like silver, carrying entablatures in which serpents entwined around mirrors.[24] Above these were statues in niches representing Prudence, Caution, Gentleness, and Gravity, each identified by insignia on their heads and bearing trophies. Other sculptures or reliefs represented the Fates, Baptism, Temptation, and the story of Tobias and the Angel, one of a series of Old Testament or Apocryphal incidents that adorned all the arches. At every arch the procession paused and rearranged itself to enjoy a performance with music that explained all the symbolism and related it to Leo. Many of the "statues" on the arches were living figures who sang in the performances. That is why the *entrata* procession took seven hours to cover less than two miles.[25]

21. Landucci, *Florentine Diary,* 279–80; Bartolomeo Masi, *Ricordanze* 163 and following; quoted in Molinari, *Spettacoli,* 25–26n33.

22. Shearman, "Entrata," 139–40.

23. Ibid., 145.

24. Landucci, *Florentine Diary,* 280–81; Shearman, "Entrata," 145n27.

25. Shearman, "Entrata," 144–45.

At Santa Felicità a second arch spanned the street. Its theme was Temperance, with eight large columns, numerous pilasters, and rich ornamentation. In niches and between the arches were statues by the best sculptors in Florence, "making people pause to consider their meaning and admire their beauty."[26] The figure of Temperance was an automaton that poured water first into one vase, then another. Above the columns and pilasters deeds of King David and other Old Testament figures occupied a "golden platform."[27] Leaving Santa Felicità, the pope crossed the Arno at the Ponte di Santa Trinità, passing through a construction that took up the entire width of the bridge and had six great columns. "These pillars," Landucci tells us, "formed a kind of portico, ornamented with many statues and so beautiful in color that one did not know how to come away; nothing else approached it."[28]

At the north end of the bridge was an obelisk, probably reproducing the one at the Vatican.[29] Just a short distance farther the Piazza di Santa Trinità was filled with a round "castle," as Landucci called it, surrounded by twenty-two square pillars with tapestries hung between them.[30] This was the theater that had been inserted into the original sequence of arches. The artist in charge of it had been experimenting with fireworks and blew himself up a few days before the pope arrived, preventing its completion.[31] In its unfinished state it seems to have puzzled observers, one of whom called it a temple, while another was certain that it reproduced the Castel Sant'Angelo in Rome.[32] In the Mercato Nuovo Baccio Bandinelli had erected a triumphal column covered with reliefs in the manner of the columns of Trajan or Marcus Aurelius—but Landucci pronounced it tasteless.[33]

In the Piazza della Signoria, which required something particularly grand, Giuliano da Sangallo had built a quadrifrons, a four-way arch, painted to resemble marble, each portal flanked by columns raised on high plinths.[34] Gilded foliage in relief decorated the upper parts of the columns, and the entablature carried palms of victory.[35] The theme of the arch was Justice, and the program called for statues of Justice, Equity, Virtue, Concord, Obedience, and Innocence. Landucci bragged that "it

26. Landucci, *Florentine Diary,* 281.
27. Shearman, "Entrata," 145n28.
28. Landucci, *Florentine Diary,* 281.
29. Shearman, "Entrata," 140.
30. Landucci, *Florentine Diary,* 281.
31. Shearman, "Entrata," 149n41.
32. Ibid., 140.
33. Landucci, *Florentine Diary,* 285; Wackernagel, *Florentine Renaissance Artists,* 198.
34. Landucci, *Florentine Diary,* 282; Andres, Hunisak, and Turner, *Art of Florence,* 2:916.
35. Shearman, "Entrata," 146n30.

would be difficult for any city to make even this one edifice."[36] Inside the Loggia dei Lanzi was a giant Hercules painted to imitate bronze, which Landucci says was "not much appreciated."[37] A few blocks past the piazza twenty-four golden columns and a profusion of gilt ornament adorned the street between the Bargello and the Badia.[38] This was the arch dedicated to Hope, though some sources specify that it was not a "true arch."[39] At the next major intersection there were four arches as tall as the houses, towering over the streets and centered on the sides of a quadrangle of twenty-seven square pillars, painted to look like porphyry, with festoons of gilt pomegranates and pine cones looped between them.[40]

The cathedral boasted a magnificent stage set front by Sansovino representing Charity, reportedly based on a design that Lorenzo il Magnifico, the pope's father, had made in 1491. It soared 141 feet above the pavement, with columns, statues, and panels imitating reliefs painted by Andrea del Sarto.[41] The decorated canopy used on the feast of San Giovanni covered the square between the cathedral and the baptistery.[42] Inside the cathedral the pope walked to the altar along an elevated runway lined with candles. Also elevated were the choir and altar, crowned with a canopy, so that everyone could behold the pope celebrating Mass. The choir and the tribunes at the sides of the crossing were completely filled with great banks of blazing candles.[43]

At the conclusion of the Mass the procession re-formed and crossed the piazza into the Via Cerretani, parading through yet another triumphal arch, higher than the houses, with four round columns, six pilasters, and "so many figures by good masters that everyone felt astounded, staring and wondering." At the Canto de' Carneschi was an arch the width of two streets and, at the entrance to the Via della Scala, a shrine honoring the Blessed Virgin. As the pope approached Santa Maria Novella there were galleries down both sides of the street and an arch at each end, with another leading to the papal quarters in the Sala del Papa.[44] Here, all the virtues were represented together on the fac-

36. Landucci, *Florentine Diary,* 282.

37. Andres, Hunisak, and Turner, *Art of Florence,* 2:916; Landucci, *Florentine Diary,* 285.

38. Landucci, *Florentine Diary,* 282.

39. Shearman, "Entrata," 146n31.

40. Landucci, *Florentine Diary,* 280–85; Shearman, "Entrata," 146n32.

41. Wackernagel, *Florentine Renaissance Artists,* 198; Andres, Hunisak, and Turner, *Art of Florence,* 2:916.

42. Andres, Hunisak, and Turner, *Art of Florence,* 2:916.

43. Landucci, *Florentine Diary,* 280.

44. Ibid., 283–84.

ing sides of the street, with "so many figures and so much ornamentation that everyone who stopped to look, lost himself in the midst of such a number of different subjects."[45] In the piazza in front of Santa Maria Novella, Landucci describes a golden horse trampling a giant.[46] At the pope's lodging a famous staircase and surrounding gates and walls had been demolished to make way for enlarged accommodation and a new staircase wide enough to be mounted on horseback.[47] The pope's chapel, redecorated by Pontormo, is the only part of the decorations for the occasion known to survive.[48] Yet Leo only stayed at Santa Maria Novella one night before moving back to his family home at the Palazzo Medici. The next day he went to Mass at San Lorenzo and departed the following morning for Bologna.[49]

Landucci was one of the few to grumble at the expense of this short-lived splendor. He estimated that two thousand men had been at work for a month, "carpenters, stone-masons, painters, carters, porters, sawyers, etc.," at what he calculated was a cost of seventy thousand florins, "all for things of no duration; when a splendid temple might have been built in honor of God and to the glory of the city."[50] He lamented "that it was a pity to see it taken down, with all those wonderful figures by good masters."[51]

Leo's *entrata* had been a special celebration that was never repeated; yet the Florentines put on a spectacle *every year* that must have been almost comparable in expense. This was the *Festa di San Giovanni,* the Feast of John the Baptist, patron of Florence, on June 24, the day that Pius had celebrated with the boat race at Capodimonte. Like other festivities, this one had been simpler in the Middle Ages. When Giovanni Villani speaks of it in 1283, the Feast of San Giovanni was still a series of private celebrations in which groups of leading citizens formed *brigate* (clubs) to play games, parade, and feast, each led by a "Lord of Love." The first horse race, or *palio,* for San Giovanni (the *palio* was the elaborate cloth or banner that was given as the prize) seems to have occurred in 1288 to bolster morale during the Florentine siege of Arezzo.[52] This race would remain, at least in theory, the climax of the festivities for

45. Ibid., 284; Shearman, "Entrata," 147.

46. Landucci, *Florentine Diary,* 284; Wackernagel, *Florentine Renaissance Artists,* 198.

47. Landucci, *Florentine Diary,* 285; Shearman, "Entrata," 148n35.

48. Shearman, 148n35.

49. Landucci, *Florentine Diary,* 285.

50. Ibid., 285.

51. Ibid., 282.

52. Cesare Guasti, ed., *Le feste di San Giovanni Battista in Firenze descritto in prosa e in rima da contemporanei* (Florence: Giovani Cirri, 1884), 2–3.

centuries to come. During the fourteenth century the feast expanded rapidly, lost its private character, and became the commune's great celebration of itself. The Feast of San Giovanni had such strong associations with the republican commune that the Medici, once their dominance was established in 1434, were uncomfortable with it. Cosimo, with his usual caution, left San Giovanni alone but promoted the Feast of the Epiphany as a competing, specifically Medicean festival.[53] His grandson Lorenzo, however, attacked not only the Feast of San Giovanni but also Carnival and all other occasions on which families other than the Medici could strut their magnificence. Lorenzo pruned back the festivals, especially the "floats," or *edifizi,* on San Giovanni—then, after 1488, he began reviving them again under the direction of the "Company of the Star," created to execute Lorenzo's own festival program.[54] The return of the *edifizi* at San Giovanni was tentative at first, with only six of them rolling in 1488; but in 1491 Lorenzo expanded San Giovanni to five days, introducing new elements designed by himself, especially the staging of the Roman triumph of Aemilius Paulus. Before June 24 came around again in 1492, Lorenzo was dead. Space does not permit tracing these developments, but four sources enable us to describe each element of the celebration as it was at the peak of its evolution. The four sources are Gregorio Dati, writing in 1410, Matteo Palmieri in 1454, Vasari's biography of Cecca, and an anonymous, undated account that may be from c. 1492 or 1514 called "Ordine e modo da tenersi nella solemnità di San Giovanni piacendo a Vostra Magnificenza" [henceforth "the 'Ordine' account"].[55]

In the months prior to San Giovanni other feasts and celebrations worked the people into a holiday frame of mind with celebrations of May Day, San Zanobi (the city's first bishop), Ascension, Pentecost, Trinity Sunday, and Corpus Christi, all with singing, dancing, banqueting, and jousts. On the streets where processions were to pass and horse races were to be run, the buildings vanished under layers of tapestries

53. Richard C. Trexler, *Public Life in Renaissance Florence* (New York: Academic Press, 1980), 423–24.

54. Trexler, *Public Life,* 451.

55. Anonymous, "Ordine e modo da tenersi nella solemnità di San Giovanni piacendo a Vostra Magnificenza," addressed to the Sforza court in Milan, hereafter cited as "Ordine," in Guasti, *Feste di San Giovanni,* 25–28. Guasti says this account is addressed to the Sforza court in Milan, which did not exist in 1513–1514, but the account mentions the burning of the *ceri,* which did not happen before the Medici restoration of 1513. It is beyond the scope of this work to resolve this contradiction which makes it impossible to be certain of the date of this document.

and rich cloths; seats and stands sprouted in front of them, also decked in gorgeous fabrics.[56] Forty feet above the Piazza di San Giovanni stretched a great blue canopy, hung from rings on the front of the cathedral, the baptistery, and the houses on the square. Vasari tells us that this canopy was embroidered all over with yellow lilies scattered around a circle in the center, which displayed the arms of the Popolo and Commune of Florence and the captain of the Guelph Party. From its edges hung banners with the arms of the various magistracies and the Marzoco lion, another emblem of the city.[57]

The first event of the San Giovanni celebrations was always the *mostra,* a display of goods by the Florentine merchants. Originally held on the Eve of San Giovanni, it was moved forward as more days of festivity were inserted in the calendar; by 1491 it was on June 21, two days before its original position. Our most detailed account of it is from Gregorio Dati in about 1410.

> early in the morning all the guilds put on the display (*mostra*) outside of the fronts of their shops, of all the rich things, ornaments, and jewels. They showed enough cloths of gold and silk to adorn ten kingdoms; so many jewels of gold and silver, and hangings, and panel paintings, and marvelous intaglios, and weaponry and armor, that it would take too long to describe them all.[58]

We would be misled if we saw this display of goods only as advertisement for the shops that displayed them or exclusively as a bragging display of the city's wealth, although it was surely both of those things. Richard Trexler has perceptively described it as a corporate act of offering, similar to the candles, torches, and *ceri* that would later be carried to the church of San Giovanni. The pedestrians viewing the displays, especially the women, were a second *mostra* of their own, sporting the riches of their fathers and husbands in yards of luxurious cloth and masses of jewelry that so encased them that an anonymous versifier said they looked more like columns than human beings.[59] In later years, the "Ordine" account tells us, on that same day there were processions of companies of men and boys and of the monastic, mendicant, and secular clergy to make costly offerings. Although this seems to have been

56. Trexler, *Public Life,* 247.
57. Vasari, "Cecca," *Lives of the Painters* I.502–3.
58. Gregorio Dati, *Storia di Firenze,* in Guasti, *Feste di San Giovanni,* 5; my translation.
59. Trexler, *Public Life,* 248–49.

merely an anticipation of the main religious procession on the morning of the Eve of San Giovanni, it possibly signified the divine acceptance and approval of the riches displayed by the shops.[60]

The next morning, June 22, came the parade of *edifizi*—ten of them in 1491, much reduced from over twice that number before Lorenzo had suppressed them. The undated "Ordine" account lists the subjects as (1) the fall of Lucifer and his followers, (2) the creation of Adam and his story, (3) the Annunciation to Our Lady with her mysteries, (4) the nativity of St. John the Baptist, (5) the nativity of Christ with its story, (6) the baptism of Christ by St. John, (7) the resurrection of Christ, (8) the ascension of Christ, (9) the assumption of Our Lady, and (10) the living and the dead.[61] Palmieri's 1454 account, before Lorenzo suppressed the *edifizi,* lists twenty-two items in this parade, which took most of the day to complete its route. It portrayed the same salvation narrative as its shorter successors, but in greater elaboration.[62] The first *edifizo* in the longer, earlier parade had two separate components. The moving *edifizo* itself showed the Archangel Michael and, above him, God the Father looking on from a cloud. But, fixed in place on the side of the piazza opposite the Palazzo della Signoria, the battle of the angels raged, with Lucifer and his cohorts falling down from heaven. Palmieri tells us about an untoward incident marring the precession of the *edifizi* in 1454. A cavalcade representing Octavian Caesar, with a sybil giving him a prophecy of Christ, drew up in front of the Signoria, who were gathered on the *ringhiera* (platform) in front of the palace. When the cavalcade arrived, "Octavian" began his performance by mounting an *edifizo* representing a temple. But a crazed German rushed up after him, ripped the idol out of the temple, and threw it into the piazza. Then, turning on "Octavian," he tossed him head over heels into the crowd. Climbing farther up a pole, the German reached some boys who were suspended above the temple and began flailing at them with a club, beating some of them severely before they managed to dislodge him. Once he fell into their midst, the multitude at once pummeled and kicked the German nearly to death.[63]

Palmieri's narrative divulges various details that we can link with Vasari's descriptions to gain a better picture of what these *edifizi* were like. The "temple" must have been built on a cart, probably propelled

60. "Ordine," in Guasti, *Feste di San Giovanni,* 25–28.

61. Ibid., 26.

62. Unnamed work, in Guasti, *Feste di San Giovanni,* 21–22.

63. Ibid.

by men hidden beneath it. The cart was probably similar to the "Car of the Mint" that Vasari praised because of "the wheels below which are pivoted [like castors], in order that the structure may be able to turn sharp corners, and may be managed in such a manner as to shake it as little as possible, particularly for the sake of those who stand fastened upon it."[64] We may picture the *edifizi,* gliding and turning without visible means of locomotion, and with numerous figures in stationary positions who, upon arriving before the priors and other officials seated on the *ringhiera,* would then perform the action appropriate to their story with sung or declaimed commentary, accompanied by trumpets and other instruments.

The superstructure that the crazed German climbed was almost certainly similar to the superstructure of the "Clouds" that Vasari describes as being invented by Cecca (Francesco d'Angelo, 1446–1488) for St. John's Eve. The "Clouds," Vasari tells us, were constructed on stout wooden platforms with reinforced legs like those of a trestle table. Above this, with firm bracing, rose a tall pole (whether of wood or iron is not clear), at the top of which "was placed a mandorla all covered with cotton wool [imitating clouds], cherubim, lights, and other ornaments, and within this, on a horizontal bar of iron, there sat or stood ... a person representing that Saint whom the particular Company principally honored." Below the mandorla,

> There radiated four or five iron bars, in the manner of the branches of a tree, and at the end of each, attached likewise with irons, stood a little boy dressed like an angel. These boys could move round and round at pleasure on the iron brackets on which their feet rested, for the brackets hung on hinges. And with similar brackets there were sometimes made two or three tiers of angels or of saints, according to the nature of the subject to be represented.

This entire apparatus could be disguised with cotton wool so that it would, indeed, appear to be a great cloud wafting down the street, or, Vasari says, it could represent a tree or a lily. Vasari asks us to believe that all of this—stout wooden platform, pole, branches, at least one fully grown person and anywhere from four to a dozen children—was lifted and carried from inside the framework by "porters or peasants, who carried it on their shoulders, placing themselves round the wooden

64. Vasari, "Cecca," *Lives of the Painters* I.506.

base [where] were fixed cushions of leather stuffed with down, or cotton-wool, or some other soft and yielding material." These "Clouds," which seem to have been predecessors of the *edifizi,* were part of the religious procession on St. John's Eve until they obtained their separate parade day in 1454.[65] It seems likely that, when the German assailant climbed the pole and attacked the boys above the top of the "temple," his victims were arranged on an apparatus similar to Vasari's description but now attached to the top of a car moving on pivoting wheels.[66]

The shortened parade of ten *edifizi* that processed in 1491 finished its route by the end of the morning. People then escaped the worst of the summer heat with a long afternoon break. If Dati's account from 1410 still applied, these breaks to dine (*desinare*) were not idle, but filled with banquets and celebrations of weddings, with so many pipers, instruments, songs, and festive dancing "that it seemed as though earth had become paradise."[67] It is unclear whether these private celebrations had continued or had expanded into all five days of the celebration by 1491.

Lorenzo de' Medici unveiled his new insertion into the San Giovanni program, the "Triumph of Aemilius Paulus," on the evening of June 22, 1491. Aemilius Paulus had been Roman consul in 168 B.C. when he won the battle of Pydna, captured the king of Macedonia, and brought home immense booty, including 150,000 slaves. It would have been injudicious for Lorenzo to identify himself with an emperor, but this republican consul who had enriched Rome was a perfect stand-in for the glorification of "il Magnifico." Lorenzo had staged neo-Roman triumphs at Carnival, but inserting a strictly classical, un-Christian event into the celebrations of San Giovanni was unprecedented.[68] It consisted of fifteen triumphal cars designed by Lorenzo himself (or artists under his

65. Vasari, "Cecca," *Lives of the Painters* I.502–4. Vasari says the clouds were in the procession of St. John's Eve—but over a century before the time he was writing.

66. There are difficulties with this reading of the sources, not least of which is that Cecca, whom Vasari credits with the invention of the "Clouds," would have been eight years old at the time of the 1454 procession that Palmieri describes, but these difficulties may derive from Vasari having misunderstood the sequence of development in the previous century and do not necessarily affect our mental picture of the *edifizi.* For other difficulties in Vasari's account of Cecca's inventions, see Orville K. Larson, "Vasari's Description of Stage Machinery," *Educational Theatre Journal* 9, no. 4 (December 1957): 287–99.

67. Dati, *Storia di Firenze,* in Guasti, *Feste di San Giovanni,* 7.

68. Trexler, *Public Life,* 452. There was a triumph of the seven planets at Carnival in 1490; see also Charles Dempsey, "Portraits and Masks in the Art of Lorenzo de'Medici, Botticelli, and Politian's Stanze per la Giostra," *Renaissance Quarterly* 52, no. 1 (Spring 1999), 5.

direction), pulled by forty to fifty pairs of oxen and escorted by five squadrons of cavalry upon richly caparisoned horses.[69] The intent to "one-up" the morning's procession of ten *edifizi* escorted by boys must have been obvious. No doubt the cars were laden with symbolic personages and attributes ingeniously contrived by Lorenzo's squadron of humanists. Tribaldo de' Rossi captured the political message when he wrote, "As Aemilius Paulus had provided such booty in the time of Caesar Augustus (*sic*), Lorenzo de' Medici provided it [now].... It was considered the worthiest thing that had ever processed on San Giovanni."[70]

The following morning, the Eve of San Giovanni, always began with the procession of the city's clergy. The clergy, along with the lay confraternities that met at each church, assembled in the cathedral and emerged from its doors at Terce (about 8:00 A.M.). Immediately all the bells in Florence began to ring and continued to do so until the procession, whose route roughly followed the line of the old city walls, had completed its circuit and reentered the cathedral.[71] Each of the fifty-two parish churches and more than a dozen monastic establishments greeted the passing procession with trumpets, incense, sprinklings of holy water, and blessings of the crowd, every group singing hymns and psalms.[72] Each company of clergy carried baldachins over their holy relics and held aloft gorgeously embroidered banners.[73] Vasari credits Cecca with the "martyrdoms" of the saints honored in this procession, "either dead or tortured in various ways, for some appeared to be transfixed by a lance or a sword, others had a dagger in the throat, and others had suchlike weapons in their bodies."[74] The spectators must have consisted mainly of females and foreigners, for most Florentine men and boys belonged to some lay confraternity and were marching along with the clergy of their church.[75]

In the evening, after *desinare,* the men and boys all paraded again, this time as representatives of the sixteen gonfalons, or wards, into which the city was divided. Early in the quattrocento the Signoria had

69. Trexler, *Public Life,* 451.

70. Tribaldo de' Rossi, *Ricordanze;* quoted in Trexler, *Public Life,* 451. The writer of the "Ordine" lists four separate triumphs for Caesar, Pompey, Octavian, and Trajan in place of the one for Aemilius Paulus; Guasti, *Feste di San Giovanni,* 26.

71. Trexler, *Public Life,* 250–51.

72. Ibid., 250–51.

73. "Ordine," in Guasti, *Feste di San Giovanni,* 27.

74. Vasari, "Cecca," in *Lives of the Painters* I.504.

75. Trexler, *Public Life,* 255.

declared that, on pain of a fine, every household must send at least two males between the ages of fifteen and sixty-five to join this procession.[76] Once the men and boys of each gonfalon assembled in their own district, they were arranged for the procession, walking two by two, beginning with the "more worthy and older," with the young and undistinguished behind.[77] We do not know who determined this order and on what basis.[78] Once everyone was in place they marched to the baptistery of San Giovanni, bearing offerings of wax candles from their district. Wax candles were a luxury; ordinary candles were tallow. In 1336 this had amounted to 3,657 pounds of wax.[79] Both the marchers and the watching women and children displayed their most sumptuous finery. In contrast to the morning's religious solemnity, the gonfalons presented "pleasure wagons" that Dati described as "Men with games of suitable enjoyment and beautiful representations."[80] In 1415 the Signoria felt compelled to outlaw obscene pictures in this procession, along with "base or undignified" words. Perhaps these were similar to the "triumphal wagons full of madmen" mentioned at other Florentine celebrations.[81] Many of the most powerful men in the city would not be marching with their gonfalon but would be part of the enormous procession of government officials bringing their own candles. This part of the procession was enlarged in 1454 to include all the officials of the city's ever-proliferating magistracies and bureaucracies, as well as the Signoria and the officers of all the guilds.[82]

At last the day of San Giovanni itself dawned. Those who went out into the streets early would have seen more of Cecca's inventions, the "Giants" and the "*spiritelli.*" Both of these were men on stilts, which, according to Vasari, were ten to twelve feet high. At this height they were prudently accompanied by a man with a tall pole on which they could steady themselves.[83] The *spiritelli* walked "without anything but their own proper form," but the Giants were enveloped in "great masks and

76. Ibid., 252.

77. Dati, *Storia di Firenze,* in Guasti, *Feste di San Giovanni,* 5.

78. Trexler, *Public Life,* 252.

79. Guasti, ed., *Feste di San Giovanni,* 3.

80. Dati, *Storia di Firenze,* in Guasti, *Feste di San Giovanni,* 5; Trexler, *Public Life,* 255.

81. Trexler, *Public Life,* 255.

82. Ibid., 260.

83. Vasari, "Cecca," *Lives of the Painters* I.505. Vasari says, "he who knows what Florentine brains are" will not be surprised to know that some could walk at this height without such assistance.

other ornaments in the way of draperies, and imitations of armor, so that they seemed to have the members and heads of giants." The pole on which they leaned was disguised as a weapon, "whether mace, lance, or a great bell-clapper, such as Morgante is said by the poets of romance to have been wont to carry."[84]

The principal event of the morning, however, was a continuation of the offerings of wax candles to San Giovanni, this time by the Parte Guelfa, the Mint, and the towns and lords subject to Florence. To Dati, around 1410, this had been the most exciting event of the festival. The Parte Guelfa had the honor of bringing its offerings first, led by its captain, followed by all the Florentine nobles as well as ambassadors and nobles visiting from other towns. Among the offerings that Dati describes were candles weighing up to a hundred pounds. About twenty of these had evolved into elaborate structures of wood, wax, and pasteboard, carried upon festive carts.[85] These constructions, called *ceri,* fell out of favor under the Medici, but were too traditional to be omitted.[86] Vasari speaks of them with contempt, and, after their restoration to power, the Medici had them burned on San Giovanni's Day.[87] The "Ordine" account says that these unfashionable objects were an "insult to the feast" but made a splendid bonfire, which took place immediately after the *desinare*—though, unfortunately, we do not know what year it was.[88] Replacing the *ceri* in the morning procession were the sumptuous palii or banners that riders on horseback displayed to the crowds in the Piazza della Signoria before carrying them to San Giovanni.[89]

When the *ceri* were reduced to embers, or in other years, after the *desinare,* preparations to run the *palio* began. This began with a parading of the *palio* that served as the prize. Jockeys and horses were naturally decked out in magnificent liveries that advertised the arms and attributes of their owners. The race still officially culminated the whole festival, but, whereas Dati describes it in detail, the "Ordine" merely says that after the *desinare* came the running of the *palio.* By then such an event would be too familiar to need explanation; Florence alone ran numerous *palii* throughout the year, often in commemoration of past

84. Ibid., I.505. Luigi Pulci, Boiardo, and Ariosto, among others, wrote of Morgante, the giant friend of Roland.

85. Dati, *Storia di Firenze,* in Guasti , *Feste di San Giovanni,* 6–7.

86. Trexler, *Public Life,* 506.

87. Vasari, "Cecca," *Lives of the Painters* I.504; Trexler, *Public Life,* 258.

88. "Ordine," in Guasti, *Feste di San Giovanni,* 27–28.

89. Dati, "Diary," in Guasti, *Feste di San Giovanni,* 6–7.

military successes. Pius's boat race at Capodimonte was simply a waterborne *palio,* and we will encounter more examples in the next chapter. The route of the *palio* would have been lined with spectators, many of whom would have money riding on the result. Thus, in one last dash of excitement, "the whole festival was crisply consummated."[90] Consummated, but not concluded; the populace would have been far too excited to go home and go to bed, so a fireworks display completed the evening.

By the time the "Ordine" was written, the *festa di San Giovanni* had been extended into the following three days as well as three days before the twenty-fourth. June 25 was the Feast of St. Eligius (San Lò to the Florentines), the patron of goldsmiths, an important guild at Florence. This observance began with a wild animal hunt in the morning and finished with another *palio* in the evening. The season concluded with a tournament over the next two days.[91] This tournament was the last participatory event to survive into the twenty-first century. In 2007, when I was in Florence for San Giovanni, businesses still closed for the day, but the tournament was suppressed for safety reasons. All that remained of the public celebrations were the evening fireworks.

In assessing this profusion of spectacles over a seven-day period, it is important to remember that this was only the largest of many annual Florentine celebrations, including May Day, Carnival, and the anniversary of the conquest of Pisa, along with the standard feasts of the Christian year: Christmas, Easter, the Assumption of the Virgin, Epiphany, and Corpus Christi, as well as a steady series of *palii* and tournaments—all of which had enjoyed explosive development since the mid-fourteenth century. Every other Italian city would have had a similar calendar of celebrations, as the splendid *palio* still run at Siena reminds us. Indeed, the proliferation of festivals, offerings, and days on which shops had to close while their owners processed in the streets amounted to a considerable economic burden. The signoria stepped in many times to reduce the number of days on which business was suspended in honor of religious precessions; it did so in the late fourteenth century and again in 1414 and 1417 and 1437. In 1460 the signoria cut the required *fifty-five* annual offerings to thirty-five because the guilds could afford neither the cost nor the lost work time. Preachers recognized the economic burden of festivity and exhorted the rich to be especially charitable on holidays to those who lost employment. Another law of 1474,

90. Trexler, *Public Life,* 262.

91. "Ordine," in Guasti, *Feste di San Giovanni,* 28.

attempting to limit the days of shop closings, observed that when men could not support their families, they were likely to curse, which was not the offering God desired.[92]

This drumbeat of legislation, like today's speed limits, is a sign not that the explosion of holidays was under control, but that it was irresistible. The appetite for spectacle had been far more restrained in the Middle Ages, but since then, the craving had grown stronger than any kind of bourgeois economic prudence. The Feast of San Giovanni and all the rest of the celebrations crowding the calendar were not expressions of calculated economic self-interest; they were, in fact, contrary to such interest. This is not to say that Florentines were uninterested in commerce, but clearly they were *even more* interested in the emotional need for distraction and escape. The continual elaboration of festivities of every kind, everywhere in Europe, implies an insatiable yearning for it at all levels of the population. The same elaboration was equally irrepressible for weddings, tournaments, state occasions, banquets, and funerals as it was for religious observances. God and his saints could have been honored and propitiated by offerings to the poor rather than by dangling children at perilous heights above the pavement. When Dati wrote that the celebrations during *desinare* were so glorious "that it seemed as though earth had become paradise," he uses almost the same words as Pius II describing Corpus Christi in Viterbo.[93] These tremendous outlays of wealth, repeated frequently year after year, suggests that rulers and ruled alike felt an obsessive need for shows that fostered the illusion that they "had assuredly entered the dwelling of gods." This lust for the mind-boggling was something almost unprecedented, brought about by the constant anxiety and painful memories from which it offered escape. Again and again, satisfied celebrators echoed Dati's and Pius's words, claiming that they felt transported in their minds from this world to Rome, to Arcady, to Camelot, to another world, to the dwellings of the gods, or to heaven—anyplace but *here.*

92. Trexler, *Public Life,* 275–76.
93. Dati, *Storia di Firenze,* in Guasti, *Feste di San Giovanni,* 7.

13

Pienza

EVEN THE PURE AIR and bucolic delights of Mount Amiata could not banish the papal gout. There were days when Pius lay suffering in bed, unable to stir. This was his condition one day when frightened cardinals burst in upon him with news of plague. Their mountain redoubt was breached; plague was in Abbadia itself, and people known to the curia had succumbed. Although "he was faint and in great pain," Pius immediately called for his litter. Before sunset he departed for Pienza across the Val d'Orcia, followed by a great train of cardinals, courtiers, and their households. Echoing his previous words at Viterbo, he wrote, "This was the end of the pleasures of Abbadia. Joy is always followed by grief."[1]

Through the long summer dusk and dark of night they carried Pius twelve miles across the valley to Pienza. Though the hour was late when they arrived, Pius says he would have liked to inspect his new buildings at once. But such eagerness was no match for the pain of his gout, and he remained confined to bed in his new palace for several days. When he was able to get up and about, he wrote many pages enthusiastically describing the buildings he had called into being. Pius had only gradually settled into the idea of converting Corsignano into a new city. On the way to Mantua in January 1459 he had thought only of a new church and palace.[2] Discussions with Alberti, Rossellino, and Biondo at Florence and during his stay in Mantua may have expanded his ideas.[3] Pienza is often called an "ideal city"; it followed Pius's sometimes ec-

1. *Comm.*, Smith, IX.597.
2. Ibid., II.147.
3. Rubenstein, "Pius II," 79–81.

centric architectural ideals and often Alberti's, but only as adapted to the very restricted site and to its intended functions as a summer home for the pope and dynastic center for the Piccolomini family.[4] Therefore, it did not follow any abstract, universal ideal that could be applied everywhere. Some egregious mistakes resulted from the great haste in construction. The architect misjudged the heights of columns in the cathedral, and the palace was well on its way toward completion before anyone noticed that it had no kitchen! They had no choice but to tack a kitchen tower onto the back in violation of the harmony between parts and whole that was the guiding principle of the design.[5] Pius, however, was perfectly content.[6] He was content also with the expense, which had been enormous—50,000 ducats, although the original estimate had been only 18,000. The Florentine architect, Bernardo Rossellino, had many ill-wishers among the Sienese, who hoped he would suffer for his extravagance. But when Pius saw the buildings he told Rossellino, "You did well, Bernardo, in lying to us about the expense. . . . If you had told the truth, neither this splendid palace nor this church, the finest in all Italy, would now be standing."[7]

Rossellino was the architect of Pienza, but some believe that Alberti's mind directed Rossellino's hand. There is no doubt, however, that Pius II directed everything, as was the patron's prerogative. In Alberti's very platonic thinking architectural beauty derives from geometry, proportion, logic, and classicism; these qualities in their purity reflect the divine forms that underlie the design of the universe; the divine soul of the observer will recognize and be moved by them.[8] The major buildings at Pienza usually follow Alberti's canons of proportion. We find the same module of length used again and again; the distance between columns on the portico at the back of the palace is the same as the distance between columns in the palace *cortile*. These are both equal to the width of the aisles of the cathedral and to the short side of the rectangles that divide the paving of the piazza.[9] But a survey of the scene at Pienza shows that Pius, the true designer of his city, used or ignored Alberti's concepts at will. To see that, we need to keep in mind some of Alberti's principles.

Churches (which Alberti calls "temples" to avoid using a nonclassical

4. Ibid., 76.

5. Ibid., 80–81.

6. *Comm.*, Smith, IX.600.

7. Ibid., IX.603.

8. Rudolf Wittkower, *Architectural Principles in the Age of Humanism* (London: Alec Tiranti, 1952), 7.

9. Rubenstein, "Pius II," 87.

word) are to be the highest embodiment of beauty and divinity. In *De re aedificatoria* ("On Building," 1450) Alberti says:

> This is why I would wish the temple so beautiful that nothing more decorous could ever be devised; I would deck it out in every part so that anyone who entered it would start with awe for his admiration at all the noble things, and could scarcely restrain himself from exclaiming that what he saw was a place undoubtedly worthy of God.[10]

Such a temple must separate itself in every way from the ordinary. It should stand apart from lesser buildings in the midst of a beautiful square on high ground, raised yet higher by a substructure or podium.[11] From inside nothing but the sky should be visible through the windows, so that no distraction from ordinary life can intrude.[12] Alberti insists upon the superiority of geometrically centralized plans: hexagons, octagons, decagons, and dodecagons, but especially the circle. "It is obvious from all that is fashioned, produced, or created under her influence that Nature delights primarily in the circle."[13] Although temples should be constructed only from the most precious materials, the color white should predominate, since "in their choice of color, as in their way of life, purity and simplicity would be most pleasing to the gods above."[14] Pienza's cathedral, its front constructed from gleaming white travertine, stands forth dramatically from the rest of the town, where almost everything else is made from the caramel-colored local tufa—in this it is perfectly Albertian.

Alberti seems to assume that the proper way to found a city is for it to spring from a virgin site at the command of a single mind.[15] Pius II's project at Pienza did not spring from fresh ground but was grafted onto the stubby stalk of old Corsignano. This was far from easy, first of all because there was not much room. The new city, like the old village, was restricted by its site on a narrow ridge of tufa. Pienza is less than a quarter of a mile long and, at its center, only 150 yards wide. Pienza has

10. Leon Battista Alberti, *De re aedificatoria* VII.3, in *On the Art of Building in Ten Books,* trans. Joseph Rykwert, Neil Leach, and Robert Taverner (Cambridge, Mass.: MIT Press, 1988), 194.

11. Alberti, *Aedificatoria* VII.3, in *Building,* 195 and 199.

12. Alberti, *Aedificatoria* VII.3, 5, 12, in *Building,* 223; Wittkower, *Architectural Principles,* 7–8.

13. Alberti, *Aedificatoria* VII.4, in *Building,* 196.

14. Alberti, *Aedificatoria* VII.10, in *Building,* 220.

15. Alberti, *Aedificatoria* IV.2, in *Building,* 95–100.

nothing like the straight colonnaded avenues of Nicholas V's plans for the Borgo; it retains the medieval street plan of Corsignano, and its narrow streets have the ambience of any Tuscan hill town until one arrives at the Piazza Pio II, with its cathedral, town hall, and palaces. Planned autocratically by one controlling mind, Pienza gives surprisingly little sense of totalitarian order, discipline, or even symmetry.

The new piazza at the center of town is only eighty-six feet by one hundred feet.[16] The shape of the trapezoidal piazza is symmetrical, but the arrangement of buildings around it is not. The cathedral, centered on the long side of the trapezoid, is Albertian in the simplicity of its form and in being exactly as tall as it is wide, but its unusually awkward use of columns as supports for arches defies one of Alberti's cherished rules. Brunelleschi and Michelozzo, pioneers of Renaissance architecture, had often built arches that sprang directly from the tops of columns. Pius followed their example in building the Piccolomini Loggia in Siena. However, in *De re aedificatoria*, Alberti decreed that, since the cross section of an arch at its springing is square, only square piers, not round columns, were appropriate supports for arches.[17] He preferred that engaged columns be applied to the outside surface of a wall pierced with arches, as the Romans had done at the Coliseum and the Theater of Marcellus.[18] Yet, on the front of the duomo at Pienza, the sides of the arched panels are actually notched back to *make* a space to insert the columns that are tucked under the arch at each side. Not only do the arches spring from columns, but the columns look as though they have rudely pushed the wall aside in order to intrude themselves. They break Alberti's rule with swagger.

To the right of the cathedral the Piccolomini Palace rises as high as the cathedral and would rival it for dominance were it not for the cathedral's contrasting whiteness. On the left side of the piazza, opposite the Piccolomini Palace, is the bishop's palace, built by Rodrigo Borgia, a humbler structure that makes no effort to balance the pope's dwelling in either size or pretension. Across the piazza from the cathedral, the town hall, an asymmetrical building asymmetrically placed, is a delightful but thoroughly medieval composition. These irregularities prevent any

16. Luciana Finelli, "Una città per il papa: Construzione e significati della piazza di Pienza," in *Pio II e la cultura del suo tempo, Atti del i convegno internazionale, 1989,* edited by Luisa Totondi Secchi Tarugi (Milan: Guerini e associate, 1991), 77.

17. Alberti, *Aedificatoria* VII.14, in *Building,* 236.

18. Wittkower, *Architectural Principles,* 30; Alberti, *Aedificatoria* VIII.7, in *Building,* 274.

Figure 13.1. Bernardo Rossellino. The façade of Pienza Cathedral. Photograph from Luke Ashworth-Sides.

symmetry in the piazza; yet they are not faults or mistakes. A formal, monumental approach in such a small place could never harmonize with little Corsignano. Alberti had recognized that irregular streets were appropriate in small cities; for them, he said, "it is better if the roads are not straight, but meandering gently like a river flowing now here, now there, from one bank to the other.... The longer the road seems, the greater the apparent size of the town."[19]

The cathedral itself is even less stylistically consistent than the square. We have seen that its white travertine is exactly what Alberti called for, and Pius speaks with Alberti's voice when he praises the whiteness and logical clarity of the interior. "As you enter the middle door the entire church with its chapels and altars is visible and is remarkable for the clarity of the light and the brilliance of the whole edifice." To preserve this lucid purity, Pius forbade tombs except in places designated for the clergy and ordered that "no one shall deface the whiteness

19. Alberti, *Aedificatoria* IV.5, in *Building,* 106.

of the walls and columns. No one shall draw pictures. No one shall hang up tablets. No one shall erect more chapels and altars than there are at present." Such restraint reflects Alberti, but his influence ends there. The plan and form of the church are not classical or even Italian. The apse end of the church is a half octagon, but nave and aisles of equal height abolish any sense of a central plan. Pius explains that he had seen this equal-height arrangement in Austria, where such hall churches are common.[20] Approaching Pienza from the south, looking up at the apse of the cathedral, one could believe that an Alpine chapel had been transplanted to Tuscany. To build the cathedral and to provide the palace with a garden, Rossellino had to widen the hill artificially with great substructures. In some places under the cathedral no firm rock existed on which to build, and cracks appeared even during construction. After building arches to bridge the weak area, Rossellino believed he could guarantee the solidity of the structure.[21] "Time will tell," Pius mused in the *Commentaries*.[22] The structure still holds, but the foundations under the apse of the church, built on the artificial extension of the hill, had to be reconstructed in the early twentieth century.[23] As one approaches the altar, the floor slopes downward very noticeably, as though the church were sliding down the bluff by slow degrees.

The cathedral's attenuated piers and the flamboyant tracery in its windows are unapologetically Gothic.[24] Pius expresses well-known Gothic aesthetics when he says that the windows make the worshippers "think that they are not in a house of stone but of glass." In his description he specifies that the purpose of the octagonal choir, the aisles and nave of equal height, and the large windows is to maximize the light in the interior. He boasts that his church is "remarkable for the clarity of the light and the brilliance of the whole edifice."[25] Alberti, on the other hand, specified that the windows of a temple should be high and small so that nothing distracting would be seen through them, but also because darkness is conducive to reverence. Excessive light, Alberti said, would overwhelm the candles on the altar, which should be the most majestic point in the church.[26]

The palace as we see it today is strikingly Florentine. Its three floors of rusticated stone, with *bifora* windows on the upper floors and pilasters

20. *Comm.*, Smith, IX.601–3.
21. Mack, *Pienza*, 77.
22. *Comm.*, Smith, IX.601.
23. Rubenstein, "Pius II," viii.
24. Hollingsworth, *Patronage*, 252.
25. *Comm.*, Smith, IX.602.
26. Alberti, *Aedificatoria VII.12*, in *Building*, 223.

Figure 13.2. Bernardo Rossellino. The Piccolomini Palace at Pienza. Photograph from Luke Ashworth-Sides.

and entablatures superimposed upon the rusticated walls, seem to derive directly from Alberti's Rucellai Palace in Florence, whose construction Rossellino directed.[27] The conventional view has always been that the Pienza building copies the one in Florence, even though Pius never refers to the Rucellai Palace in any way.[28] Some scholars, citing evidence from Giovanni Rucellai's tax records, have argued that the Rucellai Palace was not built before 1461 and that it copies the palace at Pienza rather than the reverse.[29] If the matter cannot be settled by the documents, there is a decent *prima facie* case against believing that "a knowledgeable Sienese pope would accept for his own palace a design already used for the home of a Florentine banker."[30]

According to the *Commentaries,* the severe Florentine unity that we see, which the size of the building makes almost oppressive, would not have been the original effect. For Pius tells us that on top of Rossellino's sober block, "where the smoke from the chimneys emerged, were built

27. A *bifora* window is one separated into two parts by a central column or mullion.

28. Rubenstein, "Pius II," 37.

29. Mack, *Pienza,* 47 and 200–1n11.

30. Ibid., 47.

twenty-three tower-like structures ornamented with pinnacles and buttresses and various paintings, which could be seen from a distance and added much to the splendor and charm of the building."[31] There are twenty-three bays on the three uniform façades of the palace (the garden front differs from the others); it is logical, then, to assume that each of these bays terminated at the top in one of these "tower-like structures." If so, the building's skyline would have resembled a more disciplined version of the dizzying silhouettes of the castles in the Limbourg Brothers' *Très riches heures du duc de Berry*—the sort of flamboyant Gothic buildings Aeneas would have seen serving as princely residences in northern Europe.[32] It is not unlikely that, just as he imported the Germanic hall-church plan for his cathedral, Pius would have borrowed some exuberance from the flamboyant north in his palace, leaving Rossellino the task of interpreting these forms in a classical vocabulary. Our whole image of early Renaissance architecture might be less dour if these playful fantasies on the skyline of Pienza had survived.

Apart from these vanished pinnacles, the greatest difference in design of the main palace façades from the front of the Rucellai Palace derived from Pius's yearning for light. The façades at Pienza have unusually large "cross-windows," a type very popular in Rome. In a cross-window the opening is nearly square and is divided by a stone cross into four quarters, the upper ones slightly smaller than the lower. Above the flat top of such openings at the Piccolomini Palace there is a large arch embracing two smaller ones that recall the *bifora* windows common in Florence. In contrast to the small windows of the Rucellai Palace, those at Pienza, along with their arches, fill the height of each floor. Pius leaves no doubt about the purpose of these large windows. "If, as some think, the first charm of a house is light, surely no house could be preferred to this one, which is open to all four points of the compass and lets in abundant light not only through outside windows but through inside ones looking on the inner court."[33]

Pius's love of light and natural scenery dictated the design of the garden façade, which opens up in three tiers of loggias toward the magnificent view across the Val d'Orcia to Mount Amiata. Thus every floor gave the pope an opportunity to enjoy his favorite combination of shade

31. *Comm.*, Smith, IX.598.

32. Boulting, *Aeneas Silvius*, 166. Boulting suggests that the inspiration might have come from buildings Aeneas had admired in Lübeck.

33. *Comm.*, Smith, XI.600.

and scenery. The ground-floor loggia opens onto a hanging garden as large as the palace itself, supported above the side of the cliff upon vaulted chambers that contain stabling for a hundred horses. Whereas today the garden has a windbreaking wall around it, pierced by windows for glimpsing the view, Pius describes "a balustrade breast-high ornamented with painted pinnacles, which from a distance presented a very gay appearance."[34] These "painted pinnacles" provided the south side with the same touch of flamboyance that the "tower-like structures" did on the other façades, showing that this violation of Albertian sobriety was no accident.

Pius commanded the cardinals to build houses at Pienza, showing that he intended to establish the permanent summer capital of the papacy there. The loyal Ammanati built first, his house comprising a whole block on the piazza next to the town hall. Goro Lolli laid foundations for his palace; Francesco Gonzaga, made a cardinal the previous year at age twenty, bought his property but waited for his father, the Marquess of Mantua, to supply the construction money.[35] The surprise is that the increasingly hostile Jouffroy, who had already threatened to leave the papal court, "erected a large and lofty palace behind the Vice-chancellor's," which in the 1950s was Pienza's only hotel and is now part of the splendid little museum.[36]

Those who equate Tuscan Renaissance architecture with sobriety and restraint would be shocked to see Pienza in its original state. Whereas today almost every wall has weathered down to the natural brown of the native tufa, all the prominent buildings except the cathedral and Piccolomini Palace—the Communal Palace, the Bishop's Palace, the Canonry, the palaces of the cardinals and members of Pius's family—were originally covered in plaster, etched and vibrantly colored in the technique called *sgraffito.* Plaster was applied in layers of varied colors; the artist then scratched away outer layers to reveal the colors underneath. Though it lasts much longer than paint, *sgraffito* is not permanent; still, most of the buildings in Pienza that originally had *sgraffito* retain at least a few faded patches of it from which to reconstruct the design. Usually the *sgraffito* designs were architectural: illusionistic depictions of pilasters, entablatures, and, most popular of all, quoins and rusticated masonry. For emphasis and entertainment selected spots got heraldry, garlands

34. Ibid., XI.600.

35. Mitchell, *Laurels,* 233.

36. *Comm.,* Smith, IX.604; Mitchell, *Laurels,* 233.

and swags of greenery, bucrania, sphinxes, griffins, and sometimes human figures; even the courtyard of the Piccolomini Palace sported this kind of decoration. The technique was common all over Italy and remained fashionable into the eighteenth century, but there cannot have been many places that had as much of it concentrated in a small area as Pienza.[37] If we restore this vibrant, ubiquitous decoration in our minds, the towers and pinnacles on top of the Palazzo Piccolomini no longer seem out of place, and the whole town takes on a festive, holiday atmosphere entirely appropriate to a vacation resort. The serene whiteness of the cathedral would even more effectively contrast with the visual vivacity surrounding it.

Corsignano had traditionally celebrated St. Matthew's Day on September 21 with a market and races. In 1462, inaugurating the new city, Pius provided new clothes for the leading citizens and other subsidies to ensure that the celebration was elevated to a level appropriate for the papal court, but a rustic atmosphere suited to local tastes nevertheless remained. Mass was scheduled early to permit time for the day's events. A country fair devoted to buying and selling goods and livestock consumed much of the day. Vigorous bargaining must have sharpened appetites; the crowd devoured no less than thirty roast oxen, along with many other meats. Many people must have brought meat home for latter consumption. The climactic event was traditionally a *palio*—actually four races—one for horses, one for donkeys, and separate ones for men and boys. The horse race that year was no contest, as one of the entries far outdistanced the others. In the donkey race the winner had thrown its rider, but the judges decided—as is the rule at the *palio* in Siena—that it was the mount that counted, not the rider. Each of the human races produced a foiled cheating attempt. The men, all "lusty, active youths," ran naked. "There had been a light rain and the track was slippery.... Often one or another could be seen to slip and fall and roll on the ground and mud.... In this way they ran four stades ... with very little space between the victor and the vanquished and they were so befouled with mud as to be unrecognizable." One of the pope's cooks waited somewhere along the course as a spectator; but, when the runners drew near, he stripped off his clothes except for his cloak and darted out from behind a corner, finishing first because he was fresh. The cloak and the fact that he was not muddy enough gave him away. He must have been

37. Mack gives examples in *Pienza* on pages 105, 110, 119, 121, 132, and 145, among others.

more prankster than cheat, or he would have doffed the telltale cloak. It was all taken in good humor; the judges, "shaking with laughter," gave the prize, four ells of cloth, to the real winner.[38]

By the time the boys ran, the mud, thoroughly churned by previous races, was a considerable obstacle to small legs: "They could not shake their feet clear of the sticky clay and now they would lose their breath and fall, now get it back and rise again. Their parents and siblings cheered them on with repeated shouts of encouragement." The cheater in this race was an eighteen-year-old house slave whose small stature and beardless face allowed him to pass as a boy. When he passed the fastest local boy at the finish, the defeated child "burst into tears and was furious at himself for not running faster. His mother, a very pretty woman … comforted her son with sweet words and wiped off his sweat with a towel." The prize, a goose, was about to go to the slave when his master recognized him and revealed his true age. The Pienza boy, "with fair hair and beautiful body, though disfigured with mud," "was carried home on his proud father's shoulders followed by a great crowd and greeted with joy by the entire neighborhood."[39] Pius watched the races from a high window, and is careful to say that he conducted business with the cardinals through it all. We can only guess what he thought as, elderly and crippled, he watched boys doing things he had done as a child alongside their grandfathers. So much of the boy of Corsignano still lived in him that we wonder if he would not, for at least a moment, have preferred to be running naked through the mud instead of consulting with robed prelates about the affairs of Christendom!

Well before these celebrations, probably before the dedication of the cathedral in late August, Pius would have gotten military news that profoundly improved his political position. In the previous spring Francesco Sforza had achieved an important victory affecting the Neapolitan war. Genoa, under French occupation, had been the staging post for French intervention in Naples, but the Genoese rebelled in March, and Francesco Sforza came to their aid. King René himself led an army to relieve the French garrison besieged in the fortress, but Sforza handed him a shattering defeat.[40] In the war against Sigismondo Malatesta, the fighting season had begun badly when Sigismondo captured the city of Sinigaglia that he had long besieged; but almost immediately, on August 12, Federico da Montefeltro arrived and within twenty-four hours had

38. *Comm.*, Smith, IX.605.

39. Ibid.

40. Von Pastor, *History of the Popes,* 3:113.

utterly routed and destroyed Sigismondo's army. It was only because of secret aid from Venice that Sigismondo was able to hold on for another year before surrendering.[41] Six days after Federico defeated Sigismondo, Ferrante won a crushing victory at Troia over Piccinino and Jean of Calabria. The Neapolitan nobles, whose chief interest was to be on the winning side, began to desert the gracious but unlucky Jean of Calabria and shift toward the despotic Ferrante.[42] On the same day that Pius watched the footraces in Pienza, Giovanni Antonio, Prince of Taranto, commander of the Neapolitan army, whose rebellion against Ferrante had sparked the war at the beginning, made peace with Ferrante.[43]

Pius's arthritis or gout was becoming more virulent; he would have preferred to say Mass himself on Corpus Christi at Viterbo, and certainly for the dedication of his own cathedral at Pienza, but the fact was that he could not stand long enough for the ceremony. At Easter the next year he celebrated Mass from a "device" that enabled him to do it from a seated position.[44] Sometime after the Pienza footraces Pius's tortured limbs impelled him to visit again the baths at Petriolo. He left Pienza for Petriolo in October and never saw much of his new city again. He mentions being laid up sick there for a day a few months later, and it is possible (though unrecorded) that he spent a few days there in 1464.[45] But Pienza's moment of glory—less than three months—was over forever. Among the cardinals, only Ammanati seems to have lived there in later years.[46] On his way to Petriolo Pius stopped at the almost inaccessible monastery of Monte Oliveto, mother house of the Olivetan order, a place founded by one of the Tolomei family of Siena and often enriched by the Piccolomini in their days of prosperity. Skirting a town afflicted with plague, he arrived at Petriolo, from which he made expeditions into the country and visited estates and monasteries in the neighborhood.[47]

It was well past time to return to Rome, but the plague was still raging there. Pius approached his stricken capital as far as Todi to wait for conditions in Rome to improve. With winter coming on, this windswept mountaintop town became miserably uncomfortable; it was nevertheless crowded with envoys attracted there by the pope's improved political prospects. The French ambassadors followed him to Todi, seeking a truce in Naples but giving no answer when Pius demanded a French

41. Ibid., 3:126.

42. Ibid., 3:122.

43. *Comm.*, Smith, X.637–47.

44. Mitchell, *Laurels,* 211.

45. *Comm.*, Smith, X.686; Ady, *Pius II,* 277

46. Ady, *Pius II,* 275–76.

47. *Comm.*, Smith, X.672–74.

commitment to the crusade. The French wanted to include Sigismondo in the settlement, and Florence, Milan, and Venice also sent delegations to plead for him; but toward Sigismondo, Pius was implacable. Ferrante, now on the offensive, refused to grant a truce, so negotiations led nowhere.

At length an embassy arrived from the citizens of Rome, assuring the pope that the plague was at last over and it was safe to return. It was mid-December; the ground was frozen and the roads buried in snow, but Pius would have remembered the tumults that Tiburzio had raised when he had left his capital unattended two years earlier. Pius left Todi for the difficult journey through high mountains to Rome, commenting along the way on the ancient history and military defensibility of every town.

14

Urban Dreams

A SOCIETY OF CITY-STATES obsessed with the ideal could hardly avoid visualizing the ideal city. Actually realizing an ideal at the scale of an entire city was, of course, much more problematic. The chances of actually building a new or transformed city decreased in proportion to the ambition of the builder's intentions. Pure idealists, however, were undiscouraged; if their concepts had no chance of embodiment in bricks and mortar, they set them forth in written or painted descriptions, where reality need not intrude. The concept of ideal cities had deep roots in antiquity. Plato describes one in the *Laws* having the same kind of abstraction and the same geometrical and hierarchical order that Renaissance idealists would prescribe centuries later. Aristotle also describes a town planning system in the *Politics.*[1] Porphyry, in his *Life of Plotinus,* tells how the emperor Gallienus planned to give a tract in the Campania to Plotinus to build the city of Platonopolis, governed under Plato's laws. Palace intrigue, however, scuttled the idea.[2] In the mid-quattrocento Alberti's *De re aedificatoria* prescribed the standards for an ideal city. From then on the concept of a city planned according to universal laws, with perfect buildings in perfect locations, convenient for the inhabitants, reflecting the hierarchy of society, but also conforming to the harmonious architecture of the universe, excited Renaissance imaginations.

Around 1300, simply as a practical means of controlling their expanding territory, the Florentines had begun to build new towns. Among these

1. S. Lang, "The Ideal City from Plato to Howard," *Architectural Review* 112, no. 668 (1952): 91; Aristotle, *Politics* II.5; VII.10.11.

2. Lang, "Ideal City," 92.

were Firenzuola, Scarperia, San Giovanni, Terranuova, and Castelfranco, each centered around a square dominated by a public palazzo whose design explicitly recalled the Bargello, the seat of justice in Florence.[3] An excellent example remains at San Giovanni Valdarno, founded in 1300, whose design was attributed to Arnolfo di Cambio. The government building or "Pretorium" sits between two piazzas, with the widest street passing in front of it. Other streets of two different widths divide the city into sixteen rectangular blocks, eight on each side of the central piazzas.[4] For rationality and clarity San Giovanni equals or exceeds most of the self-consciously "ideal" cities that were designed or built in the Renaissance. But the motivation of its design was efficiency more than aesthetics. After the Black Death, when populations plummeted and only slowly recovered, there was little economic impetus for creating new cities. The new cities of the Renaissance grew not from economic expansion, but from egotism or politics. None of them served significant economic functions.

Cardinal Branda Castiglione (1350–1443) made the first effort to transform a medieval village into a city conceived according to humanist principles. The village was Castiglione Olona near Varese, about twenty-five miles north of Milan, where, since the eleventh century, the Castiglione family had owned a castle perched atop a steep hill.[5] In 1287, when the Visconti were bringing this part of Lombardy under their control, they demolished this fortress.[6] At some time in the fourteenth century the Castiglione built an unfortified residence further down the hill. Beginning in 1420 Cardinal Branda extended this building as his palazzo and built a square in front of it with a small, centrally planned church. Cardinal Branda derived ideas from Pliny's description of his villa on nearby Lake Como and (inconsistently) applied the architectural ideas of Vitruvius and Brunelleschi. Pliny's influence led Cardinal Branda to give the townspeople attractive views of the surrounding landscape.[7] The church, a cube topped with only the drum of a dome, has a Brunelleschian façade articulated by fluted Corinthian pilasters.[8] Up the hill, on the site of the old castle, Branda built a collegiate church in Gothic style,

3. Goldthwaite, *Wealth,* 180; Colin Cunningham, "For the Honour and Beauty of the City: The Design of Town Halls," in Norman, *Siena and Padua,* 2:32–33.

4. Martin Kemp, "The Mean and Measure of All Things," in *Circa 1492,* edited by Jay A. Levenson, 97 (New Haven and London: Yale University Press, 1991).

5. Grafton, *Leon Battista Alberti,* 271.

6. Egerton R. Williams, *Lombard Towns of Italy* (New York; Dodd, Mead, 1914), 152.

7. Grafton, *Leon Battista Alberti,* 271.

8. Williams, *Lombard Towns,* 151.

adorned inside with frescoes by Masolino. In spite of the Gothic church, a description of Cardinal Branda's work written in 1431 by the Bolognese bibliophile Francesco Pizolpasso praises Olana's classicism. Couched as a letter to Cardinal Juan Cervantes, this description was in fact a literary work designed for wide circulation, pillaging concepts and vocabulary from both Vitruvius and Pliny to advertise its author's erudition.[9] Castiglione Olona, therefore, imitated architectural ideas from antique literature and inspired a literary description of that imitation that imitated the same literature.

Alberti was content with meandering streets in small towns, but for great and famous cities, "the streets are better straight and very wide, to add to its dignity and majesty."[10] It was Pope Nicholas V who first attempted to realize the Albertian ideal of broad, straight, colonnaded avenues laid out in a formal, symmetrical order leading to visual focal points. As we have seen, Nicholas patronized humanists, founded the Vatican Library, and embarked on an ambitious program to convert the unsanitary shambles of medieval Rome into a stately capital for the papacy—all paid for by the wealth that pilgrims brought to Rome in the Jubilee Year of 1450.[11] It is Nicholas's plans for rebuilding the Borgo Leonino, the urban area between St. Peter's and the Castel Sant'Angelo, that give him his place in the history of urban planning. Yet, since not a stone of it was built, our only knowledge of this plan comes from Giannozzo Manetti's description in his biography of Nicholas.[12]

The Borgo and the Vatican proper had been outside the walls of ancient Rome and had only been fortified by Leo IV after the Saracens sacked it in 846 (hence the name Borgo Leonino).[13] King Ladislas of Naples had sacked it again as recently as 1413, and in Nicholas's time it still lay depopulated and in ruins.[14] Nicholas proposed to demolish the entire quarter and reconstruct it on new lines.[15] Nicholas envisioned a piazza at each end of the Borgo: one adjoining the Castel Sant'Angelo and the other in front of St. Peter's. Connecting them were to be three streets, each lined with colonnades that protected pedestrians from the weather but admitted light to the shops on the ground level and to the dwellings

9. Grafton, *Leon Battista Alberti,* 271–72.
10. Alberti, *Building,* 4:5, 106.
11. Magnuson, "Project," 89.
12. Ibid., 91.
13. Stinger, *Renaissance in Rome,* 27.
14. Magnuson, *Studies in Roman Quattrocento Architecture* (Stockholm: Almqvist and Wikksell, 1958), 3–4.
15. Magnuson, "Project," 103.

above them.[16] Those approaching the new quarter would cross the Tiber on the Ponte Sant'Angelo and pass through the fortified gate in front of the castle, then turn left into the first piazza, bounded by the castle, the Tiber, new defensive walls, and the entrances to the three streets.[17] Manetti describes the three parallel streets as "broad and ample." He specifies that the central one was to lead "in a straight line" to the central door of St. Peter's. The street to the right would follow a direct axis terminating at the gate of the new Vatican Palace. The left, or southernmost street, would point to the site of the obelisk that still stood where Nero had placed it on the *spina* of his circus. Nicholas, however, intended to move the obelisk to the center of the new piazza in front of St. Peter's.[18] Replacing the transported obelisk as the new focal point of the southern street would be a "dormitory" for the canons of St. Peter. The monumental, uniform, axial streets represent a formal concept of city planning that had a long future in Paris, St. Petersburg, and Washington, D.C., among other places. Quite medieval, however, was the intent that each street would accommodate a particular hierarchy of trades: the central one to have bankers and cloth merchants, with smaller shops on the northern street and minor crafts on the southern.

The climax of the quarter would come in the great piazza in front of the new St. Peter's. Manetti says there was to be a "big and noble colonnade" along the side opposite the church, where the three streets would enter the square through archways or porticos. The obelisk, moved to the center of this piazza and surmounted by a bronze Christ, would rest upon bronze statues of the evangelists. The new basilica itself would rise from a platform raised on steps, forming, in fact, another, upper-level piazza extending the first. From there the visitor would enter the church through a great vestibule with five portals.[19] In 1450 such audacious urban planning had scarcely been seen since the founding of Constantinople. Nicholas did not build a stick of it, but Pius II may have conceived his new steps and Benediction Loggia as a first installment of his predecessor's vision. What audacious mind conceived this plan? Documents describe Bernardo Rossellino, who arrived at the curia in 1451, as the pope's "chief builder."[20] Most have considered Alberti, employed at the curia since 1432, as the moving spirit behind the design.[21] Nevertheless,

16. Magnuson, *Studies,* 93.
17. Magnuson, *Studies,* 92–93.
18. Magnuson, "Project," 102–3. This was actually done in 1586.
19. Magnuson, *Studies,* 92–94.
20. Grafton, *Leon Battista Alberti,* 297.
21. Magnuson, "Project,"89.

what we know about creative processes in the fifteenth century tells us that, just as Manetti depicts him in his biography, Nicholas himself was probably the moving spirit. We do not know whether Nicholas worked with Rossellino, Alberti, both, or neither, but we may be sure that no one worked on the plans for the Borgo independently of the pope.

Pius II's constructions on St. Peter's square were far less ambitious than those of Nicholas V but had the advantage of being at least partially achievable with the limited means at the papacy's disposal. Pius succeeded in tidying up the square, building new flights of steps and a new entrance to the Vatican Palace. Even so, his most notable building, the Loggia of Benediction, was left to his successors to finish. Facing St. Peter's square, in one of the most conspicuous locations in Christendom, the loggia embodied Alberti's most up-to-date ideas. The actual architect, as at Pienza, was probably Bernardo Rossellino.[22] Closely following the design of the Coliseum or the Theater of Marcellus, the loggia, unlike the cathedral at Pienza, obeyed Alberti's strictures on the use of columns with arches. The arches rested on segments of wall, with columns in front of the wall centered between the arches, and with the entablatures that divide the stories resting on top of the columns. In sixteenth-century views of St. Peter's square this loggia stands out as the most graceful and distinguished part of the jumble of buildings that made up the face that St. Peter's displayed to the world. We do not know how large a loggia Pius intended to build—perhaps he meant it to stretch all the way across the atrium and the palace entrance or even around the whole piazza like Nicholas's proposed colonnade—but he built only four bays of the ground floor.[23] By classical precedent and Albertian rule a facade must have an odd number of openings; thus, if Pius built a façade with four arches we can assume that he intended at least one more.[24] Nevertheless, his successor, Paul II, did not rectify this, but instead added another floor of four bays above the ones Pius had built; Rodrigo Borgia added a third level after he became Pope Alexander VI. A little over a century later Paul V, in 1610–1616, swept it all away to make way for the present façade of St. Peter's.[25]

All that remains of Pius's work in the Piazza di San Pietro are three colossal statues by Paolo Romano. One pair, a St. Paul and the St. Peter statue that moved Pius to tears when he was carrying the head of Peter's

22. Rubenstein, "Pius II," 268.

23. Ibid., 263.

24. Alberti, *Aedificatoria* VII.5, in *Building,* 200.

25. Rubenstein, "Pius II," 217 and 222–24.

brother, are now displayed among the papal tombs in the Vatican Grottoes beneath St. Peter's. Critics and art historians have generally considered them second-rate or worse, perhaps because they were too hastily executed in order to be ready for the reception of St. Andrew's head.[26] The third colossal statue, another St. Paul, now standing on the Ponte Sant'Angelo, has a much better reputation. Pius may have intended it as one of a new pair of apostles to replace the inferior ones.[27]

We have explored Pienza sufficiently in the previous chapter, but comparing it to the stately avenues that Nicholas V envisioned for the Borgo reveals how modest Pius's aspirations for his new city were. One of Pius's motives in rebuilding Corsignano was affection for his old home; he wished to glorify it, not obliterate it. His work there, inserting his new buildings and their little piazza into the existing fabric, then inviting the cardinals to do the same for their own dwellings, was not entirely different from a natural growth.

In 1465, the year after Pius II died, Antonio di Pietro Averlino, who gave himself the Greek name "Filarete" ("lover of virtue"), published an architectural treatise, *Trattato di architettura,* describing the ideal but entirely fictional city of "Sforzinda." We know little about Filarete, who was born in Florence sometime around 1400 and received his artistic training there. Although Brunelleschi influenced him and he might have learned bronze casting from Ghiberti, we know nothing specific about his education. He went to Rome to study its antiquities in 1433. The most important works from his hand are the bronze doors that Eugenius IV commissioned him to cast for St. Peter's, which were retained when the old St. Peter's was demolished and reinstalled in the new basilica. In 1451 Filarete went to Milan to serve as architect under the new duke, Francesco Sforza. Vasari says that after Francesco Sforza died in 1466 Filarete returned to Florence, but a letter from Filelfo implies that he went to Constantinople.[28] He is thought to have died in 1469. Filarete has been justly described as a man of "mixed and sketchy learning"; for composing the *Trattato,* which describes his city of Sforzinda, he had the literary help of Francesco Filelfo, then employed at the Sforza court.[29] Filarete's purpose in his *Trattato* was to introduce the new classical style of architecture to

26. Ibid., 255–56.

27. Ibid., 263.

28. Lang, "Sforzinda, Filarete and Filelfo," *Journal of the Warburg and Courtauld Institutes* 35 (1972): 391.

29. Arnaldo Bruschi, *Bramante* (New York and London: Thames and Hudson, 1977), 139.

the Milanese, who were still wedded to Gothic and would remain so into the following century.[30] "I beg everyone to abandon modern [Gothic] usage," Filarete urges his audience; "cursed be he who discovered it."[31]

The treatise itself, written between 1461 and 1464, takes the form of a narrative with dialogue about the construction of Sforzinda and its port, Plusiapolis. This form was necessary to keep his hearers entertained. They were hearers, not readers; everything about the style suggests that the treatise was meant to be read aloud to the duke and his courtiers. The architectural material is often interrupted by episodes such as travels in the country to choose the site or find materials or the visit of Lodovico Gonzaga, Marchese of Mantua and ally of the duke, to admire the new construction.[32] The core, however, is the dialogue between Francesco Sforza, the patron, and Filarete, the respectful but didactic architect.[33] While the *Trattato* does describe the practical business of construction, even that can be fanciful, as when the duke puts his army to work digging the moats of the castle and completes the excavations in a day.[34]

In contrast to Pienza, whose narrow, restricted site caused such difficulties for Rossellino, the purely fictional site of Sforzinda was a flat, blank slate. The plan, therefore, could be a complete abstraction. It is an eight-pointed star, formed by overlaying two equal squares over each other at an angle of forty-five degrees so that their intersection forms a regular octagon, a form with astrological and magical significance. The city walls form the outline of the star, which is surrounded by a circular moat.[35] The gates, located at the reentrant angles of the star, give admission to eight principal avenues, each with a canal down the middle. These avenues meet at the central piazza, where there is a great tower from which to view the surrounding countryside (though this tower disappears in the later, more detailed description of the center).[36] In addition to these eight streets, eight others lead from the center to towers at

30. Anthony Blunt, *Artistic Theory in Italy 1450–1600* (Oxford: Clarendon Press, 1971), 43.

31. Filarete (Antonio di Pietro Averlino), *Trattato di architettura* VIII, fol. 59r., in *Filarete's Treatise on Architecture,* ed. J. R. Spencer, 2 vols. (New Haven and London: Yale University Press, 1965), 1:102.

32. Filarete, *Trattato* XIII.100r., in *Treatise,* 1:xix, 175.

33. Kemp, "From 'Mimesis' to 'Fantasia': The Quattrocento Vocabulary of Creation, Inspiration and Genius in the Visual Arts," *Viator* 8 (1977): 360.

34. Filarete, *Trattato* VI.41r., in *Treatise,* I, 71.

35. Lang, "Ideal City," 96.

36. Filarete, *Trattato* I.14r., v., in *Treatise,* 1:26–27.

the points of the star. Halfway from the center to these outer points, a circular street intersects the sixteen radiating streets, with a piazza at each intersection. The piazzas on the streets leading to gates each have an economic function: straw and wood to be sold on the east side, wine and grain on the south, and so on. The churches of the monastic orders are at the piazzas on the streets leading to the towers.[37] The canals, whose purpose is to provide water transport and thus reduce the number of carts on the streets, meet in a canal that goes around the central piazza.[38] The central piazza, 150 braccia by 300 braccia (approximately 300 by 600 feet), has its short ends at the east and west. At the east end is the cathedral; at the west, the Ducal Palace. To the north of the main piazza is another piazza for merchants and to the south the general marketplace. Around these squares, in carefully arranged positions, are the law courts, prison, palaces for the *capitano* and the *podestà,* the mint, the custom house, and, south of the marketplace, taverns, inns, bordellos, and public baths.[39]

As Alberti had advised, Sforzinda's churches were centrally planned and built on raised platforms. Filarete's favorite plan was a Greek cross inscribed in a square, with a dome in the center and soaring towers at the corners. These towers have an unclassical verticality and disconcertingly resemble Chinese pagodas. All the churches are exercises in geometry and simple mathematical ratios, with little regard for liturgical needs or the functional differences between monastic churches, parish churches, the cathedral, or even a hermits' church.[40] A dialogue between the duke and Filarete about the tower of the castle illustrates the dominance of geometry and symbolism over the practical or even the possible. The duke professed himself pleased with the tower, but asked, "Why have you made so many windows and given them so many different forms, that is square, round, polygonal of eight and twelve sides?" Filarete answers:

> First of all, I made this many windows because your lordship wished it to be 365 braccia tall [roughly seventy-three stories in a modern building]. I wanted to make as many windows as the year has days. Therefore, the tower has that many windows. Since there is day and night, some are partly barred and some are partly open. These four different shapes I have given

37. Ibid., *Trattato* VI.43r., v., in *Treatise,* 1:74–75.
38. Ibid., *Trattato* VI.44r., in *Treatise,* 1:78.
39. Ibid., *Trattato* VI.42v.–43v., in *Treatise,* 1:74.
40. Bruschi, *Bramante,* 139–42.

> them are the four seasons, spring, summer, autumn, and winter. [Nevertheless, the illustration shows fewer windows, and all of them arched.][41]

Even more implausible is Filarete's revolving tower, with an equestrian statue at the top.

To provide an aura of ancient authority, Filarete claims that many of his designs came from the ancient architect "Onitoan Nolievra" [an anagram for Antonio Averlino] and were found in the "Golden Book" discovered and translated by "Iscofrance Notilento" [Francesco da Tolentino, i.e., Filelfo].[42] To illustrate the impact of Sforzinda on a visitor, Filarete has Lodovico Gonzaga visit Duke Francesco in his new city. "My lord I seem to see again the noble buildings that were once in Rome and those we read were in Egypt," Lodovico tells his host; "It seems to me that I have been reborn [back in ancient times] on seeing these noble buildings."[43] Filarete's *Trattato* presents his vision of an architectural utopia that he knew could never exist in the real world. It is architecture by "other means"—an effort to achieve architectural perfection without the annoyances of site, construction, engineering, and expense.

Brunelleschi's discovery of mathematically accurate perspective, perfected by Alberti (and very rudely approximated in Filarete's illustrations), enabled painting to serve as another alternate means of achieving architecture. Renaissance painting makes extensive use of idealized architecture as a backdrop for religious or secular narratives. A few paintings, however, exist only to present an ideal Albertian city. Three such pictures originated at Federico da Montefeltro's court at Urbino, where some of the intarsia panels on the palace doors bear similar perspective architecture. The earliest and best-known of the three paintings is the *View of an Ideal City,* still in the Urbino Palace, dated to 1470 and attributed either to Piero della Francesca, Federico's court painter, or to Federico's architect, Luciano Laurana. The second such painting, at the Walters Art Museum in Baltimore, has been dated 1480–1484 and attributed to another Urbino artist, Fra Carnevale. Francesco di Giorgio Martini, another architect of the Ducal Palace and author of a theoretical tract on architecture, is the presumed painter of the third view of an ideal city, painted about 1490–1491, now in the Gemaeldegalerie in Berlin. Three pictures of a rare type by different artists from the same

41. Filarete, *Trattato* VI.41v.–42r., in *Treatise,* 1:72.

42. Ibid., *Trattato* XIII.108v. and XXI.172r., in *Treatise,* 1:189, 293.

43. Ibid., *Trattato* XIII.100r., in *Treatise,* 1:175; bracketed part inserted by translator.

Figure 14.1. Piero della Francesca (?). *View of an Ideal City.* Galleria Nazionale delle Marche, Urbino. Photograph from Scala/Art Resource, New York.

place indicate a persistent interest from the patrons, Federico and his son, Guidobaldo.

Each of the "ideal city" paintings depicts a vast square, lined for the most part by palaces that follow Alberti's ideas. Each palace has its unique design, as if the artists intended to ring all the changes permitted within Alberti's rules. In the Urbino picture a centralized round church, embodying Alberti's ideals for a "temple," all but fills the piazza, though in the right background we glimpse a more conventional church of the basilica type. In the Baltimore picture all the buildings are built on a podium above the level of the foreground piazza, which is decorated by a central fountain and by columns in the corners topped with statues. The buildings at the sides are Albertian palaces, but the centerpiece is a Roman triumphal arch with three portals. To the right of the arch is an octagonal church that appears to be a classicized version of the Baptistery at Florence (then believed to be an ancient temple of Mars). To the left is a version of the Coliseum, updated to conform to Albertian dogmas of proportion. Through the openings of the arch we see the distant city wall with a gate on the axis of the arch, through which we glimpse hills and countryside beyond—a strong image of axial planning. The Berlin example is more scenographic than the others. A pavilion with arches at the ends and Corinthian columns on the long sides frames the view so that we see the piazza and the Albertian palazzos through its colonnade. Unlike the other pictures, the palaces at the side do not frame classical monuments but reveal a harbor with ships and distant islands.

Only the Baltimore picture shows any sign of human life. Even then, the few figures may have been added later, and their presence only emphasizes the grand scale of the architecture and the intimidating emptiness of the piazza.[44] The "Ideal Cities" are abstractions. There are no vendors and stalls, no well-dressed aristocrats parading their finery, no merchants discussing business or displaying their wares, no carts, no horses, dogs, or penned-up geese for sale; there is no princely procession to show the city on a fine state occasion. In short, the practical, the ordinary, the mercantile, the political, the imperfect, the real, and the human are rigorously excluded. What the patron wanted and the artist supplied was not a picture of this world but of another one, timeless and perfect, where a mind normally filled with the noise of war, as Federico da Montefeltro's was, or the pain of agonizing illness in Guidobaldo's case, could find peace, refreshment, renewal, and tranquility.

Federico da Montefeltro is also the probable patron of Francesco di Giorgio's *Treatise on Civil and Military Architecture,* probably written in Urbino about 1480, which contains abstract geometrical exercises in the guise of plans for cities. Francesco's hill towns, for example, are always built upon regular segments of a sphere.[45] One of Francesco's plans is for a city in the shape of a man with a church at his heart, a fortress at his head, and a tower at each extremity.[46] Francesco also perfected the kind of radial city plan that Filarete had used. Sforzinda's rectilinear center is a geometrical contradiction of its radial plan. Francesco di Georgio designed circular or octagonal central piazzas corresponding to the shapes of his cities. In one example his radial streets repeatedly cross a single, continuous street that spirals out from the center to the periphery.[47]

In the 1480s plague raged through Milan for several years, with tens of thousands of victims, perhaps a third of the population. Francesco Sforza's son, Lodovico il Moro, ruler of Milan (as regent, usurper, or duke, 1476–1499), left town and only opened his mail after it had been decontaminated by strong perfumes. Leonardo da Vinci may have concocted some of the perfumes.[48] After the plague Leonardo developed a plan for Milan that sought to improve sanitation and reduce the danger

44. Richard Krautheimer, "The Panels in Urbino, Baltimore and Berlin Reconsidered," in *The Renaissance from Brunelleschi to Michelangelo: The Representation of Architecture,* edited by Henry A. Millon and Vittorio Magnano Lamugnani, 238 39 (New York: Rizzoli, 1997).

45. Lang, "Ideal City," 97.

46. Trinkhaus, *Renaissance Humanism,* 39.

47. Horst de la Croix, "Military Architecture and the Radial Plan in Sixteenth Century Italy," *Art Bulletin* 42, no. 4 (December 1960): 270–71 and fig. 11.

48. Bramly, *Leonardo,* 193.

of plague by dividing Milan into ten cities of five thousand houses and thirty thousand lesser dwellings each. "In this way," Leonardo wrote, "you will disperse the mass of people who are now herded together like a flock of goats, filling every corner with their stench and spreading pestilential death."[49] To further promote sanitation the cities were to have a dense network of canals for transport and irrigation that would also serve to flush the streets. Each of Leonardo's cities would have an elevated section, with the canals passing under it, that would be reserved for public buildings and the residences of "gentlemen."[50] Leonardo's sanitary concerns led him to recommend spiral staircases (so that people would not relieve themselves in the corners) and plentiful lavatories of a new design with ample ventilation "so that one would be able to breathe."[51] Many would declare that such concerns indicate practicality, but that has to be seen in the context that there was not the slightest possibility of Leonardo's scheme being executed in the real world. Leonardo also participated in a project in the early 1490s to rebuild one of the poorest sections of Milan between the old and new fortifications, running from the Porta Romana to the Porta Tosa.[52] For this Leonardo collected measurements and drew detailed plans with houses having courtyards at the back and with a colonnaded market square at the center.[53] There is no evidence that anything was actually built. Leonardo, and presumably Lodovico, as well, were dreaming. At the end of his life Leonardo would revive similar fantasies for Francis I of France. Leonardo designed a palace to be built at Romorantin, near Blois, from which canals were to radiate outward to all the coasts of France.[54]

By the end of the quattrocento several Italian despots were enthusiastically redesigning their capitals or creating ideal cities following the new architectural principles. In the 1480s, when Lodovico il Moro governed Milan in the name of his nephew Giangaleazzo Sforza, the town of Vigevano, Lodovico's birthplace, was more firmly under his control than Milan and could serve him as a personal power center.[55] Here, in 1492–1494, Lodovico cleared away the old town hall, the market, and

49. Da Vinci, *Cod. Atl.* 65v. b.; quoted in Bramly, *Leonardo,* 194.

50. Bramly, *Leonardo,* 194, illustration on 195.

51. Ibid., 194.

52. Ibid., 195.

53. Carlo Pedretti, *Leonardo da Vinci: The Royal Palace at Romarantin* (Cambridge, Mass.: Harvard University Press, 1972), 14; Bramly, *Leonardo,* 196.

54. Bramly, *Leonardo,* 402–3.

55. Hollingsworth, *Patronage,* 179.

numerous houses to create a piazza 45 yards wide by 120 yards long. He preserved the cathedral at one of the narrow ends, but the other three sides he surrounded with a uniform arcade that sheltered shops and carried an upper floor of dwellings covered with antique ornament in *sgraffito.*[56] A great ramp led from this square to the castle, which received a new tower by Bramante and decorations, possibly by Leonardo, in the ducal apartments.[57] In Ferrara, Duke Ercole d'Este (r. 1471–1505) doubled his city's size with the suburb called the Ercolean Addition, begun in 1492.[58] The new quarter centered on a broad, tree-lined avenue, with wide pedestrian sidewalks, where the courtiers who resided there could promenade.[59] The other streets, all regularly laid out in straight lines and right angles, were to house merchants, artisans, and even laborers, expressing the social hierarchy as Alberti advised. The Ercolean Addition also extended the city's defenses, so that Ariosto described it as an "exquisite fortress."[60] Fine as it is (and actually built), the Ercolean Addition is little more than a simple grid plan like the Florentines had built nearly two centuries earlier at San Giovanni Valdarno. At Florence Lorenzo de' Medici had similar ideas for a new quarter and a villa for himself that would have filled some of the undeveloped space within the city walls, but it remained only a concept.[61]

At about the time of his triumphal entry into Florence in 1515, Leo X conceived a renovation of the Florentine urban fabric to embed Medici dominance into the cityscape. Demolitions in the heart of the city would have extended the Piazza San Lorenzo, in front of the Medici family's church, to the Via Larga, so that the palace Michelozzo had built for Cosimo would front on the enlarged piazza. But Leo intended another wave of demolition to double this square beyond the Via Larga so that the city's widest street would run through the middle of the now enormous but symmetrical piazza. Across the Via Larga from Michelozzo's palace would be a second Medici palace, equal in mass, but designed by Leonardo da Vinci in a more up-to-date style. Two blocks farther on, the Piazza San Marco in front of the Medici's favored convent would

56. Ibid., 180; Goldthwaite, *Wealth,* 186.

57. Hollingsworth, *Patronage,* 180; Pedretti, *Leonardo da Vinci,* 14–15.

58. Goldthwaite, *Wealth,* 187–88.

59. Cole, *Art of the Italian Courts,* 139 and 141; Nicholas Adams and Laurie Nussdorfer, "The Italian City 1400–1600," in Millon and Lamugnani, *Renaissance,* 216.

60. Cole, *Art of the Italian Courts,* 141; Alberti, *Building,* 4:1, 92–97.

61. Goldthwaite, *Wealth,* 188.

likewise be doubled to straddle the Via Larga symmetrically.[62] The sheer scale of this totalitarian vision prevented its execution.

Throughout the cinquecento writers continued to imagine ideal cities, and rulers occasionally tried to build them. Two relatively small ones attained the same kind of brief success followed by long oblivion that Pius had achieved at Pienza. Pope Paul III (r. 1534–1549) carved out a duchy from papal territories west of Lake Bolsena for his illegitimate son Pier Luigi Farnese. The tiny hamlet of Castro on an impregnable mountaintop became the duchy's capital. The architect Antonio Sangallo the Younger designed a Franciscan church and a piazza with public buildings around it.[63] Vasari says that Sangallo made plans for "palaces and other buildings for various persons, both natives and strangers, who erected edifices of such cost that it would seem incredible to one who had not seen them, so ornate are they all, so commodious, and built with so little regard for expense."[64] But when the pope obtained the richer territories of Parma and Piacenza for Pier Luigi, Castro fell into neglect. In 1649 Pope Innocent X quarreled with Pier Luigi's descendants, starved out the town, and then ordered its absolute demolition. Before the year was out nothing remained but a column with the mocking inscription, "Here was Castro."[65]

Castro's destruction makes Sabbioneta, near Mantua, the only surviving "ideal city" of the cinquecento to equal Pienza's relative success. Its creator, Vespasiano Gonzaga (1531–1591), headed a cadet branch of the ruling family of Mantua and prospered as a soldier in the service of Spain. After bringing his bride to the little *castello* and village of Sabbioneta (near Casalmaggiore) in 1550, he began building a new city there in 1556. Six years later he ordered all his subjects to move to his new town, which had thirty blocks, two piazzas, two palaces, and a mint. Vespasiano's private life, however, was scarcely less tumultuous than his battles. Discovering that his wife was unfaithful, Vespasiano had both wife and lover murdered.[66] Understandably, this plunged him into a state of anxiety about his soul. He told his cousin the Duke of Mantua that his only

62. Pedretti, *Leonardo da Vinci,* 60; Andres, Hunisak, and Turner, *Art of Florence,* 2:917.

63. Giuseppe Gavelli, *La città di Castro e Antonio da Sangallo* (Ischia di Castro: Gruppo Archeologico "Armine,"1983), 56–57, 123–27.

64. Vasari, "Antonio da San Gallo," in *Lives of the Painters* 2:111.

65. Gavelli, *Città di Castro,* 130–31. In the archeological investigation carried out on the site in the early 1980s no trace of this column was found; 138n30.

66. Alfredo Puerari, *Sabbioneta* (Milan: Istituto Editorale Domus, 1955), 4.

pleasure was to benefit his people and "to raise new walls, to give life to material works, now that I am so much reduced in the spirit."[67] In time he married again and had a son. But in January of 1580 the adolescent heir suddenly died, and the story circulated that Vespasiano had kicked him to death.[68] His original impulse to build at Sabbioneta had no obvious link to personal distress, but every time Vespasiano murdered a loved one, he reached for bricks and a trowel. After the second tragedy, the Church of Santa Maria Assunta rose on the main piazza with a dome and a façade of pink and white marble; a new octagonal church in the style of Bramante replaced an old Servite church;[69] and an elevated gallery rose across the garden from the old *castello* to display Vespasiano's collection of antiquities. So many artists and intellectuals flocked to Vespasiano's court that Sabbioneta was called the "Little Athens."[70] To accommodate the entertainment of this cultivated circle, Vespasiano brought in the architect Scamozzi, who had finished Palladio's Teatro Olimpico in Verona, to build a smaller version, the Teatro all'Antica, in Sabbioneta, the second purpose-built theater of modern times. In spite of these diversions, Vespasiano wrote, "the state of my soul is most unhappy.... The comforts of my friends are torments to me; the verses that come from everywhere to console me are annoyances. What are the good things of earth to me if I have lost those of the soul?"[71] On February 26, 1591, Vespasiano died, whispering, "I am healed."[72] In 1913 the English traveler Egerton Williams found Sabbioneta "a deserted fossil-like town of a few hundred inhabitants, within the massive walls and Renaissance palaces."[73] Today, Sabbioneta is more animated, but still a fossil—a kind of late Renaissance Williamsburg, attracting enough tourists to support a permanent population of four thousand.

At the end of the cinquecento two writers, Bartolomeo Del Bene (1515–1595) and Tommaso Campanella (1568–1639), wrote descriptions of cities that are so symbolic and astrological that they seem not to be of this earth. They embody the kind of idealized geometrical scheme that Filarete used, but their real purpose is not architectural. Del Bene's work, *Civitas Veri* ("City of Truth"), published in 1609 but written no later than 1585, is actually a topographical allegory of Aristotle's *Nichomachean Ethics.* The round city has five gates representing the senses.

67. Quoted in ibid.
68. Ibid.
69. Ibid, 4 and plates 1 and 21.
70. Ibid., 5; Masson, *Villas,* 75.
71. Quoted in Puerari, *Sabbioneta,* 2.
72. Ibid., 5.
73. Williams, *Lombard Towns,* 546.

From these gates extend five avenues symbolizing the moral virtues. The avenues pass by swamps containing the palaces of the vices, a reflection of Augustine's *Civitas terrena,* which had also influenced Filarete. The avenues converge on a mountain in the center topped by the temples of the intellectual virtues. All this Del Bene describes in a poetic narrative of a dream in which Aristotle guides Del Bene's patroness, Marguerite of Savoy, on a tour of the city.[74]

Campanella's *City of the Sun* (1602) is a radical book based on the new Copernican astronomy. This and his struggles with the Counter-Reformation church make him clearly a figure of the following age; but he does continue the architectural speculations of the Renaissance more than Del Bene does. His round city, two miles in diameter, consists of seven concentric rings representing the planets and traversed by avenues and gates aligned with the cardinal points of the compass. Each ring is a defensive wall with a range of palaces on the inner side, connected by an arcade that supports a promenade. Between each ring of the city is a clear space, seventy paces wide.[75] Although the city plan is symbolic and astrological (as becomes clear in the central temple that represents the sun), Campanella has addressed idealized solutions for architectural problems, as well.[76]

The Venetians actually built a star-shaped geometrical city at Palmanova in Friuli beginning in 1593, intended purely as a fortress-town.[77] The "star shape" comes from nine protruding bastions at the corners of a nine-sided polygon. The eighteen major streets radiate out from a hexagonal "piazza d'armi" at the center. Four other streets circle this piazza and intersect the radials. Geometry here has little to do with platonic concepts of the universe or astral symbolism. Its function is military. In the age of gunpowder artillery, bastions regularly placed around the perimeter of the fortress were the best defense. It was also important to be able to move troops quickly from one side of the town to the other and to have a clear space where they could assemble and drill. Once these factors were considered, Palmanova's geometry reveals itself as an elegant solution to practical needs. Palmanova was a precedent for other barracks-towns in which military considerations predominated over aesthetics. The military use of the radial plan marks a return to the practical goals of medieval city planning rather than an effort to produce an "ideal

74. Lang, "Ideal City," 91.

75. Ibid., 98.

76. Ibid., 96.

77. Ibid., 96; Adams and Nussdorfer, "Italian City," 228.

city." By the late cinquecento the ideal, as shown by Del Bene and Campanella, was more symbolic than urbanistic and no longer had any aspiration to be incarnated in physical reality. For Del Bene or Campanella to have included descriptions of construction methods as Filarete did for Sforzinda would have been absurd. Theory and realization had lost touch; in urban design the uneasy relationship between humanist thought and reality was resolved only by their final divorce.

15

Visits to Antiquity

By 1463 Pius had long thought of himself as old, but in that year a heightened sense of mortality was stealing over him, and the continued delay of the crusade oppressed his thoughts. In Germany disputes between Nicholas of Cusa and Duke Sigismund of Tyrol and another between Pius and Diether von Isenburg, whose election as archbishop of Mainz Pius did not recognize, prompted the anti-papal pamphleteer Gregor Heimburg to publish claims that Pius cared for nothing but his pleasures and his buildings at Pienza and that money supposedly raised for fighting the Turks was going to Ferrante.[1] Although such attacks were malicious and self-interested, they had a stinging plausibility. Pius was always sensitive to the image he would present to posterity. Would he be remembered as a pope who had talked about a crusade but done nothing? Would this negligence seem to reflect the same weakness of character as his youthful indiscretions and his heretical support for the Council of Basel? Although he had long ago written a retraction of his support for Basel, now, in April 1463, he issued a bull, *In minoribus agentibus,* repeating his previous retraction but also repenting of other lapses in his earlier life, especially his secular writings. "Remember not the sins and offences of my youth," he wrote, quoting the psalms.[2]

> We are ashamed of the error. We repent most earnestly.... But what are we to do? A written word, once published, moves irrevocably. Our writings, which fall into many hands and are read by the masses, are not in our power. Would that those that were published had languished in obscurity.[3]

1. Boulting, *Aeneas Silvius,* 310–11.
2. Psalm 25:7.
3. Pius II, *Reject/Accept,* 394.

For his error in supporting the council against the pope he offers many excuses: his youth, the example of Cesarini and other eminent men, the absence in Basel of anyone to present the papal case.[4] Even so, it is the relative *lack* of self-justification that makes *In minoribus* remarkable. Pius accepts moral responsibility for his errors, and, in spite of his great personal vanity, he repents humbly of the wrong he has done.

> We are human, and, being human, we have erred. You should not judge less harshly the things we said, wrote, and did. . . . We are compelled, therefore, beloved children, to imitate St. Augustine who, when he had introduced any errors into his books, published retractions. Such a humble and most acceptable man of genius preferred to confess and correct his follies modestly rather than defend them shamefully. We also will do likewise.[5]

Although he had mentioned Cesarini among those who had led him astray, he also credited him with pointing the way back while he himself had resisted the older man's wise counsel. He puts his most eloquent argument in favor of allowing a man to change his mind in the mouth of Cesarini. "Because we held an opinion once, you think it necessary to hold the same today, and consider us bound by a former point of view. . . . So why should we not be allowed at all times, forsaking error, to embrace the truth?"[6] "Follow what we now say," he tells his readers, "Believe the old man more than the youth; count not the private man of more value than the pontiff. Reject Aeneas, accept Pius!"[7]

The polemics of Heimburg and others in Germany were the proximate cause for this mixed outpouring of self-justification and penitence; yet, having answered all these charges before, Pius could well have treated Heimburg's fulminations with a dignified silence while leaving detailed refutation to others. Certainly a papal bull addressed to all of Christendom was an excessive response if it was only a riposte in the German pamphlet war. *In minoribus* makes more sense as a prelude to what only Pius and a few others knew was coming: a crusade led in person by the pope. To assume the role of crusader-in-chief, placing himself personally at the head of a supreme effort by united Christendom, required a pope who inspired complete confidence, a pope whose leadership and example would inspire. If he could not silence criticism, Pius could at least marginalize it. That, it seems likely, is what *In minoribus* was designed to do.

4. Ibid., 397.
5. Ibid., 394–95.
6. Ibid., 400.
7. Ibid., 396.

In May 1463, shortly after issuing *In minoribus,* Pius left Rome earlier than usual for Ostia, once the bustling port of ancient Rome, now an almost deserted fishing hamlet. In spite of old enmities and the open breach between Pius and the French cardinals, the bishop of Ostia, Guillaume d'Estouteville, Cardinal of Rouen, his former rival at the papal election, had invited him there. In the *Commentaries* Pius describes this visit and the side trip from there to Porto as the guest of its bishop, Juan de Carvajal, as interesting archeological excursions that he seems to have enjoyed. He never drops a hint about the real purpose of this expedition or reveals that he had instigated these invitations himself. This coyness was to avoid embarrassment about the real reason for the journey, which was to check out these places as sources of marble for his constructions in Rome.

Like most Italian builders, Pius freely used the apparently inexhaustible supply of high-quality building materials heaped up in former Roman cities. Even as it revered antiquity, the Renaissance consumed its remains like a hungry vulture.[8] Nicholas V had demolished the triumphal arch of Gratian, Valentinian, and Theodosius and had carted away great quantities of stone from the Coliseum, the Capitol, the Forum, and elsewhere.[9] In the hurried construction at the Piazza of St. Peter before the reception of St. Andrew's head, Pius had needed enormous quantities of marble for his flights of steps, for pavement, and for beginning the Loggia of Benediction. This marble came from demolitions of parts of the Coliseum, the Trullo, the Curia, and the Campodoglio. In 1462 the sources of marble grew even more extensive, including sites along the Via Flaminia, the Church of Saints Cosmas and Damian (originally a temple of Romulus), and the "Portico of Octavia" (probably the Baths of Antonianus).[10] Alberti was one of many who had spoken out against this kind of destruction. "I am often filled with indignation," he wrote in *De re aedificatoria,*

> when I see buildings demolished and going to ruin by the carelessness, not to say abominable avarice of the owners, buildings whose majesty has saved them from the fury of the most barbarous and enraged enemies, and

8. Magnuson, *Studies,* 5.

9. Roberto Weiss, *The Renaissance Discovery of Classical Antiquity* (New York: Humanities Press, 1969), 99.

10. Rubenstein, "Pius II," 203.

which Time himself, that perverse and obstinate destroyer, seems to have destined to eternity.[11]

Pius, no doubt, shared Alberti's principles, but he also continued to need marble. We have already seen that Pius was able to build only four bays of one floor of the Loggia of Benediction, although he intended more. One way to assure the continuation of construction after his death was to assemble onsite much or all of the marble needed for completion. This Pius succeeded in doing—to the extent that his successors were able to build two more levels of the loggia from the marble they found already awaiting them.[12]

To resolve the conflict between his ideals and his needs, Pius embarked on a plan to end the demolition of the ruins while still obtaining marble for his own projects. Pius would have known from Biondo's *Italia illustrata* that there were blocks of marble at Porto left unused by the Romans "in such quantity that one could easily build a city with them."[13] Using these quarried blocks would avoid destruction of ancient monuments. In January of 1462 Pius approached Carvajal about obtaining marble from Porto and began planning to clear the Tiber of obstacles so that it could be easily transported to Rome. At some point Ostia as well as Porto came into the picture, even though, as far as we know, it had only ruined buildings, not unused blocks. As both sites were almost entirely deserted, any destruction of ancient buildings there would go unobserved. In April, once his own supplies from Rome's ancient ports were secured, Pius issued a decree prohibiting the removal of building materials from ancient ruins.[14]

At its apex in the second century A.D. Ostia had been a flourishing city of some fifty thousand residents. By 1463 the site of ancient Ostia lay totally abandoned; the hamlet then called Ostia lay on the bank of the Tiber, east of the former Roman city. This hamlet consisted only of the old Bishop's Palace, reroofed and returned to use by Martin V, a fortified round tower also built by Martin V, the choir of the former church, and a tavern. The only citizens were the tower garrison and a few Dalmatian fishermen living in huts.[15] Cardinal d'Estouteville initiated a rebuilding

11. Alberti, *Aedificatoria* X.1, in *Building,* 320. I have preferred the clearer translation in Rubenstein, "Pius II," 205.

12. Rubenstein, "Pius II," 192–93.

13. Ibid., 190.

14. Ibid., 204–5.

15. *Comm.,* Smith, XI.751; Sonia Gallico, *Guide to the Excavations of Ostia Antica with a Section about the Renaissance Borgo* (Rome: ATS Italica Editrice, 2000), 6, 66–67.

of the church, but, since Pius makes no mention of this, the work was probably not yet begun.[16] Pius had four cardinals and their attendants with him—a minimum of about two hundred persons. The tiny Bishop's Palace could accommodate only the pope and the cardinals; their underlings had to sleep under tents or in boats on the Tiber.

Pius's description of the ruins of Ostia in the *Commentaries* tells us nothing specific. "Demolished colonnades are visible, and fallen columns and fragments of statues; the walls of temples stand, plundered of marble, that show that once they were a noble work."[17] Most of the extensive ruins we can visit today were invisible then, buried under the silt deposited by the Tiber, which had already pushed the coastline about a mile away from the formerly seaside town. Much of what Pius saw above ground in 1463 has probably been demolished, partly by Pius himself.

Soon after the papal party reached Ostia, Juan de Carvajal, Cardinal of Porto, sailed down to Ostia to invite Pius to visit the nearby remains of his titular city. Pius makes this invitation sound spontaneous, but the visits to Ostia and Porto were probably arranged at the same time. Ostia had stood next to the larger, southern mouth of the Tiber; but, even in antiquity, silting was already creating problems. Consequently, Emperor Claudius developed Porto at the smaller mouth of the Tiber two and a half miles north. Trajan later enlarged Claudius's port with a hexagonal basin located where today's *autostrada* from Rome turns to enter the Leonardo da Vinci airport.[18] When there ceased to be an imperial government to maintain a channel to the sea, both of these imperial harbor facilities clogged with mud. Today the Tiber's silt has moved the coast two miles beyond Trajan's basin.

As Pius and his companions crossed the island that separates the two mouths of the Tiber they found only the gaunt, roofless walls of Porto's former Cathedral of Santa Rufina, rising from the surrounding cow pasture, open to the coastal winds. Next to it the bell tower was intact and still stands today next to an entirely modern church. Just beneath the soil, however, Pius noted that "wherever you dig you find pieces of marble, statues, and huge columns." He gives a few details copied from Biondo's *Italia illustrata* about the markings on the rough, unpolished quarry stones and about how they were imported from Liguria for sale

16. Gallico, *Excavations,* 68. D'Estouteville lived until 1483, but the church was only completed by his successor, Giuliano della Rovere, later Julius II.

17. *Comm.,* Smith, XI.750.

18. Gallico, *Excavations,* 5.

to the Romans, but he never betrays his own interest in them.[19] Pius found Trajan's basin "choked with mud," looking like a lagoon. "Of the rows of columns around the lagoon, to which ships used to be moored, some are still standing. Nearby are arches very convenient for storing merchandise and larger workshops suitable for building or repairing ships." Pius saw ruined city walls from Constantine's time; both they and the "city gate stripped of its marbles" still stand. Although Porto offered no roof for shelter, Carvajal's servants erected canopies and "arbors of branches" under which the pope and cardinals could sit for food and entertainment.

When the papal party returned to Ostia they found that fishermen had caught a large dolphin, which was believed to portend a storm. The storm struck the following night (May 15), and Pius unleashes all his humanist rhetoric to describe it.

> A south wind churned the waters to their very depths, huge waves lashed the shore, and you could hear the ocean groaning and shrieking.... [The winds] ... fought savagely together and seemed now to rout, now to flee from one another. They tore down forests and everything in their path. The sky flashed with repeated fires, the heavens thundered, and terrible bolts shot from the clouds. One of them struck the tower bringing down a buttress and a bell which came near crushing a monk who was lying there buried in wine and sleep. Herds of cattle were stabled nearby and heifers that had just calved bellowed horribly in their anxiety for their young, either because they were terrified at the thunder or because they were afraid that wolves might attack them in the dark. The utter blackness of the night (though there were frequent flashes of lightning) doubled the terror, and such sheets of water fell that you would have said it was not rain but a deluge, as if the Creator had resolved once more to drown the human race.[20]

Boats and tents offered little shelter to the horde of servitors accompanying the pope and cardinals. Cardinal d'Estouteville's steward, finding his boat awash, jumped overboard and clung to a rope until he was rescued. One of the papal servants managed to jump from a boat to land, carrying the only lantern on board, leaving his colleagues in darkness. It was even worse for those in tents. A "whirlwind" tore through the tent housing Rodrigo Borgia's household. Pius says that it "snapped the ropes, splintered the poles, and slit the canvas to ribbons." Wandering blindly in

19. *Comm.*, Smith, XI.752; Rubenstein, "Pius II," 190.
20. *Comm.*, Smith, XI.753–54.

the dark, Borgia's servants, who had been sleeping in the nude, fell into a field of thistles that lacerated their bodies. Naked, shivering, streaming blood and water, they came staggering into the Bishop's Palace. Borgia gave them no welcome—they had abandoned his silver and gold plate! He "refused to be comforted" until men ran back to secure his valuables.

As dripping, trembling refugees crowded into the little building, Pius, unconcerned at first about the storm, was in his private room dictating to his secretary. But when he saw roof tiles flying past his window and felt the ancient walls quaking, he panicked and called for his clothes, exclaiming that "The wind is easier to bear than a falling house." It must have taken some time to find appropriate garments, because Pius was still dressing when the winds died down "as if they had been afraid to cause the Pope inconvenience."[21] With their makeshift accommodations now made uninhabitable, the papal party hurried back to Rome.

When summer brought the plague back to Rome in 1463, Pius made what would be his last *villeggiatura.* He did not go far, just to the Alban Hills south of the infected city, and his ramblings seem aimless and restless as he wandered among the Roman ruins and ancient monasteries thickly dotting that region. Pius, along with most other humanists of his time, had only an amateurish interest in archeology and ancient artifacts. The ruins of Hadrian's villa at Tivoli had elicited from Pius a meditation on the transience of the works of man, not an effort to mentally reconstruct the buildings as they had been in the imperial past. In the *Commentaries,* when he does seem specifically knowledgeable about archeological remains, he is usually quoting directly from Biondo, as he did when viewing the marbles at Porto. Throughout his life Aeneas/Pius had used archeological sightseeing as a time-filler. He sought out such places while waiting at Talamone for Eleanor of Portugal in 1451–1452, and King Alfonso had entertained him with such visits for four months not long before his election. His dilettantism does not mean that he did not enjoy archeological sites. They provided an excuse for a promenade and occupation for the mind as his litter bearers carried him through the grass and thistles or over the uneven Roman paving blocks. He enjoyed musing on the Roman achievement in general and on the evanescence of everything human, and occasionally speculated about

21. Ibid., XI.754–55.

some curious object or structure. The Alban hills, scenic, cool, punctuated with crystalline lakes, were a favorite retreat of Romans in all periods. The pope summers there at Castel Gandolfo even today.

Cardinal Ludovico Trevisan, patriarch of Aquileia, invited the pope to see his restoration of the thirteenth-century monastery of San Paolo in the city of Albano, about twelve miles southeast of Rome, on the western side of the volcanic crater lake of the same name.[22] Pius believed, like other classicists of his time, that Albano was the ancient city of Alba Longa, founded by Ascanius, the son of Aeneas. According to legend, Romulus and the first dynasty of Roman kings descended from the kings of Alba. Pius was certainly aware that one member of this dynasty, Ascanius's nephew, bore his own name, Aeneas Silvius. In the seventh century B.C. the Roman king Tullus Hostillus destroyed Alba Longa and moved its inhabitants to Rome. The site of Alba Longa certainly lies somewhere among the hills ringing Lake Albano, but archeologists have formed no consensus beyond that. Many think it was on the western side of the lake near Castel Gandolfo, while a smaller number place it near the convent of Santa Maria di Palazzolo at the lake's southeastern corner.[23]

When Pius arrived at Albano he found it bristling with Roman ruins covering an area "as large as Bologna." The "lofty arcades" of the former baths and the "traces of the channels for warm water" covered an area that Pius says was as large as the town itself. The Romans had built a theater partly cut into the hillside and partly supported on brick arches. The water supply for the ancient city depended upon reservoirs, of which Alberti had found thirty hidden in the weeds and brambles. In his own more cursory inspection Pius saw four of them; the impressive one near San Paolo, 100 feet by 160 feet in size, still stands. Five pyramids excited the pope's curiosity and prompted him to muse once more on the transience of human creations. "Time, the foe of all things, has so shaken some of the stones [of these pyramids] that they threaten to fall and in many places has allowed that foe of walls, the wild fig tree, to wedge itself in."[24] As Pius would have expected, the pyramids have now disappeared.

These were not, however, the remains of ancient Alba Longa. Some

22. Ibid., XI.758.

23. Tonino Paris, ed., *L'area dei Castelli Romani gli insediamenti storici dei Colli Albani* (Rome: Officina Edizioni, 1981), 236.

24. *Comm.,* Smith, XI.759–60.

of the ruins belonged to the immense villa that the emperor Domitian had built, which stretched between the present towns of Albano and Castel Gandolfo. Domitian's villa was itself a replacement for an older villa built by Pompey the Great.[25] Domitian (r. 81–96) had terraced the hillside into four levels, on which he built a palace, a hippodrome, cisterns, and a theater. The surrounding park, spread over almost two square miles, was dotted with gardens and nymphaea. In Constantine's time one nymphaeum from Domitian's park became the Church of Santa Maria della Rotonda, which survives today in good condition as an active church near the center of modern Albano.[26] Most of the ruins Pius would have seen were those of the town that grew up around a military camp, "Castra Albana," the headquarters of the Second Parthian Legion, built about a century after Domitian's time by Septimius Severus. This camp, where veterans often settled after retirement, became the nucleus of the medieval and modern town of Albano. It was probably Septimius Severus who built both the amphitheater, whose remains lie on a slope near the lake, and the cistern that impressed Pius.[27]

From Albano Pius made an excursion to Lake Nemi, a smaller crater lake farther south. He traveled there on the ancient Appian Way, which he says was more delightful than it had been in antiquity because of the shade of the filbert (hazelnut) trees that lined it. "Nature," he says characteristically, "is superior to any art." Unlike Lake Albano, whose shores are lined by sheer cliffs, a footpath and strip of level ground follow the four-mile circumference of Lake Nemi. On the shores and the lower slopes around the lake were orchards of apples, pears, medlars, quinces, and plums, bountiful enough in a good year, Pius says, to supply the whole population of Rome. Chestnuts, walnuts, and hazelnuts were equally plentiful. Under these trees, he tells us, "there is pleasant shade and green meadows inaccessible to the sun and obstructed by no brambles.... It is a most congenial place for poets to stroll. If the genius of a bard is listless here it will not be roused anywhere."[28]

Lake Nemi boasted an archeological curiosity in which Pius and his contemporaries took a keen interest. Local fishermen had long been familiar with a Roman ship clearly visible under the water at the northern end of the lake. In 1446 Cardinal Prospero Colonna had commissioned Alberti to raise this ship to the surface. Alberti brought in divers from Genoa who connected hooks to the hull and tried to raise the ship with

25. Paris, *Castelli Romani*, 256.
26. Ibid., 252–54.
27. Ibid., 252.
28. *Comm.*, Smith, XI.761.

ropes and hoists mounted on a raft.[29] Eugenius IV and all his court came to watch the attempt. The hoists went into action, but the resistance of the enormous ship, now firmly embedded in the lake bottom, was too much for them. Straining against the weight, the hooks and ropes wrenched some of the timbers off of the wreck, bringing only these and a piece of the bow to the surface.[30] Alberti studied these fragments and wrote a book on his findings, but both the book and the recovered timbers were later lost.[31] In 1463, when Pius came, the bits that Alberti had recovered were still on the shore for him to inspect. Pius gives a detailed account of the hull's construction, probably taken directly from Alberti's book.

The ship under the waters of Nemi continued to fascinate the historical imagination. Although only one ship was visible from the surface, there were, in fact, two of them, both among the largest wooden vessels ever built. Their subsequent history is dogged with mystery and misfortune. Like Alberti's effort, further attempts to raise the ships in 1535 and 1827 also ripped off great pieces of timber and gathered numerous artifacts—bronzes, tiles, mosaic work, bricks—all eventually lost or scattered.[32] In 1895 Eliseo Borghi, an art dealer working with government permission, discovered the second ship. From both vessels he retrieved fascinating and highly varied objects—bronze heads of lions, wolves, and Medusa, copper tiles covered in gold, pieces of mosaic, marble pavement stones, bricks, and great piles of timbers.[33] Vittorio Malfatti, a government engineer, concluded that the ships were too fragile to be raised to the surface but suggested that they might be recovered if the water level were lowered to expose them.[34]

Decades later Malfatti's proposal caught Mussolini's imagination.[35] Mussolini's engineers made use of a tunnel that their Roman predecessors had cut under the hills surrounding Nemi to irrigate a valley on the other side. Pius had noticed the entrance to this tunnel, through which he said "a stream of water of such size as a man could embrace with his arms flows into the Arrician lake."[36] Mussolini's engineers cleared, repaired, and reopened a mile of this ancient passage and used canals,

29. Guido Ucelli, *Le Navi di Nemi* (Rome: La Libreria dello Stato, 1950), 7.

30. John F. Gunmore, "The Ships in Lake Nemi," *Classical Weekly* 22, no. 13 (January 21, 1929): 97–98.

31. Ucelli, *Navi di Nemi,* 8.

32. Ibid., 9–13.

33. Ibid., 15–17.

34. Ibid., 28.

35. Ibid., 37–38.

36. *Comm.,* Smith, XI.761–62.

gorges, and natural streams to channel water from Lake Nemi all the way to the Tyrrhenian Sea. In October 1928 "il Duce" himself switched on four gigantic pumps at the lakeside to begin the drainage.[37] It took over nine months for the first ship to completely emerge, and the second was not free of water until June 1931. Conserving, moving, and studying the ships and the artifacts found with them was a mammoth archeological undertaking, followed closely by the global press. Excited scholars found unexpected revelations about Roman ship construction, pumps, and plumbing devices and about how the rowers were seated in ancient galleys.

Pius had thought that the emperor Tiberius had built the ships, but inscriptions found in the twentieth century proved that the builder was Tiberius's successor, Caligula. The ships were absurdly large for the small lake: the larger vessel was 233 feet long and 80.5 feet wide; the other measured 210 by 65.5 feet. With no practical use, the purpose of the ships was probably connected with Caligula's religious obsessions. Lake Nemi was a sacred site to the early Latins, who called it "Diana's mirror." A Roman road led from the shore near the sunken ships to a temple of Diana in the hills above. There had been such a temple since the fourth century B.C. and a sacred grove for centuries before that. A priest-king, the Rex Nemorensis, ruled these sacred precincts and defended the grove from those who came to challenge him. A challenger first plucked the "golden bough" from one of the trees and then fought to the death with the incumbent priest, who lived and reigned only so long as he remained victorious. This story became the starting point for Sir James Frazer's classic history of magic and mythology, *The Golden Bough.* Caligula had numerous religious fantasies, including belief in his own divinity. He also promoted the worship of the Egyptian goddess Isis, for whom he built a temple in Rome on the Campus Martius. Many of the objects found with Caligula's ships have associations with Diana or Isis, whom the emperor probably identified as the same goddess.[38] The mysteries of the ships' religious significance and the reason and timing of their sinking remain unsolved.

On April 21, 1940, twelve years after the draining of Lake Nemi began, a splendid museum opened on the shore with two great halls containing the hulls of the ships and displays of the other artifacts recovered

37. Ucelli, *Navi di Nemi,* 57.
38. Ibid., 287–92.

from the lake. Less than three months later Italy entered World War II as Hitler's ally. By 1944, as the Germans fought to hold Rome, the Alban hills with their antiquities, monasteries, and villas became a battleground. The Germans set up a battery of cannon about five hundred feet from the Nemi ship museum, moving the four museum attendants and their families to a cave where they could watch the building from a distance. The Americans targeted the German battery, their shells raining down, pock-marking the museum's concrete walls and shattering its windows. On the night of May 31, after the cannonading stopped, the museum officials in their cave saw a light moving around inside the building; forty minutes later the museum was a blazing inferno. An official inquiry later established that German soldiers set the fire deliberately—a judgment sometimes denied but never seriously challenged.[39]

Mussolini's museum, the Museo di Navi Romani, restored after the war, still stands at the northern tip of Lake Nemi, perhaps the most interesting museum without contents in the world. There are models, reconstructions, photographs, a few interesting artifacts, and a film (which oddly omits the destruction of the ships). It is the space itself that impresses the visitor: two great halls, each with steps leading down to sunken floors in the center. These yawning spaces, where the ships ought to be, have a powerful emptiness, a reverent display of the hole left in history by an irreversible moment of hooliganism.

After Pius returned from Nemi to Albano, Adoardo Colonna, Duke of Marsia, invited him to visit the Colonna citadel across the lake at Rocca di Papa and, if he liked it, to spend the summer there.[40] The Colonna citadel was perched on a kind of buttress protruding from the side of Monte Cavo, the second highest peak (3,117 feet) in the Alban Hills. On the way there Pius stopped at the Convent of Santa Maria di Palazzolo, which clings to a ledge on the side of the mountain overlooking the lake, straddling the route of the ancient Sacred Way that led to the temple of Jupiter Latiaris on the summit.[41] The approach to the monastery along the former Via Sacra was narrow and difficult, falling precipitously on one side toward the lake, rising in vertical cliffs on the other. Just outside the monastery gate is a Roman tomb carved in the cliff-face above the Via Sacra. The tomb displays a relief of a triumph flanked by six fasces on

39. Ibid., 312–15.

40. *Comm.,* Smith., XI.763.

41. Alberto Crielesi, *Santa Maria "Ad Nives" di Palazzolo,* ed. Luigi Devoti and Renato Mammucari, Itinerari della Campagna Romana (Vellatri, Italy: Edizioni tra 8 e 9, 1997), 10–11.

each side, probably indicating the tomb of a victorious consul. Where ivy had grown over the reliefs, Pius had it removed "to encourage the memory of antiquity."[42] Santa Maria di Palazzolo has had oscillating fortunes. A hermitage was mentioned there in 1050, but the monastery only began to flourish in the thirteenth century under the Cistercians. While the papacy was in Avignon the site became deserted and overgrown. Only in 1449 had the monastery been reactivated as a house of Observant Franciscans, but Pius still found it dilapidated.[43] In the seventeenth century Cardinal Juan da Forseca rebuilt much of the complex in the Baroque style. In the early twentieth century it came into the hands of the Venerable English College, which now runs it as a retreat center.[44]

The Colonna fortress, hanging over the mountainside town of Rocca di Papa at 2,230 feet, was on a much higher crag than Santa Maria di Palazzolo. The name "Rocca di Papa," meaning "the Pope's Castle," derives from the fortified residence where Eugenius III sometimes lived in the twelfth century. Martin V had given it to his Colonna kinsmen. Cardinal Prospero Colonna had refortified it, and Pius considered it impregnable. Nevertheless, in 1541 Pier Luigi Farnese, the bastard son of Pope Paul III for whom the city of Castro was built, had it blown up with gunpowder.[45]

Adoardo Colonna himself was not there to welcome Pius, but the castle's commandant received him "graciously and hospitably." After eating lunch Pius wandered about the high meadows and forests before turning his attention to the peak of Monte Cavo, which towered a thousand feet farther up. He says he "climbed" this summit, leaving us to wonder how a man who could not stand for the Easter Mass might have achieved this. He mentions a Roman road made of Appian flint leading to the ruins on the summit, and we must conclude that his patient bearers struggled up this path carrying his chair.[46] Here was once the temple of Jupiter Latiaris, sacred to all the Latins, first built by the last Roman king, Tarquin Superbus, in 531 B.C. In the spring and autumn, when the Latins held great festivals here, all their towns brought offerings of white bulls to be sacrificed to Jupiter while the people danced, sang, feasted, and played games to honor their god.[47] Only foundations

42. *Comm.*, Smith, XI.763.

43. Crielesi, *Santa Maria,* 11–15.

44. Ibid., 39–45.

45. Paris, *Castelli Romani,* 220.

46. *Comm.*, Smith, XI.764.

47. Severio Kambo, *I Castelli Romani: Grottaferrata e il Monte Cavo* (Bergamo: Istituto Italiano D'Arti Grafiche, n. d.), 122–23.

and fallen stones remained for Pius to see, some of which a Dalmatian hermit had used to build himself a shelter. Pius certainly knew the sacred history of this site, yet he interpreted the ruins on the summit as an ancient castle or country villa. As usual, however, it was the mountaintop view that most excited him. From this peak he could see the whole Tyrrhenian coast and even his beloved Monte Amiata, rising on the horizon beyond the peak of Monte Cimino. All the lakes, Albano, Nemi, Ariccia, and Turno, lay before him like a map. Rome itself, Tivoli, Palestrina, and the ruins of Tusculum all presented themselves to view.[48]

Far from accepting the Colonna's offer to stay the summer on the mountaintop, Pius spent only one night there before moving on to the monastery of Grottaferrata. Here, Pius was near the ruins of Tusculum, which had been one of the chief towns of the Latins, sometimes a rival, sometimes an ally of early Rome. In the late republic the heights around Tusculum had been a favorite site for aristocratic villas. In one of these Cicero wrote his *Tusculan Disputations,* a book of stoic philosophy admired by humanists for its teachings of detachment from the world and suppression of emotions. Archeologists have never identified Cicero's villa, but Pius chose to believe the local legend that it stood on the site of Grottaferrata itself.[49] There were eighteen villas near Tusculum in Cicero's day, but by the imperial period the region was blanketed with them. All of these had long ago fallen into ruin, and the town of Tusculum itself was devastated during the twelfth-century wars between the popes and the Hohenstaufen emperors.[50] Most of its people relocated to the neighboring village of Frascati, which Pius had enclosed in walls in 1460. In the sixteenth and seventeenth centuries Frascati became, like Tusculum in antiquity, the service town for a surrounding corona of magnificent villas.

Grottaferrata was unique among the monasteries that Pius visited because its monks followed the Rule of St. Basil, the form of monastic life common in the Orthodox East. Grottaferrata had been founded in 1004 by St. Nilus the Younger from Calabria (the "toe" of Italy), then a Greek-speaking, Byzantine province. Driven north by Saracen attacks, Nilus received a gift of land here for a new monastery.[51] According to legend, Nilus and his companion, while visiting here, took refuge in a cave from a storm. There the Blessed Virgin appeared to them, gave Nilus a golden

48. *Comm.,* Smith, XI.764.

49. Ibid., 765. For Cicero's villa at Grottaferrata, see Kambo, *I Castelli Romani,* 18.

50. Paris, *Castelli Romani,* 114.

51. Ibid., 132.

apple, and exhorted him to found an abbey there in her honor. The cave (*grotta*), later protected by an iron (*ferro*) gate, is the supposed origin of the name of the monastery.[52] Since there was no division between Orthodox East and Catholic West in his day, Nilus naturally founded his monastery following the rule and the liturgy of the East. These Eastern traditions have persisted down to the present. The existing church was begun in 1204, but the Romanesque exterior was "creatively" restored in the early twentieth century. The interior is mainly Baroque, but Italo-Byzantine frescoes and mosaics survive near the tops of the walls. Over the chancel arch is a splendid mosaic showing the apostles gathered around the Virgin. The Christ child sits enthroned within the Virgin's womb, an image more common in the East than the West.[53] The abbot when Pius visited Grottaferrata was a Calabrian like St. Nilus whose successes in reclaiming monastery property by means of lawsuits had made him loathed by the monastery's neighbors. Pius transferred the abbot to Sicily and turned Grottaferrata over to Cardinal Bessarion. Since Pius was finding the heat unbearable even in the Alban Hills, after lunch with the Greek monks he returned briefly to Rome.

On June 30 he departed again for Tivoli. But from this point on we hear little more from Pius about the pleasures of *villeggiatura*. That phase of his life came to an end as the political situation and the crusade absorbed all his attention. Up to this point the parts of the *Commentaries* covering 1462 and the spring of 1463 give the impression that Pius wrote or dictated them at least every few days, when little incidents, details, and immediate reactions were fresh in his mind and had an importance they would have lost had he waited a month before writing them. The last vignette of this sort comes near the end of Book XI (the division into books was made arbitrarily after Pius's death), when Pius apologetically introduces the "trifling matter" of his puppy Musetta, an ill-fated being who spent her short life trying to get herself killed. First, she fell unnoticed into a garden cistern. No one thought her barking unusual; but when the pope finally sent servants to investigate, they were just in time to fish the exhausted creature out before she drowned. The next day the pope was dining in the same garden when "a large monkey," apparently tethered or caged in the garden, escaped and attacked the dog so that the servants had to pry it out of the monkey's jaws. The third time was the evil charm: two weeks later Musetta was sitting on a

52. Kambo, *I Castelli Romani,* 17.
53. Ibid., 48.

favorite windowsill when a sudden "whirlwind" snatched her up and dashed her on the rocks below.[54]

Musetta's fate is the last of those moments of intimacy that make the *Commentaries* so much more personal than most humanist writings. Book XII and the uncompleted Book XIII focus entirely on war and diplomacy. Such matters of state had seemed intractable ever since the failure at Mantua. But suddenly, in the summer of 1463, Pius's stars seemed to align more favorably. To seize the opportunities now presented consumed Pius's time, while poor health devoured his energies. As he wrote less but acted more, he confined his writing to the great historical drama in which he believed he was playing the leading role.

The favorable turn of fortune began on the battlefields. Ferrante was finally triumphant in Naples, and Federico da Montefeltro was tearing cities from Sigismondo's grasp one by one. As Sigismondo's little state crumbled, the Venetians, to the pope's infinite fury, gave naval assistance to Sigmondo while seizing some of the border towns for themselves.[55] "What do fish care about law?" Pius fumed.

> As among brute beasts aquatic creatures have the least intelligence, so among human beings the Venetians are the least just and the least capable of humanity and naturally, for they live on the sea and pass their lives in the water . . . they are not so much companions of men as of fish and comrades of marine monsters.[56]

Nevertheless, winds from the East were finally swinging the weathervane of Venetian opinion in the direction of crusade. In September 1462 the Turks attacked the Christian island of Lesbos, informally under Venetian protection. A Venetian fleet of twenty-nine galleys watched from a distance, constrained from acting by orders from home. Two months later the Turks attacked the Venetian colony of Lepanto, though this time the Venetians drove them off. They were not so fortunate the following spring when the Turks captured Argos on April 3. A few weeks later the Turks erupted into Bosnia, where large minorities of Bogomils and other heretics supported them. The Christian king was promised his life if he surrendered his remaining fortresses, but, after he did so, the Turks decapitated him anyway.[57]

54. *Comm.*, Smith, XI.767.
55. Von Pastor, *History of the Popes,* 3:127–28.
56. *Comm.*, Smith, XI.743.
57. Paparelli, *Enea Silvio Piccolomini,* 243–44.

As the Most Serene Republic anxiously watched these assaults on her position in the East, Carvajal's diplomacy brought peace between Frederick III and Matthias Corvinus. Matthias, now the uncontested king of Hungary, could finally turn his attention to the Turkish menace.[58] During the weeks when Bosnian resistance was collapsing, Matthias sent an embassy to Venice to explore an alliance against the Turks. This time the Venetians were ready to listen. Encouraged by this, Pius sent Bessarion to the city on the lagoon as matchmaker for this alliance. After hearing impassioned speeches both for war and for peace, the Venetian Senate voted for war on July 28, 1463.[59] In September Venice and Hungary signed an alliance.[60] A few weeks later Venice signed a three-year alliance with Pius and Philip of Burgundy, promising to provide forty galleys for the pope's crusade against the Turks.[61] Venice did not wait for the crusade, however. The republic immediately launched an invasion of the Peloponnesus, strategically located both for war and for trade. None of this changed the pope's fundamental contempt for Venice; even as they joined together in war on the Turks, he wrote:

> Traders care nothing for religion nor will a miserly people spend money to avenge it. The populace sees no harm in dishonor if their money is safe. It was lust for power and insatiable greed of gain that persuaded the Venetians to equip such forces and undergo such expense.

Nonetheless, the Peloponnesus was as good a place as any to begin the assault on the Turks. Pius knew that the Venetians had recruited three thousand archers from Crete, as well as many Albanians, and believed their total ground forces amounted to over thirty thousand men.[62] The Venetians acted swiftly and at first successfully. They recaptured Argos in August and rebuilt the defensive wall across the Isthmus of Corinth called the Heximilion. As this construction went on in early September, the Venetians began a siege of Corinth. The Turks in Corinth defeated them and killed their commander on October 20. By the time the main Turkish forces arrived, the Venetians, afflicted with dysentery, had withdrawn. The Turks again demolished the Heximilion and recaptured Argos, though the Venetians successfully defended

58. Ibid., 244; Von Pastor, *History of the Popes,* 3:316.
59. Setton, *Papacy,* 2:241–43.
60. Von Pastor, *History of the Popes,* 3:319.
61. Setton, *Papacy,* 2:249–50.
62. *Comm,,* Smith, XII.775–76.

Figure 15.1. Roger van der Weyden. *Philip the Good, Duke of Burgundy*. Palais des Beaux Arts, Lille, France. Photograph from RMN-Grand Palais/Art Resource, New York.

Nauplia. Only the coming of winter saved the Venetian colonies from worse.[63] There would have been few illusions in Venice about an easy victory, but such a rapid and total defeat could only confirm the Venetian belief that the republic should risk its limited resources only for its own immediate advantage or when overwhelming support from allies made victory almost certain.

Just such an overwhelming alliance was what Pius hoped to create.

63. Setton, *Papacy*, 2:248–249.

He promised the Venetians that he would summon the Christian princes to crusade and at last sent Lorenzo Roverella, bishop of Ferrara, as envoy to France and Burgundy for this purpose. As we have seen, a few of the cardinals knew that Roverella would be secretly informing the rulers he met that Pius intended to lead the crusade in person. Even this would not secure cooperation from Louis XI. Louis had issued decrees effectively reinstating the Pragmatic Sanction, stating his intent "to defend ourselves against the aggressions of Rome, for the restoration of the ancient Gallican liberties." When Cardinal Jouffroy left the papal court in a huff, Louis welcomed him home with conspicuous favor.[64]

Philip of Burgundy seemed to offer only fair words. Philip was sixty-seven years old and on bad terms with his heir; Burgundy had no stake whatever in the fate of Hungary or the Balkans. Nevertheless, Philip understood that if Pius went in person to lead the crusade, his oath at the Feast of the Pheasant would obligate him to go as well. Lorenzo Roverella was still in Brussels when Philip suddenly fell ill, dropped into a coma, and was counted as dead. But he recovered as suddenly as he had sickened. For all his worldly shrewdness, Philip knew a sign from God when he saw one. This illness triggered one of those sudden "wake-ups" that intermittently aroused people from escapist fantasies to confront momentarily the stern realities. Although his Oath of the Pheasant had been going stale for nine years, Philip gave his commitment to join the crusade. In the *Commentaries* Pius imagines the duke speaking to his reluctant courtiers:

> Though I always meant to keep my promises, yet I delayed overmuch, beguiled by pleasures at home. . . . This has been a warning. God has called me. There is no reason for me to delay longer. Go, all of you who are my friends and who made the vow with me. Gird yourselves for the march so that when Pope Pius commands you may be ready.

To make the necessary arrangements Philip promised to send envoys to meet the pope at Rome on the Feast of the Assumption, requesting that representatives from all the Italian states also be present.[65] Pius knew that nothing in the political world was ever certain, but Philip of Burgundy, one of the great powers of Western Christendom, had bound himself to the crusade if Pius led it. Pius may have spoken for himself

64. Von Pastor, *History of the Popes,* 3:156–57.
65. *Comm.,* Smith., XII.793.

as much as for Philip when he wrote, "I delayed overmuch, beguiled by pleasures at home." But now the responsibility to save Christendom was squarely on his own shoulders. With Philip ready, Venice and Hungary on the move, Sigismondo crushed, and the king of Naples owing him his throne, it was time to lead. Pius would not allow himself to be found wanting.

16

Villas and Gardens

Pius II's summers from 1461 through 1463 do not quite fit the pattern of *villeggiatura* as it was practiced by most of his contemporaries and later generations of Italians. He was unusual in his restless migrations from place to place and in staying in borrowed quarters; most of the elite had a few, or only one, conveniently located country villa of their own, where, plague permitting, they could stay for most or all of a season, enjoying country life without the inconvenience and discomfort of long or frequent travel. Pius's palace at Pienza was presumably constructed to play this role, but Pius only made one prolonged sojourn there. It was not only that Pius was inured to travel; he apparently could not satisfy his curiosity and his appetite for natural scenery in any one place but had to continually seek new views and prospects. Compared to other Italians he also had more options from which to choose; the Papal States were a large territory including such particularly attractive areas as the Alban Hills, the environs of Viterbo, and Lake Bolsena. Pius also made free with Sienese territory at Pienza and Petriolo. Nevertheless, Pius shared his underlying love for country living and the beauties of nature with many other elite Italians.

Petrarch had established the tradition that, like lords and princes, intellectuals also needed a *hortus conclusus* in the country where they could live in solitude amidst the beauties of nature. Petrarch's first and favorite retreat was in France at the source of the Sorgue River, near Avignon in the Vaucluse. There he had a modest cottage, cared for by a single housekeeper, a garden near the house "dear to Bacchus," a shady grove a bit farther off "sacred to our Apollo," and a cave where he could escape the heat of a summer afternoon.[1] His Vaucluse property was the model for his description of the ideal intellectual retreat: "having easy access to woods and fields and, what is especially grateful to the Muses, to the bank of a murmuring stream."[2] Pius could have written these same words. In a letter of 1353 Petrarch clearly describes his joy at this refuge and his disdain for the active world outside.

> I establish here my Rome, my Athens, my spiritual fatherland. Here I have all my friends, of present and past, not only those [whom he knows personally] but those who died many centuries ago, known to me by benefit of letters.... I assemble them from every place, from every time into my narrow valley. I converse with them more eagerly than with those who presume that they are alive by discharging rank words and catching sight of their vapor exhaled on the cold air. There I wander, free and secure, alone with my chosen companions.... As much as possible I commune with myself alone.[3]

After he left France for Italy, Petrarch had several similar sanctuaries. The local tyrant in Parma tempted him to settle there with the bait of a new country retreat, a mountain aerie at Selvapiana, where Petrarch could look out across the Po Valley from the Apennines to the Alps.[4] In Milan the Visconti gave him a quiet house adjoining the church of S. Ambrogio, next to the city wall, where he could go out and wander in the countryside.[5] In 1370 he settled into his final refuge at the village of Arquà in the Euganean Hills, where the lord of Padua gave him the land to build the small but elegant house that one can still visit today.[6]

Petrarch's friend Boccaccio also valued his rural sanctuary at Certaldo in the Valdelsa, between Florence and Siena, of which he wrote:

> I ... have returned to Certaldo and here I have begun, with much less difficulty than I had thought possible, to comfort my life, and the rough clothes and the peasant fare are beginning to please me; and the absence of the ambitions and the unpleasantness and annoyances of our town-dwellers is of such consolation to my heart that, could I remain without hearing anything of them, I do believe that my repose would increase greatly.

1. Francesco Petrarca (Petrarch), *Rerum familiarium* XIII.8, in *Letters from Petrarch*, trans. Morris Bishop (Bloomington: Indiana University Press, 1966), 124.

2. Petrarch, *Solitude*, I.5–II.157.

3. Ibid., *Fam.* XV.3; Petrarca, *Letters*, 132.

4. Morris Bishop, *Petrarch and His World* (Bloomington: Indiana University Press, 1963), 172, 175.

5. Ibid., 321

6. Ibid., 360–61.

The extreme case of a humanist retreating into a *hortus conclusus* is that of Niccolò Niccoli (1364–1437). He never made himself a country seat but remained in Florence and turned his city house into a world apart. Niccoli used his house as a Petri dish in which to grow a fluorescence of classicism under controlled conditions. Niccoli was personally fastidious to the point of obsession, dressing elegantly, taking pride in serving his guests only on ancient Roman dishes, set upon the finest, whitest linen.[7] Giannozzo Manetti, who wrote his biography, described his extreme sensitivity.

> He clothed his body in fine red garments. His senses, especially those of sight and sound from which instruction was to be obtained, were so delicate that he could not bear to see or hear anything unpleasant. He would not hear a braying ass, a rasping saw or a squeaking mouse and admitted nothing to the sight of his eyes unless it was finely made, fitting and beautiful.[8]

He spent his inheritance collecting ancient manuscripts, statues, coins, vases, medals, and curios until he exhausted his resources and could only survive and continue his collection through the largesse of Cosimo de' Medici. Although he sent others to seek manuscripts all over Europe, he rarely left his own sanctum in Florence except to flee the plague. Ambitious travel plans came to nothing, and he did not even visit Rome until he was sixty.[9] Manetti, who was active in public affairs himself, nonetheless writes admiringly of Niccoli's withdrawal.

> At no time whatever ... did he give himself over to striving after public offices, ... to marriage in order to have children, but he preferred to live a happy life with his books, without much property or honors, unmarried, free of worries about transitory things, in leisure, peace, and tranquility. In this way, abstaining from public occupations, and from almost all private business, he enjoyed the leisure ... of *literati* and superior minds.[10]

On one side of his personality Niccoli seems to have been snobbish, prickly, prissy, and difficult—he was often hated, but never dull. To those who endured his peculiarities he redeemed them by his frankness,

7. Vespasiano da Bisticci, *Renaissance Princes,* 402; Michael Levey, *Florence: A Portrait* (Cambridge, Mass.: Harvard University Press, 1996), 105.

8. Holmes, *Enlightenment,* 90.

9. Ibid., 11–12, 89–90; Giuseppe Zippel, *Nicolò Niccoli: Contributo Alla Storia Dell 'Umanismo* (Florence: Fratelli Bocca, 1890), 53–54.

10. Baron, *Crisis of the Early Italian Renaissance,* 322–23.

his generosity, and his tireless efforts to assist anyone who loved antiquity. Niccoli wrote very little: his only book, on orthography, is lost, and only three letters survived into modern times, one of which is now missing.[11] Yet, after Niccoli's death, Poggio wrote to Marsuppini that "his house was always full of learned and important men who attended him every day. No-one with any knowledge visited Florence without giving priority to seeing Niccoli and his books."[12] There were always a number of young men sitting around his house, reading books he had put into their hands.[13] Those who shared his interests fell under the spell of his enthusiasm and treated his home as a temple of the muses.[14] Niccoli might have been politically passive, but he actively evangelized for classicism. He accosted Piero de' Pazzi, a wealthy young blade known for his life of pleasure, and urged him to exchange dissipation for the study of Latin. According to Vespasiano, Pazzi became a cultivated patron and collector of books and manuscripts.[15]

Niccoli's book collection was an important engine driving the discovery and collection of antique manuscripts. His network of contacts made him the clearinghouse for manuscripts, information about them, and the distribution of copies. From his sanctuary in Florence he badgered those who acted as his agents, including Poggio and Traversari, giving them lists of books to seek. After Niccoli's death Poggio claimed that most of the discoveries of lost books in his time were the product of "Niccolò's persuasion, inspiration, exhortation, and verbal pestering."[16] Vespasiano said that "He held his books rather for the use of others than of himself."[17] Niccoli assured the continuation of his work by leaving his books to Cosimo de' Medici to form a public library at the convent of San Marco.

Feudal landowners had always visited their country estates to collect their revenues, attend to their agricultural business, supervise their underlings, and enjoy the hunting. The Medici were among the first of the powerful to recast these visits in the therapeutic mold of *villeggiatura.* Cosimo de' Medici makes this explicit in an invitation he sent to the philosopher Marsiglio Ficino to join him at his Villa Careggi.

11. Zippel, *Nicolò Niccoli,* 46–48; Holmes, *Enlightenment,* 89.
12. Holmes, *Enlightenment,* 93.
13. Vespasiano da Bisticci, *Renaissance Princes,* 400.
14. Holmes, *Enlightenment,* 93.
15. Levey, *Florence,* 109–10.
16. Holmes, *Enlightenment,* 93.
17. Vespasiano da Bisticci, *Renaissance Princes,* 396.

> Yesterday I came to the villa of Careggi, not to cultivate my fields but my soul. Come to us, Marsiglio, as soon as possible. Bring with you our Plato's book *De summo bono.* This, I suppose, you have already translated from the Greek language into Latin as you promised. I desire nothing so much as to know the best road to happiness. Farewell, and do not come without your Orphean Lyre.[18]

Cosimo always used his *villeggiature* for intellectual pursuits, even building Ficino a *villetta* at Coreggio to keep his household intellectual close at hand. Ficino, who harped frequently on his own "melancholic temperament," said that only in nature could persons afflicted with such a temperament find relief; Coreggio was thus his favorite residence.[19]

A villa differs from a farmhouse because, even if it is the center of an agricultural enterprise, pleasure, not agriculture, is its primary purpose.[20] The architectural historian James Ackerman pointed out that, since antiquity, "the villa accommodates a fantasy impervious to reality."[21] Although Careggi continued to be an agricultural enterprise, its architect, Michelozzo, remodeled the old fortress into a pleasant country retreat incorporating the most crucial architectural feature of an Italian villa: the loggia—covered, but open to a garden and sufficiently protected from weather to serve for outdoor living in all but the coldest months.[22] Alberti gave his blessing to *villeggiatura* when he wrote in *Della famiglia* that at one's villa "you can live undisturbed by rumors and tales and by the wild strife that breaks out periodically in the city. You can be free of the suspicions, fears, slanders, injuries, feuds, and other miseries which are too ugly to talk about and horrible even to remember."[23] In 1484 the conclave of cardinals all signed a pledge that whoever was elected pope would allow every cardinal a country property "whither they may freely betake themselves, either for the purpose of evading the plague, or for recreation."[24]

Lorenzo de' Medici spent as much time as he could on *villeggiatu-*

18. Janet Ann Duff-Gordon Ross, *Lives of the Early Medici as Told in their Correspondence* (Boston: Chatto and Windus, 1911); quoted in Coffin, *Villa,* 9.

19. Coffin, *Villa,* 12.

20. James Ackerman, "The Villa as Paradigm," in "Paradigms of Architecture," special issue, *Perspecta* 22, no. 1 (1986): 11.

21. Ibid., 11.

22. Coffin, *Villa,* 12.

23. Alberti, *Della famiglia* III.3, in *Family,* 193.

24. Coffin, *Villa,* 23.

ra. His favorite country residence was Poggio a Caiano, located about halfway between Florence and Pistoia. A modest house there, the Villa Ambra, had been built upon the ruins of an old fortification belonging to the Strozzi and later the Rucellai. Lorenzo, who had visited there with Giovanni Rucellai, bought it from him in 1473 and commissioned Giuliano Sangallo to design the villa. Further works continued under Lorenzo's son, Pope Leo X.[25] The design was revolutionary because the fortifications were all moved to the perimeter of the grounds, permitting the villa itself to be open to its gardens. On the crest of a hill (*poggio*), Sangallo raised his two-story rectangular structure on an arcaded platform that provided a terrace for views and promenades. The most striking exterior feature is a loggia that Sangallo designed as an Ionic temple portico embedded somewhat incongruously into the stucco of the block-like building. The frieze above the columns, made by Sansovino in majolica, is full of arcane allegories.[26] In it we see Diana and Apollo in a chariot, Eternity gushing forth souls from her breast, Janus guarding the gate of the Temple of War, and much else that remains unidentified. Decoding its allegorical meanings was recreation for Lorenzo's guests but has defied the efforts of modern scholars.[27]

During the late fifteenth and sixteenth centuries the qualities of the *studiolo* extended beyond the private room to turn the entire domestic environment into a larger *hortus conclusus.* The idea of leisured contemplation, the collection of "virtuous wealth" in the form of art works and antiquities, the use of mythology to turn the daily environment into an object of contemplation, all became prominent in palaces, villas, and especially the gardens that surrounded them. What had been packed into the *studiolo* was spreading out into reception rooms, loggias, secret gardens, grottoes, and terraces in complexes where architecture, sculpture, engineering, and landscaping merged and interpenetrated one another. Some of the new spaces accommodated banquets, dramatic performances, and tournaments; but most of them, especially in the gardens, were designed for contemplation, conversation, and reading. Against the danger of boredom and satiety that always hung over the *studiolo,* the best weapons were more spaces, more variety, more objects, moving objects like fountains and automata, and, above all, motion for

25. Masson, *Villas,* 182.

26. Cloulas, *Lorenzo,* 290.

27. Jean Seznec, *The Survival of the Pagan Gods: The Mythological Tradition and Its Place in Renaissance Humanism,* Bollingen 38 (New York: Pantheon, 1953), 116.

the beholder who could stroll, wander, discover, or sit and savor at will. Finally, if it was therapeutic to be constantly planning, collecting, and commissioning new treasures for the *studiolo,* how much more effective to plan multiple buildings and acres of gardens, terraces, sculptures, and fountains?

The Villa Viridario, now called the Farnesina, built in Rome in 1507–1511 by the banker Agostino Chigi, exemplifies this next stage of this development.[28] A member of a Sienese banking family, Chigi had built up a fortune in papal finance and gained the lease on the alum mines at Tolfa. Baldassare Peruzzi designed the Villa Viridario as a rectangle with two short wings protecting the garden loggia from the weather. Its two tall stories, articulated with pilasters as Alberti would have wished, carry a whimsical frieze of terra-cotta putti and garlands concealing the mezzanine above the second story. The plain stucco walls we see today originally displayed painted male and female satyrs frolicking in mythological frescoes.[29] A descendent of the *sgrafitti* of Pienza, this playful appearance must have made a startling contrast to the massive fortress-like palazzi of Rome or Florence.

Viridario originally stood among terraces and gardens running along the Tiber. In the loggia facing the garden, Raphael and his pupils frescoed garlands of fruit and greenery from which there appear to be suspended canvas awnings painted with the story of Cupid and Psyche.[30] On the wall of another loggia facing the Tiber Raphael painted one of his masterpieces, the *Galatea,* while above it the ceiling frescoes depict astrological deities arranged in the positions of the planets and stars when Chigi was born. Together these two loggias take up about half the space on the ground floor.[31] Peruzzi, more painter than architect until he built Chigi's villa, frescoed the main room on the upper floor, the *Sala della Prospettiva,* with illusionistic paintings that seem to open up between marble columns onto a panoramic view of Rome and the countryside.[32]

The escapist message of Chigi's villa was unmistakable. Reality yields to illusion everywhere, from Raphael's bower with its suspended

28. Brigitte Hintzen-Bohlen, *Art and Architecture: Rome and the Vatican City* (New York: Barnes and Noble, 2000), 437.

29. Coffin, *Villa,* 98.

30. Georgina Masson, *Italian Gardens (*New York: Harry N. Abrams, 1961), 134.

31. Coffin, *Villa,* 91.

32. Ibid., 101–2; Hartt, *Italian Renaissance,* 479.

"awnings" to Peruzzi's panorama; but the modern visitor misses the exterior network of delicate frescoes dissolving the solidity of the walls and setting the illusionist tone from the first glimpse. Chigi seemed to enjoy illusion: at one of his banquets, after each course, he had his servants toss the silver dishes and vessels into the Tiber. He stunned his guests with this extravagance; but he had installed nets under the surface that allowed the servants to retrieve everything in the morning.[33]

Even Chigi's villa retains the box-like forms and the clear demarcation of the building from its surroundings, which were still characteristic of early Renaissance architecture, just as they had been in the Middle Ages. Roman architecture, especially Roman villas, had not been like that: indoor and outdoor spaces, architecture and garden, had interpenetrated one another.[34] Nevertheless, an artistic revolution shortly after 1500 made the cinquecento villa more garden than architecture. As so often happened during the Renaissance, the first impetus for an artistic change came from a literary work, in this case the *Hypnerotomachia Poliphili* ("The Strife of Love in the Dream of Polyphilus"), written by a Venetian, Fra Francesco Colonna, in 1467 but not published until 1499. This phantasm of imaginary architecture and landscapes conjured up a romantic vision of antiquity that we can see reflected in the more ambitious cinquecento gardens.[35] Although antiquity—Greek, Roman, even Egyptian—saturates every page of the *Hypnerotomachia,* its spirit is romantic, not classical. In form the *Hypnerotomachia* is a medieval romance, not unlike the *Roman de la Rose,* piled deep in allegories, magic, dangers, and wonders, taking place in a world that Polyphilus enters in a dream as he pines for his beloved Polia.[36] As if the reader does not have enough work to do decoding the ceaseless allegories, Colonna recounts this dream in a language of his own invention, combining Latin, Greek, and Italian, coining fantastic new words such as "hypnerotomachia" (a Greek compound: "dream-love-strife"). The efforts of Colonna's sixteenth-century English translator "R. D" (probably Robert Darlington) produce something delightfully reminiscent of Lewis Carroll's "Jabberwocky"—as when the curling hair of the "flamigerous nymphs" is "hemicirculately instrophiated" about their "divine faces."[37]

Perhaps the most unforgettable prodigy Colonna describes is the

33. Coffin, *Villa,* 108.

34. Ibid., 241.

35. Masson, *Gardens,* 66.

36. Blunt, *Artistic Theory,* 40.

37. Francesco Colonna, *Hypnerotomachia: The Strife of Love in a Dreame (1592),* trans. R. D., introduction by Lucy Gent (Delmar, N.Y.: Scholar's Facsimiles and Reprints, 1973), 96.

"Temple of the Sun," which may derive from ancient descriptions of the mausoleum at Halicarnassus.[38] The base of the temple is a square, 1,200 paces (nearly half a mile) on a side and 40 paces high. From this a pyramid rises in 1,400 steps culminating in a cube of 4 paces per side. On top of this is an obelisk that carries on its summit a gilded bronze statue of "Occasio" that pivots in the wind, emitting a terrifying sound.[39] Colonna had read the *Hieroglyphica,* supposedly written by a fifth-century A.D. Egyptian priest, Horapollo, which had been translated in 1419. Under its influence he has Polyphilus discover and decode pseudo-hieroglyphics on the Temple of the Sun.[40] One of Colonna's most influential images was a porphyry elephant carrying a hieroglyphic-covered obelisk on its back. The elephant was hollow, and Polyphilus enters it on brass steps. Inside, each end of the elephant contained an "everlasting lampe and incalcerate light" illuminating a sepulcher with a statue on top, accompanied by cryptic epigrams.[41] Bernini was almost certainly thinking of the *Hypnerotomachia* when he designed the fountain in front of Santa Maria sopra Minerva at Rome, in which an elephant carries an obelisk on its back.[42]

After many more wonders, Polyphilus encounters (in Colonna's most Jabberwockian idiom):

> a fearful Dragon shaking her trisulked and three parted tongue against me, grating her teeth, and making skritching or critching noise, her squemy and sealy hide trailing upon the flowered pavement, clopping her wings upon her wrimpled back, with a long tail folding and crinkling like an eel and never resting.[43]

This fearsome creature drives Polyphilus into a series of underground vaults and passages, from which he emerges into the land of the Nymphs of the Five Senses. The nymphs welcome him into their *hortus conclusus,* where all delights abound, "environed and walled about with steep and unpassageable rocks, by means thereof secure and free from all dangers and fear, we want not anything which may breed delight and cause a sweet content." The nymphs urge him to "cast away, shake off, and forget all afflicting sorrow and frame thyself and thy

38. Blunt, *Artistic Theory,* 41.
39. Colonna, *Hypnerotomachia,* 20–23; Blunt, *Artistic Theory,* 41–42.
40. Trinkhaus, *Renaissance Humanism,* 46.
41. Colonna, *Hypnerotomachia,* 35–39.
42. Blunt, *Artistic Theory,* 41n2.
43. Colonna, *Hypnerotomachia,* 64.

affrighted spirits to entertain of our comforts solace and pleasure."[44] The nymphs are so "flamigerous" and their curls so "hemicirculately instrophiated" that Polyphilus finds himself "lasciviously bent, and in such prurient lust" that he wished to fall upon them "like an eager and hot Falcon coming down out of the air upon a covey of Partridges."[45] The nymphs merely laugh at him and take him to the palace of their queen, an "artificious Palace, wonderful and perfinite of the Art of building, the subtlety of which, no human excogitation is able to imitate."[46] There the queen serves him a seven-course vegetarian banquet on dishes made of topaz, including such delicacies as "refined marrow, sprinkled over with Rosewater, Saffron, and the juice of Oranges, tempering the taste and gilded over, and with them six pieces of pure manchet."[47] After the entertainment, which includes a game of chess danced by live figures, Polyphilus is brought before three portals leading to the religious life, love, and worldly fame. He chooses the portal of love.[48] Passing through it, he finds Polia.[49] Together they witness the loves of Jupiter, passing by in a series of Petrarchan triumphs.[50] They have a Mass-like ceremony at the Temple of Venus, then cross the sea to Cythera, where Polyphilus attempts to embrace Polia. His gesture vaporizes her into a sweet fragrance, and he awakes.[51]

Symptomatic of Colonna's romanticism is the fact that the architectural marvels Polyphilus sees are deserted ruins—mysterious in origin, monuments of a lost world, haunting in their silent memories, and, above all, reminders of human frailty. Nature has invaded the courts and palaces of man and is as essential to Colonna's scenes as the architecture. This romantic sensuality contrasts strongly with the Florentine Renaissance of Alberti, which saw the return to antiquity as a move toward greater rationality, in conformity with the reason that governed the universe. Alberti's methods were mathematics, proportion, and exactitude in reviving architecture as Vitruvius described and the emperors had built it. Colonna's desire, as Anthony Blunt said, was "to build up a dream; and this dream, one feels, became for him more important than the ordinary conduct of life."[52] Colonna, rarely among quattrocento writers, contrasts imagination with reason and gives the prize to the

44. Ibid., 84.
45. Ibid., 96.
46. Ibid., 140.
47. Ibid., 122.
48. Ibid., 157–62.
49. Ibid., 162–67.
50. Ibid., 178–89.
51. Ibid., v–vi.
52. Blunt, *Artistic Theory,* 40.

former. Repeatedly he uses "inexcogitabile," "unthinkable," or "beyond reason" to describe his marvels.[53]

Colonna condemns the present and exalts antiquity as vehemently as any Florentine. The sight of the magnificent architecture of the imagined past makes him praise the genius of the ancients and lament that it is "buried" with them and "none [is] left for us to inherit in this age." Unlike Alberti or Palmieri, Colonna sees no gratifying return to the glories of ancient art in his own time.[54] The cause of this precipitous decline in human achievement is, in spite of Colonna's unabashed eroticism, still a moral one: it is the modern disease of greed. Just how greed becomes "the mortal enemy to good architecture" he never explains, but it provokes his fury all the same.

> This is that which accuseth horrible covetousness, the devourer and consumer of all virtue, a still biting and everlasting greedy worm in his heart that is captivated and subject to the same, the accursed let and hindrance to well-disposed wits, the mortal enemy to good architecture, and the execrable idol of this present world, so unworthily worshipped, and damnably adored. Thou deadly poison to him that is infected with thee, what sumptuous works are overthrown and by thee interdicted.[55]

When Aldus Manutius published *Hypnerotomachia* in 1499, its hieroglyphs, its beautiful woodcuts, and the artistic arrangement of the type on the page made the book itself an *objet d'art*.[56] Later painters, engravers, and sculptors sometimes represented the hieroglyphs and the sculptured reliefs that Polyphilus described.[57] The chambers inside Colonna's elephant may have inspired the grottoes inside the garden sculptures at Tivoli and Pratolino. But the most important influence of the *Hypnerotomachia* was not exercised through specific motifs. What it brought to the fore was a romantic alternative to the rational and archeological approaches to antiquity. It was this free and playful romanticism that informed the increased use of mythology in cinquecento art. It also introduced the conception of nature as an artistic medium that could be joined with sculpture and architecture to create a garden paradise, the *hortus conclusus* in the most literal sense. Finally, it legitimized ruin, no longer a misfortune to be lamented, ignored, or overcome, but the source of a sweet nostalgia tinged with mystery.

53. Kemp, "Mimesis," 365.
54. Colonna, *Hypnerotomachia,* 43–44.
55. Ibid., 58.
56. Ibid., 73; Blunt, *Artistic Theory,* 43.
57. Blunt, *Artistic Theory,* 42–43.

During his summer travels in 1461 Pius II had stayed at a dilapidated monastery in Tivoli, where the views and the orchards were beautiful but the accommodations primitive. "The house was old and tumble-down, full of rats as big as rabbits."[58] Yet this was the very building that Cardinal Ippolito d'Este (1509–1572), nephew of Isabella d'Este, would transform into the renowned Villa d'Este. Pope Julius III appointed Ippolito governor of Tivoli in 1550, by which time a previous governor had made the building habitable. Cardinal Ippolito would probably not have devoted his life to its renovation and the creation of its gardens if he had succeeded in his repeated efforts to be elected pope. His first disappointment had been at Julius III's election, just before he received the appointment at Tivoli. Six months later he was already telling his brother, the Duke of Ferrara, that he was going to find refuge from court affairs at his new residence.[59] In 1555 he once more failed to be elected pope; in fact, the new pope, Paul IV, accused him of attempting to buy the votes of his colleagues and exiled him to Lombardy until Pius IV summoned him back. In 1566 his colleagues missed yet another chance to raise him to the chair of St. Peter, and the new pope, Pius V, excluded him from power. Gathering a circle of humanists around him to entertain his leisure, he returned to Tivoli and devoted the rest of his life to developing it.[60] For this his architect was Pirro Ligorio, who had completed Bramante's Cortile del Belvedere at the Vatican, where the terraces rising up the hill to the Villa Belvedere are an obvious prototype for the gardens at the Villa d'Este.

Using the old city wall on the southwest side as a retaining wall, Ligorio created a flat section at the lowest level of his garden, with five major slopes or terraces and with many smaller terraces at the edges, rising up to the villa.[61] Visitors were meant to enter from the gate on the road, where they could see the main axis rising, terrace upon terrace, up to the large, plain building that still looks more like a monastery than a villa. Walking through the garden, the visitors were meant to experience a mounting crescendo as the terraces rose. The planting became larger, denser, and shadier until one reached the terrace in front of the villa and looked back at the view of both the gardens and the countryside.[62] In the same fashion sculptural and architectural features at Tivoli progressed from wooden pergolas to ever-larger stone constructions as the cardi-

58. Coffin, *Villa,* 26.

59. Ibid., 312.

60. Ibid., 311–13.

61. Ibid., 313–14.

62. Ibid., 325–26.

nal's guests climbed; and the fountains, just two weeping stones in the entrance pavilion, became more musical and more active, concluding at the top with roaring cascades and surprising watery assaults to soak the unwary.[63]

The lowest, most conventional level of the garden, laid out in squares, has now been entirely replaced. Beyond this was the first cross-axis, a row of pools populated by fish and waterfowl. At the left end of these pools a roaring fountain of later date now upsets the gradual introduction of sound and water effects. Above this splendid intrusion there still stands an ornate structure, originally containing a water organ, whose music was originally the visitor's first introduction to the hydraulic sound effects.[64] A water wheel operated the keys, and air was forced through the pipes by flooding a sealed chamber.[65] Beyond the cross-axis of fish pools the ground slopes steeply upward amidst a grove of trees and offers the visitor a choice of three parallel staircases, each lined at the sides by a gurgling flow of water. Halfway up the central stair one encounters the Fountain of the Dragons, an oval basin with stairs curving around it on each side and four dragons in the center spewing water in ever-changing patterns—now jets, now fan-like sprays, now sheets, now dribbles—changing the sound as well as the visual effect. Mounting the stairs around the Dragon Fountain, visitors could dip a hand into a trickling flow babbling down the middle of the stone balustrade.[66]

At the top of this stair the Hundred Fountains formed a second cross-axis that forced the visitor to go either to the left or right.[67] In either direction one followed the shade-drenched path alongside the fountains, which consisted of three channels of water rising one above the other, with stone boats, lilies, and eagles emitting sprays and jets at the top. For those turning left, the Hundred Fountains led to a shady piazza in front of the Oval Fountain. Along the back side of the oval basin is an arched passageway with statues of nymphs spewing water into the basin. At the top center of this arcade a wide, curved cascade of water thunders into the pool below. Above this cascade is a grotto containing a statue of the Tiburtine Sibyl inside an artificial hill. Higher still the hill reaches to the pinnacle of "Mount Parnassus," where the fountain of Pegasus shows the winged horse taking flight from the mountain top.[68]

63. Ibid., 327.

64. Ibid., 321.

65. John Shearman, *Mannerism* (Harmondsworth: Penguin, 1967), 133.

66. Coffin, *Villa,* 321, 327.

67. Ibid., 322.

68. Ibid., 321–22.

One could walk behind and through these fountains in the arcade along the back of the oval basin—at the risk of stepping on certain stones that sent a jet of water spurting up one's legs.

Those who went to the right at the Hundred Fountains reached another piazza in front of the Fountain of the Romella, or "Little Rome." Here, amidst noisy sprays and jets, were models of the monuments of ancient Rome. In the foreground was the "Tiber," with the island shown as a stone boat. Eager to explore, the curious visitor would hurry across the Tiber Bridge and instantly be doused by jets of water attacking from all sides. A more cautious visitor might sit on a bench to contemplate the former glories of Rome from a safe distance. There, a cold dampness worked its way inward through one's clothing, for the bench was equipped with weep holes quietly soaking its surface. Visitors emerged wet or dry according to the whim of a gardener who regulated the waterworks.[69] From the Romella one could descend along the old city wall to the fountains of the emperors, of Persephone, and of the Owl. At the last of these, before a rich architectural background, small bronze birds twittered happily in hydraulic voices until a bronze owl flew into their midst and frightened them into silence. Having explored these wonders, the cardinal's guests, whether dry or dripping, ascended though dense foliage on a series of switchback paths to the Cardinal's Walk, where there were several fountains and the Grotto of Diana. Finally, staircases led to the terrace in front of the villa from which one could look down above the garden trees at the breathtaking view toward Rome.[70]

Cardinal Ippolito's household humanist, Marc-Antoine Muret, wrote that no day passed at Tivoli without time devoted to study. At dinner the cardinal led his circle of intellectuals in conversation and then brought Muret to his bedroom to continue the discussion. If the weather was still hot after dinner, they read Horace until it got cooler.[71] Muret remembered that the villa

> was a house crammed by learned men from whose society and conversation one was always learning something. [The cardinal] himself, although of average learning, had a great and lofty spirit, and a wonderful devotion to our studies, so that his house might seem to have been an academy.[72]

69. Ibid., 327.

70. Ibid., 316–17.

71. Ibid., 335.

72. Marc-Antoine Muret, *Opera omnia,* ed. C. H. Frotscher (Leipzig: 1834), 2:140–41; quoted in Coffin, *Villa,* 336.

If we substitute these learned discussions in place of the stories told in the *Decameron,* we can see how clearly Boccaccio's fiction foretold the life to which Renaissance elites aspired in the coming centuries. The pattern is consistent. When reality disappoints or terrifies, one gathers agreeable companions, retreats to an earthly paradise, and talks. In Cardinal Ippolito's version, the loftiness of the talk makes it "virtuous," just as superb collections of curiosities became "virtuous wealth."

At least once, the romantic ruins of the *Hypnerotomachia* type achieved a physical embodiment in stone and foliage. At Bomarzo near Viterbo, between 1550 and 1584, Vicino Orsini built a garden now called "The Park of Monsters," originally a part of a larger garden, now vanished. "The Park of Monsters" was the section of the garden known as the *bosco,* or "woods," a forested area that provided the backdrop and defined the limits of most formal gardens. What may have inspired Vicino Orsini to do something unique with his *bosco* was the presence in the rugged terrain of boulders and rock outcroppings that Vicino's artists (probably directed by Pirro Ligorio) carved into sculptures and even architecture.[73] The natural randomness of the rock formations prohibits the sense of rational control in a "normal" garden of the period organized around straight axes. Everything the visitor encounters is irrational and unsettling: a giant tortoise with a statue of a woman on its back; a colossal Hercules holding Cacus upside down; a dragon fighting two lions; an elephant carrying a castle on its back, brandishing a helpless Roman legionnaire in its trunk; a three-headed Cerberus; and winged females with scaly fish or snake tails. The best-known figure is the "Orc" or "Hell-Mouth," an immense boulder sculpted into a face with a gaping mouth, over which were inscribed the words *Lasciate ogni pensiero voi ch'entrate* ("Abandon all reason, you who enter here"). The reference to Dante is obvious, but the difference between "abandon all hope" and "abandon all reason" is significant. Early Renaissance architects such as Brunelleschi or Alberti, building their architecture upon reason, would hardy have bidden anyone to abandon it when contemplating their work. The visitor who enters the Orc's mouth will find nothing more menacing than the monster's tongue with seats around it, ready to serve as a picnic table.

Other inscriptions throughout the *bosco* show Orsini's delight at his creation: "You who have traveled the world wishing to see great and stupendous marvels, come here, where there are horrendous faces, el-

73. Masson, *Gardens,* 256–57.

ephants, lions, bears, orcs, and dragons"; and again, "He who does not visit this place with raised eyebrows and tight lips will fail to admire the seven wonders of the world."[74] There have been numerous efforts to interpret the countless symbols and references at Bomarzo, but none of them are certain—as Orsini probably intended. In one of his inscriptions dated 1552, Orsini says that the *bosco* exists "only to give vent to the heart." This has led many to believe that the impetus behind the *bosco* was consolation for the death of Orsini's wife, Giulia Farnese.[75] At the highest point of elevation is Giulia's memorial, a little *tempietto* with a deep portico in the Tuscan order, vaulted down the center like a Serlian window and finishing in an octagonal domed chapel.

Like the *Hypnerotomachia,* Bomarzo pretends to be the ruin of some lost civilization. One of the rocks has been carved to resemble a fragment of entablature and pediment fallen to the ground as if it had crashed there in the overthrow of a temple; benches seem to have been assembled out of the fragments of architectural sculptures. An entire two-story house and a niche next to it containing a bench both lean at an angle as if they were settling unevenly into the earth. One of the more intriguing effects is the "mountain" from which, as at the Villa d'Este, a great Pegasus seems about to take flight. Here, where Pegasus and mountain are both cut from the natural rock, the sculptor emphasized the joints of fictitious "blocks" of which the mountain would have been made if it were actually artificial, thus making it appear that the action of the weather over centuries has revealed the seams of the man-made construction. It is "an imitation in natural rock of an imitation of natural rock, and of that imitation unmasked by the activity of nature over time." Orsini teases us with an inscription, "Tell me if such marvels are made by deceit or art."[76] Once again, as in the Urbino *studiolo,* our sense of reality becomes the artist's plaything.

The *Hypnerotomachia* is not the only literary key to Bomarzo. The constant repetition of Etruscan motifs and giant urns bearing the faces of Janus reveal the influence of Nanni da Viterbo's *Antiquities,* which asserted that Janus (whom Nanni said was the biblical Noah) had come to

74. John-Paul Stonard, "The Sacred Grove of Bomarzo," Courtauld Institute of Art: Art and Architecture, http://www.artandarchitecture.org.uk/insight/stonard_bomarzo.html, accessed September 6, 2013.

75. Battisti, *L'antirinascimento,* 126.

76. Esther Gordon Dotson, "Shapes of Earth and Time in European Gardens," *Art Journal* 42, no. 3 (Autumn 1982): 212–13.

Italy after the flood to institute a Golden Age. Bomarzo, near Viterbo, Janus/Noah's supposed capital, was the perfect place in which to counterfeit the remains of that marvelous reign.[77] Contemporaries greatly admired Bomarzo; Annibale Caro recommended it as a model for new gardens that would banish the ordinary.[78] Bomarzo eventually reverted to nature and ruin in a way that might have pleased its creator, and was only reclaimed from oblivion in the 1950s.

Any formal garden was always a *hortus conclusus,* a place apart from nature. Only in the later eighteenth century, when the threat of plague was finally lifting and when science and technology seemed to promise that the here and now was, or soon would be, the "golden age" of Reason—only then were people ready to burst through the walls around their gardens and invite wild nature in. The landscape gardens of Capability Brown or those around the *hameau* at Versailles were *horti inconclusi,* embracing and celebrating the reality of nature, no longer a defense against nature's real world.

77. Ibid., 214.
78. Ibid., 211.

17

The Crusade

PHILIP OF BURGUNDY'S ambassadors met Pius at Tivoli but delayed their formal presentation of Philip's plans until the Italian envoys gathered in Rome to hear them. Pius returned to Rome on September 19, having stopped on the way to visit Frascati, inspect the ruins of Tusculum, and revisit Grottaferrata. Pius, focusing now on the crusade, says very little in the *Commentaries* about these, his final pleasure excursions. In Rome envoys from Venice, Naples, Milan, Florence, Mantua, Modena, Siena, Bologna, and Lucca heard the Burgundians promise everything the pope could wish, including Philip's personal participation or, if illness prevented him from coming, the sending of an adequate substitute.[1] From the Italians Pius asked only that they implement the tax measures decreed at Mantua. The envoys assured the pope of their personal agreement with this program (which meant nothing) but would have to consult their governments before committing to anything.[2] The Venetians, fully engaged in the invasion of the Peloponnesus, claimed that they could hardly be asked to do more. Privately the Florentine ambassador confided his objections to the pope: The crusade would only benefit the Venetians, he said. They would claim all the land won from the Turks and thus be able to fasten their domination upon all of Italy.[3] In the *Commentaries* Pius rhetorically demolished these objections, but his arguments were irrelevant to political reality. Many Florentines hated and feared the Venetians much more than they did the Turks, and those

1. *Comm.*, Smith, XII.809; Setton, *Papacy,* 2:261.
2. Von Pastor, *History of the Popes,* 3:321–22.
3. *Comm.*, Smith, XII.813–14.

with knowledge of the East were as skeptical as ever about the crusade's chance of success. There were some crusade enthusiasts even in Florence, but most Florentines praised the project in public while nursing strong reservations in private.[4]

The day after his interview with the Florentine ambassador, Pius called together all the cardinals in a secret consistory and unveiled the plan he had divulged to the group of six in 1462—that he would lead the crusade in person. This is the longest and, he would have felt, the most important of the speeches he incorporates into the *Commentaries.* He began with a thorough review of all the wars that had distracted him from the crusade since Mantua, but, saying that these wars were now almost concluded, he announced that "We are now free to turn our arms against the Turks."[5] Then, demanding that the cardinals follow the example he was setting, he declared:

> We shall imitate our Lord and Master Jesus Christ, the holy and pure Shepherd who hesitated not to lay down His life for His sheep. We too will lay down our life for our flock since in no other way can we save the Christian religion from being trampled by the forces of the Turk. We will equip a fleet as large as the resources of the Church will permit. We will embark, old as we are and racked with sickness. We will set our sails and voyage to Greece and Asia.[6]

In contrast to his own willingness to sacrifice himself, he pointed an accusing finger at the lives of the cardinals and other clergy.

> The priesthood is an object of scorn. People say that we live in luxury, amass wealth, are slaves to ambition, ride on the fattest mules and the most spirited horses, wear trailing fringes on our robes and walk the streets with puffed out cheeks under red hats and full hoods, breed hunting dogs, lavish much on actors and parasites and nothing on the defense of the Faith. And they are not entirely wrong. There are many among the cardinals and the other members of the Curia who do these things and, if we are willing to tell the truth, the luxury and pride of our Curia is excessive. This makes us so hateful to the people that we are not listened to even when we speak the truth.[7]

Justified as this accusation may have been in the case of certain cardinals, the vehemence behind it probably sprang in part from Pius's con-

4. Black, *Benedetto Accolti,* 241–42.
5. *Comm.,* Smith, XII.818–21.
6. Ibid., XII.822.
7. Ibid., XII.823.

demnation of himself. He had enjoyed the papacy to the fullest: traveling to agreeable places; promoting the Piccolomini family and his city of Siena; enjoying exhilarating celebrations in Rome and Viterbo; above all, building a vanity city and praising its architect for hiding the costs. Meanwhile, on his watch, the Turks had conquered the Balkans—a fact intolerable to Pius's own concept of his mission. Now, with a dramatic gesture of self-sacrifice, he believed he would wipe away the stain of self-indulgence. Moreover, the tenderness of his own conscience made him believe that his act would so stir the consciences of princes that they would be compelled to drop the affairs of their states and follow the pope into a distant war that offered them every prospect of disaster and almost no hope of benefit. Anticipating the most mundane objections, he explained how the affairs of the church and the Papal States would be managed in his absence. Then he asked the cardinals what they thought.

Certainly most of the cardinals blanched before the prospect of mortal danger and acute discomfort in a distant land—but what could they say? All of them believed that God sometimes made impossible things succeed for those who sacrificed themselves and put their trust in him—yet, they also knew that sometimes he did not—as in the well-remembered case of Cardinal Cesarini at the Battle of Varna. Ruthlessly, with full understanding of the agony he was causing, Pius asked d'Estouteville to give his opinion. D'Estouteville replied with the thin sincerity of a man who has no choice. "Your Holiness," he answered, "for my part I approve your plan and admire your courage and I will follow you wherever you bid me—though nothing is harder for me than sailing. Whatever burden you impose on me I will bear." In the *Commentaries* Pius gloats that d'Estouteville "did not dare oppose the plan" and adds, "The man's nature was conquered by the nobility of the subject."[8] That was precisely the effect Pius expected to have on Europe's rulers.

While d'Estouteville offered reluctant consent, Carvajal, who believed in the crusade as much as Pius and had spent years on diplomacy in Hungary to make it possible, went into raptures. Profoundly moved, his voice broken by sobs, Carvajal cried out, "Heretofore, Your Holiness, I have thought you a man. Now I deem you an angel.... I will always be at your side, whether we must go by land or by sea. Even though you go through fire I will not desert you, since you are going straight to Heaven." Bernardo Eroli, one of the six who had known of the project

8. Ibid., XII.827.

for over a year, raised practical objections that Pius says "had already been answered a thousand times." The open hatred that Jouffroy and Pius bore each other gave Jouffroy alone the license to speak bluntly to the pope. "As I see it," he observed acidly, "this is not an open question. You have promised to go and you must go." The French, he said, regarded the crusade merely as an effort to distract them from recovering Naples for René. As for the cardinals, Jouffroy claimed they had no obligation to accompany the pope, observing frankly that "to go to martyrdom is a matter for counsel not command."[9] Once the crusade was publicly proclaimed, Jouffroy departed for France. This opposition inspired Pius to devote several pages of the *Commentaries* to blackening Jouffroy's reputation. In the standard manner of humanist invective, he recited every misdeed, real, rumored, or invented, substantive or trivial, not omitting slander about drinking bouts and courtesans.[10]

Jouffroy's opposition must have seemed irrelevant in the days following the secret consistory, as news from several quarters showed God's approval beaming like sunshine on the pope's venture. First, the city of Fano, down the coast from Rimini, held tenaciously by Sigismondo's son Roberto against a long siege by Federico da Montefeltro, surrendered on September 25, triggering the rapid surrender of several other towns that did not wish to endure a siege. Sigismondo now had nothing left but Rimini itself.[11] A few weeks later Sigismondo sent emissaries to sue for peace in the hope of saving his last town. Pius's terms piled on the humiliations—Sigismondo must acknowledge his error and heresy and could hold Rimini only by the grace of the pope and with an annual tribute of 1,000 ducats. In Rimini there were to be three days of fasting, after which there would be ceremonies where the pope's representative would deign to receive the city and its people back into the church. These were bitter pills for a proud man like Sigismondo, but they left him still a lord, if only a minor one.[12]

In Naples also, God seemed to be smoothing Pius's path. Piccinino, commanding the army of King René, was staring at final defeat. In the *Commentaries* Pius gives him a remarkable speech reflecting Pius's view of the military profession in Italy rather than anything Piccinino actually might have said. Here is Piccinino supposedly addressing the generals who are on the point of accepting his surrender:

9. Ibid., XII.827.

10. Ibid., XII.831–35.

11. Ibid., XII.828–29.

12. Ibid., XII.837–38.

> But suppose it were possible to defeat Piccinino and imprison him. I ask you, generals, whom will you defeat? ... Is it not I who support you? It is I who bestow on you wealth, luxury, and power. While I am a captain in arms and disturbing the peace of the Kingdom, you are called out to war when otherwise you would be sitting idle. It is I who have got for you the gold in which you glitter, your arms, horses, dress: and you who were but nameless I have made illustrious. Do you then persecute me who am the source of your safety?[13]

Piccinino needed no such eloquent cynicism to negotiate an agreement to abandon King René and enter Ferrante's service on highly favorable terms.[14] The great lords of Naples now fell all over each other in their rush to submit to Ferrante. René's son, Jean of Calabria, fled to the island of Ischia and returned to France in the spring of 1464.[15]

Formal negotiations between the pope, Philip of Burgundy, the Venetians, and the Hungarians concluded on October 19, 1463, with a treaty committing the parties to a three-year alliance for war against the Turks.[16] The Venetians promised in this treaty to provide forty fully armed galleys.[17] With this treaty in hand, Pius could ask other states to join an ongoing, substantial enterprise backed by important powers rather than merely gambling on a dream that might never come to pass. Two days later he could measure the results as the envoys of the Italian states, who had now consulted with their governments, reassembled in Rome to present their offers to the pope and cardinals. Rulers allied or friendly toward the pope, Ferrante in Naples, Francesco Sforza in Milan, Borso d'Este in Ferrara, and Lodovico Gonzaga in Mantua, as well as the cities of Bologna and Lucca, promised to collect the crusade taxes decreed at Mantua.[18] Ferrante offered an additional 30,000 ducats. Offers of ships for the pope's fleet, ten each from Venice and from Pius himself, two each from Borso d'Este and Lodovico Gonzaga, and the same from both Bologna and Siena, one each from Cosimo de' Medici, from Lucca, and from each of seven cardinals added up to a considerable papal fleet of thirty-seven galleys.[19] The Florentines, however, held back, saying that they had too many prominent people in Constantinople to risk offend-

13. Ibid., XII.786–87.
14. Ibid., XII.788–89.
15. Von Pastor, *History of the Popes,* 3:122–23.
16. Paparelli, *Enea Silvio Piccolomini,* 248.
17. Setton, *Papacy,* 2:249–50.
18. Paparelli, *Enea Silvio Piccolomini,* 248; von Pastor, *History of the Popes,* 3:331.
19. Paparelli, *Enea Silvio Piccolomini,* 250.

ing the sultan. Only after evacuating their citizens could they consider how to help. The answer that most infuriated the pope came from Siena, which, "after long consultation and fruitless wearing out of the senate benches," came up with only 3,300 ducats. "So much they promised their Lord Jesus Christ! So much they gave to please the Pope of Rome, their own citizen, who since his elevation had bestowed on the city of Siena more than 50,000 ducats!" The pope grumbled that he could expect no better from Florence and Siena, because such merchant republics were "traders and a sordid populace who can be persuaded to nothing noble." Siena later raised its contribution to 8,000 ducats, which Pius still considered paltry.[20] Francesco Sforza eventually convinced the Florentines that Florence and Milan should join the crusade to keep Venice from dominating it, thereby assuring themselves of a share in whatever conquests it made.[21] When spring came the Florentines allowed papal agents to preach indulgences and collect the crusade taxes in their lands; they even offered five hundred infantry and a thousand cavalry for the army. The Florentines also donated three unfinished galleys to Cardinal Forteguerri, who was outfitting the papal fleet at their town of Porto Pisano, and gave him prisoners from their jails as oarsmen.[22]

Pius wrote personally to his old friend Francesco Sforza, offering him the command of the papal armies and with it "the certainty of winning undying fame and the salvation of his soul."[23] Francesco praised the pope's heroism, but would not risk his hard-won principality in Milan for a romantic adventure. Pius seemed unable to recognize that his position as pope was fundamentally different from that of a Francesco Sforza or a Philip of Burgundy. The papacy would go on regardless of whether or not he personally succeeded; the Sforza regime in Milan and the collection of territories that Philip and his immediate forbearers had acquired depended upon a continual stream of personal successes from the incumbent ruler; any number of external and internal forces were eager to wipe these states off the map at the first misstep—which, indeed, happened to each of them in the next generation. Nevertheless, Sforza did make a substantial offer: two thousand cavalry and a thousand infantry commanded by one of his legitimate sons, but he warned the pope that the sultan could field 300,000 men himself and could draw on Muslim allies for more.[24]

20. *Comm.,* Smith, XII.829–30.
21. Black, *Benedetto Accolti,* 254–55.
22. Ibid., 257.
23. *Comm.,* Smith, XII.835.
24. Ibid., XIII.848; von Pastor, *History of the Popes,* 3:342; Setton, *Papacy,* 2:267.

The day after receiving answers from the Italian envoys, Pius formally unveiled his project and his personal participation to all of Europe in another consistory, public this time, in which Goro Lolli read Pius's bull, *Ezechielis prophetae,* proclaiming the crusade. As always, Pius boasted of the effects of his eloquence. "The decree was listened to with profound attention though its reading could barely be finished in two hours. The charm of the style, the novelty of the subject, the readiness of the Pope to offer his life for his sheep drew tears from many of those present."[25] In this speech, for the first time, Pius specified the nature of his own role:

> We do not go to fight in person since we are physically weak and a priest whom it does not befit to wield the sword. We shall imitate the holy Patriarch Moses, who when Israel was warring against the Amalekites, stood praying on the mountain. We shall stand on a high stern or on some mountain brow and holding before our eyes the Holy Eucharist, that is our Lord Jesus Christ, we shall pray Heaven for the safety and victory of our fighting soldiers. A broken and contrite heart the Lord will not despise.

Addressing the cardinals, he told them, "You too will be with us, all except the aged whom we shall permit to stay behind."[26] Carvajal, Cusa, and Bessarion were pleased to go, but others listened in varying degrees of dismay, wondering above all else how they could avoid risking their lives in this venture without seeming traitors to their religion. There are, however, notes of humility and vulnerability in *Ezechielis prophetae* that had not been present before—as in the reference to his "broken and contrite heart" (Psalm 51).[27] He acknowledged, also, that the journey was beyond his strength: "it will be a crushing burden for our old age and that we shall in a sense be going to certain death." There was also a sense that the outcome was in God's hands and might not be the one desired, as shown in expressions such as, "We are resolved to try" and "We do not refuse. We trust all to God."[28]

The reactions to this public pronouncement ranged across the same spectrum as those to the private announcements preceding it. In spite of the tepid attitude of his government, Leonardo de' Benvoglienti, the Sienese ambassador wrote, "I truly believe that God has sent this holy pontiff for the safety of his Christian people, deserted by all other Christian princes in such a great scourge as this fearful drive of the Turks,"

25. *Comm.,* Smith, XII.835.
26. Ibid., XII.826.
27. Bisaha, "Pius II and the Crusade," 50.
28. *Comm.,* Smith, XII.824.

and added, "I believe there has not been for long years a more glorious pontiff than this one!"[29] Among the more cynical, many believed that Pius really had no intention to go to the East. One rumor had him embarking at the beginning, but leaving the expedition at a south Italian port while the crusade continued without him.[30]

The most enthusiastic responses to Pius's crusade came from ordinary people all over Europe who heard and heeded crusade preachers. Bessarion was in charge of this preaching in Venice and its territories, and the detailed instructions he issued for his army of preachers in August 1463 give our best image of what the crowds all over Europe were hearing. Pius had summoned only soldiers "well-armed and fully provisioned for at least half a year," but there is little in the preaching that Bessarion outlined that seems likely to produce that result.[31] Preachers were to speak on "all feast days and such other days as they see fit" and were to give three reasons for the crusade. First was vengeance on the Turks for their "outrages and abominable injuries." For this the preachers should inflame the crowds with atrocity tales: "the men viciously slaughtered, the women ravished, the virgins raped, the nuns dishonored, the young people savagely cut down, the breast-feeding infants affixed by the sword to their mother's arms, the pregnant women run through with steel." The second reason was to assist "the numerous Christian folk most severely oppressed by the Turks and reduced by them to the most shameful slavery," and finally, "our own defense." On the third point the people would be frightened to hear that "the Turk ... is making eager preparations to subjugate the entire world, starting with Italy." Every day the Turks gained a kingdom and the Christians lost one, "so that if we are unmoved by love of religion and calamity, let us be moved by our country, our homes, our children, our family, and our wives."

Such unabashedly emotional appeals, in which the practical and the factual had no place, would strike deepest into the minds of the ignorant, the volatile, the impetuous, and the unstable. As if to reinforce this, Bessarion's preachers were to address themselves to "those who up to this point have lived badly, involving themselves in murders, thefts, rapes, arson, and all manner of crimes." Assuring them that "they now have the chance to fight in such a way that not only will they incur no

29. Quoted in Setton, *Papacy,* 2:267.

30. Bisaha, "Pius II and the Crusade," 52.

31. Von Pastor, *History of the Popes,* 3:358.

punishment for their misdeeds, but they will also enjoy the plenary remission of all their sins and eternal life." In order to receive the plenary indulgence a crusader had to serve in the crusading army for six to eight months or, for those unsuited for service, pay for the equipment and service of a substitute.[32] Lest anyone suppose that plenary indulgences obtained in the past by volunteering at the call of Nicholas V or Callixtus III might exempt them from volunteering again, past indulgences were (with some exceptions) suspended.[33]

This inflammatory preaching propelled thousands into motion, a highly combustible brew of penniless knights, younger sons, unemployed soldiers, landless peasants, vagrants, murderers, and petty thieves. A chronicler in Hamburg says that "people forsook their wagons and ploughs and hastened to Rome to take arms against the Turks."[34] Two thousand came from Lübeck; three hundred came from Ghent. In a few months Rome, Venice, and especially Ancona, the port from which the crusade would embark, were overrun by this volatile mix of the impecunious, the impressionable, and the criminal.[35]

Nevertheless, by the end of 1463, optimists might well believe that the pope's zeal and God's favor were uniting to produce a great European crusade that might turn the Turkish tide. Pius himself may have sensed that if he wanted to give the *Commentaries* a happy ending this was the time to do it. Accordingly, on the last day of 1463, Pius wrote what he intended as the conclusion of his great memoir.

> There is henceforth nothing to prevent Pope Pius from going on the crusade against the Turks and many advantages may result. Confident in this hope he is girding himself for this enterprise and preparing for the greatest of all wars. We pray that the Divine Favor may attend his undertakings. This is what we had to write about his history up to a point in the sixth year of his pontificate, in twelve books, the last of which was finished December 31 in the year of the Incarnation of the Word, 1463.[36]

Events, of course, continued to rush forward, and Pius, "weighed down by age and illness, did not discontinue any activity but rather

32. Norman Housley, ed., trans., *Documents on the Later Crusades, 1274–1580* (New York: St. Martin's Press, 1996), 147–51.

33. Ibid., 152.

34. Quoted in Ady, *Pius II,* 323.

35. Von Pastor, *History of the Popes,* 3:352–53.

36. *Comm.,* Smith, XII.841–42.

planned greater and heavier ones every day." He soon found that although he now lacked time, health, or energy for writing, as long as he continued to act, he also felt compelled to record his deeds. Thus, he admitted that "our mind recoiled from rest," and he decided to continue the history of his crusade "if life should last."[37] Not surprisingly, this continuation in Book XIII is not only unfinished, but rough and fragmentary compared to the previous twelve books.[38]

Pius knew that only Venice could supply the essential naval power, even though, in all Europe, there was no one he trusted less than these "comrades of marine monsters."[39] Seeking to bind the Serene Republic more tightly to the cause, he wrote to the doge, Cristoforo Moro, urging him to join the pope and Philip of Burgundy in leading the crusade in person. "We shall be three old men," he told the doge, "and God rejoices in a trinity. Our trinity will be aided by the Trinity of heaven, and our foes will be confounded before our eyes."[40] Moro, in his mid-seventies, was horrified. But the Venetian oligarchy, to whom their doge was a highly expendable pawn, valued the prestige of the Most Serene Republic above any individual—and, in terms of prestige, a doge heading the crusade in company with the pope was a pearl of great price. When Moro began to excuse himself, one of the senators replied, "If your Serene Highness will not embark of your own free will we will use force. We value the honor and welfare of this city more than your person."[41] The Venetians would send the doge, but how far they would go in fulfilling their promise to provide forty galleys to accompany him remained to be seen. Meanwhile, the deep reluctance behind other cities' promises was also beginning to show. Excuses and loopholes piled up much faster than food, munitions, and ships. Bologna found that, after all, it could not afford the two promised galleys. Pius had to threaten Perugia with an interdict before it would fulfill its promises.[42] Even Francesco Sforza suspended the preaching of the crusade in his lands because of the plague.[43] Soon, hope of participation from this longtime papal ally vanished; he was enmeshed in a civil war in Genoa, hoping to annex the city.[44]

Meanwhile, Rome itself once more fell into the grip of plague.

37. Ibid., XIII.845.

38. Mitchell, *Laurels,* 234.

39. *Comm.,* Smith, XI.743.

40. Quoted in Ady, *Pius II,* 323–24.

41. Quoted in von Pastor, *History of the Popes,* 3:339.

42. Mitchell, *Laurels,* 233–34.

43. *Comm.,* Smith, XIII.848; von Pastor, *History of the Popes,* 3:342.

44. *Comm.,* Smith, XIII.850–52.

Plague usually arrived in summer, but this time it struck in October, even before Pius proclaimed the crusade.[45] In early November Milanese envoys wrote home that it was increasing every day and had afflicted the households of the cardinals and leading citizens. Many cardinals and others fled; Pius himself, though suffering from gout, was determined to remain at his post, but he sent his nephews for safety to Pienza. By December plague was raging in Tuscany, as well.[46] Pius finally got away to spend Lent and Holy Week in Siena. His gout/arthritis was worse, and he suffered so much fever and such terrible pain from kidney stones that he was unable even to meet with the cardinals. Desperately, he made another trip to the healing baths at Petriolo.[47] From this point on, both Pius himself and those around him began to see him as a dying man.

Then, on Palm Sunday, he got news that struck away the principal support of all his hopes. Philip the Good, whose vows, assurances, and treaty had led directly to the bull proclaiming the crusade, wrote to say that he must delay crusading for a year. Louis XI, whose vassal he was, had forbidden him to go.[48] As recently as Christmas, Louis had seemed indifferent to Philip's proposed departure. At that time Philip's mercurial son Charles, who would later earn the name "the Rash," was in great disfavor with his father, but in February they had made up their quarrel. It now seemed likely that this unpredictable youth would serve as regent in his father's absence. Louis knew Charles too well to feel comfortable with that arrangement and immediately sought a personal meeting with Philip. At Lille on February 23 Louis told Philip to delay his journey until Anglo-French relations were settled—an almost unimaginable occurrence. Louis relied on Philip, he said, as a mediator for peace—or, if war broke out, as his most important vassal. Why should Philip be off helping the "Emperor of Greece" and leave France at the mercy of the English "who have done more harm here than the Turks have in the lands they have conquered?" Furthermore, Louis echoed Florentine opinion: there was no trusting the Venetians, who only wanted to conquer the Peloponnesus for themselves and would make peace with the Turks behind Philip's back as soon as they secured it.[49] These tendentious arguments were irrelevant. Philip's original oath required that he go only "with the agreement and permission of my lord the king"—and that

45. Von Pastor, *History of the Popes,* 3:331.
46. Ibid., 3:334–35.
47. Ibid., 3:345–46.
48. *Comm.,* Smith, XIII.852–56.
49. Vaughan, *Philip the Good,* 369–70.

agreement was now lacking.[50] Practically speaking, Louis was too formidable to antagonize. Philip was not overly scrupulous; he had waged long war against his lord the king in Louis' father's time—but then he had had the king of England at his side. He dare not be at the opposite end of Europe if Louis was in a mood to make trouble at home. How well Louis' objections chimed in with Philip's own feelings is impossible to gauge. The Milanese ambassador reported that Philip felt that, at sixty-seven, he was too old for such adventures; he hated traveling by sea and was short of cash, engrossed in his pleasures, and uneasy about entrusting his realms to his son.[51] On the other hand, Philip and his court regarded the Feast of the Pheasant and its oaths as one of the great events of his reign (it had inspired a whole spate of chivalric novels), and there is no doubt that he thirsted for crusading glory.[52] Thus, Philip promised that he would send in his place his favorite son, Antoine, Grand Bastard of Burgundy, with three thousand men.[53] When the Bastard (as he was customarily called) departed from Sluys in May 1464, Philip was still talking of following him soon with the rest of his army.[54]

Delay is forever to a dying man, as Pius knew himself to be, and the conjunction of circumstances favorable to the crusade could not be expected to last until Philip had sorted things out with Louis. The treaty with Venice and Hungary and the proclamation of the crusade had all been founded on Burgundy's promises; his withdrawal changed the perspective of every participant. The treaty in which Venice had promised forty triremes for the papal crusade was the one Philip had just broken; his force was to have been the core of the army that the Venetian galleys were intended to transport. What was the Venetian obligation now? The other contingents, such as Francesco Sforza's three thousand or Florence's fifteen hundred, as well as the amorphous hoards recruited by the crusade preachers, were intended to supplement the Burgundians, whose participation was the principal guarantee of the seriousness of the whole expedition.

On paper the cause might still seem more hopeful than it really was. Venice and Hungary were still bound by their own separate treaty to combat the Turks, and they would continue to do so. But with Sforza

50. Ibid., 297.
51. Ibid., 370.
52. Jacques Paviot, "Burgundy and the Crusade," in Housley, *Crusading,* 76–77.
53. Von Pastor, *History of the Popes,* 3:345.
54. Vaughan, *Philip the Good,* 371.

having refused command and Philip staying home, the papal venture—not just on the field of battle, but in planning, armament, supply, and logistics—lacked any prominent leader with extensive military experience. The whole affair lay in the hands of clerics, many of them elderly, few of whom had seen a shot fired in anger. All of Pius's secular, practical options had disappointed or betrayed him; only his faith in God remained. As he put it, "The less help they had from man in God's cause the more they must put their hope in the aid of Heaven."[55]

Pius could have abandoned the crusade at this point without damage to his honor. If he chose, he could say it was only a year's delay as easily as Burgundy could. But Pius knew that all over Europe people were already moving at his command and that, however reluctantly, ships were being readied and money gathered. To abandon the enterprise now would betray those who had trusted and obeyed him. If he disappointed them, how could he expect them to follow him, or another pope, the next time? In the *Commentaries* he wrote that "confidence in the Apostolic See would be utterly destroyed if its promises were not kept and Burgundy's delay would not seem to the populace a sufficient excuse." "To the populace"—Pius always judged himself through the eyes of the simple people he had known as a child; he knew their thinking and could not bear to disappoint them. Pius had enjoyed his papacy, but he had not yet fulfilled its purpose. The defeat of his enemies in Italy might have been achievement enough if either Pius or his age had been as secular as they are often portrayed, but the man who had walked through Scottish snow to fulfill a vow could not break public promises for the sake of what brief comfort old age and illness might leave to him. If we want to measure his courage (or folly) in proceeding with the crusade, we only have to look at the zeal with which others avoided it.

Even the Venetians were having difficulty finding an experienced commander to renew their assault on the Peloponnesus after their failure in 1463. With no other veteran general willing to take the job, they hired Sigismondo Malatesta to lead their armies. Pius does not mention this galling appointment in the final book of the *Commentaries,* but he must have been infuriated to find himself in alliance with the man he had so dramatically condemned to hell. Sigismondo only reached the Peloponnesus in July, by which time Pius was in Ancona expecting to embark on crusade. Sigismondo laid siege to the former Paleologian

55. *Comm.,* Smith, XIII.857.

capital of Mistra but failed to take the citadel. The Venetians never gave him adequate supply and support, and, after eighteen months of frustration and hardship, he resigned his post and returned to Italy. Pius's successor, the Venetian Paul II, received Sigismondo in Rome as a crusading hero and presented him with the Golden Rose, a symbol of special favor and gratitude reserved for the pope's most valued allies.[56]

Meanwhile, Matthias Corvinus was also pursuing Hungary's war against the Turks. He invaded Bosnia in late September 1463 and captured the city of Jajce, although it took until December to starve out the janissaries in the citadel. Matthias liberated swathes of Bosnian territory so that optimists claimed he had restored it to Christendom. He stood off a siege of Jajce led by the sultan himself during the time that Pius was in Ancona, but soon afterward succumbed to another Turkish army that brought his short-lived conquests to an end.[57]

When Pius returned to Rome in May 1464, a fever combined with pains in his bones and joints confined him to bed while the machinery he had set in motion lumbered on. Superficially, crusade preparations seemed to advance. Whatever their opinion about the crusade or its feasibility, most persons in responsible positions were willing to maintain at least an appearance of preparation and cooperation while waiting for the pope to die. The reality was that, after Philip of Burgundy's withdrawal, only a handful of loyalists around the pope and the crowds of riff-raff recruited by the crusade preachers still felt any commitment to the crusade. Pius's kinsman, Cardinal Forteguerri, commander of the papal fleet, went to Pisa to supervise the completion, equipment, and provisioning of ships, but his work lagged badly behind schedule. On June 11 Pius's nephew, Cardinal Antonio, assumed his duties as Vicar of Rome and the Papal States during the pope's absence. The archbishop of Crete went ahead to Ancona to manage the unruly mobs of crusaders already converging there from all over Europe.[58]

Pius himself departed from Rome with much ceremony on June 18, 1464. He went first to St. Peter's, where he "took the cross," a formal ritual that had evolved from the spontaneous response to Pope Urban II's announcement of the First Crusade, when the knights had pinned crosses on their clothing and shouted, "God wills it!" From St. Peter's crowds followed the papal litter to the Milvian Bridge. There Pius, along with

56. Setton, *Papacy,* 2:252–53.

57. Ibid., 2:250.

58. Ady, *Pius II,* 328–29.

Cardinal Ammanati, his nephew Antonio, three bishops, a secretary, and countless servants, boarded barges to be towed up the Tiber. It was the slowest possible means of travel, but the least painful for the aching papal joints. As he departed, Pius declared, "Farewell Rome! Never will you see me again alive."[59]

Each night when the barges stopped, everyone else went on shore; but Pius, to avoid the pain of movement, slept on his boat. His sensitivity to humble people was as keen as ever. When a young boatman fell overboard and drowned, "The Pope lay long silent," he tells us, "with tears in his eyes, praying for the departed." Another day, as the barge was being towed up the left bank, Pius learned that villagers on the right bank had turned out with elaborate preparations to greet him. He ordered the barge moved to the other side of the river to avoid disappointing them.[60] Sometime in this phase of the journey the archbishop of Crete in Ancona sent word that he was unable to control the motley crowds of hungry and disorderly adventurers pouring into the city and asked that someone of higher authority be sent. A report from Foligno said that six or seven thousand crusaders were passing toward Ancona each day.[61] Pius designated Carvajal—an elderly man, but one of the few still hot with enthusiasm for the crusade—for this crucial task. Carvajal answered him:

> Holy Father, if you consider me the person most fitted for the work, I will at once obey your command. I will follow your example, for I know that you are laying down your life for your flock. You write me to come and I am here. You bid me go, and I depart. I cannot refuse this little end of my life to Christ.[62]

Moved by the cardinal's fervor, Pius invited him and Ammanati to dine with him and spoke of nothing but his eagerness to embark. Beyond Bessarion, these three and such devoted friends as Campano and Goro Loli, how many others retained such enthusiasm?

After four days of slow progress up the river, the papal party disembarked at Otricoli and continued the journey with Pius riding in a litter. They gained nothing in speed, because Pius could only bear six or seven hours a day of lurching and jolting before he had to stop. The inveterate sightseer, whose eyes had eagerly devoured so many landscapes, rode now with the curtains of his litter drawn. One reason was to protect

59. Von Pastor, *History of the Popes,* 3:354.
60. Ady, *Pius II,* 330.
61. Von Pastor, *History of the Popes,* 3:355.
62. Quoted in Ady, *Pius II,* 331.

him from the sight of would-be crusaders who, having found no food, shelter, or pay in Ancona, were already plodding home.[63]

At Terni cardinals Borgia, Eroli, and d'Estouteville joined the party.[64] The caravan was supposed to continue on to Spoleto, but, along the way, Pius found he could go no farther. The others continued, but left Pius and Ammanati at a wayside house. The previous night in Terni, Ammanati had caught a chill but said nothing about it; the drafty tent where he slept at their improvised stop turned his chill into a serious illness. He and the pope caught up with the main party at Spoleto, but by that time Ammanati had such a fever that he could not continue.[65] Pius himself rallied a bit in Assisi and pressed on to Fabriano, where he met Federico da Montefeltro, who had come to beg him to stop his suicidal journey. Federico no doubt knew his pleas were useless, but would have wanted to see his old friend one last time.[66]

Pius's last stop before Ancona was the shrine of Our Lady at Loreto, where he donated a chalice. Many believed that this shrine contained the very house in Nazareth where the Blessed Virgin grew up, received the annunciation of the angel, and raised the young Jesus. Legend says that to protect it from Muslim infidels in 1291 angels transported it to Tersato in Croatia and three years later to Italy, and shortly thereafter to Loreto. Paul II, Pius's successor, made the first known mention of the shrine's miraculous origin; there is no authenticated document claiming it was transported by angels until 1472.[67] Pius's gift shows his faith in the shrine's importance, though we cannot know exactly what he believed about it.

As Pius approached, Ancona was descending into chaos. Pius sent d'Estouteville ahead to assist Carvajal, just as he had sent Carvajal to help the archbishop of Crete. The mob in Ancona, the harvest of the crusade preachers, came from all over Europe, with the largest contingents from Spain and France. Pius had summoned only soldiers "well-armed and fully provisioned for at least half a year," but most of those who made it to Ancona were ne'er-do-wells whose chief pastime was fighting among themselves.[68] The Venetian ships were supposed to be waiting for the pope, but, since they had not arrived, there was no place to put the excited, hungry, and impatient crowds any more than there

63. Ady, *Pius II,* 331.

64. Mitchell, *Laurels,* 235.

65. Ady, *Pius II,* 331–32.

66. Mitchell, *Laurels,* 236.

67. *Catholic Encyclopedia,* s.v. "Santa Casa di Loreto (Holy House of Loreto)."

68. Von Pastor, *History of the Popes,* 3:358.

were supplies to feed them or even a way to sort the potential soldiers from the utterly useless. No doubt there were still tardy crusaders arriving in Ancona, but many more were departing, selling their arms and other goods at a fraction of their value to pay for their return home.[69] The beleaguered citizens of Ancona, seeing their food and other essential supplies evaporating, made fake corpses out of straw and carried them on biers through the streets, trying to convince their visitors that plague was rampant. The plan was clever but quickly unmasked.[70] On one thing citizens and crusaders could agree—their troubles were the fault of Pope Pius II.[71]

Pius reached Ancona on July 19. It was an entrance into a city like no other he had experienced during his papacy. There were no welcoming celebrations; no arbors of branches, no tapestries, no flowers strewn in his path or fountains flowing with water and wine. Crowds there were, but sullen, hostile ones that might turn violent in a flash. Helpless in his litter, the pope's passage through the streets must have been harrowing. Perhaps his guards ensured his safety, or perhaps they smuggled him furtively into the city by back alleys—no record informs us. At least the drawn curtains kept him from seeing the hostility seething through the streets. Pius was deposited at last in the Bishop's Palace, safely isolated on the high promontory of Monte Guaso next to the twelfth-century Cathedral of San Ciriaco. High above the surly streets, the palace had the kind of magnificent view Pius loved, overlooking the ancient harbor built by Trajan, but Pius could not rise from his bed to see it. From his window he could have seen six papal ships riding at anchor, but not the forty Venetian triremes, now long overdue. With no word from Venice of the fleet's movements or intentions, the conviction grew that they would never come at all. The papal half of the fleet was also missing. In Pisa Cardinal Forteguerri seemed unable to hasten the equipping of the pope's ships. When Forteguerri and the fleet finally departed, contrary winds delayed them even more; eventually word arrived in Ancona that plague among the crews had forced them to turn back.[72]

Once Cardinal Ammanati recovered from his fever he hastened from Spoleto to Ancona, where he arrived on July 25. On the eve of his arrival Ammanati dreamed of the pope's death. He found Pius still alive, lying

69. Boulting, *Aeneas Silvius,* 353–54.

70. Ady, *Pius II,* 332.

71. Von Pastor, *History of the Popes,* 3:358.

72. Ibid., 3:362.

on a couch in the Episcopal Palace, still hard at work. Ammanati had witnessed the long decline in his friend's health but was still shocked at his latest deterioration. His face looked as though it had fallen in on itself—yet he still talked eagerly of embarking for war.[73] Pius and Carvajal discussed departing immediately with the six ships in the harbor to relieve a threatened Turkish siege of Ragusa (now Dubrovnik). Ammanati tried but failed to discourage them until word came that the Turks had withdrawn.[74] With the coming of August the heat in Ancona intensified and brought with it genuine plague; the bodies carried through the streets were no longer made of straw. It swept mercilessly through the remaining crusaders and attacked the households of the cardinals. Borgia immediately fled, but the other cardinals stayed—a few, like Carvajal and Bessarion, were still intent on the crusade; some, like Ammanati, wanted to be at their friend's bedside; but many remained simply because there was no place to go: the plague had engulfed the whole region.[75]

On August 12 gallantly decorated Venetian galleys rowed into Trajan's harbor, their pennants and garlands almost mocking the fact that there were a mere dozen of them instead of forty.[76] Delay had made them irrelevant; because of the plague there was no army left for them to transport. The delay, it turned out, was due to the reluctant doge, who had put off departure as long as possible and then took his ships to Istria for further equipping instead of making directly for Ancona.[77] Pius insisted on being carried to the window to witness their stately arrival; some report him saying, "Up till now there was no fleet for me, and now a fleet has come, but I shall not be here."[78] After nightfall the pope's condition worsened so decisively that everyone realized that he was now in the clutches of death. Ammanati would have preferred to stay at his bedside, but the imperatives of ceremonial required him to accompany two bishops to welcome the doge.[79] It was a surreal occasion. The Venetians did not want to be there; a few weeks earlier their senate had discussed making peace with the Turks. As they belatedly and inadequately fulfilled their promises, they speculated among themselves that Pius must be sorry they had come because it would force him to fulfill his own promise to embark.[80]

Two days after the Venetians arrived was the Vigil of the Feast of St.

73. Ibid., 3:361–62 .
74. Ady, *Pius II,* 333.
75. Von Pastor, *History of the Popes,* 3:361.
76. Ibid., 3:363.
77. Ibid., 3:367–68.
78. Boulting, *Aeneas Silvius,* 355.
79. Ady, *Pius II,* 334.
80. Ibid. 236–37.

Mary's Assumption. After vespers, Pius gathered the cardinals around his bed. In a letter, Ammanati records Pius's last speech.

> My beloved brethren, my last hour approaches; God calls me hence; I die in the Catholic Faith in which I have lived. Believe me that until this day I have done my utmost for the flock, and have spared myself neither toil nor danger. I have not the power to finish what I have begun, the rest must be left to you. Persevere in this work of God, and do not allow the cause of religion to languish through your negligence.[81]

After further admonitions, he asked them to forgive any offenses he might have committed against them. The cardinals, the loyal few, stood silently weeping until Bessarion said that it was only the pope's humility that led him to ask for pardon because "he had always been a kind and indulgent father, and they had no cause for complaint against him." His passing, Bessarion said, would be a loss both to them and to Christendom. Each cardinal in turn knelt to kiss the pope's hand and ask God's blessing upon him. He asked them all to reassemble in the morning for the Mass of the Assumption, but Ammanati says that "as the sun sank, Pius too began to sink." After the rite of extreme unction, Ammanati, Goro Lolli, Andrea Piccolomini, and the three bishops of the papal household kept vigil at the bedside. Pius asked Ammanati to pray for him, prayed himself for divine mercy, and then turned to Ammanati and charged him solemnly: "Keep the continuation of our holy enterprise in the mind of the brethren, and aid it with all your power. Woe unto you, woe unto you, if you desert God's work." Ammanati was silent. What could he say? The "holy enterprise" was dead, and he could do nothing to revive it. Seeing his face, Pius's kindness overcame his desire to impose his will on the future. He comforted his friend, saying, "Do good my son, and pray God for me." The prelates continued to read prayers commending his soul to God until about three hours after sunset, when "he surrendered his spirit to God so peacefully that he seemed to have passed into sleep and not into death."[82]

On the fifteenth, the day of the Assumption, Pius's body lay in state in the Cathedral of San Ciriaco. The doge, Cristoforo Moro, came to pay his respects, then met with the cardinals to liquidate the crusade. Bessarion, Carvajal, and Ammanati might have wanted to continue, but even

81. Ibid., 334.
82. Ibid., 335–36.

they had no immediate hopes. Everyone else, the doge and the cardinals, were quietly buoyant with relief at escaping obligations they had never wanted to assume. The cardinals gladly gave the six papal ships in the harbor to the doge to use against the Turks, along with the 40,000 ducats raised for the crusade, which were to be passed on to the Hungarians.[83]

Two days later Pius's heart and viscera were removed and buried in the choir of San Ciriaco under a marble slab in the choir.[84] Today visitors no longer see this slab; when the altar was moved out from the wall in compliance with the reforms of Vatican II, the memorial ended up behind the new position of the altar. On my visit, no one seemed to know where it was until I rousted a senior clergyman from his office, who showed it to me. The rest of Pius's body was sent to Rome for burial in the Chapel of St. Andrew. The next day the doge, whose brief expedition had netted six new ships for Venice, departed for home. The cardinals returned to Rome for the conclave. Before they elected the Venetian cardinal Pietro Barbo as Pope Paul II they prepared, as was customary, a capitulation by which the cardinals hoped to direct the policy of the next pope. Continuing the crusade was included, but alongside it was a provision that the pope-to-be must agree that he would leave Rome only with the consent of a majority of the cardinals and that to leave Italy would require their unanimous support.[85] Thus the cardinals registered their displeasure at Pius's constant wanderings and guaranteed that the next pope would never go crusading and try to drag them along.

Pius's nephew, Cardinal Francesco Todeschini-Piccolomini, spent a thousand ducats building a marble tomb for Pius in the Chapel of St. Andrew. When he himself died in 1503 after serving a few days as Pope Pius III, he got his own monument in the same chapel. But the chapel itself only survived until 1610, when it was demolished to make way for Carlo Maderno's extension of the nave of St. Peter's. Cardinal Francesco had built a palace in Rome that a later heir gave to the Theatine Order. On its site Maderno was then building a new church, Sant'Andrea della Valle, for the Theatines. The Piccolomini's past connection to the property made the new church an appropriate site for reburying the two Piccolomini popes. The two papal monuments, already removed from their demolished chapel, were reassembled in the new church in 1614. The bodies, however, remained in temporary quarters in the crypt of

83. Ibid., 338.

84. Von Pastor, *History of the Popes,* 3:372.

85. Ibid., 4:10.

St. Peter's for nine more years. On the night of January 6, 1623, they were moved "without ceremony," as a witness says, to the tombs that had so long stood empty.[86] The design of Pius II's tomb is fussy and undistinguished, consisting of four relief panels stacked up vertically like a pile of bricks, each level flanked by a pair of virtues. The topmost relief shows St. Paul presenting the kneeling Pius to the enthroned Madonna and Child, while St. Peter hands him the papal keys. Below this is a bier with Pius's body lying in state. The third layer down shows Pius receiving the head of St. Andrew, while the lowest stratum carries an inscription. This uninspired monument is on the side of the nave, seen only at a distance high above the visitor's head, and lacks the poignancy of that hidden slab at Ancona.

Pius's crusade—anachronistic, grandiose, and impractical—typifies many aspects of the Renaissance. It was anachronistic because many of the conditions that led to the success of the First Crusade—a large pool of trained fighters with no binding commitments at home, Muslim disunity, superior Western military technique, and naïveté about the dangers involved—had vanished or reversed themselves. Pius shared his blindness to changed circumstances with Petrarch, Cola di Rienzo, Biondo, and Machiavelli, among others, who believed that this or that aspect, or even the entirety, of Roman antiquity could be resurrected as if the intervening millennium had left no trace. It was grandiose in piling moral, spiritual, historical, and theological baggage onto the back of a border war on the fringe of Western Christendom. With territories of scant value at stake, Pius visualized a clash of cosmic significance that must unite Europe, save souls, remit time in purgatory, and culminate in the martyrdom of a pope. This political and military disproportion paralleled the disproportion seen in the ceremonies at the reception of St. Andrew's head and at Corpus Christi in Viterbo, the disproportionate canonizing of Sigismondo to hell, or even in Leonardo's plan to defeat Pisa by diverting the Arno. Impractical? No one ever summarized its impracticality better than Aeneas Silvius did a decade earlier when he pointed out Christendom's fragmentation and mutual hostility. "What eloquence," he had asked, "could draw such dissentient antagonistic powers together in battle-array?" Yet he had repeatedly applied his own eloquence to that very task! He was the one who had observed, "Let some small army embark in the sacred cause and it will be annihi-

86. Ady, *Pius II*, 340.

lated . . . ; let a great host set forth and its internal enmities will destroy its organization, and its end will be general ruin."[87] Using all the powers at his disposal, he had not gotten a single soldier on board a ship.

The common element in crusade, festival, building Pienza, and much else was the disproportion of means to ends. Cost/benefit analysis worked very strangely in a period when honoring the feast of Corpus Christi required acres of tapestries and tooled leather, ingenious stage machinery, and gunpowder explosions, not to mention man-hours spent on design, labor, and rehearsal or the risks to children dangled high above the piazza's pavement. Would returning Constantinople to Christian hands be worth the tens of thousands of men, the hundreds of triremes full of groaning oarsmen, and the pyramids of coinage required for success? If Florence could have lifted the Arno to the mountaintops, would discomfiting Pisa have justified the labor and expense? Festivals, wars, and hydraulic engineering are a heterogeneous assortment of activities, yet it is difficult to miss the parallel disproportions in the ways that fifteenth-century Italians chose to approach them. Parallels of this sort, repeated throughout the whole range of human activities, reveal the mindset of a nation or an age. In this case it reveals a persistent problem in perceiving and heeding the dictates of reality and a willingness—even an eagerness—to be seduced by noble delusions.

87. ASP to Leonardo Benvoglienti, July 5, 1454, in *Opera,* Epistle 127; quoted in Boulting, *Aeneas Silvius,* 207–8.

18

The Art of Copiousness

Pius II was an eager patron of architecture, but used sculpture and painting only as adjuncts to his buildings. Painting, however, paid ample homage to him after his death, giving him a memorial that has done as much as any of his own achievements to keep his memory green. This, of course, is the Piccolomini Library at Siena Cathedral, which we glanced at early in our journey and where we must return at its end. In 1502 Pius's nephew, Cardinal Francesco Piccolomini-Todeschini, commissioned Pinturicchio (Bernardino di Betto, c. 1456–1513) to paint the room that the cardinal had built to house his uncle's library. By that time sumptuousness and fantasy were integral elements of Renaissance style—and these were the qualities for which Pinturicchio was best known. Pinturicchio was then at what turned out to be the rather brief height of his fame, and the Piccolomini Library, one of the most prestigious and lucrative commissions of its time (the contract was for 1,000 gold ducats), was the kind of commission such a prominent artist expected to command.

A native of Perugia, Pinturicchio probably trained there as a miniaturist.[1] Miniature painting had preserved the whimsy and sensuality typical of late Gothic style, and these qualities became Pinturicchio's trademarks. Pinturicchio first gained prominence as principal assistant to his fellow citizen Perugino in the Sistine Chapel. There, Sixtus IV (r. 1471–1484), who built the chapel, commissioned frescoes from Perugino, Botticelli, Ghirlandaio, and the now-forgotten Cosimo Roselli. Perugino must have thought very highly of Pinturicchio's talents, since he put two of the three frescoes allotted to him in the hands of

1. Carli, *Pintoricchio,* 17; Mancini, *Pintoricchio,* 266.

his young assistant. Thus, *Moses's Journey into Egypt* and *The Baptism of Christ* are mainly Pinturicchio's work. With the reputation they gave him, Pinturicchio went on to paint fresco cycles at Santa Maria in Aracoeli in Rome. Then, in 1492, Pinturicchio won the most desirable commission of the day—painting the Vatican apartments of Pope Alexander VI (who, in Pius's day, had been Cardinal Rodrigo Borgia). Such a commission stamped Pinturicchio as one of Italy's foremost artists, a position he held for the rest of his life. Raphael worked as his assistant at the Piccolomini Library; Pope Julius II consulted him on the decoration of the rooms now known as Raphael's *Stanze;* the painter Signorelli was a godfather of his child; and he was chosen as a prior in the government of his native Perugia.[2]

Alexander VI was an especially desirable patron: he spared no expense, demanded unprecedented opulence, and encouraged—perhaps prodded—his artist to experiment in seeking daring new effects. As a cardinal Rodrigo Borgia outshone his peers with the ingenuity and magnificence of his festival tableaux at the reception of St. Andrew's head and at Corpus Christi in Viterbo; now he meant to outshine all previous popes in the splendor of his living quarters. He paid Pinturicchio to hire an army of assistants to speed the work, since he wanted instantaneous results. Alexander's friend, the humanist Nanni da Viterbo, whose bizarre theories later inspired the monsters of Bomarzo, provided the themes and symbolism for the pope's chambers.[3] Identifying the Borgia family emblem, a bull, with the sacred bull Apis worshipped in ancient Egypt, Nanni concluded that the Borgias were descendents of Osiris and Isis. These Egyptian deities therefore came to preside over the private chambers of the Vicar of Christ.[4] Such is the proliferation of bulls on Pinturicchio's ceilings that the visitor feels he is standing beneath an overhead Pamplona..

Alexander's appetite for opulence contributed to the fall of Pinturicchio's reputation in later generations. Both painter and patron had a gift for flamboyance; together, they produced the Los Vegas of quattrocento art—impressive, but vulgar to those of delicate tastes. Goaded on by the pope, Pinturicchio obsessively piled on gold and ultramarine, the most expensive pigments. His experiments began with the plaster surfaces themselves. Bits of stucco relief, covered in gold, pop out from these surfaces in clothing, in haloes, on architecture, and on fountains

2. Carli, *Pintoricchio,* 65.
3. Mancini, *Pintoricchio,* 128–30.
4. Ibid., 134.

and sculptures. Painters normally use two dimensions to create the illusion of three; but if the real third dimension intrudes, the illusion often crumbles. The Borgia apartments frequently fall into this trap. In *The Resurrection of Christ,* in which Pope Alexander kneels beside Christ's tomb, the fresco seems afflicted with gilded acne. In Christ's mandorla the protruding dots of gilded plaster work rather well; but the golden pox spreads outward to every highlight in the fresco—on rocks, trees, the edges of the sarcophagus, on armor, on halberds, even in the grass. The jewels and pearls on the pope's magnificent cope are a Braille text of raised plaster superimposed on a background of gilded filaments that do not so much depict cloth of gold as crudely reproduce it. The razzamatazz splendor of the Borgia apartments perfectly expressed the greed, corruption, and vanity of Alexander's scandalous papacy and shared in the reaction against him following his death. Julius II, who succeeded to the papacy after the eighteen days of Pius III, refused to live in the rooms of his despised predecessor and commissioned Raphael to decorate new rooms on the floor above, where, today, Raphael's *Stanze* (rooms) are second only to the Sistine Chapel on the must-see lists of the Vatican's millions of visitors. On the floor below, Pinturicchio's faded and flaking frescoes loom in the shadows above the Vatican's modern art collection, where visitors are rare.[5]

Pinturicchio's excesses were repugnant to the High Renaissance of the early cinquecento, which preferred to leave backgrounds in shadow, concentrating attention on idealized figures (preferably nude) in geometrically unified compositions. In the mid-sixteenth century Giorgio Vasari, whose *Lives of the Most Excellent Painters, Sculptors, and Architects* became the basis for all later histories of Renaissance art, turned up his nose at Pinturicchio, holding even his successes against him. "It is clearly manifest," Vasari says,

> that [Fortune] acknowledges as her children those who depend upon her without the aid of any talent, since it pleases her to exalt by her favour certain men who would never be known through their own merit; which is seen in Pinturicchio of Perugia, who, although he made many works and was assisted by various helpers, nevertheless had a much greater name than his works deserved.[6]

5. The Vatican has recently restored the Hall of the Mysteries of the Faith; Claudia La Malfa, *Pintoricchio* (Florence: Giunti Editore, 2008), 39.

6. Vasari, "Pinturicchio," *Lives of the Painters*, 1:571.

Figure 18.1. General view of the Piccolomini Library in Siena Cathedral. Photograph from Luke Ashworth-Sides.

Even Vasari, however, acknowledges the beauty of the Piccolomini Library. I will always remember the first time I stepped through a narrow door into the blazing color-fest of that high, nobly proportioned hall. The two large windows at the far end, their glare softened by linen curtains, seemed insufficient to admit so much brilliant light. The frescoes covering the walls and ceiling are as fresh today as if the paint were still wet, even though they have never been cleaned or retouched. Cardinal Francesco, who had paid for Pius's tomb, began construction of this room in 1492, intending it as a memorial to his uncle and to house the deceased pope's library. Pius's books have since vanished; the beautifully illuminated quattrocento psalters and anthem books that now line the room came from the cathedral sacristy.[7] Cardinal Francesco commissioned Pinturicchio to fill the ceiling with "fantasies, colors, and compartments" in what was called the "grotesque style" and to cover the walls with ten scenes from his uncle's life, both before and during his

7. Carli, *Siena Cathedral and the Cathedral Museum* (Florence: Scala, 1999), 71.

papacy.[8] The next year Cardinal Piccolomini was elected pope, taking the name Pius III, but died after only eighteen days. At Pius III's death his surviving brother, Andrea, had Pinturicchio depict Pius III's papal coronation in the cathedral aisle over the door to the library. For a few years Pinturicchio did other work for the cathedral, returning to finish the library frescoes between 1505 and 1507, receiving his final payment in 1509.[9]

Vasari lists the subjects of the ten frescoes in the Piccolomini Library but gets many of them wrong. He minimizes Pinturicchio's role and credits the cartoons and compositions to Raphael, then Pinturicchio's assistant.[10] Two surviving Raphael drawings show his involvement in some of the figures but not in the backgrounds. Raphael's drawing for the first fresco of the series, the *Departure for Basel,* shows a rather sexy Aeneas Silvius, who was decorously smothered under an immense cloak in the executed fresco. The background in Raphael's drawing, however, is not nearly as interesting as the one in Pinturicchio's fresco.[11]

The contract between Cardinal Francesco and Pinturicchio gave the artist no choice of subjects, but great freedom in depicting them.[12] The specified subjects were:

1. Aeneas Silvius Departs for the Council of Basel
2. Aeneas Silvius at the Court of Scotland
3. Aeneas Silvius Crowned Poet Laureate by Frederick III
4. Aeneas Silvius Makes his Submission to Eugenius IV
5. Aeneas Silvius, Bishop of Siena, Presents Eleonora of Portugal to Frederick III
6. Aeneas Silvius Receives the Cardinal's Hat
7. The Newly Crowned Pius II enters the Lateran Basilica
8. Pius II at Mantua Proclaims the Crusade against the Turks
9. Pius II Canonizes Catherine of Siena
10. Pius II Arrives in Ancona to Launch the Crusade

All but the first and last of these subjects depict dry court ceremonies—one or two figures carrying out simple, stylized actions while a

8. Mancini, *Pintoricchio,* 209; Carli, *Pintoricchio,* 66.

9. Alessandro Cecchi, *The Piccolomini Library in the Cathedral of Siena* (Florence: Scala, 1982), 10.

10. Vasari, "Pinturicchio," *Lives of the Painters,* 1:571.

11. Carli, *Pintoricchio,* 72.

12. Cecchi, *Piccolomini Library,* 9.

collection of officials, courtiers, and soldiers pay varied degrees of attention. With so little for these bystanders to do, most of the figures are studies of the art of loitering. Rare indeed is a face registering any emotion. We could easily concoct a more entertaining subject list that might include "Aeneas Silvius Prays for Deliverance during a Storm," or "Aeneas Silvius Walking in the Snow in Scotland," or "Pius II Drinks the Milk of the Cowherd"; but the cardinal was only interested in displaying the trophies of his uncle's career, not in penetrating his character. To offset the lack of emotion and action Pinturicchio dresses his figures in the most sumptuous costumes consistent with their rank. Frederick III and his bride, Eleonora of Portugal, wear actual sheets of gold, over which the artist painted the pattern of the brocade and the shadows of the folds.

Pinturicchio displays his inventiveness in the varied backgrounds that prevent us from realizing how repetitious the actions are; some scenes are in the open air, some in churches, others in pavilions opening upon lyrical landscapes. The nineteenth-century art historian Giovanni Morelli described Pinturicchio's style as a "miraculous weaving of fairy tales, dreams, whims, stratagems, and daring."[13] These qualities abound, for example, in the fairytale Scotland Pinturicchio imagines in the second fresco. The only hint of the real Scotland is in the long, narrow bay, stretching for miles between mountains, which might be interpreted as a firth. But Pinturicchio defies the facts of Scottish climate and culture in placing James I's court in an open loggia, richly decorated with classical motifs and supported on gleaming marble columns with composite capitals. Typically for Pinturicchio's style, he creates dramatic effects by cheekily violating the laws of proportion and perspective. Gargantuan trees tower against the sky; one example, not the tallest, is seven times higher than the length of the galley anchored at its base. If this galley were a small one, say thirty feet long, the tree would be no less than 210 feet tall. Gothic towers, proportioned like chess pieces, with structurally insupportable turrets poking out of their sides, stab at the sky like spikes on a security fence. Overshadowing these towers are enormous rocks piled up precariously in defiance of tectonic laws, with patches of grass growing on top like thatched roofs. Out of this thatch, with only inches of soil, sprout more enormously tall trees. The next picture is less wild, but no less whimsical: a delightful classical pavilion

13. Quoted in Mancini, *Pintoricchio,* preface, unnumbered.

Figure. 18.2. Pinturicchio. *Aeneas Silvius at the Court of Scotland.* Piccolomini Library in Siena Cathedral. Photograph from Scala/Art Resource, New York.

rises up behind Frederick III as he bestows the poet laureate's wreath upon the kneeling Aeneas. A variety of figures, including a man beating his wife, populate the pavilion. In this and many of the other frescoes we ignore the principal actors while our eyes lovingly explore the background and linger over the loitering foreground figures, whose saucy, mincing poses seem like freeze-frames of a mildly erotic dance.

Some of the backgrounds recognizably represent real places; when Aeneas introduces Frederick III to his Portuguese bride, the Sienese would have recognized one of their city gates, the Porta Camillia, and the column they had erected to commemorate the event. In the far distance they would note their cathedral, including the *facciatone* of the unfinished "New Cathedral." But the bizarre proportions in this scene make it almost as unnatural as Pinturicchio's Scotland. There was probably never an umbrella pine outside Siena's walls whose trunk was taller than the cathedral dome, and the luscious date palm in the foreground elaborates considerably on nature's simple symmetries. This transformation of recognizable places into physically impossible whimsies is common in quattrocento art. St. Francis received the *stigmata* at a hill called La Verna, now an important pilgrimage site. In Ghirlandaio's fresco of the *Stigmatization of St. Francis* in the Sassetti Chapel at Santa Trinità in Florence, St. Francis kneels in front of an amazing mountain shaped like a muffin or cupcake. It is nearly circular, rising for half its height in outward-slanting cliffs and above that in an almost symmetrical mound. A few buildings cling to the tops of the cliffs, with the mound rising behind them. I was amazed to find a scholarly analysis that called this background "a quite realistic view of La Verna."[14] A comparable photograph of La Verna shows that there is indeed a cliff, almost vertical, not overhanging, that runs for about a hundred yards along part of the side of the hill. This cliff, along with the general grouping of the buildings and the church tower, does, indeed, make a recognizable relationship between photograph and fresco, but I cannot imagine any sense in which the cupcake mountain could be called "quite realistic."

The most beautiful and effective background in the Piccolomini Library—it catches the eye as soon as you enter the room—is in the first fresco, the cover illustration of this book, showing Aeneas departing for Basel with Cardinal Capranica. The reader may remember that the de-

14. Eve Borsook, *Francesco Sassetti and Ghirlandaio at Santa Trinità, Florence: History and Legend in a Renaissance Chapel* (London: Davaco, 1984), 28.

Figure 18.3. Domenico Ghirlandaio. Fresco of *St. Francis Receiving the Stigmata*. Sassetti Chapel, S. Trinità, Florence. Photograph from Scala/Art Resource, New York.

parture from Piombino was not easy; Aeneas spent the night in the open on the island of Elba, after which a storm drove their ship (almost to Africa, Pius claims in the *Commentaries*) before they made it safely to a Genoese port. Pinturicchio implies all of this in the background of the fresco. The right background shows Piombino, rising up its hill toward the castle, enjoying peaceful weather. To the left we catch glimpses of Elba under a golden glow of sunlight piercing through great shrouds of grey rain—perhaps the most striking depiction of weather anyone had yet painted. Finally, a golden rainbow arches across the sky from the storm back to Piombino, implying a safe return. Piombino is recognizable in the limited sense that La Verna is recognizable in the Sassetti Chapel, but its dozen or so distinct buildings look like a toy village under a Christmas tree and defy every rule of perspective.

The contract with Cardinal Francesco required Pinturicchio to cover the ceiling with "fantasies, colors, and compartments" in the grotesque style. The name "grotesque" came from the ancient paintings in Nero's "Golden House" (Domus Aureus), the palace the emperor built upon the ruins of Rome's Great Fire. About ten years later the emperor

Figure 18.4. Pinturicchio. Pendentive with grotesque ornament on the ceiling of the Piccolomini Library in Siena Cathedral. Photograph from Scala/ Art Resource, New York.

Titus simply buried Nero's palace in order to build on top of it. When the Domus Aureus was rediscovered beneath the streets of Rome during the quattrocento, the buried chambers seemed like caves (*grotte*), and their ornaments were therefore called *grotteschi.* These *grotteschi* were a mother lode of fanciful motifs combining body parts from human, animal, and mythical creatures interwoven with plants, flowers, urns, and amphorae in ways that continually surprise and delight. In 1477, in a chapel he painted at Santa Maria del Popolo, Pinturicchio became the first artist since antiquity to make use of this fanciful decoration.[15]

The Piccolomini Library was the greatest display yet seen of this entertaining ornament. The ceiling is a felicitous riot of grotesques, while gold and black pilasters covered with grotesques divide the segments of wall. Within each panel symmetry stabilizes the whimsy. On a black background in one of the triangular pendentives in the cove of the ceiling we find the following creatures duplicated symmetrically on each side: a plump man with the legs of a goat, a frog-legged person with

15. La Malfa, *Pintoricchio,* 12–13.

wings instead of arms, three completely different species of dragons, a winged horse with plants growing out of its head, a fat baby, a winged, human-faced lion, and, in the center top and bottom, masks whose beards turn into foliage. These creatures inhabit a jungle of curling acanthus leaves, garlands, scepters, and urns. On the pilasters stacks of urns form the central axis, giving some variants of this kind of decoration the name "candelabra ornament."

If we compare the Piccolomini Library to the emotional insight that Leonardo and Michelangelo bring to their religious art, we have to recognize that Pinturicchio is not in their league. Perhaps the comparison is unfair; this is a library, not a chapel, but then Pinturicchio's chapels have similar qualities. Pius II had more religious depth than he generally gets credit for, but in other respects the Piccolomini Library fits the personality of the man it commemorates. The subjects his nephew selected are little different from the ones Pius would have chosen himself. Except for the unavoidable submission to Eugenius IV, we never see Aeneas/Pius in a vulnerable moment. In reality, of course, the entrance into Ancona was an extremely vulnerable moment. But, although Pius looks aged in this fresco, Pinturicchio shows him borne aloft in triumph, not hidden behind the curtains of his litter. Accompanying him in painted plaster are the doge, who kneels before the pope; Thomas Paleologus, who brought the head of St. Andrew from Greece; Hassan Zaccaria, deposed prince of Samos; and Calapin Bajazet, pretender to the sultan's throne, then held as a papal hostage. The tragic reality of Ancona (which might have made a wonderful picture) becomes a triumphal procession—which, we are intended to assume, will carry Pius beyond Ancona into the gates of paradise.

Vasari and many writers following his lead have tended to interpret the history of Renaissance painting as the simple advance of naturalism—the artists' ability to make objects appear as they do in nature. Not only does this miss the interplay of Gothic, Byzantine, and classical styles, but the growth in naturalism itself followed more than one path. We can gain important insights into the origins of the Renaissance itself by looking at some of the forces that brought painting to the point it reached in the Piccolomini Library.

Vasari claims Cimabue (1240–1302) as "the first cause of the renovation of the art of painting,"[16] but he credits Giotto di Bondone (1266–

16. Vasari, "Cimabue," *Lives of the Painters,* 1:57.

1337), who studied under Cimabue, as the artist who rediscovered the "correct" way of painting:

> [Giotto] alone, although born among inept craftsmen, by the gift of God, revived that art which had come to a grievous pass, and brought it to such a form as could be called good. And truly it was a great miracle that that age, gross and inept, should have had strength to work in Giotto in a fashion so masterly, that design, whereof the men of those times had little or no knowledge, was restored completely to life by means of him.[17]

Giotto's verisimilitude had been attracting praise for over two centuries before Vasari. Here, for example, is Boccaccio:

> Giotto was a man of such outstanding genius that there was nothing in the whole of creation that he could not depict with his stylus, pen or brush. And so faithful did he remain to nature (who is the mother and motive force of all created things, via the constant rotation of the heavens), that whatever he depicted had the appearance, not of a reproduction, but of the thing itself, so that one very often finds, with the works of Giotto, that people's eyes are deceived and they mistake the picture for the real thing.[18]

Vasari established Giotto's reputation as the founder of Renaissance painting entirely on the basis of his realism, but, in fact, Giotto has only a very indirect connection to the Renaissance at all. The generations of painters after Giotto did not follow his style, and a quite different style, the International Gothic, dominated painting in Italy and all across Europe in the later fourteenth and early fifteenth centuries. The next painter to continue Giotto's stolid, earthy, unpretentious naturalism was Masaccio, whose earliest known work was painted some eighty-five years after Giotto died. Instead of connecting Giotto with developments of the following century, we ought to see how he fits into the trends of his own time.

The return to naturalism in Western art did not wait for the Italian Renaissance; it was well established in the cathedrals and mendicant churches of the High Middle Ages. The rapidly expanding economy of that time produced an urban lay population very concerned about their eternal destiny but also deeply engaged in gathering material wealth in this world. A faith that offered only withdrawal from the world through

17. Vasari, "Giotto," *Lives of the Painters,* 1:96.
18. Boccaccio, *Decameron* VI.5.494.

asceticism could not engage them. Religious leaders like St. Francis and St. Dominic in the thirteenth century responded to this challenge by launching the mendicant friars, a movement intended to bring Christianity into the everyday world of the laity. Mendicant friars lived in the cities and involved themselves in the lives of their neighbors, even living off their charity ("mendicant" means "begging"). The mendicant orders—the Franciscans, Dominicans, Carmelites, Augustinians, Servites, Umiliati, Valambrosani, and Silvestrini, among others—spread throughout Europe but developed most intensely in Italy.[19] Dominating the universities, Dominicans and Franciscans became the leading scholastic theologians, rationalized the faith, and encouraged the study of natural science. Their response to secularism was to co-opt it.

The naturalistic painting of Cimabue, Giotto, and others was a direct expression of this new religious impetus. Making Christianity present, palpable, and immediate to urban lay people required putting religious ideas into easily visualized form. St. Francis, in particular, urged his followers to translate their religious thoughts into specific, concrete mental pictures.[20] To the Franciscans the study of scriptures consisted of forming a picture in the mind of what it would have been like to be physically present at the holy event. To help people visualize the nativity of the Savior, Francis himself made the first crèche at Greccio for the Christmas Eve Mass of 1223.[21] Under the influence of the mendicants, Christ, the Pantocrator, came down out of his dome and became the "Man of Sorrows" who lived in the midst of a human, physical world whose dangers and pains he shared. The suffering figure on the cross suddenly replaced the triumphant one in the middle of the thirteenth century. New, more emotional subjects, such as the *pietà,* the Virgin Mary holding the dead Christ, appeared in sculpture and painting.[22] Franciscans believed that "a congregation's weeping was more important than its words."[23]

We see the direct emotional appeal advocated by St. Francis in Cimabue's crucifixion fresco in the transept of the upper church of St. Francis at Assisi, painted after 1279. Cimabue sets the crucifixion in a howling wind, wildly whipping the Savior's loincloth in contrast to the heavy slump of his corpse. Below, Mary Magdalene and Longinus, the

19. Goldthwaite, *Wealth,* 94; Andres, Hunisak, and Turner, *Art of Florence,* 1:50.
20. Paoletti and Radke, *Art in Renaissance Italy,* 77.
21. Ibid., 78.
22. Goldthwaite, *Wealth,* 140.
23. Holmes, *Florence, Rome,* 153–54.

centurion, seem to claw the air in desperation. Angels fly frantically about, driven hysterical by the horror of the event. Only St. Francis, kneeling and clinging to the foot of the cross, has found serenity, presumably because he knows about the resurrection to come.[24]

The Florentine bias of Vasari and many of our other sources has distracted attention from Cimabue's contemporary, the crucially important Sienese painter Duccio di Buoninsegna (fl. 1278–1318/19), whose work was the point of departure for the International Gothic style. Duccio was an eclectic who borrowed from all the influences around him, including the French Gothic and the Byzantine style that had long dominated Italian painting. His sense of the solidity of figures and his sophisticated handling of drapery came from the sculptors Niccolà and Giovanni Pisano and Arnolfo di Cambio. His own touch, which united these elements, was delicate, sensitive, and luxurious.[25] Duccio's greatest work, the largest panel painting of the fourteenth century, with over seventy panels on front and back, is his *Maestà,* commissioned by the commune of Siena and installed on the high altar of the cathedral.[26] On the front was the *Maestà* itself, a picture of the Madonna and Child enthroned amidst the Court of heaven. Its figures have volume and overlap in ways that lock them into coherent spatial relations to each other. Instead of flat blue or gold backdrops, the narrative events take place within a background scene—sometimes a room, sometimes architecture, often a rocky landscape, all showing more depth and perspective than previous paintings.[27]

The majority of Giotto's works, even those commissioned by laymen, were for churches belonging to mendicant orders, including the Church of St. Francis in Assisi (a disputed attribution), the Church of St. Anthony in Padua, and the churches of Santa Maria Novella and Santa Croce (Dominican and Franciscan respectively) in Florence. He carried Duccio's sense of depth and his interactions among figures to even greater lengths, while shedding Duccio's Gothic delicacy, flowing lines, and soft, gentle faces.[28] Giotto's naturalism is actually quite limited: it is true that he and Duccio created "picture space" in which to deploy their figures, but Giotto's backgrounds give little sense of depth beyond that; his perspective is primitive, his rocks are white and gray

24. Paoletti and Radke, *Art in Renaissance Italy,* 76.

25. Holmes, *Florence, Rome,* 209.

26. Paoletti and Radke, *Art in Renaissance Italy,* 98; Holmes, *Florence, Rome,* 206, 212.

27. Paoletti and Radke, *Art in Renaissance Italy,* 98.

28. Holmes, *Florence, Rome,* 216–17.

patterns, and his trees look like sprigs of broccoli. His naturalism is concentrated in his figures, with their sense of weight and roundness, with the emotions they register, and with their interactions, which clearly convey the story.[29] His picture space, the physical solidity of his figures, and his emotional realism all exist to fulfill a specifically religious purpose—to make biblical, apocryphal, or legendary stories seem real and palpable. Giotto was so rigorously focused on this mission that he pruned away anything that did not contribute directly to this purpose. In contrast to the mixture of stylistic element in Duccio, Giotto's style was to have *no* style, rejecting classic and Gothic alike. Giotto embodies mendicant spirituality in art; critics today appraise his technique; his contemporaries experienced an intensified devotion.

Giotto died a decade before the Black Death. During the eighty-five years that separate the death of Giotto from the earliest works of Masaccio, Giotto's techniques for depicting volume and depth in space survived, but individualized characterization and emotion shriveled; the sense of everyday physical reality faded. Instead, there was mysticism expressed as an unbridgeable gulf separating the divine from the human; piety became more abject and pleading; the church became stern and authoritative, more insistent upon doctrinal conformity.[30] The period between Giotto and Masaccio has not attracted much study, but Millard Meiss, one of the great art historians of the last century, made it the focus of his book *Painting in Florence and Siena after the Black Death* (1951). Meiss attributed this change from earthy realism to a severe kind of mysticism to the plague.

A God remote from man, rigid and inflexible, impervious to man's pleas and his suffering, is the God whom Gabriele de' Mussis in Piacenza heard during the Black Death saying: "I bid you weep. The time for mercy has passed."[31] Such a God and his minions, the saints and the clergy, would have little patience with everyday, fleshly, human reality. Any contact between ordinary humans and these intractable holy beings could only emphasize the exalted power on one side, the helpless insignificance on the other. The rituals, rubrics, laws, and hierarchy of the church, the only channel of communication between divine and human, took on the same unyielding rigidity.

29. Charles Harrison, "The Arena Chapel: Patronage and Authorship," in Norman, *Siena, Florence and Padua* (1995), 2:102.

30. Meiss, *Painting in Florence,* 165.

31. De' Mussis, *Historia de Morbo,* in Horrox, *Black Death,* 18.

In the post-plague period almost every department of cultural expression saw an escalation in ostentation, ornamentation, elaboration, and enrichment. Clothing, for example, tended toward caricature as sleeves hung almost to the ground or were puffed up like balloons; men wore codpieces and women wore variations on the dunce-cap-with-scarf so beloved of cartoonists; minor arts such as jewelry went in the same direction. In architecture northern Europe developed the Flamboyant Gothic, in which pinnacles, crockets, tracery, ogives, pendants, and statuary burst out in tropical profusion to obscure the structural logic that High Gothic had accentuated. In painting, Meiss noted, this enrichment was another wedge between divine and human. Divine figures now inhabited realms gleaming with gold and furnished with sparkling, luxurious objects and wore rich cloth and elaborate jeweled crowns, whereas laymen and lesser figures wore the ordinary clothes of their period.[32]

There is a painting style more or less equivalent in time, patronage, and expression to Flamboyant Gothic in architecture: it is the International Gothic style, which sought sumptuous luxury and an almost erotic sensuality. The International Gothic grew from Duccio by way of his Sienese follower, Simone Martini (1284–1344), who was never interested in depicting realistic space but learned much from Duccio and Giotto about painting figures and their interactions. In his later years Simone went to Avignon, where the frescoes in the Palace of the Popes seem to be the work of his disciples.[33] International Gothic is a courtly style whose painted manuscript pages on the secular themes of chivalry, courtly love, or hunting are as well-known as its magnificent altarpieces. No example typifies the style better than the *Très riches heures* manuscript made by the Limbourg Brothers for the Duc de Berry in 1412–1416 and completed by Jean Colombe for Duke Charles I of Savoy in 1485–1489. The willowy figures in International Gothic manuscript paintings sway erotically from side to side as their extravagant costumes fall into elegant linear patterns. Everywhere sinuous, serpentine lines wind and slither with sensuous self-indulgence. The narrative always seems to find its way into a garden in which diverse species of plants and remarkably tame animals dwell in an enchanted peaceable kingdom. International Gothic is the perfect expression of the *hortus conclusus.* It

32. Meiss, *Painting in Florence,* 45 and following.

33. H. W. Janson, *History of Art: A Survey of the Major Visual Arts from the Dawn of History to the Present Day* (Englewood Cliffs, N.J.: Prentice-Hall; New York: Harry N. Abrams, 1963), 273, 280.

is hard to visualize the gardens in Boccaccio's *Decameron* illustrated in any other style. Except for the flowing bonelessness of the figures, International Gothic is quite naturalistic, especially in its precisely observed and rendered details; but the exquisite preciousness that pervades everything is the opposite of realistic. The world it shows us seems mythical and exotic, even when it shows peasants at their labors and dukes at their banquet tables.

In Italy, painting was the last of the major arts to come under humanist-inspired classicizing influence. Even after Donatello had produced classically inspired sculpture and Brunelleschi had built the first classically inspired buildings, painting, of which there were no Roman examples to copy, remained untouched. Naturalism in human figures had made great progress, but there was less development toward creating the illusion of a real space in which these figures could move. Since International Gothic satisfied the needs of patrons for escapist art, the delay in the arrival of classicism in painting might have continued indefinitely if Brunelleschi had not made a revolutionary technical discovery. Brunelleschi seems to have been the first builder in Florence to use measured plans and elevations worked out on paper. Using measured grids for his horizontal and vertical planes and applying the principle of proportionally similar triangles, Brunelleschi was able to create the first mathematically accurate linear perspective.[34]

The new technique redefined the goals of painting. The ability to depict things exactly as they would actually appear from a given spot, at a given moment, soon persuaded many painters to accept that kind of portrayal as the norm.[35] The International Gothic could not coexist with this technique because the strict naturalism of the picture space created by perspective would make the attenuated proportions, liquid spines, and serpentine limbs of International Gothic figures seem absurd. The new techniques could make a scene look exactly as it would if the viewer were *there*—in a particular place, looking at particular objects in a particular moment in time, just as we do in ordinary experience. This built-in ordinariness affected representations of the supernatural as much as the natural. Now the mendicant goal was achieved: the supernatural would look as though it were happening in our world—but it became subject to most of the physical laws of our world and could look only marginally different from the natural. This fact has led

34. Andres, Hunisak, and Turner, *Art of Florence,* 1:329.
35. Holmes, *Enlightenment,* 211–12.

Figure 18.5. Limbourg Brothers. *April*, from the *Très Riches Heures du Duc de Berry* (1416). Musée Condè, Chantilly, France. Note the extravagant costumes typical of the period. Photograph from RMN-Grand Palais/Art Resource, New York.

generations of observers to believe that Renaissance paintings—no matter how clearly religious their intent and message might be—are inherently "secular" compared to earlier art. It is this response in the eyes of modern viewers, and not anything the humanists wrote (which only scholars read), that convinces most modern people that the Renaissance was a radical secularization of European society.

Brunelleschi's friend Tommaso di Ser Giovanni di Simone, called Masaccio (1401–1428?), was the first to apply Brunelleschi's invention in painting. If the new technique impelled Masaccio toward the stripped-down earthy realism of Giotto, his personality (as far as we know it) was pushing in the same direction. The name "Masaccio," itself, is revealing. "Maso" is a diminutive for "Tommaso." The form "Masaccio" implies roughness and crudity. Suggested translations include, "Sloppy Tom,"[36] "Careless Tom," "Hulking Tom,"[37] "Big Lug Tom," "Klutsy Tom," "Great Guy Tom," and "Rascally Tom."[38] All of these, except perhaps the last, harmonize with the fleshly heaviness of his painted figures and their mundane settings. Masaccio's first *Madonna and Child with Saints* (1422) is almost defiantly harsh. The Virgin is no beauty; the Child stands with awkward stiffness on her lap with two fingers thrust into his mouth. The feathers on the wings of the kneeling angels are "as disheveled as those of street sparrows."[39] The saints on the sides scowl morosely. Every hint of Gothic grace and delicacy is banished.

Masaccio's brutalist style reaches its fullest development in the Brancacci chapel of the church of Santa Maria del Carmine in Florence, which depicts the life and miracles of St. Peter. In most scenes the apostle moves among real, but now unidentified, Florentine citizens. Vasari confirms that they are portraits, highly individualized and depicted with psychological perception varying from the amusing to the profound.[40] Not everything in the chapel is Masaccio's; he collaborated with an artist of very different personality, Tommaso di Cristofano di Fino, known as Masolino, whose nickname implies gentleness and delicacy and can be translated "Adorable Tommy," "Elegant Tommy," or "Little Tommy."[41]

36. Andres, Hunisak, and Turner, *Art of Florence,* 1:450.

37. Vasari, "Masaccio," *Lives of the Painters*, 1:318 fn.

38. Rona Goffen, ed., *Masaccio's Trinity* (Cambridge: University of Cambridge Press, 1998), 11.

39. Hartt, *Italian Renaissance,* 155.

40. Vasari, "Masaccio," *Lives of the Painters*, 1:321; Levey, 96; Holmes, *Enlightenment,* 220–21.

41. Goffen, ed., *Masaccio's Trinity,* 11.

Among the Brancacci frescoes, *St. Peter Healing the Sick with His Shadow* exemplifies Masaccio's place in the development of the Renaissance mentality. A robust and solemn Peter strides sternly and with fiery eyes down the middle of a very Florentine street, looking neither to the right nor the left. The rapt attention that the suppliants focus upon Peter, in contrast with his refusal to notice them, emphasizes the distance between the Prince of Apostles and the wretched of the earth. The eyes of the bald, scantily clad cripple near the front have just a spark of hope; the slightly parted lips seem to tremble with expectation, while the humble gesture of the crossed arms and the gentleness of the relaxed hands seem to be already receiving the apostle's healing power. The streetscape, seen in two-point perspective, is more consistent with the scale of the figures than any architecture in earlier Italian art.[42] Masaccio's Brancacci frescoes use a very limited palette of earth tones typically found in Florence and the Tuscan countryside.[43] To contemporaries this must have been a stark contrast with the coloristic effects beloved of International Gothic painters like Lorenzo Monaco and Gentile da Fabriano, who dominated painting at the time.

Except in their technical advances, the Brancacci frescoes belong more to the medieval mendicant tradition than to the classically inspired, escapist mentality of the Renaissance. That changes, however, in Masaccio's latest surviving work, the *Trinity* on the left wall of Santa Maria Novella, painted in 1425 or 1427. In the 1560s Vasari himself covered the *Trinity* with a stone tabernacle and a new painting, but at the same time he preserved its memory by describing it in his *Life* of Masaccio. When the *Trinity* was rediscovered behind Vasari's work in 1860–61, it was removed from the wall and considerably damaged. The lower part, not mentioned by Vasari, was left behind.

In painting the mystery of the Trinity, Masaccio, the earthiest of artists, was called upon to paint the most celestial of subjects. There already was a traditional composition for this subject that Masaccio would be expected to follow: it depicts Christ on the cross with God the Father standing behind him, arms outstretched to support the cross, and the dove of the Holy Spirit hovering between them.[44] In Masaccio's version the Virgin Mary and St. John flank the Divine Persons and are enclosed along with them in a classical chapel. The donors, Domenico Lenzi on the left, his wife on the right, are outside this sacred space, kneeling out-

42. Andres, Hunisak, and Turner, *Art of Florence,* 1:491.

43. Ibid., 1:447.

44. Goffen, ed., *Masaccio's Trinity,* 16.

side and slightly below the chapel, in our worldly space. The classical chapel is Masaccio's solution to the knotty problem of how to depict divine space (heaven, containing the Trinity) using techniques so closely tied to representing earthly things. No one had ever depicted heaven in classical style before. But Masaccio's humanist friends insisted that classical Rome was the ideal—a perfection that could not be exceeded. Therefore, a classical heaven was a proper and natural way to elevate the ideal world of divinity far above the human and ordinary.

What Vasari admired, and what initially strikes a modern viewer, is not the figures but the classical architecture, especially the perspective view of the coffered barrel vault in the chapel. An outer pair of Corinthian pilasters frames an arch resting on approximations of Ionic columns. Behind the arch we see a coffered barrel vault receding dramatically backward to an arch at the back matching the one in front.[45] When classical architecture and perspective were both new, these features would have conveyed a stunning majesty. The perspective is so perfect that it has been suggested that Masaccio worked from a set of plans (presumably by Brunelleschi himself) projected to scale according to Brunelleschi's methods.[46] The perspective of the chapel is lifted well above the viewer's head, increasing the dignity of the figures it contains and making the rapid recession of the vault above their heads even more startling.[47] To viewers who had never seen accurate perspective before, the sense of depth and reality must have seemed almost miraculous.

Within the chapel, St. John's expression of sorrow and devotion is beautifully tender, but not a new conception.[48] The Virgin Mary is more radical. Gone is the graceful, courtly lady; in her place is a massive, formidable woman glaring at us and gesturing toward her son and his sacrifice. Her stare reproaches us, condemning the sins that required her son to suffer. Mary gazes at the point where we are meant to stand in order for our viewpoint to match the perspective in the picture. When we meet her gaze, her gesture directs us to the religious mystery upon which we are to meditate.[49] She is the first example of a type of figure that Alberti advocated: an interlocutor whose eye contact with the viewer and gesture toward the action forms a bridge between us and the figures in the painting.[50]

45. Andres, Hunisak, and Turner, *Art of Florence,* 1:487.

46. Holmes, *Enlightenment,* 187.

47. Ibid., 218.

48. Goffen, ed., *Masaccio's Trinity,* 48.

49. Ibid., 7, 18.

50. Leon Battista Alberti, *De pictura* II, in *On Painting,* trans. John R. Spencer (1956; repr. New Haven and London: Yale University Press, 1966), 78.

Figure 18.6. Masaccio. *The Trinity* (1427). Santa Maria Novella, Florence. Photograph from Erich Lessing/Art Resource, New York.

The full meaning of this fresco remained hidden until it was returned to its original position in 1952 and the lower section was revealed. Only then could we see that the ledge on which the donors kneel is the upper surface of a tomb in which lies a skeleton accompanied by an inscription, "What you are, I was; what I am you will be." It is clear that a real altar, probably supported on columns similar to those painted at the edges of the tomb, once sat in front of the fresco. A worshipper kneeling in front of this altar would see beneath it, at his own eye level, the tomb and skeleton.[51] This grim *momento mori* existed in the worshipper's own space along with the real altar and the donors kneeling above, who were themselves dead and buried beneath the floor. For kneeling worshippers the skeleton would make the most immediate impression of any part of the fresco, telling them that in their world there was only death, but that beyond that world was a divine world in which the crucified Christ transcended death. One more detail ties the worldly and heavenly realms together. A trickle of Christ's blood runs down the cross, over a tiny mound symbolizing Calvary, and over the ledge on which the donors kneel, where it meets the surface of the now-missing altar precisely at the point where the priest placed the chalice in which Christ's blood became miraculously present.

The central concepts of this book are all embodied here in Masaccio's *Trinity.* The skeletal reminder of death is the unbearable reality that everyone in fifteenth-century Europe knew, but from which they sought escape. The crucified Christ and the trickle of his blood represent the hope the church offered to her anguished people. Yet the impassive face of the Father and the accusing glare of Mary were disturbing reminders that God is not always kind. The classical architecture of heaven reminded viewers that, once upon a time, when Rome was great, this human world was a better place and might be again if they could only recreate what the Romans once achieved. A heaven that resembles Rome shows that reviving Rome would be an offering pleasing to God, as Manetti says Nicholas V believed. Finally, the naturalism of the figures and the unprecedented power of perspective made the divine world so strikingly real that viewers felt they could touch it, enter it, participate in it, live in it.

Well before the middle of the quattrocento, artists and patrons would realize that the naturalistic space created by perspective enabled

51. Goffen, ed., *Masaccio's Trinity,* 14–15.

them to transport the mind to other times and places even more effectively than the humanists could do in words—and without the labor of learning classical Latin. In fact, the panel painting or fresco with perspective was the ideal instrument for creating a *hortus conclusus* that one could look into even if one could not live in it. The frame of the picture that divided the pictured reality from the one we inhabit thus became a new kind of wall around a new and infinitely variable *hortus conclusus* in which the mind could refresh itself.

In 1436 Alberti wrote a handbook on painting, *De pictura,* in which he laid down the rules for painting, just as he did for architecture in *De re aedificatoria* (1452) and sculpture in *De statua* (1462). He continued to see imitation of nature as the guiding principle in painting, but only if nature were idealized and perfected so as to conform more closely than she actually does to the *ideal* of beauty. Alberti recommends the practice of the ancient painter Zeuxis, who, when commissioned to make a painting of Helen, took the five most beautiful girls in the city of Croton and selected for his painting the most perfect features of each.[52] This principle of selection, the "Zeuxis principle," became the accepted means by which Renaissance painters remained "true" to nature while also idealizing it. Alberti urged painters to strive for variety and copiousness. "I say that *istoria* [narrative painting] is most copious in which in their places are mixed old, young, maidens, women, youth, young boys, fowls, small dogs, birds, horses, sheep, buildings, landscapes and all similar things." Nevertheless, he requires moderation so that the picture does not seem to be in "tumult."[53]

Alberti's advice took root, not because of his authority, but because "copiousness" and the unreal made to seem real were what patrons wanted. A contract between Giovanni Tornabuoni and the artist Ghirlandaio for decorating the main chapel at Santa Maria Novella specifies the scenes to be painted and the materials to be used and requires Ghirlandaio to embellish the scenes with "figures, buildings, castles, cities, villas, mountains, hills, plains, water, rocks, garments, animals, birds, and beasts."[54] In this we recognize the same proliferation of entertaining detail that we have seen in the backgrounds at the Piccolomini Library, in the *studioli,* at the festivals, and in the villas and gardens of

52. Alberti, *Painting,* 3;93.

53. Ibid., 2:75–76.

54. Jeanne K. Cadogan, *Domenico Ghirlandaio: Artist and Artisan* (New Haven: Yale University Press, 1984), 240.

the quattrocento and cinquecento. The backgrounds of quattrocento paintings by Mantegna, Ghirlandaio, Filippino Lippi, Benozzo Gozzoli, and countless others abound in improbable mountains, geological marvels, disproportionate trees, and Roman architecture enriched with rare marbles, carved reliefs, statuary, and, after Pinturicchio, grotesque ornament.

What we do not see is as significant as what we do. In Italy the world inside the picture frame rarely features everyday scenes. Landscapes may include recognizable cityscapes or locations, but these are usually distorted and idealized, as La Verna was in the Sassetti Chapel, or as Siena and Piombino are in the Piccolomini Library. Isolated exceptions exist, but only rarely and inconspicuously do we see peasants going about their labors as they do in the *Très Riches Heures du Duc de Berry;* we seldom see craftsmen at work, or household servants or wool workers, or merchants at their counters, or carts loaded with foodstuffs or merchandise. We see beggars only when they are the subjects of miracles. Unless they have symbolic meaning, these things are never a center of attention. Yet, medieval cathedrals had frequently, sometimes prominently, displayed such vignettes in stained glass and sculpture; the eighteenth and nineteenth centuries would make such genre painting a whole department of art; but the Renaissance was interested only in the ideal. Pinturicchio's style, even in the Borgia apartments, is simply the extreme end of the spectrum of enrichment and fantasy typical of the period. In the end it is not painting, or literature, or clothing, or festival, or architecture, or city planning that define and display the mentality of a period—it is all of them together. There are exceptions, of course, in every art—people do not universally conform to a common model in any age—but the straining to escape from the real to the ideal in Italian Renaissance culture is too persistent and too consistent with the culture of northern Europe at the same period to be any longer ignored.

Conclusion

Pius and His Period

THE UNIQUENESS of every human being prevents any individual from being a perfect exemplar of a period—or perhaps of any other broad category. Pius II possessed characteristics such as his affection for humble people that were quite atypical of his time and status. He also lacks characteristics that are essential for understanding his age, such as his indifference to painting or the comparative rarity of his reflections on death. Yet, by presenting a broad hypothesis and an individual example simultaneously, I hope I have been able to show how such theories and examples can work together, each illuminating the other. I will begin this conclusion by pointing out some other ways in which our understanding of the Renaissance aversion to reality illuminates the life of Pius II. All of the previous biographies of Pius have largely left his pleasures and summer travels alone, regarding them (apparently) as tangential to his life. Yet the large spaces he devotes to them in the *Commentaries* surely indicate that they were not tangential to him. Similarly, most histories of the Renaissance omit its manic appetite for festivity. Historians of art and architecture have given some attention to villas and gardens, *studioli,* and ideal cities (real and imaginary), but no one that I know of has related them to the core characteristics of the period. Those who see the Renaissance primarily as a precursor of modernity usually ignore the strong presence of chivalry and ascetic religion.

All the varied forms of the Myth of the Renaissance share the assumption that the important thing about the Renaissance is that it is the beginning of modernity. Under the guidance of this assumption we have not been truly open to all the kinds of evidence we might find;

instead we sift through the evidence, ignoring what seems un-modern, while looking for little bits of the present embedded in the past as if they were precious ore locked in a rock formation. These ore-bearing rocks then wind up monopolizing our attention. I have to admit that my own process has been analogous; I have looked at the Renaissance with my eyes peeled for examples of morbidity and escapism. But for escapism, at least, I have not had to look very hard. It is inevitable and even proper that a historian, like a scientist, will seek out what is relevant to his or her hypothesis. One of the many reasons we cannot dispense with metanarratives is that our hypotheses at the metanarrative level determine what we look for in our particular researches. But certainly those hypotheses should not consistently derive from a period centuries removed from the one we are trying to understand. The Myth of the Renaissance has been a procrustean bed, made to the measure of the present, with the Renaissance cut or stretched to fit. I do not claim that the rhythm of morbidity and escapism was the only thing going on in the Renaissance. We must never forget that people and periods are infinitely varied. But I am confident that, as a diagnostic tool, this interpretation will prove more enlightening than the Myth and more fruitful than pretending to have no hypothesis at all.

I chose Pius II as the hero of this book primarily as an example of Renaissance escapism. Because he was also fully engaged in the affairs of his time, we can see what he was escaping *from* as well as what he was escaping *to.* We can observe times when this experienced man of affairs sacrificed real-world priorities to escapist ones, such as when he let Tiburzio Maso run riot in Rome while he bathed at Petriolo, or when he spent much of his reign ignoring the crusade while wandering among the pleasant spots of central Italy, and, most egregiously, when he spent thousands that he needed for the crusade on building the vanity city of Pienza.

But Pius's disjuncture from practical reality was embedded in the core of his character, influencing not only his amusements but some of the most crucial decisions of his life, such as the decision to become a humanist and the decision to launch a crusade, along with the subsequent decisions the crusade entailed. When he first left Corsignano for Siena he was a penniless youth who had to make his way in the world and was attending a university whose only academic strength was in law. By all rights he ought to have studied law and stuck with it. Then as now, a law degree guaranteed a comfortable living and opened doors that might lead to power and opulence. Humanist studies could also be the basis for a career, but there were too many competitors for the available posts as secretaries or tutors to the powerful, and Aeneas's provincial origins and training were a competitive handicap. He chose the humanities over law simply because he enjoyed them. In this first independent decision he made for himself, the enjoyable already trumped the practical.

What has seldom been realized and never explicitly spelled out is that humanism was *intrinsically* escapist; it *necessarily* led out of this world and into another. If humanism sometimes led its followers into conducting practical business, as Leonardo Bruni's chancellorship in Florence did, it might just as well take them where it led his contemporary, Niccolò Niccoli, who withdrew from the outside world into the house that he had made into a museum of antiquities and manuscripts. We have seen that Petrarch, rightly regarded as the father of Renaissance humanism, is very explicit about the escapist value of humanist studies. "I have dwelt single-mindedly on learning about antiquity, among other things because this age has always displeased me, so that . . . I always wished to have been born in any other age whatever, and to forget this one and I always tried to transport myself mentally to other times."[1] For Petrarch, Aeneas, and many others, the ancient world, already idealized by its own writers, was an irresistible siren calling them away to a better world available to the mind, if not to the body. When Aeneas complains of the boorishness of his companions in Germany, he is lamenting, among other things, that their constant presence blocks his escape tunnel to that better classical world.

In Pius's mind the crusade was always the pressing mission of his papacy. But we have to ask whether the whole concept of the crusade derived from confronting reality or from the world of chivalric imaginings. The answer is clear enough in the case of Philip of Burgundy and his court. Crusades were an integral part of the pageant of chivalric make-believe, which the whole Burgundian court continually enacted. As we have seen, the oaths taken at the Feast of the Pheasant savor more of chivalric epic than preparation for war. We can see that there was some seriousness to these oaths because, nine years later, when Philip recovered after nearly dying, he immediately made plans to carry out his vow. How little that seriousness actually amounted to we see in Philip's withdrawal from the crusade before the next Easter.

1. Petrarch, "To Posterity," *Sen.* XVIII.1, II.673–74.

Philip's vacillation makes Pius's earnestness stand out more boldly; but was the crusade ever a realistic response to the Turkish problem? In practical terms, what was the actual danger to Western Christendom from the Turkish conquests? The Turks put the Venetian and Genoese possessions and trade in the eastern Mediterranean in immediate peril. Without outside help, these outposts were certain to be lost sooner or later. If the Turks captured the whole of the western Balkans, as they had done by 1464, they gave the Kingdom of Hungary a dangerous neighbor and put counties like Austria and Bohemia on notice that Hungary stood as their only bulwark. This would seem to dictate a policy of doing everything possible to shore up Venice and Hungary.[2] In the case of Hungary, the first priority would be to end the debilitating succession dispute between Frederick III and Matthias Corvinus. Papal diplomacy helped to accomplish this by 1462. In the case of Venice, however, the Venetians' policy of short-term opportunism and Pius's prejudices against their city prevented any effective long-term cooperation between them. As for Venice and Genoa cooperating against the common foe, there was more likelihood of the sultan converting to Christianity.

A crusade was only useful if it scored a crushing military success. A limited success, picking up a province or two, would be useful only if it substantially strengthened the frontline states of Venice, Genoa, and Hungary. More probable was that the Turks would reverse any such local success once the crusading army returned home. To have lasting effect the crusade would have to shatter the Turkish fighting force and drive it out of any substantial foothold in the Balkan Peninsula, an outcome that could hardly be realized without the direct intervention of the heavenly hosts. Barring celestial assistance, how possible was it even to launch a crusade? Local powers such as Venice and Hungary could wage their own wars against the Turks, but for anything beyond that, Aeneas Silvius had spoken the final word in a letter written three years before he became pope. "Christendom has no head that all men will obey," he had written. "Each state has its own ruler; each ruler is dominated by his own particular interest." His military assessment was equally acute and equally pessimistic: a small army would be annihilated; a large one would break apart from internal dissension. On this basis he had asked, "What ground do you find for hope?"[3]

2. Genoa's obsequious submission to the Turks made it ineligible for such backing.

3. ASP to Leonardo Benvoglienti, July 5, 1454 (*Opera*, Epistle 127); quoted in Boulting, *Aeneas Silvius*, 207–8.

Since Aeneas wrote this analysis in 1455 nothing had changed except that the Turks had strengthened themselves with further conquests. It is unlikely that Pius had forgotten anything that Aeneas had understood so well. Why proceed with the crusade, then? Would not the more direct, more prudent policy of supporting the Hungarians and Venetians be the better choice? It would be, except that it was not heroic and it had no historic resonance—it lacked charisma. The crusade had plenty of charisma, therefore Pius chose it. Chivalric romance was separating minds away from reality long before Don Quixote. Pius's mind, like those of all his educated contemporaries, was overstuffed with tales of heroism, both ancient and medieval. The chivalric hero could be shrewd and calculating, outsmarting his foes, but he was never prudent. To avoid battle simply because there was nothing to gain by it was disgraceful. In the chivalric world there was *always* something to be gained in battle—the chance for heroism even in defeat. King Władysław at the Battle of Varna likely would have considered his own death and that of thousands of his companions to be a just price to pay for a hero's fame. This warrior code, which goes back at least as far as the *Iliad,* was proclaimed with equal gusto in the literature of Rome and of chivalry. Even that supposed realist Machiavelli, in his *Discourses,* never tires of giving Roman examples of self-sacrificing heroism. As for historic resonance, everyone in Europe knew that the crusades were the Christian equivalent of the fight for Troy or the Punic wars. In the First Crusade Godfrey of Bouillon had earned his place among the "Nine Worthies," the greatest heroes of history, alongside Alexander, Caesar, David, Joshua, and King Arthur. Crusades had earned sainthood for King Louis IX of France. Every town and village had memories of their own crusaders and treasured the sacred relics they had brought home from the Holy Land. Every Muslim advance since the First Crusade had called forth a new crusade. The loss of Edessa prompted the Second Crusade; the fall of Jerusalem generated the Third; the conquest of Acre led to the Fourth—was Constantinople to go unavenged?

In the light of all this heroic and historic pressure, did Pius have any option *but* a crusade? These pressures certainly would have forced him to *talk* eloquently about a crusade, but he did not actually have to *have* one. To talk much and do little would have put him in company with many prominent contemporaries and probably would have satisfied everyone except Bessarion and Carvajal. This was essentially the policy of Nicholas V, who suffered no ill effects from it. The examples of Venice and Genoa show that an unheroically pragmatic policy, one that could sometimes even cooperate with the Turks, was within reach of any who chose to use it. Of course, this was one of the reasons Pius despised the Venetians as "companions of fish." Pius *could* have chosen a more prudent policy; the reasons he did not lie deeper than his humanist education in the aspects of his character that first attracted him to humanism rather than law—a preference for what is imagined over what is concrete.

That the crusade was unrealistic does not necessarily make it escapist; Pius perceived it as real in a way that he knew that the Corpus Christi show at Viterbo was not. But the fact that he carried on with it after Philip of Burgundy pulled out, even when he knew himself to be dying—that he even contemplated rescuing Ragusa with six ships and the rabble assembled at Ancona—these things show more than an unrealistic policy: like King Władisław charging at the sultan's janissaries, they are a defiant gauntlet cast in reality's face. From March 25, when Pius learned of Burgundy's withdrawal, until June 18, when he departed for Ancona, he had ample time to assess the realities of the situation and make a strategic retreat from the crusade. Even after that, he could have made the choice to stop the painful charade. Yet in his last hours he solemnly charged Ammanati to continue the fantasy. In the concluding act of his life, Pius at Ancona is the Greek tragic hero; his flaw, the refusal to concede to reality, is also the source of his heroism.

So it is with the Renaissance itself: if refusing to face "things as they are" is a flaw, then it is that very flaw that produced what is great in the Renaissance. The Italian Renaissance has left us a few writings and a great many works of art that have permanently enriched our lives, but these very works derive from people's refusal to accept the reality they were given and their insistence on making or resurrecting from the past an alternative reality that, like all counterfeits, had to be made to *seem* real. That this was no easy task we can see by the extraordinary measures people were willing to employ to make festivals seem like heaven. If these expressions seem shrill, it is because only the shrill can shout down the real. The realities of a life exposed to the continual, unpredictable menace of plague, the almost equally fickle fortunes of war, and the arbitrary will of a God apparently enraged against mankind *could not* be faced in a calm, pragmatic spirit. There was nothing cowardly about escape from reality under such circumstances. When real events proclaimed the worthlessness of human life, an irrational defiance of reality was the only way to maintain the individual and collective dignity of humanity. Humans cannot carry on without a sense of dignity and must find it where they can.

There is, indeed, a significant step toward secularism during the Renaissance, one that comes through with startling clarity in Pius's *Commentaries.* In reading the memoirs of a pope, we might expect to find God on every page. God is not entirely absent from the *Commentaries;* he appears when Aeneas is in danger and beseeches God to save him. God frequently smites the pope's enemies as he did in leveling L'Aquila with an earthquake.[4] God will surely fight for the Christians against the Turks. But God is *not* visibly woven into the pope's daily life. If Pius prayed for guidance in crucial decisions, he keeps it secret from his readers. Pius gives many examples of his own eloquence, but there is not a single private prayer in the thirteen books of the *Commentaries.* Nowhere in Pius's descriptions of the beauties of nature does he hymn the Creator for his wondrous works. He does not thank God for victories or beg mercy in defeat. If Pius prayed for healing as he bathed at Petriolo, we do not know it. In reality, Pius probably did all this and more in his daily prayers, but, unlike his orations, he does not record his prayers for posterity. In part this reflects the conventions of humanist writing that required adherence to Roman models. Most Roman writing and most humanist writing avoids admitting readers into the interior life of the writer. Internal conflicts, doubts, hesitations, and fears were "unmanly" and are seldom exposed to view. Petrarch, in such explicitly religious writings as "The Ascent of Mont Ventoux" and *The Secret* (whose title implies that it will show what is normally hidden), confesses sinful inadequacies, but only in such general terms that he reveals no more than what Christian doctrine ascribes to all people. It did not have to be that way: St. Catherine of Siena is only one of many mystical writers who had established a rich language to express the inner life of a Christian. Such language was readily available for Pius and other humanists to use, but they avoided it because it had no Roman precedent. Courtly love literature also presented a rich fund of language for the expression of subjective feelings. Even though such literature was contrived and conventional and seldom expressed the author's actual state of mind, its language could, in theory, have given voice to sincere feelings, as well. But, since it was a vernacular literature outside the classical canon, the

4. *Comm.,* Smith, V.398.

humanists avoided it—except when they were explicitly writing in that genre. Humanists apparently believed that whatever was written in Latin must always imitate the ancients and can never express kinds of content the ancients did not address. Not only the new medieval genres of mysticism and courtly love, but potentially any new content foreign to the mind of antiquity, could only appear in the vernacular. This, over time, doomed Latin to extinction.

Escapism often intruded into Renaissance expressions of religion. The backgrounds of Mantegna's or Ghirlandaio's religious pictures are as full of improbabilities as the frescoes in the Piccolomini Library. On the other hand, Christianity almost never invades the places of escape—villas, gardens, and *studioli,* where ancient myth was always welcome.[5] By sending the plague, God made himself unwelcome in times and places of refuge. God appears, for example, at the beginning of the *Decameron* as the young ladies gather at Santa Maria Novella to pray for an end to the plague, but he makes few intrusions into the *horti conclusi* into which they retreat afterward. God was *reality* for Renaissance Italians and was closely connected with reality's grimmest aspects. To create an escape from reality meant carving off a God-free zone. This is a very significant development, but, as a step toward modern secularism, it is only one rung on a long ladder—a ladder whose feet are planted firmly in the Middle Ages. The Middle Ages had already established vast areas of statecraft, war, and commerce in which Christ had only the smallest, most superficial share. Even by the end of the Renaissance, there is no appreciable movement toward unbelief, not even an avowed unbeliever. In the latest phase of the Renaissance, Benvenuto Cellini, a thug with numerous murders on his account, believed he had had a divine vision that left him with a halo on his head![6] The Reformations show that the power of faith had barely been scratched by the Renaissance. It is significant, however, that in those Reformations both Catholics and Protestants felt obliged to squelch Renaissance art—Catholics by strict regulation, Protestants by outright abolition.

Those who are accustomed to hearing the Renaissance lauded as the birth of everything desirable in modernity—of individualism, practi-

5. The festivals are a partial exception to this, since many of the largest, the reception of St. Andrew, Corpus Christi, and the feast of San Giovanni were specifically religious occasions. God does not seem conspicuous at the festivities Pius enjoyed at Capodimonte and Pienza in 1462.

6. Benvenuto Cellini, *Autobiography,* trans. George Bull (London: Penguin, 1956), 231.

cality, secularism, science, even human nature as we recognize it—are probably offended at this book for attempting to topple such idols. I do not mean to imply that these qualities were never present in the Renaissance, but, generally speaking, they had already been well established in the Middle Ages. We owe much more than we have ever admitted to that much-maligned period. Perhaps, for the next few generations, every book on the Renaissance ought to begin with an apology and a humble appreciation addressed to the Middle Ages! Nevertheless, there are certain things that originated or grew dramatically during the Renaissance that eventually contributed to modernity. I would emphasize two specifically Renaissance contributions that were particularly important for the future: they are *counterfactual imagination* and the *embrace of change.*

The Middle Ages, much more than the Renaissance, was notable for down-to-earth practicality. Most medieval artifacts are exactly what they need to be to accomplish their purpose, no more, no less. Until well into the fourteenth century, castles, however romantic they look to us, were entirely practical applications of military science, accommodating their denizens in what passed for comfort and convenience and enabling them to hold off almost any kind of enemy except starvation. Medieval clothes kept people warm and modest. Greater skill and richer materials went into the most regal outfits, but their fundamental design was as practical as the garb of the humble. We have already glanced at some of the practical machines developed before 1348. Trade routes, banking, international mercantile companies, instruments of credit, double-entry bookkeeping, and limited liability partnerships all originated in the Middle Ages. Even the great churches and cathedrals that seem to us to have absorbed such a disproportionate share of the wealth are entirely practical if you grant medieval people their assumption that Catholic Christianity is true. If God actually was who the church said he was; if he had done for human salvation what the church said he did; if nonetheless, each individual's eternal bliss or eternal torment remained a delicately balanced question—then building cathedrals and monasteries and pouring wealth into their endowment was the only sensible response.

Here is a test of practicality that the vast majority of medieval artifacts pass but that most of the characteristic products of the Renaissance do not: medieval artifacts rarely pretend to be something they are not. Humanist neo-Latin and Albertian architecture quite clearly strive to be counterfeits of antiquity. Sculptors and painters gave Roman bodies to their figures, dressed them in Roman drapery, and disported them in Roman settings. This element of pretense is intrinsic even in the increased naturalism of painting. A medieval or Byzantine icon of the Blessed Virgin is unmistakably an *image* that *represents* the Virgin without actually *being* the Virgin. It "represents" her as a delegate, somewhat as an ambassador represents a king. This sense of delegation can include delegated power, so that such images are often believed to have supernatural powers, received from the holy person represented. But a naturalistic, Renaissance painting of the Virgin seeks to be something it is not; it seeks to convince the viewer that he or she is actually seeing the Virgin's physiognomy. Perhaps because its literalness confines the image to the physical, or perhaps because of the element of deception (however innocent), this type of picture is rarely ascribed any supernatural power. This Renaissance pretense, in which artworks consistently sought to be what they were not, lasted until the artistic revolution of the twentieth century. Until then railroad terminals posed as Roman baths, law courts as Greek temples, chimneys as campanile, and prisons as Egyptian tombs. Paintings and sculptures hoped to preserve and continue the techniques of exact naturalism, just as Vasari said they should. "Modern" art was a reversion to the unpretendingness of the Middle Ages. As in the Middle Ages, "form follows function"; as a castle had been a military machine, a house was now a *machine á habiter.* Paintings frankly admitted that they consisted of paint on canvas; sculptures displayed themselves as assembled objects.

The Renaissance development of counterfactual imagination is something much broader than art. By counterfactual imagination I mean the ability to imagine something as intensely real, even though you know that it is not only unreal but impossible. Imagination exists to some extent in all of us; the hunter who imagines killing a prey that will feed his family, the farmer who imagines the future harvest are exercising this faculty. But these imaginings are entirely consistent with the factual situation. Fiction, which has existed in every culture, requires imagination, but the Renaissance expanded the ways in which imagination was applied. Ancient and medieval fiction and myth are chock full of things we regard as imaginative—metamorphoses, Medusa, Fates, sirens, nymphs, flying horses, dragons, wizards, enchantments—but the agents of all these imagined things and events are almost always supernatural. Humans, in ancient and medieval literature, unless they have supernatural aid, do only things that humans actually do; the impossible, the counterfactual, is done by the gods or other supernatural agents.

On many fronts people in the Renaissance began imagining impossible, counterfactual things done by humans. First among these was the restoration of Rome. The reality was that Rome's political dominion, its language, and its culture were over and gone and, in many important respects, forgotten, lost, and unknown. But Cola di Rienzo, Petrarch, and Biondo imagined that they could live again. Cola's vision of restoring Rome's political domination was absurdly impractical and cost Cola his life. Petrarch supported Cola but was primarily interested in restoring Rome's language and culture. This dream, though ultimately impractical, attracted support from generations of humanists, artists, architects, and their patrons and, in arts and letters, if nowhere else, enjoyed a surprising degree of success. Trying to view humanists as proto-modern instead of neo-antique has dimmed our perception of their radicalism. Alexander the Great, at the height of his power, had visualized a merger of Greek and Persian cultures; with that exception, no one in Western history had ever conceived the idea of changing the established course, not of a state, but of a *culture.* That the people who conceived this radical idea were mere writers with no direct access to coercive power is even more remarkable. Their partial success, though limited to arts, letters, and entertainments, was still momentous. Above all, it provided a precedent and prototype for other intellectuals and artists to attempt similar radical departures from prevailing norms in later centuries. Some such attempts have been mere fashions, others complete failures, but some, the Protestant and Catholic Reformations, the eighteenth-century Enlightenment, and the modern movement in art, have been turning points that are unlikely to be reversed.

During the trecento, quattrocento, and cinquecento, as plague and war made present reality frequently unendurable, people became habituated to rejecting it. Nothing could be done about plague, and those who might do something about wars were only interested in winning them. Nevertheless, it became more common to propose or attempt relatively drastic changes to the facts on the ground. Some of them, such as Pius II's idea to fill the Val d'Orca with a lake and Leonardo's to reroute the Arno over the mountains, were literally changes to the ground itself. The earth and its rivers were too much for the technological and financial resources of the day, but the fact that Brunelleschi, Alberti, Francesco di Giorgio, Leonardo da Vinci, and others sought technological solutions to geographical inconveniences was an expansion, at least in thought, of medieval technological successes that had by-and-large been applied to the pedestrian tasks of producing and transporting goods.

Imaginations in the quattrocento sometimes soared into realms where there was no hope that reality would ever follow. At least occasionally, the dreamer, undeterred by this, put his fancies in the form of an illustrated book. Filarete's *Sforzinda* and Colonna's *Hypnerotomachia Poliphili* are a new kind of literature altogether. It is a rare designer who will laboriously work out in full detail an immense and complex design that he knows can never be realized. What did they hope to achieve? Colonna, a monk, but probably a wealthy one, connected his book with a frustrated love, but that may be simply a conventional fig leaf to excuse his eccentricity. Filarete, an architect, may have hoped to win favor from Francesco Sforza that would lead to real-world commissions, but there were surely more efficient ways of achieving that aim. For both authors, the motive could only have been that they personally thirsted to engage in the very *acts* of imagining and writing. In both cases, especially for Filarete's enormous volume, the author had to subtract innumerable hours from attention to real-world concerns.

What *Sforzinda* was in the expenditure of its author's time Pienza was in the expenditure of papal funds. To look at the tiny, boorish backwater of Corsignano and envision a shining city was a stunning feat of counterfactual imagination, but to spend money that could have paid for constructing seven or eight war galleys for the crusade was to sacrifice the pressingly real for a chimerical dream—though, of course, the crusade was also, in its own way, a chimera.[7] That the papal court spent three months in Pienza and never returned again makes the unreality of the entire venture embarrassingly obvious. It is as impossible to imagine a medieval king spending his resources that way as it is to picture a modern democracy doing so.

A corollary to the expansion of imagination was an increased tolerance for change. This was still far short of the modern enthusiasm for unceasing change, but it was perhaps the first stage in moving away from the *fear* of change that seems to be natural to humans and that has predominated in most human civilizations except post-Renaissance Europe and its offshoots. Art and architecture give us vivid illustrations. Egyptian, Ancient Mesopotamian, Classical, Indian, Chinese, Japanese, Islamic, Byzantine, and medieval arts and architecture are very far from

7. This estimate derives from the 50,000 ducats that Pius is supposed to have spent on Pienza and Alan Ryder's estimate that constructing a war galley in the time of Alfonso the Magnanimous cost 6,000 to 7,000 florins; Ryder, *Kingdom of Naples,* 303.

being uniform and monolithic, but, with rare exceptions, their changes are evolutionary. The change from Romanesque to Gothic style was unusually drastic, but it was a natural outgrowth, not a repudiation of the past. We do not find, before the Italian Renaissance, an example of an angry rejection of a well-established, long-prevailing style of art replaced by another style drawn from a distant age that is proclaimed to be uniquely "correct." In the nineteenth century, when Pugin, Ruskin, Viollet-Le-Duc, and others tried to undo the Renaissance and return to Gothic, they were attempting to perform the same kind of angry rejection of the prevailing art and its replacement by a revived, "correct" older style. Their limited success made architecture, their main interest, into a cafeteria of past styles from which patrons and architects could choose at will. Less than a century later another "angry rejection" occurred in architecture, introducing another "correct" set of artistic principles, the central one being never, ever to revive anything from the past! Nothing like this narrative has occurred in any other civilization. The ideas that art can be "correct" or not and that a campaign of literary propaganda demonstrated by examples can produce a revolutionary change in the arts of many nations is new to the Renaissance and—if we were not used to seeing it actually happen—more than a little bizarre. It is a prototype, however, of other revolutionary changes effected largely by literary propaganda backed by examples—among them, the Protestant and Catholic Reformations, the Enlightenment, and the more amorphous destruction of the Enlightenment that has changed modern into postmodern.

The humanists' proclamation of the need for change and their partial success in effecting it was an important precedent in establishing change as the expected norm in the West, but we should not conclude that the humanists and the artists influenced by them embraced the *idea* of change itself the way modern people do. To them, "change" meant the disaster of Rome's collapse: it was an aberration from the norm, a defection from an eternal, unchanging correctness that, once reestablished, must never be allowed to change again. Vasari, for example, recognizes the existence of change in the history of the arts both in the collapse of Roman norms and in the three stages of development into which he divides the *rinascita.* But in the "Preface to the Third Part," he says that Michelangelo has "given *final* form [my emphasis] to these three most noble arts" (painting, sculpture, and architecture).[8] Vasari

8. Vasari, *Lives of the Painters,* 1:622.

is clear that the duty of artists is to continue channeling Michelangelo until the end of time. Change destroyed the correct forms of art; change has reestablished them; now change must stop.

For both humanists and Protestant reformers, the source of authority lay in the ancient past, especially in ancient texts. It took the exploration of the Americas and the Copernican revolution to fatally undermine the authority of antiquity. If the ancients were ignorant about the existence of half the earth and if their concept of the heavens was dead wrong, and if it is the present that has revealed these errors, then the authority of the ancients as guides to the present becomes unsustainable. Not until authority moves to the present and hope focuses on the unprecedented future rather than revival of the past is it possible to speak of the arrival of modernity; but those very movements brought an end to the Renaissance, whose foundation rested squarely on the authority of the past. It was not the Renaissance itself but the factors that ended it that introduced modernity.

Appendix

Plague in Italy, 1347–1700

This appendix is based on Biraben, *Les hommes et la peste,* appendix 4, 1:394–99. I have modified Biraben's list by placing Florence and Tuscany at the beginning of each year's list in which they occur to enable the reader to see at a glance how frequently the plague returned to this important center of Renaissance culture. Biraben's list is certainly incomplete, since it omits plagues in Rome, Viterbo, and Abbadia in 1462 and in Rome and Ancona in 1464 that figure prominently in the life of Pius II.

Cities and regions experiencing outbreaks:

1347	Naples, Genoa, Cagliari, Reggio di Calabria, Sardinia, Elba, Messina, Syracuse, Sciacca, Trapani, Agrigento, Catania
1348	Florence, Tuscany, Rome, Venice, Siena, Pisa, Padua, Lucca, Perugia, Ferrara, Bologna, Genoa, Verona, Piacenza, Cesena, Trento, Sardinia, Faenza, Kingdom of Naples, Rimini, Ancona, Parma, Modena, Piombino, Trapani, Friuli, Mouro, Varese, Reggio nell Emilia, Malta
1349	Siena, Naples, Kingdom of Naples, Bologna, Catania, Parma, Trieste, Udine
1350	Venice, Pisa, Milan, Genoa, Messina, Modena, Kingdom of Naples, Valletidone
1351	Venice
1357	Tuscany, Venice, Venetia, Milan, Friuli
1358	Venetia
1359	Florence, Venice, Friuli, Aquileia
1360	Venice, Venetia, Genoa, Piacenza, Istria, Friuli
1361	Venice, Milan, Lombardy, Genoa, Umbria, Ferrara, Piacenza, Trento, Piemonte, Parma, Romagna
1362	Tuscany, Milan, Bologna, Padua, Verona, Brescia
1363	Florence, Tuscany, Milan, Pisa, Bologna, Verona, Abruzzi, Sicily

1364	Northern Italy
1369	Milan, Genoa, Venice
1371	Florence, Padua, Verona, Piemonte, Trento
1372	Venetia, Genoa
1373	Milan, Lombardy, Perugia, Trento
1374	Florence, Milan, Pisa, Orvieto, Bologna, Rimini, Parma, Piacenza, Reggio, Modena, Budrio
1377	Venice, Genoa
1381	Bologna, Friuli
1382	Venice, Venetia, Vicenza, Padua, Ferrara, Naples, Abruzzi, Udine
1383	Florence, Venice, Milan, Siena, Pisa, Lucca, Genoa, Bologna, Verona, Perugia, Aquileia, Pavia, Piemonte, Udine, Abruzzi
1384	Pavia
1385–86	Piacenza
1387	Milan, Piacenza, Vicenza, Bologna
1388	Milan, Lombardy, Venetia, Parma, Pavia, Piacenza, Reggio
1389	Tuscany, Rome, Piacenza, Bologna, Romagna, La Marche, Pistoia, Arezzo
1390	Florence, Genoa, Liguria, Piacenza, Perugia
1391	Florence, Venice, Piacenza
1393	Venice
1394	Gaeta?
1397	Venice, Venetia, Genoa
1398	Venice, Venetia, Genoa, Ferrara
1399	Florence, Lombardy, Perugia
1400	Florence, Tuscany, Rome, Venice, Siena, Milan, Naples, Pistoia, Bergamo, Umbria, La Marche, Piacenza, Como, Siena
1402	Florence, Pavia
1403	Venice
1404	Lombardy
1405	Padua
1406	Milan, Genoa, Savoy
1409	Pisa
1410	Florence, Venetia, Ferrara, Bologna, Mantua
1411	Florence, Tuscany, Venice, Siena, Genoa
1413	Venice
1414	Venice, Rimini
1415	Venice, Rimini

1416	Piemonte, Romagna, Chieri, Forli
1417	Florence, Arezzo
1418	Tuscany, Perugia, Bologna, Castel del Pieve
1419	Siena, Viterbo
1420	Siena, Chieri
1422	Florence, Tuscany, Naples, Genoa, Romagna, Sicily, Budrio, Forli
1423	Tuscany, Venice, Lombardy, Bologna, Romagna, Parma
1424	Venice, Venetia, Verona, Lombardy, Alghero
1425	Romagna, Rimini
1427	Venice, Trieste
1428	Rome, Venice, Padua, Lombardy, Treviso, Arecia
1429	Florence, Venice, Genoa, Lucca, Otranto, Castro, Lecce, Neritto, Jattipoli (?)
1430	Florence, Genoa, Lucca
1431	Venetia, Verona, Lombardy, Pavia, Piemonte, Asti
1432	Padua, Como
1433	Siena
1435	Rome, Venice, Rimini, Perugia, Gaeta
1436	Tuscany, Genoa, Ferrara
1437	Tuscany, Venice
1438	Tuscany, Venice, Verona, Venetia, Ferrara, Genoa, Brescia
1439	Florence, Lombardy, Genoa, Ferrara, Umbria, Brescia
1440	Ferrara
1444	Budrio
1446	Ancona
1447	Venice, Perugia
1448	Florence, Venice, Rome, Milan, Parma, Romagna, La Marche
1449	Florence, Rome, Milan
1450	Florence, Rome, Lombardy
1451	Milan, Pavia, Bologna
1452	Milan
1456	Florence, Tuscany, Venice, Venetia, Naples, Ravenna, Piscenium, La Marche, Romagna, Palermo, Velletri
1457	Rome, Venice, Bologna, Perugia, Udine, Osimo, Ancona, Forlimpopoli, Brindisi, Nerito, Lecce
1458	Genoa, Naples
1460	Venice

1461	Venice
1462	Venice, Gubbio, Aquileia
1463	Padua, Ferrara, Aquileia
1464	Venice, Perugia
1466	Lucca
1467	Bergamo, Lucca
1468	Rome, Venice, Mantua, Parma, Piacenza, Perugia, Messina
1471	Aosta
1474	Verona
1476	Rome, Velletri, Recanati, Perugia, Viterbo, Iglesies
1477	Venice, Recanti, Friuli?, Sassari
1478	Florence, Tuscany, Rome, Venice, Milan, Naples, Pisa, Perugia, Parma, Verona, Mantua, Bologna, Sicily, Brescia, Aquileia, Gubbio, Udine, Alessandia, Bergamo, Cremona, Modena, Romagna
1479	Florence, Venice
1480	Rome, Venice, Verona, Bologna
1481	Rome, Venice, Lombardy, Naples, Parma, Pouilles
1482	Venice, Milan, Ferrara?, Otranto
1483	Venice, Milan, Ferrara?, Velletri
1484	Venice, Milan, Modena, Vercelli, Velletri
1485	Venice, Milan, Ferrara, Bologna, Pavia, Lodi, Como, Velletri, Brescia
1486	Milan, Lombardy, Pavia, Siena, Lodi, Como, Parma, Reggio, Velletri, Brescia
1487	Lombardy
1490	Venice, Venetia
1491	Udine
1493	Rome, Genoa, Naples, Palermo, Sicily
1494	Florence, Rome, Perugia, Ancona
1495	Venice, Naples?
1496	Naples
1497	Florence, Tuscany, Naples, Ferrara, Mantua, Assisi
1498	Venice
1499	Rome, Genoa, Ferrara, La Marche, Ravenna, Forli, Perugia, Cortona, Arezzo?
1500	Rome, Siena?, Verona?, Sicily
1501	Milan, Lombardy, Genoa, Como, Modena, Messina
1502	Milan
1503	Rome, Venice, Piacenza, Ferrara, Fermo, Apulia

1504	Rome, Naples, Perugia, Reggio nell Emilia
1505	Florence, Rome, Siena, Perugia, Ferrara, Recanati
1506	Venice? Mantua, Cremona?, Pizzighettone
1509	Florence
1510	Venice
1511	Venice, Verona, Udine, Cremona
1512	Milan, Verona
1513	Sicily, Noto, Crema
1514	Milan, Venetia, Lombardy
1516	Milan
1517	Verona
1519	Malta
1522	Florence, Rome, Milan, Lombardy, Naples, Perugia, Orvieto, Noto, Syracuse, Sicily, Cremona, Viterbo, Sardinia, Ancona
1523	Florence, Tuscany, Rome, Milan, Umbria, Bologna, Modena, Sicily, Sardinia, Sartone, Saluzzi, Alessandria, Sorpello
1524	Florence, Rome, Milan, Lombardy, Genoa, Liguria, Pavia, Mantua, Modena, Parma, Piacenza, Cremona, Sicily, Sardinia, Vercelli, Novarra, Alessandria, Budrio
1525	Florence, Rome, Milan, Lombardy, Naples, Genoa, Liguria, Perugia, Parma, Piacenza, Cremona, Pavia, Mantua, Modena, Sicily, Sardinia, Vercelli, Novarra, Alessandria, Modena, Camerino, Budrio
1526	Florence, Rome, Milan, Lombardy, Naples, Genoa, Liguria, Pavia, Mantua, Parma, Piacenza, Perugia, Cremona, Vercelli, Novarra, Alessandria, Modena, Camerino, Ancona, Sicily, Sardinia
1527	Florence, Rome, Naples, Siena, Bologna, Aquileia, Ancona, Camerino, Viterbo, Alessandria, Reggio nell Emilia, Perugia, Sicily, Sardinia, Varese, Budrio, Pouilles
1528	Florence, Venice, Milan, Naples, Genoa, Bologna, Mantua, Ferrara, Modena, Cremona, Ancona, Camerino, Padua, Sicily, Sardinia, Pouilles
1529	Rome, Naples, Ancona, La Marche, Sicily, Sardinia
1530	Florence, Sicily, Sardinia
1531	Florence
1532	Venice
1533	Venice
1536	Casale
1537	Belluno
1547	Budrio

1550	Milan
1551	Messina
1552	Messina
1555	Venice, Padua
1556	Venice, Padua, Udina, Capo d'Istria
1560	Padua
1564	Piemonte, Rivoli, Chiavonne, Avigliana
1565	Avigliana
1566	Milan
1567	Desenzano?
1568	Milan
1571	Messina
1572	Ferrara, Modena, Massa Lombarda
1573	Messina
1574	Trento
1575	Venice, Milan, Verona, Palermo, Trento, Siacca, Messina, Palazzo Adriano, Giuliona
1576	Venice, Venetia, Milan, Lombardy, Pavia, Verona, Mantua, Padua, Palermo, Messina, Calabria, Pouilles
1577	Venice, Milan, Verona, Padua, Vicenza, Pavia, Palermo, Messina, Sicily, Trapani, Trento, Bergamo, Friuli, Iseo
1578	Milan, Pavia, Friuli
1580	Genoa, Sardinia, Sassari
1581	Sardinia
1582	Sardinia
1583	Sardinia
1584	Brissago
1586	Malta
1590	Bari, Apulia
1591	Rome, Trento, Bari, Apulia, Malta
1592	Bari, Apulia, Malta
1593	Malta
1598	Turin, Piemonte, Friuli, Civdde, Udine
1599	Turin, Piemonte, Udine, Astigiano, Casale
1601	Istria, Trieste
1612	Fiuli
1613	Milan

1623	Malta
1624	Palermo, Messina, Trapani, Sicily
1625	Palermo
1629	Venice, Milan, Turin, Parma, Vicenza, Plaisance, il Corrasco, Lecce, Risane Chiusa, S. Michele della Chiusa, Chiomande
1630	Florence, Venice, Milan, Cento, Modena, Pistoia, Pisa, Liguria, Budrio, Guastella, Plaisance, Parma, Ferrara, Fiuli, Livorno, Pavia, Busto Arsizio, Reggio, Treviso, Padua, Vicenza, Abbadia, Pancalieri, Suza, Piedmont, Montferrat, Bologna, Lucpuco, Mantua, Turin, Fermossi, Imola, Lugo, Alessandria, Chieri, Cremona, Verona, Bergamo, Brescia
1631	Florence, Venice, Milan, Friuli, Portogruaro, Marano (Murano?), Turin, Chieri, Vicenza, Padua, Urbino, Sorriva, Bassano, Ferrara, Livorno
1632	Florence, Milan, Imola, Sospello, Turin, Livorno, Parma, Pisa
1633	Florence, Sospello, Lucques.
1634	Bozen, Meran
1636	Levico, Bozen, Brixen
1637	Milan, Verona, Levico
1638	Levico
1639	Levico
1640	Levico
1646	Naples
1648	Messina
1652	Alghero, Sassori, Sardinia
1653	Sardinia
1654	Sardinia
1655	Sardinia, Malta, Sicily
1656	Rome, Naples, Genoa, Ischia, Liguria, Montefiascone, Viterbo, Rieti, Savone, La Spezzia, Voltaggio, Sestri, Bisagno, Palaterino, Velletri, Nettuno, Civitavecchia, Papal States, Kingdom of Naples, Sardinia, Gorifalco, Panormiti, Amaroni, Cosenza, Torre Annunziata, Torre del Greco, Resina, Somma, Puzzolo, Città del Lettere, Capri, Procido, Aversa, Sessa, Sacerra, Arienzo
1657	Naples, Genoa, Viterbo, Montefiascone, Rieti
1663	Malta
1675	Malta, La Valette
1676	Malta
1682	Gorizia
1691	Bari, Monopoli

Bibliography

Ackerman, James. "The Villa as Paradigm." In "Paradigms of Architecture." Special issue, *Perspecta* 22, no. 1 (1986): 10–31.

Adams, Nicholas, and Laurie Nussdorfer. "The Italian City 1400–1600." In *The Renaissance from Brunelleschi to Michelangelo: The Representation of Architecture,* edited by Henry A. Millon and Vittorio Magnano Lamugnani, 205–32. New York: Rizzoli, 1997.

Adembri, Benedetta. *Hadrian's Villa.* Translated by Eric De Sena. Milan: Ministero per i Beni e le Attività Culturali and Electa, 2011. Originally published in 2000.

Ady, Cecilia M. *Pius II (Aeneas Silvius Piccolomini): The Humanist Pope.* London: Methuen, 1913. Bibliolife reprint.

Alberti, Leon Battista. *The Family in Renaissance Florence: A Translation by Renee Neu Watkins of "I libri della famiglia," by Leon Battista Alberti.* Columbia: University of South Carolina Press, 1969.

———. *On the Art of Building in Ten Books.* Translated by Joseph Rykwert, Neil Leach, and Robert Taverner. Cambridge, Mass.: MIT Press, 1988.

———. *On Painting.* Translated by John R. Spencer. New Haven and London: Yale University Press, 1966. Originally published in New Haven in 1956.

Andres, Glenn M., John M. Hunisak, and A. Richard Turner. *The Art of Florence.* 2 vols. New York: Artabras; London: Abbeville, 1994.

Antal, Frederick. *Florentine Painting and Its Social Background: The Bourgeoise Republic before Cosimo de' Medici's Advent to Power; XIV and Early XV Centuries.* London: Routledge and Kegan Paul, 1965. Originally published in 1948 by Kegan Paul, Trench Trubner.

Bak, János M. "Hungary and Crusading in the Fifteenth Century." In Housley, *Crusading,* 116–27. 2004.

Barber, Malcolm. *The Two Cities: Medieval Europe, 1050–1350.* New York: Routledge, 1992.

Barbini, Bruno. *Viterbo: History and Masterpieces.* Sesto Fiorentino: Bonechi Edizioni "Il Turismo," 2009.

Barker, Sheila. "The Making of a Plague Saint: Saint Sebastian's Imagery and Cult Before the Counter-Reformation." In *Piety and Plague from Byzantium to the Baroque,* edited by Franco Mormando and Thomas Worcester, 90–131. Kirksville, Mo.: Truman State University Press, 2007.

Baron, Hans. *The Crisis of the Early Italian Renaissance.* Princeton: Princeton University Press, 1966. Originally published in 1955.

Battisti, Eugenio. *L'antirinascimento, con una appendice di manoscritti inediti.* Milan: Feltranelli, 1962.

Bean, J. M. W. "The Black Death: The Crisis and Its Social Consequences." In Williman, *Black Death,* 23–38. 1982.

Benedictine Monks of Subiaco. *The Sanctuary of the Sacred Cave, Subiaco.* Subiaco, Italy: Monastery of St. Benedict, n.d.

Benedictow, Ole J. *The Black Death, 1346–1353: The Complete History.* Woodbridge, Suffolk, UK: Boydell Press, 2004.

Benporat, Claudio. *Feste e banchetti: Convivialità Italiano fra tre e quattrocento.* Florence: Leo S. Olschki Editore, 2001.

Benton, Tim. "The Design of Siena and Florence Duomos." In Norman, *Siena, Florence and Padua,* 2:129–44. 1995.

———. "The Three Cities Compared: Urbanism." In Norman, *Siena, Florence and Padua,* 2:4–7. 1995.

Bernardo, Aldo S. "The Plague as Key to Meaning in Boccaccio's *Decameron.*" In Williman, *Black Death,* 39–64. 1982.

Biraben, Jean-Noel. *Les hommes et la peste en France et dans les pays européens et mediterranéens.* 2 vols. Paris: Mouton, 1975.

Bisaha, Nancy. "Pope Pius II and the Crusade." In Housley, *Crusading,* 39–52. 2004.

Bishop, Morris. *Petrarch and His World.* Bloomington: Indiana University Press, 1963.

Black, Robert. *Benedetto Accolti and the Florentine Renaissance.* New York: Cambridge University Press, 1985.

Blunt, Anthony. *Artistic Theory in Italy 1450–1600.* Oxford: Clarendon Press, 1971.

Boase, T. S. R. *Giorgio Vasari: The Man and the Book.* National Gallery of Art. Bollingen Series 35. Princeton: Princeton University Press, 1979.

Boccaccio, Giovanni. *The Decameron.* Translated by G. H. McWilliam. London: Penguin, 1972.

Borsook, Eve. *Francesco Sassetti and Ghirlandaio at Santa Trinità, Florence: History and Legend in a Renaissance Chapel.* London: Davaco, 1984.

Boulting, William. *Aeneas Silvius (Enea Silvio de' Piccolomini): Orator, Man of Letters, Statesman, and Pope.* London: Archibald Constable, 1908. Bibliolife reprint.

Bowsky, William M. "The Impact of the Black Death upon Sienese Government and Society." *Speculum* 39 (1964): 19–34. In Bowsky, *Black Death* (revised and adapted), 114–21. 1971.

———, ed. *The Black Death: A Turning Point in History?* Melbourne, Fla.: Robert E. Kreiger, 1971.

Bramly, Serge. *Leonardo: The Artist and the Man.* Translated by Sian Reynolds. London and New York: Penguin, 1991.

Branca, Vittore. *Boccaccio: The Man and His Works.* Translated by Richard Monges and Dennis J. McAuliffe. New York: Harvester Press, 1976.

Brucker, Gene. *Florentine Politics and Society 1343–1378.* Princeton: Princeton University Press, 1962.

———. *The Civic World of Early Renaissance Florence.* Princeton: Princeton University Press, 1977.

Bruni, Leonardo. *The Humanism of Leonardo Bruni: Selected Texts.* Edited by Gordon Griffiths, James Hankins, and David Thompson. Binghamton, N.Y.: Renaissance Society of America, 1987.

Bruschi, Arnaldo. *Bramante.* New York and London: Thames and Hudson, 1977.

Burckhardt, Jacob. *The Civilization of the Renaissance in Italy.* Translated by S. G. C. Middlemore. Introduction by Peter Burke. London: Penguin, 1990.

Burke, Peter. *The Italian Renaissance: Culture and Society in Italy.* Cambridge: Polity Press, 1986.

Burroughs, Charles. "A Planned Myth and a Myth of Planning: Nicholas V and Rome." In Ramsey, *Rome in the Renaissance,* 197–208. 1982.

Cadogan, Jeanne K. *Domenico Ghirlandaio: Artist and Artisan.* New Haven: Yale University Press, 1984.

Caferro, William. *Mercenary Companies and the Decline of Siena.* Baltimore and London: Johns Hopkins University Press, 1998.

Calzona, Arturo. "Mantova in attesa della Dieta." In Calzona et al, *Il Sogno, 529–78.* 2000.

Calzona, Arturo, Francesco Paolo Fiore, Alberto Tenenti, and Cesare Vasoli, eds. *Il Sogno di Pio II e il vaiggio da Roma a Mantova: Atti del convegno internazionale, Mantova, 13–15 aprile 2000.* Mantova: Leo S. Olschki, 2000.

Campbell, Stephen J. *The Cabinet of Eros: Renaissance Mythological Painting and the Studiolo of Isabella d'Este.* New Haven and London: Yale University Press, 2004.

Capellanus, Andreas. *The Art of Courtly Love: With Introduction, Translation, and Notes by John Jay Perry.* New York: Columbia University Press, 1990.

Carli, Enzo. *Il Pintoricchio.* Milan: Electra, 1960.

———. *Siena Cathedral and the Cathedral Museum.* Florence: Scala, 1999.

Carpentier, Elisabeth. "Autour de la peste noire: Famines et epidemies dans l'histoire du XIVe siècle." *Annales. Economies, Societes, Civilisations* 17 (1962): 1080–83. Translated by William M. Bowsky. Excerpt reprinted in Bowsky, *Black Death,* 35–37. 1971.

———. *Une ville devant la peste: Orvieto et la Peste Noire de 1348.* Paris: S.E.V.P.E.N., 1962, 192–95, 222–25. Translated by William M. Bowsky. Excerpts reprinted in Bowsky, *Black Death,* 108–13. 1971.

Cartellieri, Otto. *The Court of the Dukes of Burgundy.* New York: Haskell House, 1925.

Castiglione, Count Baldesar. *The Book of the Courtier.* Translated by Leonard Eckstein Opdycke. New York: Horace Liveright, 1929.

Cecchi, Alessandro. *The Piccolomini Library in the Cathedral of Siena.* Florence: Scala, 1982.

Cellini, Benvenuto. *Autobiography.* Translated by George Bull. London: Penguin, 1956.

Chambers, David S. *Popes, Cardinals and War: The Military Church in Renaissance and Early Modern Europe.* London: I. B. Tauris, 2006.

Chironi, Giuseppe. "Pius II and the Formation of the Ecclesiastical Institutions of Pienza." In Von Martels and Vanderjagt, *Pius II "el più expeditivo pontifice," 171–86.* 2003.

Christianson, Gerald, Thomas M. Izbicki, and Christopher M. Bellitto, eds. *The Church, the Councils, and Reform: The Legacy of the Fifteenth Century.* Washington, D.C.: The Catholic University of America Press, 2008.

Clark, James M. *The Dance of Death in the Middle Ages and Renaissance.* Glasgow: Jackson, Son, 1950.

Cloulas, Ivan. *Lorenzo, il Magnifico.* Translated by Cesare Scarton. Rome: Salerno Editrice, 1986.

Coffin, David R. *The Villa in the Life of Renaissance Rome.* Princeton: Princeton University Press, 1979.

Cohn, Samuel K. *The Black Death Transformed: Disease and Culture in Early Renaissance Europe.* London: Arnold, 2002.

———. *Cultures of Plague: Medical Thinking at the End of the Renaissance.* Oxford: Oxford University Press, 2010.

Cole, Alison. *Art of the Italian Courts: Virtue and Magnificence.* London: Everyman Art Library, 1995.

Colonna, Francesco. *Hypnerotomachia: The Strife of Love in a Dreame (1592).* Translated by R. D. Introduction by Lucy Gent. Delmar, N.Y.: Scholar's Facsimiles and Reprints, 1973.

Corradi, Alfonso, *Annali delle epidemie occorse in Italia dale prime memorie fino al 1850: Compilati con varie note e dichiarazioni.* Edited by U. Stefanutti. Bologna: Ristampa fotomeccanica, 1972. Originally published in Bologna: Formi Editore, 1863.

Crielesi, Alberto. *Santa Maria "Ad Nives" di Palazzolo.* Edited by Luigi Devoti and Renato Mammucari. Itinerari della Campagna Romana. Vellatri, Italy: Edizioni tra 8 e 9, 1997.

Cunningham, Colin. "For the Honour and Beauty of the City: The Design of Town Halls." In Norman, *Siena, Florence and Padua,* 2:29–54. 1995.

Da Bisticci, Vespasiano. *Renaissance Princes, Popes, and Prelates: The Vespasiano Memoirs; Lives of the Illustrious Men of the XVth Century.* Translated by William George and Emily Waters. New York: Harper Torchbooks, 1963.

Dal Pogetto, Paolo. *Guide to the Galleria Nazionale delle Marche in the Ducal Palace at Urbino.* Urbino: Gebart Srl, 2007.

De la Croix, Horst. "Military Architecture and the Radial Plan in Sixteenth Century Italy." *Art Bulletin* 42, no. 4 (December 1960): 263–90.

Delatouche, Raymond. "La crise du XIVe siecle en Europe occidentale." *Les Etudes Sociales* n.s., nos. 42–43 (1959): 1–2, 4–6, 8–17. Published by the Societe d'Economie et de Science Sociales. Translated by William M. Bowsky. Excerpt reprinted in Bowsky, *Black Death,* 47–55. 1971.

D'Elia, Anthony F. *A Sudden Terror: The Plot to Murder the Pope in Renaissance Rome.* Cambridge, Mass.: Harvard University Press, 2009.

Della Mirandolla, Giovanni Pico. *Oration on the Dignity of Man.* Translated by A. Robert Caponigri. Washington, D.C.: Renery Gateway, 1956.

Della Tuccia, Niccolà. *Chronica di Viterbo et di altre città.* In *Cronache e statute della città di Viterbo,* edited by Ignazio Ciampi, 1–272. Bologna: A Forni, 1976.

De' Medici, Lorenzo. *The Autobiography of Lorenzo de' Medici.* Translated by James Wyatt Cook. Medieval and Renaissance Texts and Studies 129. Binghamton: State University of New York at Binghamton, 1995.

Dempsey, Charles. "Portraits and Masks in the Art of Lorenzo de'Medici, Botticelli, and Politian's Stanze per la Giostra." *Renaissance Quarterly* 52, no. 1 (Spring 1999), 1–42.

Di Tura, Agnolo. *Cronaca senese attribuita ad Agnolo di Tura del Grasso detta la Cronica Maggiore.* In *Cronache senesi: Rerum Italicarum Scriptores,* edited by A. Lisini and F. Iacometti. Bologna: 1931–37. Excerpt reprinted in Bowsky, *Black Death,* 13–14. 1971.

Dotson, Esther Gordon. "Shapes of Earth and Time in European Gardens." *Art Journal* 42, no. 3 (Autumn 1982): 210–16.

Ferguson, Wallace. *The Renaissance in Historical Thought: Five Centuries of Interpretation.* New York: Houghton Mifflin, 1948.

Ferretti, Lodovico. *Saint Catherine of Siena.* Siena: Edizioni Cantagalli, 1996.

Filarete (Antonio di Pietro Averlino). *Filarete's Treatise on Architecture.* Edited by J. R. Spencer. 2 vols. New Haven and London: Yale University Press, 1965.

Finelli, Luciana. "Una città per il papa: Construzione e significati della piazza di Pienza. In Tarugi, *Pio II e la cultura del suo tempo,* 77–84. 1991.

Fiore, Francesco Paolo. "La loggia di Pio II per I Piccolomini a Siena." In Calzona et al, *Il Sogno,129–42.* 2000.

Franci, Aldo. "Pio II e Pienza." In Tarugi, *Pio II e la cultura del suo tempo,* 39–46. 1991.

Gallico, Sonia. *Guide to the Excavations of Ostia Antica with a Section about the Renaissance Borgo.* Rome: ATS Italica Editrice, 2000.

Gasquet, Francis Aidan. *The Black Death of 1348 and 1349.* London: George Bell, 1908.

Gavelli, Giuseppe. *La città di Castro e Antonio da Sangallo.* Ischia di Castro: Gruppo Archeologico "Armine," 1983.

Geanakoplos, Deno John. *Byzantine East and Latin West: Two Worlds of Christendom in the Middle Ages and Renaissance.* New York: Harper Torchbooks, 1966.

———. *Constantinople and the West: Essays on the Late Byzantine (Paleologian) and Italian Renaissances and the Byzantine and Roman Churches.* Madison: University of Wisconsin Press, 1989.

Gertsman, Elina. "Visualizing Death: Medieval Plagues and the Macabre." In *Piety and Plague: from Byzantium to the Baroque,* edited by Franco Mormando and Thomas Worcester, 23–89. Kirksville, Mo.: Truman State University Press. 2007.

Giglioli, Alberto. "Il cammino di conversion di E. S. Piccolomini." In Tarugi, *Pio II e la cultura del suo tempo,* 29–38. 1991.

Gilbert, Felix. *Machiavelli and Guicciardini: Politics and History in Sixteenth Century Florence.* Princeton: Princeton University Press, 1965.

Gill, Joseph. *The Council of Florence.* Cambridge: Cambridge University Press, 1959.

Gimpel, Jean. *The Medieval Machine: The Industrial Revolution of the Middle Ages.* Aldershot, UK: Wildwood House, 1988.

Goffen, Rona, ed. *Masaccio's Trinity.* Cambridge: University of Cambridge Press, 1998.

Goldthwaite, Richard A. *Wealth and the Demand for Art in Italy 1300–1600.* Baltimore: Johns Hopkins University Press, 1993.

Gottfried, Robert S. *The Black Death: Natural and Human Disaster in Medieval Europe.* New York: Free Press, 1983.

Grafton, Anthony. *Leon Battista Alberti: Master Builder of the Renaissance.* New York: Hill and Wang, 2000.

Greene, Thomas M. "Resurrecting Rome: The Double Task of the Humanist Imagination." In Ramsey, *Rome in the Renaissance,* 41–54. 1982.

Grendler, Paul F. *The Universities of the Italian Renaissance.* Baltimore and London: Johns Hopkins University Press, 2002.

Griffiths, Gordon, James Hankins, and David Thompson, eds. *The Humanism of Leonardo Bruni: Selected Texts.* Binghamton N.Y.: Renaissance Society of America, 1987.

Guasti, Cesare, ed. *Le feste di San Giovanni Battista in Firenze descritto in prosa e in rima da contemporanei.* Florence: Giovanni Cirri, 1884.

Gundersheimer, Werner L. *Ferrara: The Style of a Renaissance Despotism.* Princeton: Princeton University Press, 1973.

Gunmore, John F. "The Ships in Lake Nemi." *Classical Weekly* 22, no. 13 (January 21, 1929): 97–98.

Harrison, Charles. "The Arena Chapel: Patronage and Authorship." In Norman, *Siena, Florence and Padua,* 2:83–104. 1995.

Hartt, Frederick. *History of Italian Renaissance Art: Painting, Sculpture, Architecture.* New York: Abrams, 1969.

Haskins, Charles Homer. *The Renaissance of the Twelfth Century.* Cleveland, Ohio: Meridian, 1968. Originally published 1927.

Hauser, Arnold. *The Social History of Art.* Translated by Stanley Goodman. 2 vols. New York: Knopf, 1951.

———. *Mannerism: The Crisis of the Renaissance and the Origin of Modern Art.* New York: Knopf, 1965.

Hay, Denys. *Flavio Biondo and the Middle Ages.* Oxford: Oxford University Press, 1960.

Helmrath, Johannes. "The German *Reichstage* and the Crusade." In Housley, *Crusading,* 53–69. 2004.

Herlihy, David. *Medieval and Renaissance Pistoia.* New Haven, Conn.: Yale, 1967, 112–20. Excerpt reprinted in Bowsky, *Black Death,* 60–64. 1971.

———. *The Black Death and the Transformation of the West.* Cambridge, Mass., and London: Harvard University Press, 1997.

Herlihy, David, and Christiane Klapisch-Zuber. *Tuscans and their Families: A Study of the Florentine Catasto of 1427.* New Haven: Yale University Press, 1985.

Hintzen-Bohlen, Brigitte. *Art and Architecture: Rome and the Vatican City.* New York: Barnes and Noble, 2000.

Hollingsworth, Mary. *Patronage in Renaissance Italy.* Baltimore: Johns Hopkins University Press, 1994.

Holmes, George A. *The Later Middle Ages, 1272–1485.* New York: W. W. Norton, 1962, 136–48. Excerpt reprinted in Bowsky, *Black Death,* 91–99. 1971.

———. *The Florentine Enlightenment.* Oxford: Clarendon, 1969.

———. *Florence, Rome and the Origins of the Renaissance.* Oxford: Clarendon, 1986.

Horrox, Rosemary, trans., ed. *The Black Death.* Manchester, UK, and New York: Manchester University Press, 1994.

Housley, Norman. *Crusading in the Fifteenth Century: Message and Impact.* London: Palgrave Macmillan, 2004.

———. "Giovanni da Capistrano and the Crusade of 1456." In Housley, *Crusading,* 94–115. 2004.

———, ed., trans. *Documents on the Later Crusades, 1274–1580.* New York: St. Martin's Press, 1996.

Huizinga, Johan H. *The Autumn of the Middle Ages.* Translated by Rodney J. Payton and Ulrich Mammitzsch. Chicago: University of Chicago Press, 1996.

Hussey, J. M. *The Orthodox Church in the Byzantine Empire.* Oxford: Oxford University Press, 1986.

Imber, Colin. *The Crusade of Varna, 1443–45.* Aldershot, UK: Ashgate, 2006.

Izbicki, Thomas. "'Reject Aeneas!' Pius II on the Errors of his Youth." In Von Martels and Vanderjagt, *Pius II "el più expeditivo pontifice,"* 187–204. 2003.

Iurlaro, Sabrina. "Il *De curialium miseriis* nell'ideologia politica do Pio II: Dal Concolio alla Crociata." In Calzona et al, *Il Sogno,* 517–28. 2000.

Janson, H. W. *History of Art: A Survey of the Major Visual Arts from the Dawn of History to the Present Day.* Englewood Cliffs, N. J.: Prentice-Hall; New York: Harry N. Abrams, 1963.

Jenkins, A. D. Fraser. "Cosimo de' Medici's Patronage of Architecture and the Theory of Magnificence." *Journal of the Warburg and Courtauld Institutes* 33 (1970): 162–70.

Jocelyn, Henry David. "The Unclassical Aspects of Aeneas Silvius Piccolomini's *Chrysis.* In Tarugi, *Pio II e la cultura del suo tempo, 215–28.* 1991.

Kambo, Severio. *I Castelli Romani: Grottaferrata e il Monte Cavo.* Bergamo: Istituto Italiano D'Arti Grafiche, n.d.

Kedar, Benjamin Z. *Merchants in Crisis: Genoese and Venetian Men of Affairs and the Fourteenth Century Depression.* New Haven and London: Yale University Press, 1976.

Kelly, John. *The Great Mortality: An Intimate History of the Most Devastating Plague of All Time.* New York: Harper Collins, 2005.

Kemp. Martin. "From 'Mimesis' to 'Fantasia': The Quattrocento Vocabulary of Creation, Inspiration and Genius in the Visual Arts." *Viator* 8 (1977): 347–98.

———. "The Mean and Measure of All Things." In *Circa 1492,* edited by Jay A. Levenson, 95–111. New Haven and London: Yale University Press, 1991.

Kieckhefer, Richard. *Unquiet Souls: Fourteenth Century Saints and their Religious Milieu.* Chicago: University of Chicago Press, 1984.

King, Catherine. "Effigies: Human and Divine." In Norman, *Siena, Florence and Padua,* 2:105–28. 1995.

———. "Women as Patrons: Nuns, Widows and Rulers." In Norman, *Siena, Florence and Padua,* 2:243–66. 1995.

Kirkbride, Robert. *Architecture and Memory: The Renaissance Studioli of Federico de Montefeltro.* New York: Columbia University Press, 2008.

Krautheimer, Richard. "The Panels in Urbino, Baltimore and Berlin Reconsidered." In *The Renaissance from Brunelleschi to Michelangelo: The Representation of Architecture,* edited by Henry A. Millon and Vittorio Magnano Lamugnani, 233–58. New York: Rizzoli, 1997.

Kristeller, Paul Oskar. *Renaissance Thought: The Classic, Scholastic and Humanist Strains.* New York: Harper Torchbooks, 1955.

———. *Renaissance Thought and Its Sources.* Edited by Michael Moony. New York: Columbia University Press, 1979.

———. "Teorie umanistiche della Vita attiva e dalla Vita contemplative." In Tarugi, *Pio II e la cultura del suo tempo,* 13–28. 1991.

LaCroix, Jean. "I *Commentarii* di Pio II fra storia e diaristica." In Tarugi, *Pio II e la cultura del suo tempo,* 133–50. 1991.

La Malfa, Claudia. *Pintoricchio.* Florence: Giunti Editore, 2008.

Landucci, Luca. *A Florentine Diary from 1450 to 1516 by Luca Landucci Continued by an Anonymous Writer til 1542, with Notes by Iodoco del Badia.* Translated by Alice de Rosen Jervis. Hallandale, Fla.: New World, 1971. Originally published in Freeport N.Y.: Books for Libraries Press, 1927.

Lang, S. "The Ideal City from Plato to Howard." *Architectural Review* 112, no. 668 (1952): 91–104.

———. "Sforzinda, Filarete and Filelfo." *Journal of the Warburg and Courtauld Institutes* 35 (1972): 391–97.

Larner, John. *Culture and Society in Italy, 1290–1420.* New York: Scribner's, 1971.

Larson, Orville K. "Vasari's Description of Stage Machinery." *Educational Theatre Journal* 9, no. 4 (December 1957): 287–99.

Levey, Michael. *Florence: A Portrait.* Cambridge, Mass.: Harvard University Press, 1996.

Lopez, Robert. *The Three Ages of the Italian Renaissance.* Charlottesville: University Press of Virginia, 1970.

Luongo, F. Thomas. *The Saintly Politics of Catherine of Siena.* Ithaca and London: Cornell University Press, 2006.

Machiavelli, Niccolò. *The Letters of Machiavelli: A Selection of His Letters.* Edited and translated by Allan Gilbert. New York: Capricorn, 1961.

Mack, Charles R. *Pienza: The Creation of a Renaissance City.* Ithaca: Cornell University Press, 1987.

Magnuson, Torgil. "The Project of Nicholas V for Rebuilding the Borgo Leonino in Rome." *Art Bulletin* 36, no. 2 (June 1954): 89–115.

———. *Studies in Roman Quattrocento Architecture.* Stockholm: Almqvist and Wikksell, 1958.

Mallett, Michael. *The Florentine Galleys in the Fifteenth Century.* Oxford: Clarendon, 1967.

———. *Mercenaries and Their Masters: Warfare in Renaissance Italy.* Totowa N.J.: Rowman and Littlefield, 1974.

———. "Venezia, I Turchi e il Papato dopo la pace di Lodi." In Calzona et al, *Il Sogno,* 237–46. 2000.

Mancini, Francesco Federico. *Pintoricchio.* Milano: Silvano, 2007.

Martines, Lauro. *The Social World of the Florentine Humanists 1390–1460.* Princeton: Princeton University Press, 1963.

———. "The Gentleman in Renaissance Italy." In *The Darker Vision of the Renaissance: Beyond the Fields of Reason,* edited by Robert S. Kinsman, 77–94. Berkeley: University of California Press, 1974.

———. *Furies: War in Europe, 1450–1700.* London and New York: Bloomsbury Press, 2013.

Masson, Georgina. *Italian Villas and Palaces.* New York: Harry N. Abrams, 1959.

———. *Italian Gardens.* New York: Harry N. Abrams, 1961.

Maxwell, Hope. "'Uno elefante grandissimo con lo castello di sopra': Il trionfo Aragonese del 1423." *Archivio storico italiano* 150, no. 3 (1992): 847–75.

Mazzocco, Angelo. "Rome and the Humanists: The Case of Biondo Flavio." In Ramsey, *Rome in the Renaissance,* 185–96. 1982.

McNeill, William H. *Plagues and Peoples.* New York: Anchor, 1977.

Meiss, Millard. *Painting in Florence and Siena after the Black Death.* Princeton: Princeton University Press, 1951.

Meserve, Margaret. "From Samarkand to Scythia: Reinventions of Asia in Renaissance Geography and Political Thought." In Von Martels and Vanderjagt, *Pius II "el più expeditivo pontifice,"* 13–40. 2003.

———. "Italian Humanists and the Problem of the Crusade." In Housley, *Crusading,* 13–39. 2004.

———. *Empires of Islam in Renaissance Historical Thought.* Cambridge, Mass., and London: Harvard University Press, 2008.

Mitchell, Rosamund Joscelyne. *The Laurels and the Tiara: Pope Pius II, 1458–1464.* Garden City, N.Y.: Doubleday, 1962.

Molinari, Cesare. *Spettacoli fiorentini del Quattrocento: Contribute allo studio delle sacre Rappresentazioni.* Venice: Neri Pozza Editore, 1961.

Montecalvo, Rolando. "The New Landesgeschichte: Aeneas Silvius on Austria and Bohemia." In Von Martels and Vanderjagt, *Pius II "el più expeditivo pontifice,"* 55–86. 2003.

Naphy, William, and Andrew Spicer. *The Black Death and the History of Plagues 1345–1730.* Stroud, Gloucestershire: Tempus, 2000.

Nicholas, David. *The Later Medieval City, 1300–1500.* London: Longman, 1997.

Nohl, Johannes. *The Black Death: A Chronicle of the Plague.* Translated by C. H. Clark. New York: Ballantine, 1960. Originally published in London by Allen and Unwin, 1926.

Norman, Diana. "The Art of Knowledge: Two Artistic Schemes in Florence." In Norman, *Siena, Florence and Padua,* 2:217–42. 1995.

———. "'Hail Most Saintly Lady': Change and Continuity in Marian Altarpieces." In Norman, *Siena, Florence and Padua,* 2:217–42. 1995.

———. "'Love Justice, You Who Judge the Earth': The Paintings of the Sala dei Nove in the Palazzo Pubblico, Siena." In Norman, *Siena, Florence and Padua,* 2:145–68. 1995.

———. "'A Noble Panel': Duccio's *Maesta.*" In Norman, *Siena, Florence and Padua,* 2:55–82. 1995.

———. "Those Who Pay, Those Who Pray and Those Who Paint: Two Funerary Chapels." In Norman, *Siena, Florence and Padua,* 2:169–94. 1995.

———, ed. *Siena, Florence and Padua: Art, Society and Religion 1280–1400.* Vol. 2. New Haven and London: Yale University Press, 1995.

O'Brien, Emily. "Aeneas Sylvius Piccolomini and the Histories of the Council of Basel." In Christianson, Izbicki, and Bellitto, *The Church, the Councils, and Reform,* 60–81. 2008.

O'Brien, Emily, and Kenneth Bartlett, eds. *The Two Lovers: The Goodly History of Lady Lucrece and her Lover Eurialus.* Ottawa: Dovehouse, 1999.

Paoletti, John T., and Gary M. Radke. *Art in Renaissance Italy.* New York: Harry N. Abrams, 1997.

Paparelli, Gioacchino. *Enea Silvio Piccolomini: L'umanessimo sul soglio di Pietro.* Ravenna: Longo Editore, 1978.

Paris, Tonino, ed. *L'area dei Castelli Romani gli insediamenti storici dei Colli Albani.* Rome: Officina Edizioni, 1981.

Partner, Peter. *The Lands of Saint Peter: The Papal State in the Middle Ages and Early Renaissance.* Berkeley and Los Angeles: University of California Press, 1972.

Patetta, Luciano, "Enea Silvio Piccolomini e l'architetto Rossellino." In Tarugi, *Pio II e la cultura del suo tempo,* 59–76. 1991.

Paviot, Jacques. "Burgundy and the Crusade." In Housley, Crusading, 70–80. 2004.

Pedretti, Carlo. *Leonardo da Vinci: The Royal Palace at Romarantin.* Cambridge, Mass.: Harvard University Press, 1972.

Pellegrini, Marco. "Pio II, il Collegio cardinalizio e la Dieta di Mantova." In Calzona et al, *Il Sogno,* 15–76. 2000.

Pertici, Petra. "Il viaggio del papa attroverso il territorio senese: le tappe do una vita." In Calzona et al, *Il Sogno,* 143–62. 2000.

Petrarca, Francesco. *The Life of Solitude by Francis Petrarch.* Translated by J. Zeitlin. Urbana: University of Illinois Press, 1924.

———. *The Triumphs of Petrarch.* Translated by Ernest Hatch Wilkins. Chicago: University of Chicago Press, 1962.

———. *Letters from Petrarch.* Selected and translated by Morris Bishop. Bloomington: Indiana University Press, 1966.

———. *Rerum familiarium libri I–VIII.* Translated by Aldo S. Bernardo. Albany: State University of New York Press, 1975.

———. *Letters of Old Age: Rerum senilium libri, I–XVIII.* Translated by Aldo S. Bernardo, Saul Levin, and Reta A. Bernardo. Baltimore and London: Johns Hopkins University Press, 1992.

Piccolomini, Aeneas Silvius. *See* Pius II.

Pierini, Marco. *Pienza, Guide to the Town and Surroundings: Corsignano, Spedaletto, Monticchiello, Sant'Anna in Camprena.* Siena: Nuova Immagine, 2007.

Pitti, Buonaccorso, and Gregorio Dati. *Two Memoirs of Renaissance Florence: The Diaries of Buonaccorso Pitti and Gregario Dati.* Edited by Gene Bruckner. Translated by Julia Martines. New York: Harper Torchbooks, 1967.

Pius II. *The Commentaries of Pius II.* Translated by Florence Alden Gragg. Introduction and notes by Leona C. Gabel. In *Smith College Studies in History.* 13 Books. Northampton, Mass.: Smith College, 1936–1957.

———. *Memoirs of a Renaissance Pope: The Commentaries of Pius II.* Translated by Florence Alden Gragg. Edited by Leona C. Gabel. New York: Putnam, 1959.

———. *Selected Letters of Aeneas Silvius Piccolomini.* Translated and edited by Albert R. Baca. Northridge, Calif.: San Fernando Valley State College, 1969.

———. *Epistola ad Mahomatem II [Epistle to Mohammed II].* Translated by Albert R. Baca. New York: Peter Lang, 1990.

———. *Enee Silvii Piccolominei, postea Pii PP II, De viris illustribus.* Edited by Adrianus Van Heck. Vatican City: Biblioteca Apostolica Vaticana, 1991.

———. *Commentaries.* Edited by Margaret Meserve and Marcello Simonetta. I Tatti Renaissance Library. 2 vols. Cambridge, Mass.: Harvard University Press, 2003, 2007.

———. *Reject Aeneas, Accept Pius: Selected Letters of Aeneas Silvius Piccolomini (Pope Pius II).* Introduction, with a translation by Thomas M. Izbicki, Gerald Christianson, and Philip Krey. Washington, D.C.: The Catholic University of America Press, 2006.

———. "The Education of Boys." In *Humanist Educational Treatises.* Edited and translated by Craig W. Kallendorf, 65–132. Cambridge Mass.: Harvard University Press. 2008.

Poliziano, Angelo. *The Stanze of Angelo Poliziano [Stanze Cominciate per la Giostra del Magnifico Giuliano de' Medici].* Translated by David Quint. Amherst: University of Massachusetts Press, 1979.

Polzer, Joseph. "Aspects of the Fourteenth-Century Iconography of Death and the Plague." In Williman, *Black Death,* 107–30. 1982.

Porçal, Peter. "Le Allegorie del Correggio per lo *Studiolo* di Isabella d'Este a Mantova." *Mitteilungen des Kunsthistorischen Institutes in Florenz* 38, no. 2 (1984): 225–76.

Postan, Michael M. "Histoire Economique. Moyen Age." In *IXe Congres international des sciences historiques. Paris 28 aout–3 septembre 1950. Rapports* 1 (1950): 232–36. Excerpt reprinted in Bowsky, *Black Death,* 56–59. 1971.

Puerari, Alfredo. *Sabbioneta.* Milan: Istituto Editorale Domus, 1955.

Ramsey, P. A., ed. *Rome in the Renaissance: The City and the Myth.* Papers of the Thirteenth Annual Conference of the Center for Medieval and Early Renaissance Studies. Binghamton, N.Y.: State University of New York at Binghamton, Center for Medieval and Early Renaissance Studies, 1982.

Raymond of Capua. *The Life of Catherine of Siena.* Edited and translated by Conleth Kearns. Wilmington, Del.: Michael Glazier, 1980.

Renouard, Yves. "La Peste Noire de 1348–50." *La Revue de Paris* (March 1950): 107–19. Translated by William M. Bowsky. Excerpt reprinted in Bowsky, *Black Death,* 25–34. 1971.

Rinaldi, Rinaldo. "L'Italia "romana" del Piccolomini." In Calzona et al, *Il Sogno,* 109–28. 2000.

Robin, Diana. *Filelfo in Milan: Writings 1451–1477.* Princeton: Princeton University Press, 1991.

Roth, Cecil. *The Last Florentine Republic.* London: Methuen, 1925.

Rotondo, Pasquale. *The Ducal Palace of Urbino: Its Architecture and Decoration.* New York: Transatlantic Arts, 1969.

Rowe, John Gordon. "The Tragedy of Aeneas Sylvius Piccolomini (Pope Pius II): An Interpretation." *Church History* 30, no. 3 (1961): 288–313.

Rubenstein, Ruth Olitsky. "Pius II as a Patron of Art with Special Reference to the History of the Vatican." Ph.D. diss., Courtauld Institute of Art, University of London, 1957.

Ryder, Alan. *The Kingdom of Naples under Alfonso the Magnanimous: The Making of a Modern State.* Oxford: Clarendon, 1976.

Sarton, George. "Science in the Renaissance." In *The Civilization of the Renaissance,* edited by James Westfall Thompson, George Rowley, Ferdinand Schevill, and George Sarton, 75–98. Chicago: University of Chicago Press, 1929.

Schevill, Ferdinand. *Siena: The Story of a Medieval Commune.* New York: Charles Scribner's Sons, 1909.

Schiferl, Ellen. "Iconography of Plague Saints." *Fifteenth Century Studies* (1983): 205–25.

Setton, Kenneth Meyer. *The Papacy and the Levant (1204–1571).* Vol. 2, *The Fifteenth Century.* Philadelphia: American Philosophical Society, 1978.

Seznec, Jean. *The Survival of the Pagan Gods: The Mythological Tradition and Its Place in Renaissance Humanism.* Bollingen 38. New York: Pantheon, 1953.

Shearman, John. *Mannerism.* Harmondsworth: Penguin, 1967.

———. "The Florentine Entrata of Leo X, 1515." *Journal of the Warburg and Courtauld Institutes* 38 (1975): 136–54.

Sidwell, Keith. "Aeneas Silvius Piccolomini's *De curialium miseriis* and Peter of Blois." In Von Martels and Vanderjagt, *Pius II "el più expeditivo pontifice,"* 87–106. 2003.

Siena, Province of, the Municipalities of Asciano, Buonconvento, Monteroni d'Arbia, Rapolano Terme, San Giovanni d'Asso, and the Tourist Board of Siena. *Le Crete.* Siena: APT Siena, n.d.

Simonetta, Marcello. "Il Duca alla Dieta: Francesco Sforza e Pio II." In Calzona et al, *Il Sogno,* 247–86. 2000.

———. "Pius II and Francesco Sforza: The History of Two Allies." In Von Martels and Vanderjagt, *Pius II "el più expeditivo pontifice,"* 147–70. 2003.

Stinger, Charles L. *The Renaissance in Rome.* Bloomington: Indiana University Press, 1985.

Stonard, John-Paul. "The Sacred Grove of Bomarzo." Courtauld Institute of Art: Art and Architecture. http://www.artandarchitecture.org.uk/insight/stonard_bomarzo.html. Accessed September 6, 2013.

Strocchia, Sharon T. *Death and Ritual in Renaissance Florence.* Baltimore: Johns Hopkins University Press, 1992.

Strong, Roy. *Art and Power: Renaissance Festivals, 1450–1650.* Berkeley: University of California Press, 1984.

Tarugi, Luisa Totondi Secchi. *Pio II e la cultura del suo tempo: Atti del i convegno internazionae, 1989.* Milan: Guerini e associate, 1991.

Tenenti, Alberto. *Il senso della morte el'amore della vita nel Rinascimento (Francia e Italia).* Turin: Giulio Einaudi Editore, 1957.

Thompson, James Westfall. "The Aftermath of the Black Death and the Aftermath of the Great War." *American Journal of Sociology* 26 (1921): 565–72. Excerpt reprinted in Bowsky, *Black Death,* 19–24. 1971.

Thornton, Dora. *The Scholar in His Study: Ownership and Experience in Renaissance Italy.* New Haven and London: Yale University Press, 1997.

Trapp, J. B. "The Poet Laureate: Rome, *Renovatio* and *Translatio Imperii.*" In Ramsey, *Rome in the Renaissance,* 93–132. 1982.

Trexler, Richard C. *Public Life in Renaissance Florence.* New York: Academic Press, 1980.

Trinkhaus, Charles Edward. *The Scope of Renaissance Humanism.* Ann Arbor: University of Michigan Press, 1983.

Ucelli, Guido. *Le Navi di Nemi.* Rome: La Libreria dello Stato, 1950.

Valcke, Louis. "Il *De pace fidei*: Niccolò da Cusa ed Enea Silvio Piccolomini." In Tarugi, *Pio II e la cultura del suo tempo,* 301–12. 1991.

Van der Haegen, Anne Mueller, and Ruth Strasser. *Art and Architecture in Tuscany.* New York: Barnes and Noble, 2001.

Vasari, Giorgio. *Lives of the Painters, Sculptors and Architects.* Translated by Gaston du C. de Vere. 2 vols. New York: Knopf/Everyman, 1996.

Vasoli, Cesare. "Dal *De pace fidei* alla Dieta di Mantova." In Calzona et al, *Il Sogno,* 457–80. 2000.

Vaughan, Richard. *Philip the Good: The Apogee of Burgundy.* London: Longmans, Green, 1970.

Vigo, Pietro. *Le Danze Macabre in Italia.* Bergamo: Istituto Italiano D'Arti Grafiche, 1901.

Villari, Pasquale. *The Life and Times of Machiavelli.* Translated by Linda Villari. St. Claire, Mich.: Scholarly Press, 1969. Originally published in London by Ernest Benn, 1891.

Viti, Paolo. "Osservazioni sul *De viris aetate sua claris* di Enea Silvio Piccolomini." In Tarugi, *Pio II e la cultura del suo tempo,* 199–212. 1991.

Vollmann, Benedikt Konrad. "Aeneas Silvius Piccolomini as Historiographer: *Asia.*" In Von Martels and Vanderjagt, *Pius II "el più expeditivo pontifice,"* 41–54. 2003.

———. "*Enkyklios paideia* in the Work of Aeneas Silvius Piccolomini." In Von Martels and Vanderjagt, *Pius II "el più expeditivo pontifice,"* 1–12. 2003.

Voltaire (Francois-Marie Arouet). *Essai sur les moeurs et l'esprit des nations.* Paris: Editions Garnier Frères, 1963.

———. *Siècle de Louis XIV.* Paris: Flammarion, n.d.

Von Martels, Zweder. "The Fruit of Love: Aeneas Silvius Piccolomini About His Illegitimate Child." In Von Martels and Vanderjagt, *Pius II "el più expeditivo pontifice,"* 229–48. 2003.

———. "'More Matter and Less Art': Aeneas Silvius Piccolomini and the Delicate Balance between Eloquent Words and Deeds." In Von Martels and Vanderjagt, *Pius II "el più expeditivo pontifice,"* 205–28. 2003.

Von Martels, Zweder, and Arjo Vanderjagt, eds. *Pius II "el più expeditivo pontifice": Selected Studies on Aeneas Silvius Piccolomini (1404–1464).* Brill's Studies in Intellectual History. Brill, Leiden, and Boston: Brill, 2003.

Von Pastor, Ludwig, Freiherr. *The History of the Popes from the Close of the Middle Ages, Drawn from the Secret Archives of the Vatican and Other Original Sources.* Vols. III, IV. Translated by Frederick Ignatius Antrobus. St. Louis: B. Herder, 1898.

Wackernagel, Martin. *The World of the Florentine Renaissance Artists: Projects and Patrons, Workshop and Art Market.* Princeton: Princeton University Press, 1981.

Waley, Daniel. *The Italian City-Republics.* New York: McGraw-Hill, 1969.

Watanabe, Morimichi. "Pope Eugenius IV, the Conciliar Movement, and the Primacy of Rome." In Christianson, Izbicki, and Bellitto, *The Church, the Councils, and Reform,* 177–93. 2008.

Weiss, Roberto. *The Renaissance Discovery of Classical Antiquity.* New York: Humanities Press, 1969.

White, Lynn. "Death and the Devil." In *The Darker Vision of the Renaissance: Beyond the Fields of Reason,* edited by Robert S. Kinsman, 25–46. Berkeley: University of California Press, 1974.

———. *Medieval Technology and Social Change.* New York: Oxford, 1978. Originally published in 1962.

Wilkins, Ernest Hatch. *A History of Italian Literature.* Cambridge, Mass.: Harvard University Press, 1966.

Williams, Egerton R. *Lombard Towns of Italy.* New York: Dodd, Mead, 1914.

Williman, Daniel, ed. *The Black Death: The Impact of the Fourteenth Century Plague.* Papers of the Eleventh Annual Conference of the Center for Medieval and Early Renaissance Studies. Binghamton, N.Y.: State University of New York at Binghamton. Center for Medieval and Renaissance Texts and Studies, 1982.

Wittkower Rudolf. *Architectural Principles in the Age of Humanism.* London: Alec Tiranti, 1952.

Woodhouse, John Robert. *Baldesar Castiglione: A Reassessment of "The Courtier."* Edinburgh: Edinburgh University Press, 1978.

Woodward, William H. *Studies in Education During the Age of the Renaissance, 1400–1600.* Cambridge: Cambridge University Press, 1906.

Ziegler, Philip. *The Black Death.* New York: John Day, 1969.

Zippel, Giuseppe. *Nicolò Niccoli: Contributo Alla Storia Dell'Umanismo.* Florence: Fratelli Bocca, 1890.

Index

Plague and Pleasure: The Renaissance World of Pius II was designed in Agmena and composed by Kachergis Book Design of Pittsboro, North Carolina. It was printed on 60-pound House Natural Smooth and bound by Sheridan Books of Dexter, Michigan.